Jeff,
I don't know what your plans are for after high school, but After hearing you express your passion for law, I went home and dug up the text book I used for my Bu[illegible] law classes that I took at Suffolk in [illegible] accounting [illegible] had an amazing [illegible] profe[illegible]

STUDY GUIDE

by Ramona Atkins

for *Contemporary Business and Online Commerce Law*, Fifth Edition
by Henry R. Cheeseman

Custom Edition for Suffolk County Community College

I believe his name was Stephen Russell. We didn't use the study guide or the text for that matter... He gave us amazing notes which I will continue to look for. Anywho, I thought you might have more of an interest in them than me. No matter what you decide to do in life, just remember to love what you do and do what you love. You will learn sooo much in the next decade about yourself... Life is great! Keep yourself surrounded with positive people and do what feels the best in your heart ♡!

Miss Skilton

Date: 22nd of March 2014

Taken from:
Study Guide
by Ramona Atkins
for *Contemporary Business and Online Commerce Law*, Fifth Edition
by Henry R. Cheeseman

PEARSON Custom Publishing
PEARSON Prentice Hall

Cover Art: *Boston: Int'l Place with Lamp* by Kay Canavino

Taken from:

Study Guide
by Ramona Atkins
for *Contemporary Business and Online Commerce Law*, Fifth Edition, by Henry R. Cheeseman

Published by Prentice Hall
Upper Saddle River, New Jersey 07458

This special edition published in cooperation with Pearson Custom Publishing.

Printed in the United States of America

10 9 8 7 6 5 4 3 2

ISBN 0-536-32312-7

2006160133

EC

Please visit our web site at *www.pearsoncustom.com*

PEARSON Custom Publishing

PEARSON CUSTOM PUBLISHING
75 Arlington Street, Suite 300, Boston, MA 02116
A Pearson Education Company

Contents

Chapter 1	Legal Heritage and Critical Legal Thinking	1
Chapter 2	Constitutional law for Business and Online Commerce	9
Chapter 3	Traditional, Alternative, and E-Commerce Dispute Resolution	16
Chapter 4	Torts and Privacy	26
Chapter 5	Intellectual Property and Internet Law	38
Chapter 6	Business and Cyber Crimes	47
Chapter 7	Ethics and Social Responsibility of Business	59
Chapter 8	Nature of Traditional and Online Contracts	68
Chapter 9	Agreement and Consideration	75
Chapter 10	Capacity and Legality	88
Chapter 11	Reality of Consent and Writing	97
Chapter 12	Third-Party Rights and Discharge	110
Chapter 13	Remedies for Breach of Traditional and Online Contracts	120
Chapter 14	Formation of Sales and Lease Contracts	131
Chapter 15	Performance of Sales and Lease of Contracts	140
Chapter 16	Remedies for Breach of Sales and Lease Contracts	149
Chapter 17	E-Commerce, Domain Names, and Internet Law	161
Chapter 18	Warranties and Product Liability	172
Chapter 19	Creation and Transfer of Negotiable Instruments	181
Chapter 20	Holder in Due Course and Liability	190
Chapter 21	Checks and Digital Banking	199
Chapter 22	Credit, Secured Transactions, and Surety Agreements	209

Chapter 23	Bankruptcy and Reorganization	217
Chapter 24	Agency	225
Chapter 25	Sole Proprietorships and Partnerships	238
Chapter 26	Formation and Operation of Domestic and Multinational Corporations	247
Chapter 27	Corporate Directors, Officers, and Shareholders	258
Chapter 28	Corporate Mergers and Acquisitions	267
Chapter 29	Limited Liability Companies	276
Chapter 30	Franchises, Licensing, and Strategic Alliances	286
Chapter 31	Investor Protection and Online Securities Transactions	293
Chapter 32	Antitrust Law	302
Chapter 33	Consumer and Environmental Protection	312
Chapter 34	Labor and Employment Law	324
Chapter 35	Equal Opportunity in Employment	333
Chapter 36	Personal Property and Bailments	342
Chapter 37	Real Property and Landlord-Tenant Relationships	350
Chapter 38	Insurance, Wills, and Estates	360
Chapter 39	International and Comparative Law	372

Chapter 1

LEGAL HERITAGE AND CRITICAL LEGAL THINKING

Chapter Overview

This chapter provides a detailed look at the concept of law and its functions in our society. Even though the meaning of law is vast, law in general is a set of standards and rules that we justify our actions by and which is the basis of consequences as well as sanctions. The philosophy of law, various schools of thought on its development and the importance of flexibility in its application are also examined. The history and development of our laws and courts along with interpretation as it pertains to technology, growth of commerce and the standards of society are what bring about changes and new laws.

Objectives

Upon completing the exercises that follow, you should be able to:

1. To describe law based upon its function.
2. To recognize and compare the major schools of jurisprudence.
3. To understand and appreciate the history of American law.
4. To differentiate between a law court, equity court and a merchant court.
5. To recognize the sources of modern law in the United States.
6. To understand and recognize key terminology when briefing a case.
7. To understand how to recognize legal and ethical issues when briefing a case.

Practical Application

You should be able to understand the need for law as well as flexible interpretation and the framework by which laws are established.

Helpful Hints

You should read each chapter and complete or read the corresponding study sheet. Next, a Refresh Your Memory exercise will determine what materials you need to place more emphasis on. The Critical Thinking exercise that follows will help to assess your ability to analyze and apply the legal concepts you have learned to the facts. Finally, a Sample Quiz consisting of true/false, multiple choice and short answer questions is provided as a means of assessing your mastery of the chapter.

Essentials For a Well-Written Critical Thinking Exercise

Critical Thinking Exercises should be approached in a methodical way. Each exercise should be read twice, the first time to get a feel for the facts and determine what is being asked of you, and the second to spot the issues presented. Once you know what the question is asking you to do, you can mark up the facts with a pen and place possible applicable legal terms from the chapter you have just studied next to the fact it pertains to. In order to stay organized, it's best to outline the answer to the exercise. State your issues to be discussed and place them in the order that they will be presented. Demonstrate how the facts in your exercise meet the requirements of the legal principle(s) you are discussing.

Remember, every story has two sides, as does every argument. When applicable, give reasoning for both sides. Also, if you are applying case law that you have studied, be sure to show how the case(s) apply to the facts you've been given, based upon the similarity of both scenarios. Further, if the case is not supportive of your analysis, you may indicate this point with a brief explanation and continue with the issues you have strong support for.

Finally, make sure that you have utilized all of the relevant facts and applied the pertinent law in analyzing these facts. Remember, it is your reasoning and application of the main objectives of the chapter that will help to determine your competency of the information given to you. If you approach these types of exercises as challenging, fun and practical, you will begin to appreciate their usefulness in your every day life. A sample answer is given at the end of the chapter and is to be used as a guide. Answers will vary based on the law and analysis applied by individual students.

Study Tips

Law is a set of standards and rules that we justify our conduct and actions by and that, which is subject to consequences and sanctions.

Functions of the law include the following:

- To shape moral standards.
- To maintain the status quo.
- To facilitate planning.
- To maximize individual freedom.
- To keep the peace.
- To promote social justice.
- To facilitate orderly change.
- To provide a basis for compromise.

Various scholars have stated their philosophies on the development of the law. There are several schools of jurisprudential thought. You can remember the main ones by the following mnemonic:
A cranky squirrel commands natural history!

A - The **A**nalytical School asserts that the law is formed by logic.
C - The **C**ritical Legal Studies School does not believe in rules for settling disputes, but applying rules of fairness to each circumstance.
S - The **S**ociological School believes that law is a way to form social behavior and attain sociological goals.
C - The **C**ommand School espouses that the law changes when the ruler changes.
N - The **N**atural Law School maintains that the basis of law should be on morality and ethics.
H - The **H**istorical School believes that changes in societal norms are eventually demonstrated in the law. These scholars rely on precedent to solve modern problems.

Foundation of American Law

The American common law was derived from England and its laws. The English system of law was the foundation that helped to build our common law in America.

English Common Law (Court of Chancery)

These laws developed from judge issued opinions that became precedent for other judges to decide similar cases.

Law Courts

The judges issued their opinions in cases that later set the precedent for deciding the same types of cases.

Equity Courts

A court that investigates the merits of a case and one that is based on fairness when deciding cases.

Merchant Courts

A court that dealt with just the law of merchants. Eventually this court was combined with the regular court system.

Sources of Law

- Constitution - The supreme law of the land that provided for the structure of the federal government. This structure established the legislative, executive and judicial branches of government.
- Treaties - Compacts or agreements between two or more nations.
- Statutes - A set of state or federal laws that describes conduct that must be followed by those the statute was designed to protect.
- Ordinances - Laws that are created and enforced by local governments including counties, school districts and municipalities.
- Executive Orders - These are laws that are made by the President or state governors.
- Judicial Decisions - Federal and state issued decisions about individual lawsuits.

The Doctrine of Stare Decisis

A rule of law set forth by higher courts, which becomes precedence for lower court decisions. In addition to the benefit of helping to establish uniformity of law, this doctrine makes it easier for individuals and businesses to determine what the law is.

Key Terms

Plaintiff is the one who originally brings the lawsuit

Defendant is the party who is being sued or whom the suit is brought against.

Petitioner or Appellant is the party (plaintiff or defendant) who has appealed the decision of the lower court or trial court.

Respondent or Appellee is the party (or person) who must answer the appeal brought by the petitioner or appellant. The respondent or appellee may be either the plaintiff or defendant based on which party is the petitioner.

Essentials for briefing a case

Case name, citation and the court
Important case facts briefly and concisely stated
Issues presented to the court
Rules of law
Analysis of the facts with incorporation of the law
Conclusion or holding of the court hearing the case

Refresh Your Memory:

The following exercise will give you the opportunity to test your memory of the principles given in this chapter. Read the question twice and place your answer in the blanks provided. Review the chapter material for any question that you are unable to answer or remember.

1. Audrey has been given a set of rules and consequences for breaking those rules if she does not follow them. These legally binding guidelines are referred to as the ______________________.

2. Realists believe that under this jurisprudential school of thought, the purpose of law is to shape social behavior. ______________________________

3. What jurisprudential philosophy would you apply if you based your decisions on laws that are enforced by a ruling party? ______________________________

4. Past courts decisions that are used in deciding future cases become ____________________.

5. Laws enacted by local government such as traffic laws, building codes and zoning laws are known as ________________.

6. Establishment of an Office of Homeland Security within the Executive Office is an example of ________________________.

7. Alex has an appellate lawsuit served on Sylvia. What term describes Alex's role? ____________.

8. Which court dealt primarily with merchants? ______________________________

9. A legal scholar who basis his or her thought on logic would follow which legal school of thought? ______________________________

10. The doctrine that helpted establish uniformity of law is known as ______________________.

Critical Thought Exercise

Following the genocide, torture, rape, and murder of thousands of civilians in Rwanda in 1994, sixty-three individuals were tried for genocide and crimes against humanity. Numerous persons were sentenced to life sentences.

Many of those prosecuted objected to being tried outside Rwanda for acts committed within Rwanda. The accused further objected to being prosecuted for acts that were not deemed criminal by their own leaders or national laws.

You are asked to address a large convention sponsored by a nationalist group that argues against any person ever being subjected to criminal punishment by an international court for acts committed within their home country.

Your argument should address the following issues while trying to explain whether or not you feel prosecutions by an international body are lawful and justified:

1. What law is being violated when someone commits a crime against humanity?
2. Who has the authority to enforce laws against genocide and crimes against humanity?
3. Should a citizen of a sovereign nation be subjected to punishment by an international tribunal for acts committed within their home country?
4. Who is responsible for the prosecution of these crimes?

Answer. ____

Practice Quiz

True/False:

1. ____ Laws consist of rules that govern the conduct of individuals, but not businesses and organizations that function with it. [p 2]

2. ____ Businesses are not like individuals, however they still owe no duty to society. [p 2]

3. ____ The U.S. Constitution is often called "a living document" as it is so flexible and adaptive. [p 9]

4. ____ The term stare decisis has nothing to do with precedence or predictability of law for businesses or individuals. [p 12]

5. ____ The Constitution of the United States gave all power to the federal government thereby leaving states with their own constitutions to establish state power. [p 9]

6. ____ Legal philosophers who use past legal decisions to solve contemporary problems follow the beliefs of the Law of Economics. [p 7]

7. ____ The case of *Brown v. Board of Education* challenged the separate school systems of four states. [p 5]

8. ____ An equity court emphasizes the procedure of a case versus the merits of a case. [p 8]

9. ____ A merchant court is one that emphasized legal procedure in order to grant an appropriate remedy. [p 8]

10. ____ Judicial opinions are written opinions that often interpret statutes as well as ordinances. [p 11]

Multiple Choice:

11. Some of the primary functions of the law in our country are: [p 3]
    a. promoting social justice, encouraging legal decisions, and interpreting judicial decisions.
    b. facilitating change, providing a basis for compromise and developing legal reasoning.
    c. keeping the peace, shaping moral standards, minimizing individual freedom.
    d. none of the above.

12. The Sociological School of Jurisprudence maintains that [p 6]
    a. the law is a set of rules enforced by the ruling party and the law changes when the ruler changes.
    b. the rules of law are unnecessary and subjective decisions made be judges are permissible.
    c. the purpose of law is to achieve, advance and shape social behavior.
    d. the law is an evolutionary process.

13. The term codified law refers to [p 9]
    a. statutes enacted by the legislative branches of state and federal governments that are arranged by topic in code books.
    b. a written agreement made between the United States and another nation.
    c. administrative rules and regulations.
    d. all of the above.

14. The term stare decisis means: [p 12]
    a. to interpret statutes and make a decision.
    b. to predict the legal decision in a case.
    c. to stand by the decision.
    d. to adopt and regulate the conduct of others.

15. Provisions of state established constitutions are valid unless [p 14]
    a. they are patterned after the U.S. Constitution .
    b. they have an executive branch of their governments.
    c. they apply to evolving social, technological and economic conditions.
    d. they conflict with the U.S. Constitution or any valid federal law.

Short Answer:

16. What was the primary example that was set in the case of *Brown v. Board of Education?* [p 5]

    ____

17. Distinguish between a law court and a Chancery (equity) court. [p 8] ____________________

    ____

18. What were the rules known as the Law of Merchants based on? [p 8] ____________________ and ____________________

19. Jurisprudence is. [p 5] ____________________________

    ____

20. Which school of jurisprudential thought promotes market efficiency as being the central goal of legal decision making? p 6] ____________________________

21. Why will treaties become increasingly more important to business? [p 9] ________________
____

22. Administrative agencies are created to enforce and interpret statutes. Give two examples of these types of agencies. [p 11] ____

23. Which state bases its law on the French Civil Code? [p 15] ________________________

24. What is a judicial decision? [p 11] ____
____

25. What purpose do administrative agencies serve? [p10] ______________________________

26. Which doctrine provides for adherence to precedence? [p 11] __________________________

27. What type of court emphasized legal procedure over merits? [p 8] ______________________

28. Why are statutes written? [p 9] ____

29. What jurisprudential school of thought do realists follow? [p 6] _______________________

30. What types of agencies are the Securities and Exchange Commission and the Federal Trade Commission? [p 11] ____

Chapter 2

CONSTITUTIONAL LAW FOR BUSINESS AND ONLINE COMMERCE

Chapter Overview

This chapter provides a solid overview of the legal framework that our government operates under. As you read through this chapter, you will gain a better understanding of the concept of federalism as well as separation of powers and the federal government's power to regulate foreign, interstate and even local commerce. Additionally, you will become familiar with the First Amendment on the Internet. The concepts of substantive and procedural due process, equal protection and the constitutional limits on e-commerce are also analyzed.

Objectives

Upon completion of this chapter's exercises, you should be able to:

1. Recognize the function of the powers granted to the state and federal government.
2. Understand the importance of the supremacy clause and its application.
3. Understand the federal government's authority and rationale for regulating interstate commerce.
4. Understand the protection speech is afforded under the First Amendment.
5. Apply the first amendment freedom of speech protection to situations involving the Internet.
6. Analyze and understand substantive and procedural due process.
7. Understand the constitutional standards applicable in equal protection cases.

Practical Application

You should be able to understand the importance of the commerce clause as well as the government's reasoning behind regulation of commerce. You should also be able to understand what types of speech are protected as well as the limitations on speech. Finally, you should be able to understand and apply the various standards of review in equal protection cases.

Helpful Hints

This chapter should be approached in a manner much like you would approach the weighing as well as need for various elements in a scientific laboratory. The chapter begins with a discussion on the powers given to the federal government and those that are reserved for the states. Next, the chapter discusses the creation, need and function of balancing the three branches of government. The impact of the commerce clause on the government and its role in business are also emphasized. Further, the limitations on the First Amendment Freedom of Speech based on the type of speech as well as restrictions on the government concerning Freedom of Religion are also discussed. The important balancing of classification as set forth in a government regulation against governmental standards in equal protection cases are carefully examined as well. As you review the study tips section followed by the various chapter exercises, it is helpful as well as beneficial to weigh the governmental interest against what is being protected.

Study Tips

Federalism

This refers to our country's form of government. The states and the federal government share powers. Sometimes the federal law and state law conflict. When this happens, the federal law prevails.

Branches of the Federal Government

You should familiarize yourself with the legislative, executive and judicial branches of government and know what function each branch serves, as well as how each affects one another.

State and Local Government Regulation of Business – "Police Power"

States are able to regulate intrastate and a large amount of interstate business that takes place within its borders. The police power given to the states allows the states to make laws that protect or promote the health, safety, morals and welfare of its citizens.

Bill of Rights

You should know that the Bill of Rights is the ten amendments to the United States Constitution. Also, the two rights that are heavily emphasized are the Freedom of Speech and the Freedom of Religion as per the First Amendment.

Freedom of Speech

It is important to realize that this freedom extends only to speech and not conduct. You should also familiarize yourself with the types of speech. It is helpful to list them and place the protection each is given next to them. The following demonstrates an easy way to do this.

Political Speech – fully protected

Commercial Speech – An example would be advertising. Speeches used by businesses are subject to time, place and manner restrictions.

Offensive Speech – Speech that is offensive to a lot of people is also subject to time, place and manner restrictions.

Unprotected Speech includes: dangerous speech, fighting words, defamatory language, child pornography, and obscene speech.

Note that with obscene speech, the states can define the meaning of obscene speech. It has been stated that obscene is where the average person's prurient interest is appealed to, and the work is patently offensive thereby describing the sexual conduct in accordance with the state law and the work is in need of serious literary, artistic, political or social value.

Freedom of Religion

The Constitution mandates that the local, state and federal governments be neutral regarding religion.

The two religion clauses in the First Amendment that you should know the difference between are the Establishment Clause, which prohibits the government from establishing a state religion or promoting one religion over another and the Free Exercise Clause. The Free Exercise Clause prevents the government from making laws that inhibit or prohibit people from participating in or practicing their chosen religion.

Commerce

This is a very important term to know. As you may recall, the Commerce Clause of the Constitution has the greatest impact on business than any other clause. In order to fully appreciate as well as understand this importance, you need to know the following:

- The difference between interstate and intrastate commerce is that interstate involves instrumentalities of trade moving across state borders. Compare this to intrastate where commerce is moving within the state.

- The traditional role of government in regulating interstate commerce was to regulate only commerce that moved in interstate commerce. Whereas modernly the federal government may regulate local commerce if it has an impact on commerce as a whole.

- If state law burdens interstate commerce, then the law is declared void and unconstitutional.

The Equal Protection Clause

This clause of the Fourteenth Amendment states that a state cannot, "deny to any person within its jurisdiction the equal protection of the laws." Though it primarily applies to state and local governments, it also applies to federal government action as well. You must know the three standards for review of equal protection cases. They are:

1. *Strict Scrutiny*, which is applied when there is a classification that is a suspect class such as race.
2. *Intermediate Scrutiny*, which is applied when the classification is based on a protected class that is not race, such as age and sex.
3. Finally, the *Rational Basis Test* is applied when neither a suspect nor protected class is involved. All that is needed is a justifiable reason for the law trying to be enacted.

The Due Process Clause

This clause is provided for in the Fifth and Fourteenth Amendments as both have a due process clause. The Fifth Amendment applies to the federal government whereas the fourteenth amendment applies to state and local government. The crux of this clause is that no individual shall be deprived of life, liberty or property without due process of law. There are two types of due process, substantive and procedural. Substantive refers to the content of the law. It must be clear, not too broad and worded in such a way that a "reasonable person" could understand the law in order to obey it. The procedural aspect requires a person be given notice and an opportunity to be heard before his/her life, liberty or property is taken. Note, within this aspect is the Just Compensation Clause, which states the government, must pay to the owner just compensation for taking an individual's property.

Privileges and Immunities Clause

This clause prohibits states from enforcing laws that unduly favor their own residents thereby resulting in discrimination against residents of other states.

Refresh Your Memory

The following exercise will enable you to refresh your memory of the main principles given to you in this chapter. Read each question twice and placed your answer in the blank(s) provided. If you do not remember, go to the next question and come back to the one you did not answer. It is also helpful to look over the section(s) in the study tips again, and then try to answer what you may be having difficulty with.

1. Our country's type of government is known as ___________________.

2. The powers delegated to the federal government by the states ratification of the Constitution are known as ________________ __________________.

3. What are the three branches that the federal government is divided into? ______________________ ____.

4. The United States Constitution's system of ______________ and ______________ prevents any one of the three branches of the federal government from becoming too powerful.

5. The ____________ Clause has a greater impact on business than any other provision of the Constitution.

6. _____________ commerce refers to commerce that moves within a state or that affects commerce between the states.

7. The police power given to the states allows the states to regulate both private and business activity within their borders is known as ________________ ________________.

8. The Bill of Rights is the first ______ amendments to the United States Constitution.

9. Under the incorporation doctrine, many of the fundamental guarantees set forth in the Bill of Rights are also applied to ____________ and ____________ government action.

10. The First Amendment's Freedom of Speech Clause protects ______________ and not conduct.

11. The preemption doctrine refers to federal law taking precedence over ___________ and _____________ law.

12. Any intrastate activity that has an effect on interstate commerce is subject to _____________ regulation.

Critical Thought Exercise

Larry Brown is a very religious person and is very active in the anti-abortion movement. While Brown travels the streets of his hometown of Westerfield, Illinois, he plays taped sermons and spiritual music that support his religious and political views. The City of Westerfield enacted an ordinance that prohibited the playing of car sound systems at a volume that would be "audible" at a distance greater than fifty feet. Brown was arrested and convicted for violating the ordinance. Brown appealed his conviction on the grounds that the ordinance violated his right to free speech and free exercise of his religious beliefs. The City of Westerfield countered that noise coming from Brown's car could pose a hazard if he and other drivers were unable to hear emergency vehicles as they approached, and as such, the ordinance was a proper exercise of the police power possessed by the State of Illinois.

Was the playing of sermons by Brown protected by the Free Speech and Free Exercise Clauses of the First Amendment to the United States Constitution?

Answer. ____

Practice Quiz

True/False:

1. ___ State laws may burden interstate commerce. [p 30]

2. ___ The part of the government that consists of Congress is the legislative branch. [p 26]

3. ___ The Equal Protection Clause also applies to federal government action. [p 36]

4. ___ Commercial speech is subject to proper time, place and manner restrictions. [p 38]

5. ___ Government classifications based on a suspect class are subject to the strict scrutiny test. [p 36]

6. ___ Substantive due process requires the government to give a person proper notice and a hearing before depriving the person of life, liberty, or property. [p 37]

7. ___ The Free Exercise Clause prohibits the government from either establishing a state religion or promoting one religion over another. [p 35]

8. ___ In addition to the Bill of Rights, 17 other amendments have been added to the U.S. Constitution. [p 30]

9. ___ Police power permits states to enact laws that regulate the conduct of business. [p 29]

10. ___ Conduct is also protected by the First Amendment. [p 31]

Multiple Choice:

11. Enumerated powers are [p 6]
    a. the part of the government that consists of the Supreme Court and other federal courts.
    b. sequentially numbered laws.
    c. powers delegated to the federal government by the states.
    d. None of the above.

12. The Commerce Clause is intended to [p 28]
    a. deregulate commerce with foreign nations.
    b. foster development of a national market and free trade among the states.
    c. authorize state governments to authorize trade with the Indian tribes.
    d. be the supreme law of the land.

13. The concept of federal law taking precedence over state or local law is called [p 27]
    a. the supremacy clause.
    b. interstate commerce regulation.
    c. the preemption doctrine.
    d. All of the above

14. Interstate commerce refers to [p 28]
    a. commerce that crosses state borders.
    b. commerce that occurs within a state.
    c. commerce that occurs across state borders and within a state.
    d. commerce that occurs only in a limited local area.

15. Offensive speech is an example of [p 31]
    a. speech that is given excessive protection.
    b. speech that has time, place and manner restrictions.
    c. speech that will incite the overthrow of the government.
    d. speech that is fully protected.

16. The test of whether substantive due process has been met is whether [p 37]
    a. proper notice and a hearing.
    b. clear laws and not be overly broad in what they cover.
    c. a reasonable person could understand the law and comply with it.
    d. none of the above

17. The privileges and immunities clause prohibits [p 68]
    a. states from giving the same privileges to out-of-state residents.
    b. prevents out-of-state residents from owning property in other states
    c. the government from enacting laws that unduly discriminate in favor of their own

residents.
d. federal government from regulating commerce that moves in interstate commerce.

Short Answer:

18. These clauses state that no person shall be deprived of "life, liberty, or property." [p 36]

19. The __________ __________ __________ of the Fifth Amendment applies to federal government action. [p 36]

20. A test that is applied to classifications based on protected classes other than race is known as the [p 36] ________________ ________________ test.

21. What does the substantive due process clause require of government statutes, ordinances, regulations or other laws? [p 37] ____

22. The Rational Basis test is used in reviewing Equal Protection cases that do not involve a [p 36] ____________ or ______________ class.

23. Offensive speech is subject to ____________, ____________, and ____________ restrictions. [p 31]

24. This clause prevents the government from enacting laws that either prohibit or inhibit individuals from participating in their chosen religion. [p 35]

25. Which clause prohibits states from enacting laws that unduly discriminate in favor of their residents? The ________________ and ______________ Clause. [p 68]

26. Under the _______ _____________ _______, the government must pay the owner for taking his or her property? [p 37]

27. Give examples of unprotected speech [pp 32 -33] ______________________________
____

Chapter 3

TRADITIONAL, AND E-COMMERCE DISPUTE RESOLUTION

Chapter Overview

This chapter examines and compares the state court systems and the federal court system. It also provides a clear overview of the types of cases the various courts can hear as well as jurisdictional issues that web site operators face. Emphasis is also placed on the importance of a cost-benefit analysis when bringing, maintaining and defending a lawsuit. The pre-trial litigation process, court use of e-filings and the stages of a trial are thoroughly explained along with the nonjudicial alternatives of arbitration and medication.

Objectives

After completing the exercises that follow, you should be able to:

1. Compare the state court systems and the federal court system.
2. To analyze various factors when conducting a cost-benefit analysis in deciding whether to bring or defend a lawsuit.
3. To recognize jurisdictional issues and their application to state and federal court.
4. To understand jurisdictional issues web site operators face.
5. To understand the pre-trial litigation process.
6. To comprehend the stages of a trial.
7. To be aware of the nonjudicial alternatives of arbitration and mediation.

Practical Application

You should be able to be familiar with the costs and benefits of bringing and defending a lawsuit. You should be able to know which is the proper court and system to hear particular cases as well as be able to decide whether the benefits outweigh the costs of litigation. Additionally, you should have a broader understanding of the pre-trial litigation process and the various procedural requirements. Finally, you should be able to understand the sequence of events associated with a trial and be aware of the nonjudicial alternatives available to you.

Helpful Hints

This chapter may be a little confusing, as there appear to be so many different types of courts, all of which hear different types of cases. It is recommended that you diagram the state and federal court systems, branching each of the various courts off of the applicable state or federal court system. Page 2-3 of your text gives an example of how one diagram can be utilized.
You should also place two to four main points next to each type of court. For example, if you are working on the state court systems, in particular the limited-jurisdiction trial court, you may want to note

that they are sometimes called inferior trial courts, hear matters that are specialized and list some of the examples of the types of cases that are heard in this type of court. As you proceed in this manner, you will find that you have created a flow chart of the courts that will be easy to visualize when determining the answers to text and real life situations. Next, review this chapter's study sheet, complete the Refresh Your Memory exercise followed by the Critical Thought Exercise and Sample Quiz.

Study Tips

The laws and their development that you became familiar with in Chapter One as well as the court systems you are learning about in this chapter are analogous to the base layer of a specialty cake. It is by knowing the appropriate law and court within the proper court system that you will be able to apply the correct legal principles to situations as they occur. The areas of law in the chapters that follow will provide the upper layers and frosting to this unique cake. The essential ingredients of adhering to the proper time and procedural requirements along with satisfying the essential substantive elements for various legal actions are what provide balance to this legally created pastry if you will.

Litigation as you know is the process of bringing, maintaining and defending a lawsuit. The question to be answered however is where should litigation take place? There are two main court systems to choose from in the United States, the federal and the state court systems. It is important to know which court system has the proper jurisdiction to hear the case that has been prepared. The following list breaks down each court system highlighting some important points to remember about each court system as well as the courts within each system.

State Court Systems

A general fact about the state court systems is that every state as well as the District of Columbia has one. Additionally the majority of states have at least four types of state court systems that are discussed below.

Limited *-Jurisdiction Trial Court (Inferior Trial Courts).* These trial courts in most cases can hear specialized cases such as those involving family law, probate, traffic matters, juvenile issues, misdemeanors, and civil cases that do not exceed a set dollar amount. An attorney trying a case in this type of court may introduce evidence and illicit testimony. If the case does not result in a favorable outcome for one of the parties to the lawsuit, that party may appeal his/her case to an appellate court or a general-jurisdiction court. Many states also have a small claims court wherein a party on his/her own behalf brings a civil case worth a small dollar amount. If a party in a small claims case loses, then that party may also appeal to the general-jurisdiction trial court or an appellate court.

General*-Jurisdiction Trial Court.* A general-jurisdiction trial court can be found in every state. The trial testimony and evidence that is preserved on record allow these courts to be called the courts of record. This court hears felonies, cases above a certain dollar amount and cases not heard by the inferior trial courts.

Intermediate Appellate Court. This court hears appeals from trial courts and decides if the trial court erred thereby justifying a reversal or modification of the decision. The entire trial court record or just the important parts of the record may be reviewed. At this level of the court system, a party may not introduce new evidence or testimony. The decision of this appellate court may be appealed to the highest state court.

Highest State Court. The majority of states have a supreme court, which is the highest court in the state court system. The job of a state supreme court is to hear appeals from the intermediate appellate court. Once again, no new evidence or testimony is allowed. Once this court has made its decision, it becomes fine. However, if there is a question of law, then the state supreme court's decision Mt be granted review by the U.S. Supreme Court.

Federal Court System

The United States Constitution states that the federal government's judicial power lies with the Supreme Court. In addition to this judicial power, Congress was allowed to establish inferior, or special courts that include the U.S. District court and the U.S. courts of appeal.

Special Federal Courts. The nature of these courts is to hear limited types of cases such as those involving federal tax laws, law suits against the United States, international commercial disputes and cases involving bankruptcy.

U.S. District Courts. These courts are the federal courts general jurisdiction courts.

U.S. Courts of Appeal. These courts are the intermediate appellate courts of the federal court system. The U.S. Courts of Appeals hear appeals from the cases already heard by the U.S. District Courts. As with the state court systems, no new evidence or testimony may be introduced by a party.

Court of Appeals for the Federal *Circuit*. Even though this is a United States Appellate Court, its jurisdiction is special as it is able to review the decisions made in the Patent and Trademark Office, the Court of International Trade and the Claims Court.

The U.S. Supreme Court. This high court of our land is administered by a president appointed chief justice and is made up of nine nominated justices. This court hears cases from the federal circuit courts of appeals, from some federal district and special federal courts as well as the highest state courts. A special note of interest is that a petition for certiorari must be made to the Supreme Court if a petitioner wants his/her case reviewed. If the court decides to review the case, then a writ of certiorari is issued provided there is a constitutional or other important issue involved in the case. Remember, no new evidence or testimony may be introduced at this level.

Federal and State Courts Jurisdiction

In order for a federal court to hear a case, the case must involve a federal question, or diversity of citizenship. It's important to distinguish these two concepts. A case involving a federal question deals with treaties, federal statutes and the U.S. Constitution. Also, there need not be a set dollar amount to bring this type of case. Compare this to cases involving diversity of citizenship whereby the cases need to be between citizens of different states or a citizen of a country and a citizen of a state or a citizen of a state and a foreign country with the foreign country acting as the plaintiff in a law suit. These types of cases require that the controversy exceed $75,000.00. If the dollar amount isn't met, then the appropriate state court must hear the case.

Court Jurisdiction to Hear a Case

In order to bring a lawsuit, a person must have a stake in the outcome of the lawsuit. This is known as standing.

The court must also have the proper jurisdiction to hear the case. You must be familiar with *subject matter jurisdiction, in personam, in rem,* and *quasi in rem* jurisdiction. Finally you must be familiar with the use of the *long-arm statutes* and when they are permitted over nonresidents.

Which court is the proper venue to hear my case?

The law mandates that lawsuits be heard by the court with jurisdiction that is closest to where the incident happened or where the parties live.

What are the advantages and disadvantages of bringing and defending a lawsuit?

It is very important to consider all of the factors involved when deciding to sue or defend a lawsuit. This is known as the cost-benefit analysis. This is a common sense decision that can be made by weighing how much money will be won or lost in light of your chances of winning or losing against the costs to litigate, expenses associated with employees being released from work, as well as pre-judgment interest provided by the law. Other emotional considerations such as the impact on the relationship of the parties and their reputations as well as the mental aggravation and turmoil that may manifest itself should also be factored in. Further, a caveat of the potential for error in the legal system must not be discarded in balancing whether or not it is wise to bring or defend a lawsuit.

When can a lawsuit be brought?

This refers to federal and state government time limitations regarding the period of time the plaintiff has the right to sue a defendant. Statutes of limitations will vary depending on the type of lawsuit involved.

What is involved in the pretrial litigation process?

The pretrial litigation process is an essential ingredient in the foundational layer of the legal process. You must be familiar with the various important pleadings of complaint, answer, cross-complaint and reply when initiating and responding to a lawsuit. Additionally, you will need to know about the different types of discovery and what activities both parties may participate in to discover facts of the case from one another as well as witnesses before trial. The primary types of discovery are depositions, interrogatories, production of documents and physical and mental examinations. Also, a familiarity with the pretrial motions of judgment on the pleadings, and motion for summary judgment should be developed to create an understanding that some lawsuits in whole or in part should not go to trial. Finally, you should be aware of the purpose of a settlement conference and realize that if a settlement is not forthcoming, this tool is important in identifying the main trial issues.

What are the stages of a trial?

A legal trial is much like a performance at a theater. There are those who are performing the case in a methodical fashion from beginning to end. In using this comparison, the program of a trial would read in the following order: jury selection, opening statements, the plaintiff's case, the defendant's case, rebuttal, rejoinder, closing arguments, jury instructions, with the jury deliberation and the entry of judgment acting as the end of the show. The sequel to the trial in a civil case is the appeal, which can be brought be either the plaintiff or the defendant. In a criminal trial, the appeal can only be brought by the defendant. Opening and responding briefs may be filed with the court. The drama of this performance is in the appellate court finding an error of law in the record, in which case the lower court decision will be reversed.

What other choices does a person have?

Sometimes using the court system to resolve disputes results in a great expenditure of money and time. In order to alleviate these concerns, alternative dispute resolution methods are being utilized to resolve disputes rather than using litigation. Some of the alternatives that are available include mediation, conciliation, mini-trial, fact-finding, and a judicial referee.

Refresh Your Memory

The following exercise will enable you to refresh your memory on the rules and principles presented to you in this chapter. Read each question twice and place your answer in the blanks provided. Review the chapter material for any question you miss or are unable to remember.

1. The process of bringing, maintaining and defending a lawsuit is known as ___________.

2. What are the two major court systems in the United States? The _______ and _________.

3. An inferior trial court is also known as a __________________________.

4. What types of cases do general-jurisdiction trial courts hear? ______________________.

5. What types of courts hear civil cases involving small dollar amounts? ____________________.

6. Attorneys who receive a percentage of the amount recovered for the plaintiff upon winning or settling a case are working under a ____________________ agreement.

7. Which courts review the trial court record to determine any trial errors that would mandate reversal or modification of the trial court decision? ________________________________

8. The Court of Appeals for the Federal Circuit has special appellate jurisdiction to review what types of decisions? ____

9. Name four types of special federal courts that have limited jurisdiction? _______________, _______________, _______________, _______________.

10. Who is responsible for the administration of the Supreme Court? ______________________ ____________________________.

Critical Thought Exercise

You are a District Manager of marketing for Intestine Smart, Inc., a California corporation, makers of Colon Grenade, a colon-cleansing drug. You have negotiated the sale of over 4 million dollars worth of this product from Prescript Co, another California corporation, which operates pharmacies under the names of Col On, Goodstuff Co. and Drugs 2 Go. These pharmacies are located primarily in California, but Prescript Co has now expanded into 22 states including Utah.

Enticed by a Goodstuff add in the Utah Free Press for Colon Grenade, Alice Thinstone bought the drug at Goodstuff Co. and used it. Within a week, Thinstone suffered a ruptured colon. Alleging that the injury was caused by Colon Grenade, Thinstone sued Prescript Co and Intestine Smart in a Utah state court.

You have received a letter from the CEO of Intestine Smart, Ms. Sheila Snob, threatening to fire you and demanding to know why Intestine Smart is being subjected to a lawsuit in Utah, since she has never been informed of any sales of the product to companies outside of California.

Your assigned task is to ***draft a memo to your boss***, Ms. Snob, and explain to her whether Intestine Smart must respond to the suit and defend against it in Utah. Explain the legal theory and the reasons for your opinion.

Answer: ____

____

____

____

Practice Quiz

True/False:

1. ___ The U.S. Supreme Court usually hears cases concerning major constitutional questions. [p 46]

2. ___ A plurality opinion decides a case but is not precedent. [p 49]

3. ___ There is a set dollar amount on federal question cases that can be brought in Federal Court. [p 50]

4. ___ Writs of certiorari issued by a court deciding to review a case are granted in all types of cases. [p 48]

5. ___ Andy's friend Wanda is injured when a wrecking ball controlled by Bart is dropped on her. Wanda has standing to sue Bart. [p 52]

6. ___ A court may not hear a case unless it has subject matter jurisdiction. [p 52]

7. ___ A plaintiff who obtains a judgment against a defendant in one state cannot try and collect the judgment by attaching a defendant's property located in another state. [p 52]

8. ___ Long arm statutes limit a state's jurisdiction to residents who have moved out of state. [p 52]

9. ___ A deposition is oral testimony given by a party or witness before trial. [p 57]

10. ___ Once a summons has been filed, the court issues a complaint. [p 55]

11. ___ A judge who decides a motion for Judgment on the pleadings cannot consider any facts extraneous to the pleadings. [p 58]

12. ___ One of the purposes of a pretrial hearing is to organize and address the issues of the case so that the trial will be professionally presented. [p 58]

13. ___ The defendant bears the burden of proof to persuade the trier of fact on the merits of the case. [p 60]

14. ___ A plaintiff's attorney may rebut a defendant's case once the defendant's attorney has finished calling witnesses. [p 60]

15. ___ A court may not overturn a verdict if mere bias is shown. [p 61]

Multiple Choice:

16. State jurisdiction is limited to [p 44]
    a. bankruptcy cases.
    b. small claims cases.
    c. matters not subject to federal jurisdiction.
    d. suits against the United States.

17. A party who disputes the jurisdiction of a court cannot [p 52]
    a. enter a claim in the forum state's small claims court to recover expenses of the dispute.
    b. make a special appearance in that court to argue against the merits.
    c. appeal to the state supreme court and ask that the suit be dismissed.
    d. be served a complaint if he or she makes a special appearance in the court to argue against imposition of jurisdiction.

18. The bringing, maintaining, and defense of a lawsuit is known as [p 44]
    a. discovery
    b. litigation
    c. a cross-complaint
    d. a summons

19. A law that establishes the period within which a plaintiff must bring a lawsuit against the defendant is known as [p 56]
    a. a statute of limitations
    b. a complaining period
    c. an e-filing of pleadings
    d. none of the above

20. A deposition is [p 57]
    a. written testimony given by a party or witness prior to trial
    b. oral testimony given by a party or witness prior to trial
    c. a pleading alleging ultimate allegations of fact
    d. all of the above

21. Which of the following situations refers to the production of documents refers to [p 57]
    a. Alice's attorney submits written questions to Jeff, the party to whom she is suing.
    b. Ed brings a motion for a mental and physical examination of Bob, a party to the lawsuit.
    c. Jan brings a motion for the assembly of legal documents
    d. Fred, one party to a lawsuit requests that Barney, the other party produce all documents that are relevant to the case prior to trial.

22. The term rejoinder refers to [p 60]
    a. when the plaintiff's attorney calls witnesses and puts forth evidence to rebut the defendant's case
    b. the making of a closing argument by each party's attorney
    c. the reading of jury instructions to the jury
    d. the calling of additional witnesses and introduction of other evidence to counter the plaintiff's rebuttal

23. When a court overturns a verdict based on bias or jury misconduct, this is known as [p 60-61]
    a. a judgment on the pleadings
    b. an entry of judgment
    c. a judgment notwithstanding the verdict
    d. all of the above.

24. The responding party in an appeal is known as [p 62]
    a. the respondent
    b. the appellant
    c. the defendant
    d. the plaintiff

Short Answer:

25. Define the meaning of discovery. [p 57] ____
____

26. What are interrogatories? [p 57] ____

27. When one party requests another party to produce all documents relevant to the case prior to trial is known as the __________________ of ____________________. [p 57]

28. A party can make a motion to try to dispose of all or part of a lawsuit prior to trial is known as a _______________ _______________. [p 58]

29. The jury in a jury trial and the judge where there is not a jury trial is known as the __________________ of __________________. [p 59]

30. A person chosen as a neutral third party who acts as a conveyor of information between the parties and helps them to try and reach a settlement of the dispute is known as a ___________________. [p 64]

31. When the parties hire a neutral person to investigate the dispute, this person is known as a ________________ ________________. [p 64]

32. Federal and state courts have concurrent jurisdiction to hear cases that involve __________ of ________________ and ________________ ________________. [p 50]

33. A plaintiff must have _______________ to sue before he/she can bring a lawsuit. [p 52]

34. In rem jurisdiction refers to a court's jurisdiction over _______ _______. [p 52]

35. Under a ____________________ fee arrangement, the lawyer receives a percentage of the amount recovered for the plaintiff upon settling or winning the lawsuit. [p 46]

36. A summons is issued once a ____________ has been filed with the court. [p 55]

37. The __________ must file an answer once he/she is served with the complaint. [p 55]

38. The defendant may assert ________________ __________________ when answering the plaintiff's complaint. [p 55]

Chapter 4
TORTS AND PRIVACY

Chapter Overview

This chapter provides a good understanding of the intentional torts against persons as well as property. Additionally, the tort of negligence as well as applicable defenses to this cause of action is explained in a very methodical fashion. The special negligence doctrines such as negligence per se, negligent infliction of emotional distress and res ipsa loquitur are also examined. Further, the torts of unfair competition, disparagement and fraud are also discussed. Finally, the issue of punitive damages and the doctrine of strict liability are reviewed as well.

Objectives

Upon completion of this chapter's exercises, you should be able to:

1. Differentiate between the different types of intentional torts against persons and against property.
2. Understand the elements that are necessary in a cause of action based on negligence and apply those elements to given fact situations.
3. Be familiar with the defenses associated with a negligence action.
4. Understand the special negligence doctrines and how they differ from one another.
5. Understand the business torts of unfair competition and disparagement.
6. Understand the purposes of punitive damages and the application of punitive damages in lawsuits involving the tort of bad faith.
7. Understand the doctrine of strict liability and its application.

Practical Application

You should be able to identify the different types of intentional torts as well as negligence and apply the elements associated with each to real life as well as hypothetical situations. Additionally, you should have a greater understanding of the concept of strict liability as well as why and when punitive damages are asked for.

Helpful Hints

This chapter lends itself towards organization in that you can sort the intentional torts by their application to individuals, property or business. Also, the elements of the tort of negligence are easily remembered if you list the elements vertically and diagram causation horizontally. This is displayed for you in the study tips section of this chapter. Further, the tort of misrepresentation is easily remembered by using the mnemonic given under the study tips section. Once you have these organizational skills mastered for the main sections in this chapter, the other information given is very easy to remember. Many of the cases you will review in this chapter will be easy for you to understand as they pertain to many companies that you may be familiar with.

Study Tips

The first organizational step you should take is to learn the intentional torts based upon their application. You should also be cognizant of some of the fine nuances associated with some of these torts. It is often easier to list the elements of the tort rather than state its technical definition. Student learning styles will vary, and as such, both methods are given. The pages that follow will assist you in studying the torts that are discussed in this chapter.

Tort

A tort is a civil wrong for which an individual or business may compensation for the injuries that have been caused. Compensation for these injuries may include damages for mental distress, loss of wages, pain and suffering, past and future medical expenses and in some situations, punitive damages. In a tort situation where the victim dies, a wrongful death action may also be an option.

Intentional Torts Against Persons

Assault – The intentional threat of immediate harm or offensive contact or any action that arouses reasonable apprehension of imminent harm.

Assault list of elements with special nuances

- *intentional*
- *placing of another*
- *in immediate* – Note that future threats are not actionable.
- *apprehension* –The victim must be fearful of what appears to be an inevitable contact. The victim must be aware of the tortuous act. The victim's reaction must be one of fear as opposed to laughter which would negate the element of apprehension.
- *of harmful or offensive contact*

Battery – The intentional, unauthorized harmful or offensive touching of another without consent or legal privilege.

Battery list of elements with special nuances

- *intentional*
- *unauthorized*
- *harmful* or *offensive* – A kiss may be considered offensive by some
- *touching* – The touching of an accessory such as a purse that is attached to the victim may be enough to satisfy this element.
- *of another*
- *without consent* or *legal privilege* – You should be aware of the merchant's protection statutes, which sometimes have a role in the privilege arena of this tort.

Other interesting notations on battery are that the victim does not have to be aware of the battery in order for the tort to occur. Also, the victim may be sleeping when it happens or have his or her back turned when the battery occurs. Battery and assault can occur together, however, the victim would need to show awareness in order to fully prove the elements of assault.

Transferred Intent Doctrine - When one individual intends to injure one person but instead injures another individual, the law transfers the perpetrator's intent from the person the harm was originally meant for to the actual victim. The actual victim may then bring a lawsuit against the wrongdoer.

False Imprisonment – The intentional mental or physical confinement of another without consent or legal privilege.

False Imprisonment list of elements with special nuances:

- *intentional*
- *mental* or *physical* – An example of mental confinement may be through an assertion of legal authority or by one in a superior position. Physical confinement may include barriers or threats of physical harm.
- *confinement* – Be careful with this element as future threats or moral pressure does not satisfy this element. Also, if there is a reasonable means of escape, this element may be difficult to prove.
- *of another*
- *without consent* or *legal privilege* – This element will be difficult to establish if a merchant is involved. This aspect of tort law is discussed below.

Merchant Protection Statutes - Since many merchants lose thousands of dollars every year from shoplifters, many states have enacted statutes to protect them. These statutes are often referred to as shopkeeper's privilege. There are three important aspects of this type of statute that will absolve a merchant from liability of false imprisonment allegations.

Merchant Protection Statutes nuances

- There must be reasonable grounds for detaining and investigating the shoplifter.
- The suspected shoplifter can be detained for only a reasonable time.
- The investigations must be conducted in a reasonable manner.

Defamation of Character- This tort involves an intentional or accidental untrue statement of fact made about an individual to a third party.

Defamation of Character list of elements with special nuances

- *intentional* or *accidental* – may be overheard accidentally
- *untrue statement of fact* – Be careful as truth is always a defense.
- *published to a third party* – The third party can see or hear the untrue statement.

You should be aware of some of the other important aspects of defamation of character. For example, libel is written defamation and slander is oral defamation. Some types of media such as television and radio broadcasts come under the category of libel, as the courts view them as permanent in nature since the original scripts were composed prior to broadcasting the defamatory content. Also, opinions are not actionable, as it is not considered to be an untrue statement of fact. Finally, public figures such as movie stars, celebrities and other famous people must show that the statement was knowingly made or with reckless disregard of the statement's falsity. In other words, malice must be shown.

Misappropriation of the Right to Publicity – This tort is an attempt by another to appropriate a living person's name or identity for commercial purposes. A classic example of this would be individuals who sell cheaper versions of a famous performer's concert merchandise.

Invasion of the Right to Publicity

- A violation
- of an individual's
- right to live his/her life
- without unwarranted or undesired
- publicity

Truth is not a defense to this tort, as the fact does not have to be untrue. If the fact is one of public record, this tort cannot be claimed. Examples include wiretapping, reading hand delivered as well as the e-mail of another.

Intentional Infliction of Emotional Distress

- intentional or reckless
- extreme and outrageous conduct – The conduct must go beyond the bounds of decency.
- by one individual
- against another
- that causes severe emotional distress – Many states require a physical injury, illness or discomfort. However, states that are more flexible in their interpretation of this element have found that humiliation, fear and anger will satisfy this element. Some states no longer require that the severity of the emotional distress be shown.

Negligent Infliction of Emotional Distress

Though this is not an intentional tort, it is being placed here as it is a tort that is not only against individuals, but is one that some courts are recognizing when defendant's negligent conduct causes the plaintiff to suffer severe emotional distress. This tort requires the plaintiff's relative was injured or killed and that plaintiff suffered the severe distress at the same time he or she observed the accident. Some jurisdictions require the plaintiff suffer some sort of physical injury while other states do not mandate this element.

Intentional Torts Against Property

The two torts in this area are trespass to land, which is real property, and the trespass to personal property, which involves those items that are movable. The tort of conversion is also discussed along with trespass to personal property.

Trespass to Land

- *intentional* – It is not intentional if someone else pushes an individual onto someone else's land
- *entry*
- *onto the land*
- *of another*
- *without consent* or *legal privilege* –Rescuing someone from danger is not considered trespass. By the same token, remaining on someone's land after the invitation has expired is trespass.

Trespass to Personal Property

- *intentional*
- *injury* or *interference with* – An example of this would be breaking someone else's glass vase.
- *another's enjoyment*
- *of his or her personal property*

Conversion of Personal Property

- *intentionally*
- *depriving* – Note that the failure to return borrowed property can satisfy this element.
- a true *owner*
- of the *use and enjoyment*
- *of his or her personal property*

The rightful owner can bring a cause of action to get the property back. If the property is destroyed or lost, the true owner can recover the property's value.

Negligence

In order to be successful in a negligence cause of action, one must show that a duty of care was owed to the plaintiff, that the defendant breached this duty, that the defendant was the actual and proximate cause of plaintiff's injuries and that the plaintiff suffered damages.

Duty of Care

You should know the general duty of care which states that we all owe one another a duty of due care so as to not subject others to an unreasonable risk of harm. This duty is based on the reasonable person standard. An example of when this general duty of care is owed is the situation involving an invitee. An invitee is one who is invited onto the land of another for the mutual benefit of both people. The duty of ordinary care is also owed to licensees. A licensee is one who with consent comes onto the land of another for his or her own benefit. An example of a licensee would be an encyclopedia salesperson. Note, an owner does not owe a general duty of care to a trespasser; however, an owner of property does owe a duty not to willfully or wantonly injure a trespasser. Also, children are measured against other children of similar age and experience.

There are certain situations however where a higher standard of care is owed. They involve the professionals, innkeepers, common carriers, tavern and bartenders, social hosts and paying Passengers riding in a vehicle of another.

Professionals are held to the standard of a reasonable professional. Liability is known as malpractice. You should be cognizant of the medical professional who acts as a good Samaritan. Medical professionals are relieved of liability for injury caused by their ordinary negligence when rendering aid to victims in need of emergency care.

Innkeepers owe a duty of utmost care and have to provide security for their guest.

Common carriers also owe a duty of utmost care for their guests.

Tavern and bartenders are liable to third parties who are injured by a patron who was served too much alcohol or who was served alcohol when he/she was already intoxicated. Social Hosts are held liable for injuries caused by guests who are served too much alcohol.

The Danger Invites Rescue Doctrine allows those who are injured while going to someone's rescue to sue the person who caused the dangerous situation. Compare this to the Fireman's Rule where the fireman who is injured while putting out a fire may not sue the person who caused the fire as not only does the job imply that injury may occur, but people would be reluctant to call for help if they thought they might be sued in doing so.

Breach of Duty

If a duty, albeit general and or special has been established and it is found that the defendant has not acted as a reasonable person would, the court may find a breach of the duty of care.

Causation
It is important to remember that the plaintiff must show that the defendant was the actual (factual) and proximate (legal) cause of the plaintiff's injuries. Further, the defendant must be the direct cause of the plaintiff's injuries. If this cannot be established, plaintiff must show that the injuries that occurred were foreseeable in that it would be the type of injury one would expect from the activity the defendant was engaged in. It is best to diagram this element horizontally in order to remember its nuances. Please see below.

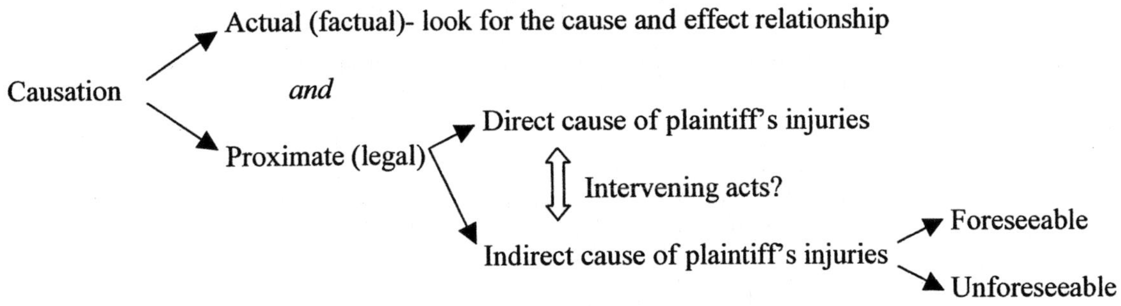

Damages
The plaintiff must nave actually suffered an injury or damages.

Defenses
Contributory negligence states that if a plaintiff is partially at fault for causing his or her own injuries, then the plaintiff is barred from recovering damages.

Comparative negligence doctrines assess damages by the plaintiff's percentage of fault. This is nown as pure comparative negligence. If however, the plaintiff is in a jurisdiction that adopts The partial comparative negligence doctrine, then plaintiff must be less than fifty percent negligent in causing his or her injuries. If the plaintiff is over fifty percent negligent, then recovery is barred and the defendant is not liable.

Assumption of the Risk is a defense that states that a defendant may assert indicating that the plaintiff knowingly and voluntarily entered into a risky activity that resulted in injury.

Special Negligence Doctrines

Negligence per se and **res ipsa loquitur** are special negligence doctrines that are important to be aware of as they are special in their establishment of the element of duty as well as assisting in the plaintiff's burden of proof in a negligence case.

Negligence Per Se – This doctrine involves the violation of a statute that proximately causes the plaintiff's injuries. There must be a statute that was enacted to prevent the type of injury suffered by the plaintiff and the plaintiff must be within the class of persons the statute was designed to protect.

Res Ipsa Loquitur – This doctrine means, "the thing speaks for itself." This is an important doctrine as there is a presumption of negligence where the plaintiff proves that the defendant had exclusive control of the instrumentality or circumstances that caused the plaintiff's injuries and the injury that the plaintiff suffered wouldn't have ordinarily occurred, "but for" someone's negligence.

Business Torts

Entering into a business or profession without a license can subject the violator to civil and criminal penalties.

Unfair Competition – This tort is also known as palming off whereby one company tries to "palm off" its products as those of a rival. Plaintiff must show the defendant used the plaintiff's symbol, trademark, logo, etc and that there is a likelihood of confusion as to the product's origin.

Disparagement – This tort involves an untrue statement made by a person or business about another business' reputation, services, products, etc. This tort is also known as product disparagement or trade libel. The defendant must have made the statement intentionally to a third party knowing that what he or she was saying was not true.

False Advertising – When companies use untruthful comparative advertising to compare the qualities of their products to those of their competitors, this is known as false advertising. False and misleading advertising is a violation of part of the federal statute known as the Lanham Act.

Intentional Misrepresentation (Fraud) – This tort lends itself nicely towards a mnemonic that will assist you in remembering its elements. The mnemonic is MIS JD.

M Misrepresentation of material fact that was false in nature
I Intentionally made to an innocent party
S Scienter (knowledge) of the statement's falsity by the wrongdoer
J Justifiable Reliance on the false statement by the innocent party
D Damages were suffered by the injured party

Intentional Interference With Contractual Relations – There must be a valid and enforceable contract that a third party knows about. The third party induces one of the contracting parties to breach the contract with the other party.

Breach of Implied Covenant of Good Faith and Fair Dealing – Parties to a contract must adhere to the express terms of a contract and also to the implied term of "good faith." When a party to a contract acts in bad faith, this gives rise to the tort of Breach of Implied Covenant of Good Faith and Fair Dealing.

Punitive Damages – These types of damages are recoverable in torts involving fraud, intentional conduct and are in addition to actual damages. Punitive damages are awarded not only to set an example for others, but to prevent the defendant from the same or similar conduct in the future and to punish the defendant for his or her actions.

Strict Liability – This is a tort that involves liability without fault if the activity that the defendant is engaged in places the public at risk of injury despite reasonable care being taken. Examples of activities that qualify for this categorization include fumigation, storage of explosives, and blasting. Punitive damages are also recoverable in strict liability cases.

Refresh Your Memory

The following exercise will enable you to refresh your memory on the rules and principles presented to you in this chapter. Read each question twice and place your answer in the blanks provided. Review the chapter material for any question you miss or are unable to remember.

1. Tor is a French word that means ________.

2. The main purpose that punitive damages are awarded is to _________ the defendant.

3. The tort of assault requires reasonable apprehension of _______________ ___________.

4. Which doctrine applies when an individual acts with the intent to injure one person but actually injures another? The doctrine of _____________ _____________.

5. Actual malice means that the defendant made the false statement knowingly or with ___________ ___________ __ __ ___________.

6. Slander is an ____ defamatory statement.

7. The tort of misappropriation is also known as the tort of ________________.

8. __________________ is an example of the tort of invasion of the right to privacy.

9. Interference with an owner's right to exclusive possession of land constitutes the tort of ______________ to ____________.

10. _________ of care refers to the obligation not to cause any unreasonable harm or risk of harm to others.

11. When proving causation in a negligence action, what are the two types of causation that must be proved before the plaintiff may prevail? ___________ in fact and ___________ _______.

12. A professional who breaches the reasonable professional standard may be found liable based on __________________ __________________.

13. The doctrine of res ipsa loquitur raises the _________________ of negligence.

14. Under which type of act may a tavern and bartender be civilly liable for too much alcohol? _________ ________ act.

Critical Thought Exercise

Chip North is a 22-year-old racing enthusiast who went to a car race at Trona International Speedway. North was excited because he had obtained a seat close to the track near the finish line. North's ticket came with five others in a sealed envelope that was imprinted in a large font with the following:

"WARNING!
Your seating for this event is in a very
DANGEROUS AREA

Debris and fluids from race cars may be ejected or sprayed from the race surface into your seating area in the event of a crash or malfunction of a race vehicle. Please ask to change your seating if you do not desire to ASSUME THE RISK OF SERIOUS INJURY."

The envelope is opened by North's younger brother, who does not pay any attention to the envelope and discards it after removing the tickets. During the race a car crashes into the wall in front of North's seat and sprays him with burning gasoline, causing severe injuries. North sues Trona Speedway for negligence for subjecting him to a known danger by seating him and others so close to the racetrack. Trona Speedway denies any liability based upon the warning on the envelope and the known risk that spectators take when attending a race.

At trial, which side should prevail?

Answer. ____

____

____

____

____

____

____

____

____

____

____

____

____

____

____

____

____

Practice Quiz

True/False

1. ___ Fred can sue Sam for assault for threatening to beat him to a pulp right now. [p 73]

2. ___ Direct physical harm between the perpetrator and the victim is needed when proving the tort of battery. [p 73]

3. ___ Truth is not an absolute defense to a charge of defamation. [p 76]

4. ___ Angie attempt by another person to used Jennifer Aniston's picture to advertise her new real estate agency without Jennifer's permission. Jennifer does not have any cause of action to sue

Jennifer for as she should assume her popularity will be used in such things as advertising. [p 75]

5. ___ Threats of future harm as well as moral pressure are both considered to be forms of false imprisonment. [p 74]

6. ___ The tort of conversion can not happen when someone who initially was given possession of personal property fails to return it. [p 79]

7. ___ A person who is the cause of a car accident because he or she fell asleep while driving is not liable for any resulting injuries caused by his or her carelessness as his or her actions were not intentional. [p 80]

8. ___ Under the reasonable person standard, the courts try to determine how a subjective, careful, and unconscious person would have acted in the same circumstances, and then measure the defendant's conduct against this standard. [p 80]

9. ___ Actual cause is the same principle as proximate cause. [p 82]

10. ___ Since there have been an increase in malpractice law suits, almost all states have enacted the Good Samaritan laws that relieve medical professionals from liability for injury caused by their ordinary negligence in such circumstance. [p 86]

11. ___ Dram Shop Acts do not hold tavern and bartenders civilly liable for injuries caused to or by patrons who are served too much alcohol. [p 86]

12. ___ The fireman's rule provides that a fireman may not sue the party whose negligence caused the fire for any resulting injuries from putting out the fire. [p 86]

13. ___ Under the social host liability rule, a social host is liable for injuries caused by guests who are served alcohol at a social function. [p 87]

14. ___ Common carriers and innkeepers owe a duty of utmost care to their passengers and guests. [p 88]

15. ___ If a plaintiff knows of and voluntarily enters into or participates in a risky activity that results in injury, the law acknowledges that the plaintiff assumed the risk involved. [p 89]

Multiple Choice:

16. A tort that states that a person whose extreme and outrageous conduct intentionally or recklessly causes severe emotional distress is known as [p 76]
    a. intentional infliction of emotional distress.
    b. res ipsa loquitur.
    c. extreme negligence.
    d. invasion of right to privacy.

17. Jane spray painted George's red corvette purple and dented the passenger door. Which tort has Jane committed? [p 92]
    a. false imprisonment.

b. trespass to personal property.
c. stinginess.
d. negligence.

18. If Jane took George's red Corvette and sold it, this would be considered the tort of [p 79]
a. trespass to personal property.
b. conversion of personal property.
c. trespass to land.
d. strict liability.

19. In determining the standard of care owed by an attorney, the court will measure the defendant's conduct against [p 81]
a. a reasonable person.
b. a reasonable brain surgeon.
c. a reasonable attorney.
d. a reasonable child.

20. A breach of duty of care is [p 80]
a. a fulfillment to act as a reasonable person under the same or similar circumstances.
b. an expectation in certain circumstances.
c. the failure to act as a reasonable person would.
d. immaterial in assessing liability.

21. If two or more individuals are liable for negligently causing the plaintiff's injuries, both or all can be held liable to the plaintiff if each of their acts is a [p 83]
a. proximate cause of plaintiff's injuries.
b. substantial factor in causing the plaintiff's injuries.
c. inconsequential cause of plaintiff's injuries.
d. None of the above.

22. Sally, a bystander who witnessed the injury of Charlie, her brother that was caused by Kaitlin's negligent conduct may bring a cause of action against Kaitlin for [p 85]
a. negligent death.
b. intentional infliction of emotional distress.
c. battery.
d. negligent infliction of emotional distress.

23. Liability for a surgeon who braches the reasonable professional standard of care is known as [p 84]
a. negligence per se.
b. res ipsa loquitur.
c. professional malpractice.
d. social host liability.

24. Violation of a statute that proximately causes an injury is referred to as [p 85]
a. negligence per se.
b. negligent infliction of emotional distress.
c. the "Danger Invites Rescue" doctrine.
d. unfair competition.

25. If Andrea Smith, a registered nurse sees Ida Victim laying helplessly in the line of traffic and decides to render aid, but, in doing so causes her ankle to be bruised, which statute will relieve Andrea of liability for Ida's injuries? [pp 85-86]
    a. Assumption of the risk
    b. Dram shop acts
    c. Good Samaritan law
    d. Strict liability

Short Answer:

26. If Terry wants to sue Cyrina for defamation of character, wht must Terry prove? [p 76]

____

____

27. Briefly describe the difference between real property and personal property. [p 78]

____

____

28. What are the necessary elements that Shelly must prove in order to establish a cause of action for negligence against Andrew? [p 79]

____

____

____

29. What is the difference between actual cause and proximate cause? [p 82] ______________

____

____

30. Why isn't opinion actionable in terms of defamation of character? [p 76]

____

____

31. If Harold wants to sue Archie for Intentional Misrepresentation, what elements must Harold prove? [p 92] ______________________________

____

32. What must a plaintiff show in order to succeed in a cause of action for disparagement? [p 92] ______________________________

____

33. If Wendy intended to hit Marie, but hit Jeff instead, what must Jeff show under the doctrine of transferred intent? ______________________________

____

34. Explain the liability concept under a cause of action for strict liability. [p 93]

____

____

Chapter 5
INTELLECTUAL PROPERTY AND INTERNET LAW

Chapter Overview

This chapter provides information about the various types of intellectual property. Intellectual property consists of trade secrets, patents, trademarks, copyrights, computer law and domain names. You will learn a wealth of information concerning this type of property including the remedies for infringement of the rights that are attached to them. Further, you will become familiar with the protection that is attached to technology based intellectual property.

Objectives

Upon completion of the exercises in this chapter, you should be able to:

1. Define what intellectual property consists of.
2. Explain the business tort of misappropriating a trade secret.
3. Explain the process for obtaining a patent
4. Discuss the types of writings afforded protection under copyright laws.
5. Differentiate between trademarks, service marks and certification marks.
6. Explain what international protection is given to intellectual property rights.

Practical Application

You should be able to differentiate between a copyright, trademark and patent and know whether or not an infringement has occurred. Further, you will be more familiar with the various intellectual property acts and what they apply to. This chapter provides a clearer understanding of what is involved in intellectual property and which acts and laws will afford the greatest protection to the creator.

Helpful Hints

Since there is a wealth of information with the various intellectual property acts, the easiest way to study the material is to categorize all of the information and acts in a methodical fashion that is consistent throughout the chapter. The Study Tips section that follows attempts to organize the information for you so that studying becomes more manageable.

Study Tips

Each intellectual topic area is organized in the same fashion so that it becomes habit for you to learn the information in a logical manner. When studying, it will help you to have someone ask you the questions under each heading to determine what you have learned.

Trade Secrets

What is a trade secret? A product, formula, pattern, design compilation of customer data or any other business secret. Note, the federal definition includes,

What is considered a violation of a trade secret? The defendant, usually an employee must have obtained the trade secret through unlawful means, such as theft, bribery, etc.

Does an owner of a trade secret have any obligations under the law? Yes, he or she must take all reasonable protections to protect his or her trade secret. If the owner does not protect his or her trade secret, then there is no protection under the law for it.

What laws afford protection of a trade secret?
State unfair competition laws, which may include the Uniform Trade Secrets Act.
The federal Economic Espionage Act of 1996 makes it a federal crime to steal another person's trade secrets.

What may the owner recover if he or she is successful in a trade secret action?
The owner may recover profits, damages and procure an injunction to stop the offender from using or revealing the trade secret.
Under the Economic Espionage Act, organizations may be fined up to $5 million dollars per criminal act and $10 million if the act benefited a foreign government. Also, individuals may get up to 15 years of prison time per violation increasing to 25 years if the act benefited a foreign government.

Patents

What is required to get a patent? An invention that is novel, useful and nonobvious.

What types of things can be patented? Processes, machines, improvements of existing machines, compositions of matter, asexually reproduced plants, designs for an article of manufacture, living material invented by a person

How does an individual get a patent? Briefly stated, an individual applies for a patent with the Patent and Trademark Office and is assigned a number. While waiting for approval, the individual may affix the terminology, "patent pending" on the thing to be protected.

What other laws are available to help inventors? Under the *American Inventors Protection Act* of 1999, an inventor may file a provisional application with the Patent and Trademark Office pending the final completion and filing of a patent application. The inventor has "provisional rights" for three months pending the filing of a final application.

Federal Law and Patents – The *Federal Patent Statue* protects patented inventions from infringement. There are no state patent laws.

Changes in Patent Laws- In 1994, the General Agreement on Tariffs and Trade extended patent protection from 17 to 20 years. Also, the patent term now begins to run from the date that the application is filed instead of when the patent is issued.

Cyber Business Plans and *financial models* that are used over the Internet are protected by patent law.

Law to be aware of - The *Public Use Doctrine* (also called the one-year "on sale" doctrine) states that a patent may not be granted if the invention was used by the public for more than one year prior to the filing of the patent application. This law encourages timely patent applications.

What may the patent holder recover in a successful patent infringement action? A patent holder may recover money equal to a reasonable royalty rate on the sale of infringed article, damages such as loss of customers, an injunction preventing future infringing action and an order requiring destruction of the infringing material. If the court finds that the infringement was intentional, then it may award treble the damages.

Copyrights

What can be copyrighted? Only tangible writings that can be physically seen may be copyrighted. This includes, books, sermons, greeting cards, jewelry, and glassware.

What is required in order to get a copyright? The work must be the original, tangible work of the author. Notice is not required, however it is recommended that notice be place on the work so as to prevent the claim of innocent infringement. Registration with the U.S. Copyright Office is needed as well.

What laws afford protection of an individual's work?
Copyright Term Extension Act of 1998 - This act added 20 years to existing copyrighted work and to future copyrighted works. For individual copyright holders, copyright protection is for the life of the author plus 70 years. For a Corporate copyright holder, protection is ninety-five years from the year of first publication or 120 years from the year of creation, whichever is the shorter of the two.

Computer Software Copyright Act – Computer programs were added to the list of tangible items protected by copyright law. It has been held that the creator of a copyrightable software program obtains automatic copyright protection. The *Judicial Improvement Act* allows for the acceptance and recordation of any document relating to computer software. Finally, the *Semiconductor Chip Protection Act of 1984* provides protection of a computer's hardware components, and masks that are used to create computer chips.

The Digital Millennium Copyright Act – This act " prohibits the unauthorized access to copyrighted digital works by circumventing the wrapper or encryption technology that protects the intellectual property." Civil and criminal penalties are imposed under this act. Actual damages, treble damages, attorney's fees, and injunction and statutory damages are some of the remedies available. Criminal penalties in the form of fines and prison time may also be ordered. The level of protection of digital copyrighted works has risen as a result of this act.

The World Intellectual Property Organization prompted the *Copyright Treaty* that "protects computer programs and their data and grants the copyright holders the exclusive right to make their works available on the Internet and other wireless means". The *Phonogram Treaty* gives "performers and producers the exclusive right to broadcast, reproduce, and distribute copies of their performances by any means, including video recording, digital sound, or encryption signal."

The *No Electronic Theft Act (NET act)* provides from criminalizing certain types of copyright infringement. It "prohibits any person from willfully infringing a copyright for either the purpose of commercial advantage or financial gain, or by reproduction or distribution even without commercial advantage or financial gain, including by electronic means where the retail value exceeds $1,000. Up to one year imprisonment and fines up to $100,000 are the penalties for violating this act.

<u>Can work be used even if it is copyrighted?</u> Under the *Fair Use Doctrine,* certain limited, unauthorized use of copyrighted materials is permitted without it being an infringement. Quotations from a review or criticism of a work, brief news report quotations, a small reproduction of a work by a teacher in order to teach a lesson and reproduction of a work in a judicial or legislative hearing are considered fair use.

<u>What may an individual recover in a successful copyright infringement action?</u> The plaintiff may recover any profit made by the infringer, damages suffered by the plaintiff, an order to impound or destroy the infringing work, an injunction to prohibit future infringement and statutory damages in lieu of actual damages may be awarded.

Trademarks

<u>What can be trademarked?</u> Marks such as distinctive marks, symbols, names, words, mottos or slogans can be trademarked. Color may even be trademarked when it is associated with a particular good.

<u>Note the difference between a trademark and other marks, such as a service mark, certification mark or a collective mark</u>

Service mark – Used to set apart the services of the holder from the competition. *Ex: Weight Watchers*
Certification mark – A mark used to certify that goods are of a certain quality or come from a certain geographical location. *Ex: Santa Maria Tri-Tip Sandwiches*
Collective mark –A mark used by associations or cooperatives, etc. *Ex: Big Brothers of America*

<u>What is the purpose of a trademark?</u> To protect the owner's investment and good will in a mark.

<u>What is needed to qualify for protection of a mark?</u> The mark must have acquired secondary meaning and be distinctive. Both of these aspects must be present or the mark will not be protected. A term that becomes descriptive loses its distinction and its protection.

<u>How does an individual register a trademark?</u> Trademarks are registered with the U.S. Patent and Trademark Office in Washington D.C. The original mark is valid for 10 years and renewable for an unlimited number of 10-year periods. The registered user ma y use the trademark symbol, however, it is not necessary. Registration is permitted if a mark was in used in commerce or the Individual verifies a good faith intention to use the mark within six months of registration.

<u>What laws protect a trademark?</u>
The *Federal Lanham Trademark Revision Act of 1998* which made it easier to register trademarks, but more difficult to maintain them.

The *Federal Dilution Act of 1995* protects famous marks from dilution. There are three requirements under this act that must be met. The mark must be famous and used for commercial purposes by the other party. Also, the use must cause dilution of the distinctive aspect of the mark. The purpose of this act is to stop those who try to benefit from others monetary and creative efforts in promoting their famous marks. Many situations that call for the use of this act's protection are domain name cases.

The *Agreement on Trade-Related Aspects of International Property Rights* requires that member nations of the WTO must comply with the "international treaties and conventions protecting copyrights in traditional works, computer programs, and digital works, and related intellectual property laws." If one country thinks that another country is not complying with this law, a nation can file a charge with the WTO.

State antidilution statutes allow companies and individuals to register service marks and trademarks in an effort to prevent infringement on and dilution of a mark that has been registered. Local businesses take advantage of registering under the state's protection.

Refresh Your Memory

The following exercise will enable you to refresh your memory on the rules and principles presented to you in this chapter. Read each question twice and place your answer in the blanks provided. Review the chapter material for any question you miss or are unable to remember.

1. What types of writings are subject to copyright registration? ____________________

2. Give examples of the term writing. ____

3. What did the Sonny Bono Copyright Term Extension Act of 1998 do?
____
____

4. Define the meaning of a trade secret? _______________________________________
____.

5. Explain the main purpose of enacting the federal Espionage Act of 1996? __________
____

6. Which law intended to provide an incentive to investors? _____________
____

7. What three aspects must be present for an invention to be patented? The invention must be ___________________, ____________________, and ___________________.

8. Give an example of three things that may be patented. (1) ______________________
(2) ____________________________ (3) _________________________

9. What is meant by trade dress as per the protection afforded it in the Lanham Act?
____
____

10. What does the public use doctrine state? ______________________________
____

Critical Thought Exercise

Lindsey and Tony decide to establish an Internet business called Our Business is E-Business (OBE) in Greenport, while enrolled a Green Valley College. The business sells electronic equipment including computers, CD players, home theater systems, and PDA's. The merchandise is high quality, but sales have been in a slump due to competition. They need more sales to keep the business operating. Lindsey and Tony add you as a partner with a 1/3 interest for you investment of $20,000. Lindsey comments that if all the students who were listening to the latest hits from artists like Linkin Park, O-Town, and Sheryl Crow would buy apiece of equipment from them, OBE would be an overnight success. Lindsey purchased CDs from twelve popular music artists and establishes a link for listening to this music once an item is purchased from OBE. For every $100 spent on OBE merchandise, the customer can listen to an hour of music for free. Lindsey and Tony have not been making very mush profit on each individual sale, especially since many items sold by OBE are relatively inexpensive, such as remote controls, surge protectors, CD cases, and audio/video cables. As a partner, you are worried that there may be something wrong with using the artist's music to help sell OBE merchandise. You ask Tony and Lindsey to remove the link to the free music from the OBE Internet site. Mainly because sales have increased by 30% since the music link was added to the OBE site, they vote against you and insist that the music link remain part of the site unless you can prove to them that it is not in the best interest of OBE to continue with the "free music" offer.

Prepare a memorandum to your partners on the intellectual property rights that may be involved in your situation and the consequences of any infringement for OBE.

Answer. ____
____
____
____
____
____
____
____
____
____
____
____
____
____
____
____
____
____

Practice Quiz

True/False:

1. ___ There are state patent laws. [p 103]

2. ___ The issuance of a patent may not be challenged. [p 104]

3. ___ Improvements to existing machines can be patented. [p 104]

4. ___ An injunction is one remedy that is not available for patent infringement. [p 105]

5. ___ An idea by itself is not copyrightable. [p 108]

6. ___ One of the things the American Inventors Protection Act does not permit is for an inventor to file a provisional application with the Patents and Trademark Office. [p 106]

7. ___ The Digital Millennium Copyright Act imposes both civil and criminal penalties. [p 112]

8. ___ A brief quotation in a news report is subject to fair use. [p 109]

9. ___ Cyber business plans and financial models are not subject to patent protection. [p 105]

10. ___ The creator of copyrightable software programs does not obtain automatic copyright protection. [p 109]

11. ___ The copyright holder may not recover for infringement where fair use is found. [p 109]

12. ___ It is legal to access copyrighted material by breaking through the digital wrapper that protects the work. [p 112]

13. ___ If Sam Sly copies a very tiny part of the back of your business law text and places it in his text entitled, "Business Law for Numbskulls!," he will be held liable regardless of the amount of work he copied. [p 109]

Multiple Choice:

14. In order for an invention to receive a patent, it must [p 104]
    a. be novel, useless, and non-obvious.
    b. be novel, useful and non-obvious.
    c. be novel, useful and obvious.
    d. be novel, functional and clandestine.

15. Examples of trade secrets include [p 119]
    a. patterns, designs, and slogans.
    b. formulas, patterns and designs.
    c. postcards, tapestries, and glass
    d. maps, books, and tangible writings.

16. A trademark is good for [p 112]
    a. 10 years and can be renewed for one more ten year period.
    b. 10 years.
    c. 10 years and can be renewed for an unlimited number of 10 year periods.
    d. 20 years plus the life of the creator.

17. What federal act specifically provides protection for trademarks, service marks and other marks? [p 112]
    a. The Lanham Trademark Act
    b. The Landon Act
    c. The Mask Work Act
    d. The Sony Bono Term Extension Act

18. Explain to Marko what are the state trademark statutes called? [p 117-118]
    a. Distinct and secondary meaning statutes
    b. Public use doctrine statutes
    c. No electronic theft statutes
    d. Antidilution statutes

19. If Ann came into your office with the following items, which one would you tell her is not afforded copyright protection under the law? [p 117]
    a. Photographs
    b. Poems
    c. Color
    d. Maps

Short Answer:

20. A distinctive mark that has acquired secondary meaning qualifies for ___________ protection. [p 114]

21. If Rosa steals the secret recipe to Betty's Blueberry Bagels and opens up his own bagel shop, what should Betty's cause of action against Rosa be based on? [p.119]

    ____

22. If Chandler finds out that Robby stole his recipe by hacking into his computer files, what federal act will give Chandler the best chance of recovering his economic damages from Robby? [p 119] The federal _________________ __________________ __________

23. What does the No Electronic Theft Act Provide? [p 120] ________________________
____

24. What is the definition for generic name? [p 116] _______________________________

25. Wilson Wickes sues Tammy Teacher for copyright infringement based on Tammy's use of Wilson's poem to provide an example of iambic pentameter for her class. What is Tammy's best defense to a lawsuit brought by Wilson? [p 109]

26. Prudential Insurance Company's "Own a Piece of the Rock" is an example of a ____. [p 112]

27. "Boy Scouts of America" is an example of a ______________ ______________. [p 113]

Chapter 6
BUSINESS AND CYBER CRIMES

Chapter Overview

This chapter gives an insightful presentation of business and online crimes. You will be able to know the difference between a felony and a misdemeanor as well as know how the various crimes are defined and what elements are necessary to establish liability for each. Additionally, the chapter provides a thorough overview of criminal procedure from arrest through trial. The Racketeer Influenced and Corrupt Organization Act (RICO), Foreign Corrupt Practices Act and the safeguards provided in the Fourth, Fifth, Sixth and Eighth amendments to the U.S. Constitution are also examined. Finally the law as it pertains to the computer and Internet crimes is reviewed.

Objectives

Upon completion of this chapter's exercises, you should be able to:
1. Describe the difference between a felony and a misdemeanor.
2. Discuss the elements of a crime.
3. Discuss criminal procedure beginning with the arrest and ending with the trial.
4. Differentiate between crimes against persons and property as well as those involving white-collar crimes and criminal fraud.
5. Understand the safeguards inherent in the Fourth, Fifth, Sixth and Eighth Amendments to the United States Constitution.
6. Familiarize you with the laws affecting the computer and crimes involving the Internet.

Practical Application

You should be able to identify the different types of crimes, including those involving the computer and the Internet as well as identify the elements necessary to establish liability. Further, you should be able to understand and explain the criminal process beginning with the arrest through to trial. In addition, you should be able to access the application of the safeguards that are afforded under the United States constitution.

Helpful Hints

It is helpful to distinguish between what a felony is versus a misdemeanor. This chapter lends itself toward categorization. It is easier to remember the crimes that are involved if you categorize them based on whether the crimes are against individuals, property or the computer and Internet. In order to remember the aspects of criminal procedure that accompanies the crime itself, it is helpful to draw a horizontal time line listing the various stages of the criminal process. Further, it is important to be aware of the various statutory acts such as Racketeer Influenced and Corrupt Organization Act and the Foreign Corrupt Practices Act.

Study Tips

Background Information
- ✓ The United States leads the world in terms of humanity and sophistication in the criminal law system.
- ✓ A person is presumed innocent until proven guilty.
- ✓ Guilt must be established beyond a reasonable doubt.
- ✓ The United States Constitution gives the accused certain safeguards.

Crime
A crime is a violation of a duty owed to society that has legal consequences and which requires the individual to make amends to the public.

Sources of Criminal Law
- ✓ Statutes are the main source
- ✓ Penal codes – These are detailed, well-defined criminal activities along with punishment for the same if committed.
- ✓ State and federal regulatory statutes.

Parties to a criminal action
- ✓ The government is the plaintiff in a criminal action and is represented by an attorney called a prosecutor.
- ✓ The accused is the defendant and is represented by a defense attorney. The government will provide a free attorney if the defendant is unable to afford representation.

Important facts to know about felonies:
- ✓ They are the most serious types of crimes.
- ✓ Crimes that are inherently evil (mala in se) are considered to be felonies.
- ✓ Crimes such as murder, rape, bribery and embezzlement are felonies in a majority of jurisdictions.
- ✓ Imprisonment is the usual punishment, however, the death penalty is imposed in some jurisdictions for the crime of first-degree murder.
- ✓ Federal law requires mandatory sentencing for certain crimes.
- ✓ Some states require mandatory sentencing for certain crimes.
- ✓ A number of statutes provide for the degrees of crime and the penalties for each.

Important facts to know about misdemeanors:
- ✓ They are less serious than felonies.
- ✓ Crimes that are prohibited by society (mala prohibita) are categorized as a misdemeanor.
- ✓ Crimes such as burglary, regulatory statute violations, and robbery are examples of misdemeanors.
- ✓ These types of crimes have punishments that are less severe than felonies.
- ✓ Punishment includes imprisonment for less than a year and/or a fine.

Violations are neither a felony nor a misdemeanor.
- ✓ Examples of a violation include jaywalking and traffic violations. A fine is the only punishment allowable unless a jury trial is granted.

Elements of a Crime
Two necessary elements to be shown when proving a person is guilty of a crime:

Criminal Act

- ✓ The defendant must have performed the wrongful act. The performance of the wrongful act is also known as the actus reus.
- ✓ The performing or failure to do a certain act can satisfy this element.
- ✓ A defendant's thought of doing the crime will not satisfy the criminal act element. The wrongful act must have been carried out.
- ✓ An interesting notation is that criminal acts can bring about civil law actions that have their basis in tort.

Criminal Intent

- ✓ The defendant must have the necessary state of mind (specific or general intent) when he/she performed the act. This intent is also referred to as the mens rea.
- ✓ It is important to differentiate between specific and general intent. Specific intent is demonstrated when the accused intentionally or with knowledge or purposefully performs the prohibited act. General intent is proven where there is a lesser amount of culpability.
- ✓ The jury may deduce the type of intent based upon the defendant's actions.
- ✓ There is no crime where there is no mens rea. If the act that was performed was an accident, then mens rea cannot be established.
- ✓ Strict or absolute liability for a prohibited act means that mens rea is not required. A violation of an environmental statute would be an example where absolute liability would be imposed.

Crimes Affecting Business

The most common crimes that affect business are those given below. It is important for you to be aware of the necessary elements of a particular crime in order to prove that it has or has not been committed. When you are given a certain set of facts, it is important to analyze them and determine their applicability to each of the requisite elements of the crime you are trying to prove.

Robbery

- ✓ The taking of personal property of another using fear or force.
- ✓ Note that a pickpocket does not qualify as a robbery as there is no fear or force.

Burglary

- ✓ At common law, burglary was the "breaking and entering a dwelling at night" with the intent to commit a felony therein.
- ✓ Compare the common definition to the modern expansion, which includes daytime thefts of offices and commercial buildings. Further, the breaking element is no longer a requirement in many jurisdictions. If there has been an unauthorized entry through an unlocked door or window, this will be sufficient.

Larceny

- ✓ At common law, larceny was the "wrongful and fraudulent taking of another person's personal property."
- ✓ Personal property includes trade secrets, computer programs, tangible property and other types of business property.
- ✓ Examples of larceny include automobile theft, car stereo theft and pick pocketing.
- ✓ The perpetrator need not use force or go into a building in order to commit this crime.
- ✓ Some jurisdictions categorize the larceny as either grand or petit based upon the value of the goods that were taken.

Theft
- ✓ In those jurisdictions that do not categorize their crimes in terms of robbery, larceny and burglary, the crimes of this nature are under the heading of theft. These jurisdictions then label the theft as petit or grand depending on the value of the goods taken.

Receiving Stolen Property
- ✓ If a person knowingly receives stolen property with the intent to deprive its rightful owner of that property, they may be found to have committed the crime of receiving stolen property. The stolen property may be personal property, money, stock certificates or anything tangible.
- ✓ An important notation is that the element of knowledge may be inferred from the circumstances.

Arson
- ✓ The crime of Arson at common law was defined as "the malicious or willful burning of the dwelling house of another person."
- ✓ Modernly, the term dwelling includes all buildings including public, commercial and private ones.

Forgery
- ✓ This crime involves the fraudulent making or alteration of a written document, which affects the legal liability of another person.
- ✓ Examples include falsifying public records and counterfeiting as well as imitating another person's signature on a check or altering the amount of the check. Note, that one spouse may sign his or her spouse's check and deposit it into a joint account without it being designated as forgery. There is no intent to defraud in this situation.

Extortion
- ✓ Extortion involves the obtaining of property of another with or without his or her consent by use of actual or threatened force, violence or fear.
- ✓ The truth or falsity of the information does not matter.
- ✓ Examples of extortion include when one person threatens another that a piece of information will be exposed unless money or property is given to the extortionist. This is known as blackmail.
- ✓ Extortion of public officials is referred to as extortion "under color of official right."

Credit-Card Crimes
- ✓ Many jurisdictions have made it a crime for the misappropriation and use of another person's credit cards.
- ✓ Some states prosecute credit-card crimes under their forgery statutes.

Bad Check Legislation
- ✓ A majority of jurisdictions hold that an individual who knowingly makes, draws, or presents a check for which there are insufficient funds in the individual's account to cover the amount of the check has committed a crime.
- ✓ Some jurisdictions require that proof of the intent to defraud be shown.

White- Collar Crimes otherwise known as Crimes Usually Committed by Businesspersons
- ✓ These are usually called white-collar crimes and involve deceit.
- ✓ Embezzlement, Criminal Fraud, and Bribery are examples of white-collar crimes.

Embezzlement
- ✓ A statutory crime involving the fraudulent conversion of property by a person to whom another individual's property was entrusted.
- ✓ Employer's representatives, agents or employees usually commit this crime.

- ✓ The main element to be aware of is the fact that the property was entrusted to the individual whom ultimately absconded with it.

Criminal Fraud

- ✓ This crime is known as false pretenses or criminal fraud or deceit as the accused obtains title to the property through trickery.
- ✓ Included under this crime is the crime of mail and wire fraud. The government will prosecute a suspect if the mail or wires are used to defraud another individual.
- ✓ It is important to be aware of the Identity Theft and Assumption Deterrence Act of 1998. This act makes it a crime the stealing of another's identity. This crime imposes a penalty of prison sentences from three to twenty-five years. The Federal Trade Commission also appoints a representative to assist in restoring victims credit and expunge the consequences of the imposter.

Bribery

- ✓ When one individual gives money, property, favors or anything of value to another in exchange for a favor in return, this is known as bribery. This is often referred to as a kickback or a payoff.
- ✓ Intent is an essential element of this crime.
- ✓ If the offeree accepts the bribe, he or she is then also guilty of the crime.
- ✓ The offeror can be guilty of the crime without the offeree accepting the bribe.
- ✓ The Foreign Corrupt Practices Act of 1977 requires firms to keep accurate records as they pertain to foreign transactions. Additionally, American companies may not bribe a foreign official, political party or candidate in an attempt to influence new business or retention of a continuing business. Knowledge is a key element in making the conduct as described above a crime. Punishment includes fines and imprisonment.

The Racketeer Influenced and Corrupt Organizations Act (RICO)

- ✓ It is a federal crime to acquire or maintain an interest in or conduct or participate in an "enterprise" through a "pattern" of "racketeering activity."
- ✓ Examples of racketeering activity include gambling, robbery, arson, deals involving narcotics, bribery, mail fraud, etc.
- ✓ Punishment includes fines, imprisonment, and forfeiture of any property or business interests that were obtained as a result of the RICO violations.
- ✓ The government can also seek business reorganization, dissolution, and the dissolution of the defendant's interest in an enterprise as part of civil penalties for RICO violations.

Inchoate crimes

- ✓ Nonparticipants commit these crimes.
- ✓ Conspiracy is an inchoate crime, which is defined as two or more individuals who enter into an agreement to commit a crime. An overt act in furtherance of the crime is needed.
- ✓ Attempt to commit a crime is a crime requiring an act in furtherance but not completion of a crime.
- ✓ Aiding and abetting the commission of a crime is a crime that occurs when an individual supports, assists or encourages the commission of a crime.

Corporate Criminal Liability

- ✓ At common law, the courts held that corporations lacked the mens rea needed to commit a crime.
- ✓ Modernly, corporations are being held criminally liable for the acts of their managers, employees, and agents. Since imprisonment is not feasible, they are being fined or having their franchise or license taken away.
- ✓ The corporate officers, employees or directors are held personally liable for crimes that they Personally commit regardless if it was done for personal gain or for the corporation. Further,

if a corporate manager fails to appropriately supervise his or her subordinate, the manager may be held criminally liable for the subordinate's criminal activities.

Criminal Procedure

There are several pretrial procedures as well as the trial itself that you need to be familiar with. The pretrial procedure involves the arrest, indictment, arraignment and plea-bargaining.

Arrest

- ✓ The police must have a warrant based upon probable cause before a person can be arrested. Probable cause has been defined as the existence of objective, articulated facts that would raise in the mind of a reasonable person that a crime has been committed or is about to be committed.
- ✓ A search without a warrant is allowed when the crime is in progress, those involved in the crime are fleeing from the scene or there is a great chance that the evidence will be destroyed. Probable cause is still required even in the absence of a warrant.
- ✓ After the accused is arrested, a booking take place. The booking involves the recording of the arrest as well as the standard fingerprinting.

Indictment or Information

- ✓ The indictment or information involves the formal charges that must be brought against the accused before being brought to trial,
- ✓ The government evaluates those charged with serious crimes. If there is enough evidence to hold the accused for trial, an indictment is then issued and the accused is held for trial.
- ✓ For crimes with a lesser magnitude, a judge will determine if there is sufficient evidence to hold the accused for trial. An information is issued upon confirmation that the evidence is sufficient and the accused is then held over for trial.

Arraignment

- ✓ Once an information or indictment is issued, the accused is informed of the charges against her or him and is requested to enter a plea.
- ✓ The accused may enter a guilty, not guilty or nolo contendere plea. If the latter is chosen, the accused does not admit guilt, but agrees to a penalty. Nolo contendere pleas may not be used later on in a civil proceeding. Acceptance of the nolo contendere pleading is optional.

Plea Bargaining

- ✓ This involves an agreement between the government and the accused whereby the accused admits to a lesser offense in exchange for the government's imposition of a lesser penalty.
- ✓ The rationale behind plea bargaining is to minimize overcrowding of prisons, avoid trial risks, and to save costs associated with trial.

The Criminal Trial

- ✓ All jurors must agree unanimously before the accused is found guilty.
- ✓ The defendant may appeal if he or she is found to be guilty.
- ✓ Even if one juror disagrees, the accused will not be found guilty.
- ✓ If the defendant is innocent, the government can not appeal.
- ✓ If a unanimous decision does not come to fruition, the jury will be hung in terms of what they decided. The government then has the option of retrying the case before a new jury or judge.

Constitutional Safeguards

- ✓ The **Fourth Amendment** plays an important role in protecting corporations and persons from *unreasonable searches and seizures* by the government. "It permits people to be secure in their person, houses, papers and effects." Note that regulated businesses as well as those who are involved in hazardous industries are subject to warrantless searches.

Searches may not go beyond the area specified in the warrant. If evidence is obtained as a result of an unreasonable search or seizure, it will be considered tainted. This evidence may not be used against the accused, but can be used against other individuals.

The "good faith" exception to the exclusionary rule states that illegally obtained evidence may be used against the accused if the police officers that obtained the evidence believed in good faith that they were acting in accordance with a lawful search warrant.

✓ The **Fifth Amendment** states "no person shall be compelled in any criminal case to be a witness against himself."

The *privilege against self-incrimination* is applicable to individuals, not corporations and partnerships. Be aware though that private papers such as personal diaries of businesspersons are protected from disclosure.

✓ **Immunity from Prosecution**
The government consents to not use any evidence given by an individual against that person. Immunity is usually granted when the government wants information from an individual who has asserted his or her Fifth Amendment privilege against self-incrimination. If immunity is granted, the individual loses his or her Fifth Amendment protection.

✓ Fifth Amendment Protection Against **Double Jeopardy**
The Fifth Amendment via its double jeopardy clause states a person may not be tried twice for the same crime. Compare this to where the accused has committed several crimes. The accused may be tried for each of the crimes without being in violation of the double jeopardy rule. Also, if the acts are violations in different jurisdictions, each jurisdiction may try the accused.

The *attorney-client privilege* is provided for in the Fifth Amendment. The Fifth Amendment also recognizes the psychiatrist/psychologist-patient privilege, priest/minister/rabi-penitent privilege, spouse-spouse privilege and parent-child privilege.

✓ Sixth Amendment Right to a **Public Jury Trial**
The Sixth Amendment gives the accused the right to be tried by an impartial jury, to cross-examine witnesses against the accused, to have a lawyer's assistance and to have a speedy trial.

✓ Eighth Amendment Protection against **Cruel and Unusual Punishment**
This amendment protects the accused from abusive or torturous punishments.

✓ **Accountant-Client Privilege**
Many states have enacted statutes that have created an accountant-client privilege. This law states that an accountant may not be called as a witness against a client. Note that there is no federal law that provides for the accountant-client privilege.

Federal Antiterrorism Act of 2001

✓ Congress enacted this act to help the government in prevention and detection of terrorist activities and with the investigation and prosecution of terrorists.

- ✓ Special Intelligence Court – This part of the act provides authorization for the issuance of expanded wiretap orders and subpoenas.
- ✓ Nationwide Search Warrant- Instead of using the traditional warrant that specified certain areas that a search warrant was good for, the act now provides for a nationwide search warrant to gather evidence of terrorist activities.
- ✓ Roving Wiretaps- Any person suspected of involvement in terrorism may have a roving wiretap placed on the use of multiple telephones, including cellular phones in order to monitor their activities. Former law required separate permission for each telephone that was used.
- ✓ Sharing Information – Evidence that is obtained by the multiple government agencies such as the Federal Bureau of Investigation, Central Intelligence Agency, etc. may share with one another. Prior law restricted what information was being shared.
- ✓ Detention of Non-citizens – A nonresident of the United States may be detained for up to seven days if he or she is suspected of terrorist activities. If an individual is a threat to national security, he or she may be held for up to six months. Nonresidents who raise revenue to support terrorist activities and organizations may be deported.
- ✓ Bio terrorism Provision – Biological or chemical weapons may only be used for peaceful purposes. Possession for any other use is illegal.
- ✓ Anti-Money Laundering Provision – This aspect provides for the discovery, tracing and impounding of bank accounts that are being used to fund terrorist activities. The banks are required to divulge information regarding sources of large overseas bank accounts. Failure to do so will result in sanctions or forfeiture of the banks' licenses to do business.

Refresh Your Memory

The following exercise will enable you to refresh your memory on the rules and principles presented to you in this chapter. Read each question twice and place your answer in the blanks provided. Review the chapter material for any question you miss or are unable to remember.

1. A ______ is defined as any act done by an individual in violation of those duties that he or she owes to society and for the breach of which the law provides that the wrongdoer shall make amends to the public.

2. The ___________ is represented by an attorney called the prosecutor in a criminal lawsuit.

3. Felonies are the _____ _______ kinds of crimes.

4. What are three examples of felonies that are usually punishable by imprisonment? ___________, _____________, and ______________________.
5. _____________ are crimes that are less serious than felonies.

6. The two elements that must be shown for a person to be found guilty of most crimes are criminal _____ and criminal _________.

7. When the police obtain an arrest warrant, it usually must be based upon ___________ _________.

8. _____________ persons must be formally charged with a crime before they can be brought to trial.

9. If a grand jury determines that there is enough evidence to hold the accused for trial, it will issue an __________________.

10. ____________ is defined as the taking of personal property from another person by the use of fear or force.

11. The wrongful and ____________ taking of another person's personal property is the definition for the crime of larceny.

12. The _________ Amendment protects the rights of the people from unreasonable search and seizure by the government.

13. The ___________________ rule prohibits evidence from an unreasonable search and seizure from being introduced at trial or an administrative proceeding against the person searched.

14. The ___________ Amendment guarantees criminal defendants the right to be tried by an __________ _________.

15. The __________ _____________ _________ of 2001 assists the government in detecting and preventing terrorist activities and prosecuting businesses.

Critical Thought Exercise

Build-Rite Construction Company of Santa Maria, Jamaica receives a copy of an invoice for $160,000 of supplies from Hayward Lumber. Tom Cheat, owner of Build-Rite, notices that the invoice states that the company name is Build-Right Contractors and gives the company office address as Santa Maria, California. The invoice contains three different account numbers that Cheat discovers are all assigned to Build-Right. Cheat pays the invoice but does nothing to correct the account numbers.

During the next 14 months, Cheat has his employees order over $800,000 worth of materials from Hayward Lumber via the Internet, using the account numbers assigned to the California company. When the bills come due each month, Build-Right pays for the materials sent to Build-Rite, thinking that they have been shipped to one of their own construction sites. Cheat builds over 200 luxury vacation homes in Jamaica and has the funds from the sale of the homes send to his accounts in the Bahamas, where his brother runs a one-person bank. The credit of Build-Right is ruined when they discover the misuse of their account numbers and refuse to pay the balance of over $300,000 charged to their accounts. Several banks pull their funding of Build-Right projects and equipment is seized. Build-Right has to temporarily lay off 180 employees.

What crime, if any, has been committed by Tom Cheat or his company? Who may be prosecuted? What law will apply? What steps should Build-Right take to help it recover financially and prevent this from happening again in the future?

Answer. ____

____

____

____

____

____

____

____

____

Practice Quiz

True/False:

1. ___ In a criminal lawsuit, the government is the defendant. [p 126]

2. ___ The actual performance of the criminal act is called the mens reus. [p 126]

3. ___ General intent is where there is a showing of a higher degree of mental culpability or recklessness. [p 126]

4. ___ To be found guilty of a crime, the state of mind of the accused when the act was committed is relevant. [p 126]

5. ___ Cody Cop, a policeman arrived at an apartment building where Sam Speed was burglarizing Doris' apartment. Cody may arrest Sam Speed even if he does not have a warrant to do so. [p 128]

6. ___ If the defendant is not found guilty, he or she may not appeal. [p 130]

7. ___ Robbery is defined as the forceful and fraudulent taking of another person's personal property. [p 131]

8. ___ If Randy lies to Wanda in order to get her new Microsoft computer program, Wanda may be able to have Randy charged with larceny. [p 131]

9. ___ Anne signed her soon-to-be ex-husband George's paycheck one Friday evening, knowing she wanted to take him for as much as she could. Anne has not committed any crime, as she and George are not divorced yet. [p 133]

10. ___ The fraudulent conversion of property by a person to whom the property was entrusted is known as embezzlement. [p 133]

11. ___ Under the exclusionary rule, evidence that is tainted cannot be prohibited from introduction at a trial or administrative proceeding against the person searched. [p 138]

12. ___ Any confessions or statements obtained from a suspect before he or she is read his or her Miranda rights may be included as evidence at trial. [p 140]

13. ___ When a suspect is offered immunity from prosecution, the government agrees to use the evidence given by a person granted immunity against that person. [p 141]

14. ___ The Eighth Amendment prohibits cruel and unusual punishment. [p 141]

15. ___ The government may deny immunity from prosecution if a suspect asserts his or her Fifth Amendment privilege against self-incrimination. [p 141]

Multiple Choice:

16. What type of crimes has Edna committed if she has traffic violations and has jaywalked? [p 126]
    a. Violations
    b. Felonies
    c. Misdemeanors
    d. Trespass

17. A magistrate who finds there is enough evidence to hold the accused for trial of a lesser crime will issue an [p 129]
    a. information.
    b. indictment.
    c. injunction.
    d. intentional tort.

18. Carol has purchased real estate with money she obtained from robbing a local bank. Which act has Carol violated? [p 135]
    a. Identity Theft and Assumption Deterrence Act of 1998
    b. The Racketeer Influenced and Corrupt Organization Act
    c. Money Laundering Control Act
    d. Civil False Claims Act

19. Warrantless searches are allowed only when [p 128]
    a. they are incident to an arrest.
    b. where evidence is in "plain view."
    c. where it is likely that evidence will be destroyed.
    d. all of the above.

20. If Trenton threatens to tell Kyle's wife about Kyle's affair unless Kyle gives him money, this is an example of [p 132]
    a. Forgery
    b. Extortion
    c. Receiving stolen property
    d. Larceny

Short Answer:

21. What is the usual punishment for felonies that are committed? [p 126] ______________

____

22. What are the two elements that must be proven for a person to be found guilty of most crimes? [p 126] ____

23. Why would a person injured by a criminal act not sue the criminal to recover civil damages? [p 127] ____

24. Who usually evaluates the evidence of serious crimes? [p 129] ______________

25. Please tell what it means when the government grants a suspect immunity from prosecution. [p 141] ____

____

26. What is the definition for the crime of robbery? [p 131] ______________________

____

27. What is required for the crime of receiving stolen property? [p 131] ______________

____

28. Mr. Sly convinces Suzy Sweet to withdraw all of her money and invest in his water well that he claims to bottle as the water of youth. He has Suzy believe that her investment will triple in a month. Mr. Sly takes her money and flees the country to live in Barbados. What crime has Mr. Sly committed? [p 134] ____________________________

29. What does the Fourth Amendment protect persons and corporations from? [p 138] __________

____

30. How may an accused be prosecuted twice or more without violating the double jeopardy clause of the Fifth Amendment? [p 141] ____________________________________

____

Chapter 7

ETHICS AND SOCIAL RESPONSIBILITY OF BUSINESS

Chapter Overview

This chapter provides a clear understanding of the moral principles that determine the conduct of individuals or a group. The five main theories of ethics are thoroughly discussed with case law providing an excellent example of each.

Objectives

Upon completion of the exercises that accompany this chapter, you should be able to:

1. Define the meaning of ethics.
2. Define and compare the five main theories of ethics.
3. Compare the traditional role of social responsibility of business to the modern trend.
4. Describe corporate citizenship.
5. Describe the corporate social audit and discuss its importance in business today.
6. Observe the differences in ethical standards from country to country.

Practical Application

You should be able to recognize the types of ethical behavior being utilized in business based upon your knowledge of the various ethical principles. Additionally, you will have a greater appreciation for the history of this area of the law.

Helpful Hints

It is important to become familiar with the key terms and phrases associated with ethics. Additionally, it is helpful to be familiar with a case example for the theory you are trying to remember. The study tips given below have been organized by theory accompanied by a case or an example to enforce the principles it applies to.

Study Tips

Utilitarianism

The concept behind this theory is that people have to choose or follow the rule that provides the greatest good to society.

Example of utilitarianism - The case of Charter *Township of Ypsilanti Michigan v. General Motors Corporation,* No. 161245 (Mich. App. 1993) involved a General Motors Chevrolet production plant that decided to move from Ypsilanti, Michigan to Arlington Texas. The Charter Township of Ypsilanti brought a suit against General Motors alleging that it had given the automaker $13 million dollars in tax abatements, and that without the plant 4,500 people would be out of work. The trial judge appeared to apply the concept of utilitarianism in this case by ruling that just because General Motors thinks it can make the cars cheaper elsewhere does not make it right to desert the workers and their families. Further that the tax abatements given to the automaker could have been given toward education. Unfortunately, the appellate court reversed holding that there was no quid pro quo (this for that) agreement between the parties.

Kantian Ethics

This theory of ethics is also referred to as duty ethics. In other words, "do unto others as you would have them do unto you. In terms of business under this theory, an obligated party must keep his or her part of the bargain as he or she has a moral duty to do so regardless of any detriment that the party may suffer.

Rawl's Social Justice Theory

Under this theory, each person in society is presumed to have entered into a social contract with society in an effort to promote peace and harmony. Those following this theory agree to abide by the rules as long as everyone else also keeps to the rules.

Example of Rawl's social justice theory – The Sears and Robuck Co. "bait and rip off" scheme wherein Sears distributed discount brake job coupons to consumers and upon redemption of the same would convince the consumer that he or she needed additional repairs. The customers presumed that Sears would act ethically until many became upset with being overcharged. Thereafter California officials became aware of the situation and threatened to revoke Sears auto repair license. Sears settled all lawsuits against it. In this case forty-one states voiced complaints thereby evoking anger and conflict versus peace and harmony as per this ethical theory.

Ethical Relativism

Under this moral theory, individuals have to determine what is ethical using their own intuition or feelings as to what is right or wrong. Due to the subjectivity of what the moral standard is, an individual who adopts ethical relativism cannot be criticized for the way he or she feels. Most philosophers do not find this theory a satisfactory one when it comes to applying it to morals.

Example of ethical relativism - The case of *McNeil-P.C.C. inc. v. Bristol-Meyers Squibb Co. 938F.2d 1544 (1991)* illustrates this theory as McNeil sued Bristol –Meyers based upon the theory of false advertising. Bristol Meyers had advertised that Excederin worked better than Tylenol. After testing both products, it was found that they were basically the same and that Bristol-Meyers violated the Lanham Act, which prohibits false advertising. If Bristol-Meyers were applying ethical relativism to their claims regarding their product, they may claim that in their opinion, its products is better than that of McNeil-P.C.C. and that there should be no conflict on this point based upon how they feel. Therefore, even though the court found that fraud was committed, under this theory, Bristol-Meyer's thought would in fact be ethical.

Business and its Social Responsibility

More than ever we are looking at the impact as well as the social responsibility those businesses owe to society as a whole. Traditionally all that was viewed was a cost-benefit analysis and how a business' actions affected profits. Modernly however corporations are being held responsible for their actions. The four theories of social responsibility are the maximization of profits, the moral minimum, the takeholder's interest, and corporate citizenship all of which are discussed individually.

Maximizing Profits

The traditional rule regarding a business and its social responsibility was that it should maximize its profits for the shareholders. Proponents of this theory affirm this philosophy by adding that a business should participate in activities that will increase its profits as long as long as it is without any fraud or deception.

Example of maximizing profits – The case of *Mangini v. R.J. Reynolds Tobacco Company* involved R.J. Reynolds Tobacco Company's use of Joe Camel, a cartoon character that attorney and plaintiff Janet Mangini claimed was using unfair business practices. The defendant utilized the defense of freedom of speech under the First Amendment. However the plaintiff showed that R.J. Reynold's advertising was targeted at youth who were unable to make an informed choice knowing what the health risks are. R.J. Reynold's marketing ploy was designed to make money regardless of the existing and potential harm it was causing to those it wanted to sell to. It appears that this case is a classic example of the theory of maximizing profits.

Moral Minimum

This theory states that a business' social responsibility is met as long as it either avoids or corrects any social injury it causes. In other words, a corporation may make a profit, if it does not cause harm to others while doing so.

Example of the moral minimum- The case of *In re Union Carbide Corporation Gas Plant Disaster at Bhopal, India, in December 1984, 634 F.Supp. 842 (S.D.N.Y. 1986); 804 F.2 195 (2d Cir. 1987); cert. Denied, 484 U.S. 871 (1987)* involved a leakage of Methyl isocyanate, a toxic gas used to produce pesticides. The winds blew the gas into a heavily populated residential area causing many deaths and over 200,000 people to be injured. After determining that the Indian legal system would decide the cause of the event, Union Carbide was ordered to set up a fund of $470 million dollars for the claimants. Many issues were raised in this case, however, the main ethical one appears to be, did this fund correct the injuries it caused? Opponents argue that it did not as the settlement amounted to less than a thousand dollars per claimant.

Stakeholder Interest

Businesses have to consider the impact its actions will have on its stockholder, employees, suppliers, customers, creditors and the community as a whole. All of these individuals have a stake in the business.

Example of the stakeholder interest theory - As per your text, if employees of a business were seen only as a means to acquire wealth for the stockholders, this would not take into consideration the impact it would have on those employees.

Corporate Citizenship

This theory maintains that a business has a responsibility to do well. Under this theory, Businesses are under a duty to help solve social problems that it had minimum or no association with. The rationale behind this theory is because of the social power society has given to businesses. Opponents of this theory tend to lean toward moderation as society will always have some sort of social problem that needs to be solved. Businesses have limits too.

Example of corporate citizenship – Corporations owe a duty to fund a cure for a local child suffering from a rare disease.

Principles for International Business

The Caux Round Table developed Principles for International Business which is a code that states the responsibilities of business beyond shareholders toward stakeholders as well as the economic and social impact of business toward innovation, justice and world community.

The Corporate Social Audit

Generally speaking, audits are usually conducted to examine the financial health of a business. However, it has been suggested that a moral check up be conducted as well. Included in the ethical check up would be an examination of employee adherence to the company's code of ethics, whether the corporation has fulfilled its duty of social responsibility, promotion of worker safety, employment opportunities, etc. An independent firm should conduct the audit in an effort to assist in determining how the company can move toward the goal of social responsibility.

Refresh Your Memory

The following exercise will enable you to refresh your memory on the rules and principles presented to you in this chapter. Read each question twice and place your answer in the blanks provided. Review the chapter material for any question you miss or are unable to remember.

1. Ethics is a set of ________ principles or _________ that governs the conduct of an individual or group.

2. The moral theory of __________________ states that people must choose the actions or follow the rule that provides the greatest good to society.

3. What ethical theory is being implemented if Cathy believes that by treating others with respect, they should treat her in the same manner? ____

4. A theory that promulgates that each person is presumed to have entered into a social contract with all others in society to obey moral rules that are necessary for people to live in peace and harmony is known as __________ __________ ___________ theory.

5. If Willy, a customer of Food Inc. sees Fred drop a $20.00 bill while checking out of the store, and Willy's first instinct is to inform Fred of it., Willy would be applying the ethical theory of __________________.

6. If a sewage treatment plant that causes damage to a local lake and camp site offers to clean the lake and camp site, the plant would be applying the theory of _____________________________.

7. Utilizing the suggestions of the Sarbanes-Oxley Act of 2002, state how senior officers of public companies should act. ____

8. The social responsibility owed by businesses that states that business should maximize profits is known as the ____________________ view.

9. The stakeholder theory states that a corporation should consider the effects that its __________ have on other ________________.

10. A businesses responsibility to help solve social problems that it may not have caused would have its foundation in the theory known as ________________ ________________.

11. The corporate social audit refers to an audit of the corporation's ___________ health.

12. If Mary looks to the Bible for ethical rules or commands to guide him, he would be supporting the theory of ______________ ____________________.

13. Corporations have some degree of __________ ________________ for their actions.

14. Those following the theory that a corporation's duty is to make a profit while avoiding causing harm to others is known as the ____________ ____________theory.

15. The corporate citizenship theory of social responsibility states that businesses have a ____________________ to do good for ___________.

Critical Thought Exercise

You are an employee in the public relations department of Preciso, the luxury European automobile manufacturer. Preciso's sales have skyrocketed since the handcrafted vehicles were introduced to the United States ten years ago. Preciso's president has announced that Preciso will stop buying wood products from endangered forests following the example last year of Challenger Motor Company. Preciso will immediately stop buying wood from Canada's Great Bear Forest in British Columbia and phase out purchases of other wood from endangered forests. Instead, Preciso would like to use a "manmade wood-like product" for the interior parts (steering wheels, door panels, shifter knobs, etc.) of the autos it designs and builds.

There is no law against using wood from endangered forests and it is highly profitable to include these rare woods as part of the interiors of Preciso's cars. Shareholders are furious with the decision and are considering suing the Board of Directors and the officers of Preciso for wasting profits.

You are asked by the President of Preciso to draft a speech that she will deliver t the annual shareholders meeting which will explain the ethical business decision that was made and persuades the shareholders to not pursue a suit against the company.

Answer. ____

Practice Quiz

True/False:

1. ___ The corporate social audit should be designed to inspect the corporation's moral health. [p 165]

2. ___ The moral minimum theory states that a corporation's social responsibility is to rectify the soe social injury that it causes. [p 162]

3. ___ When a person looks to an outside source such as the Koran or the Bible for ethical rules, he or she is utilizing ethical fundamentalism. [p 150]

4. ___ Under Rawl's Social Justice Theory, one must enter into a formal written contract in order to enforce rules that are necessary for people to live in peace and harmony. [p 154]

5. ___ Kantian ethics refers to an individual's own feelings as to what is right or wrong. [p 154]

6. ___ Ethical standards are the same in each country. [p 159]

7. ___ Under the maximizing profits theory, the interest of others such as employees, suppliers, and local residents are not important in and of themselves. [p 160]

8. ___ There is an international ethics code in existence due to the many transnational values. [p 159]

9. ___ If a corporation pollutes the waters and then refuses compensation to those whom it injures, it has met its moral minimum duty of social responsibility. [p 162]

10. ___ The stakeholder interest theory is not widely accepted, as it is challenging to harmonize the conflicting interests of the stakeholders. [p 163]

11. ___ In the past, many businesses have made business decisions utilizing a small factor analysis. [p 160]

12. ___ Ethical relativism would apply in the situation of one company making what it feels is an dishonest comparison to a competitor's product even though the comparison is invalid. [p 157]

13. ___ It is unethical for a company to purposefully create partnerships in order to appear profitable and use these partnerships in an effort to borrow money to engage in speculative business dealings. [p 157]

14. ___ Proponents of the corporate citizenship theory contend that the duty of a corporation to do good is limited and cannot be expanded beyond certain limits. [p 164]

15. ___ Consistency and reversibility are two main principles espoused in deontology's universal rules. [p 154]

Multiple Choice:

16. A moral theory that states that people must choose the actions that will provide the greatest good to society is [p 154]
    a. Kantian ethics.
    b. maximizing profits.
    c. Utilitariansim.
    d. corporate social audit.

17. Which theory proposes a social contract theory of morality? [p 156]
    a. Stakeholder interest
    b. Rawl's Social Justice Theory
    c. Ethical relavtivism
    d. Ethical fundamentalism

18. Which theory indicates that the use of fraud is all right if the perpetrator honestly thought it was in fact ethical? [p 160]
    a. Rawl's distributive justice theory
    b. Maximizing profits
    c. Principles for International Business
    d. Ethical relativism

19. What type of ethics have many multinational corporations around the world adopted? [p 159]
    a. Principles for International Business
    b. Moral minimum
    c. Corporate citizenship
    d. All of the above

20. Edward brought a $15.00 discount coupon off of his next oil change to Sam Slick's garage. Fred, an employee of Sam Slick's garage convinces Edward to have a variety of other services performed, which in turn causes Edward's final bill to be over $500.00. What ethical theory would Sam Slick allege if his "bait and switch" scheme is questioned?
[p 157]
    a. Utilitarianism
    b. Ethical fundamentalism
    c. Ethical relativism
    d. Stakeholder interest

21. If a computer manufacturer decided to close one of its manufacturing plants in Burlington, Vermont because the employees were not assembling the computers fast enough which in turn was causing sales to drop, which ethical theory would this manufacturer be violating? [p 163]
    a. Stakeholder interest
    b. Utilitarianism
    c. Kantian ethics
    d. All of the above

22. Under which ethical theory could an individual be considered to act unethically if he or she went to extremes in following the code of conduct promulgated by this theory? [p 153]
    a. Ethical fundamentalism
    b. Maximizing profits
    c. Corporate citizenship
    d. Corporate audit

Short Answer:

23. Kantian Ethics is a set of universal rules that establishes __________ ________. [p 154]

24. Corporations that conduct __________ __________ will be more likely to prevent illegal and unethical conduct by employees, managers, and agents. [p 165]

25. What is the international ethics code that is based on transnational values from the East and West? [p 159] ________________ for ________________ ________________

26. If Joshua, a Brinks driver follows the commandment, "Thou shall not steal," he most likely follows __________ ____________________as the basis for his conduct. [p 154]

27. If Cigarette Co. uses a thirteen year old smoking a cigarette at a party in one of its ads, what ethical theory might it be utilizing? ____________________ [p 160]

28. The Environmental Safe Company promotes the safe dumping of toxic materials into our nation's waters. On one particular instance, Environmental caused the deaths of hundreds of sea lions. Its only response to the tragedy was that there are plenty of sea lines to mate with one another. Further, the population will be back in no time. If Environmental would have complied with the ____________ ____________theory, it would have met its duty of social responsibility by cleaning up the waters where the toxic materials were dumped and provide for safe dumping in the future so that other marine life are saved. [p 162]

29. Which theory says that a corporation must consider the effects its actions have on individuals other than its stockholders? [p 163] The ___________ ____________ theory.

30. What is the code of conduct that includes the respect for national sovereignty as well as adherence to socio-cultural objectives and values called? [p 159] The ______________________________ ____________________ code of conduct for ____________________ ____________________.

31. Businesses that make their decisions solely on a cost-benefit analysis owed a certain amount of ________________ ________________ for their actions as their decisions may have negative consequences for others. [p 160]

32. The theory of utilitarianism states that people must choose the actions or follow the rule that provides the ______________ ______________ ____ ______________. [p 154]

Chapter 8

NATURE OF TRADITIONAL AND ONLINE CONTRACTS

Chapter Overview

There are a variety of situations in which an individual will enter into a contractual situation in his or her lifetime. This chapter will provide you with a broad overview of the different types of contracts, the requirements for contract formation, the sources of contract law and technology's role in contract law.

Objectives

Upon completion of the exercises in this chapter, you should be able to:

1. Define what a contract is.
2. Describe the necessary elements to form a valid contract.
3. Differentiate between a bilateral and unilateral contract.
4. Differentiate between an implied-in-fact contract and an express contract..
5. Describe the difference between a valid, void, voidable and unenforceable contract.
6. Discuss equity and its applicability to contracts.

Practical Application

You should be able to recognize whether or not a contract has been formed, as well as the type of contract that is involved. You should also be able to recognize whether or not equity will play a role in the situation you are assessing. Finally, you should be more aware of the difficulties that individuals face when entering into electronic contracts and the licensing of computer information as well as the importance of the Uniform Computer Information Transaction Act in these matters.

Helpful Hints

This chapter lends itself toward organization. As you attempt to learn the area of contract law, it is first helpful to know what a contract is as well as the necessary requisites for its formation. Then it is beneficial to list the various types of contracts along with an example of each to help you remember and differentiate between them. As you study various fact situations, it is especially important in contract law that you read the hypotheticals and or cases line by line being careful to examine the facts as they may or may not be controlled by the contract principles that you have learned. In contract law, slight variations in wording or sequence of events can change the outcome.

Study Tips

The following study tips have been organized in a manner that will assist you in easily learning the concepts involved in this chapter.

Contract

- Defined: An agreement between two or more parties that is enforceable in equity or a court of law.

- Parties to a contract: The offeror whom is the one making the offer, and the offeree who is the individual to whom the offer is made.

- Requirements to have a valid contract: In order to have a valid contract, there must be:
  1. An offer and acceptance, both of which equate to an agreement.
  2. Consideration that is a legally sufficient bargained-for- exchange. Be careful with this element, as gift promises, moral obligations, past consideration and illusory promises are considered insufficient consideration.
  3. Contractual capacity to enter into the contract. This is another area to watch for issues in, as minors, intoxicated individuals and those who have been adjudged insane may not have the requisite capacity to understand the nature of the transaction they are entering into.
  4. Lawful object. Contracts to accomplish illegal goals are contrary to public policy and are void. An example of this would be a contract entered into to kill another individual in order to receive an insurance policy's proceeds.

- Sources of Contract Law: There are three sources of contract law. They are as follows:
  1. Common law of contracts – This law was developed from early court decisions that eventually became precedent for subsequent decisions. Many of the principles developed under the common law are still the same today.
  2. Uniform Commercial Code (U.C.C.) – The purpose of this law is to establish a uniform system of commercial law in the United States. It is important to note that the U.C.C. takes precedence over common law.
  3. Restatement (Second) of Contracts – Though this compilation of contract law principles is law, it is used more often as a guide due to its statutory nature as opposed to law.

- Types of Contracts: There are a variety of contracts, each of which have differences that you must be aware of.
  1. ***Bilateral contract*** – This type of contract involves a promise for a promise. For example, "I promise to wash your car if you promise to take me to the movies." Acceptance is in the form of a promise.
  2. ***Unilateral contract*** – This type of contract involves a promise for performance. For example, "If you mow the lawn, I will pay you $10.00." There is no contract until the offeree performs the requested act of mowing the lawn. Acceptance is in the form of performance.
  3. ***Express contract*** – Simply stated, these are either oral or written agreements between two parties. An example would be an oral agreement to buy someone's radio and a written agreement to buy someone's home.
  4. ***Implied-in-fact contracts*** – This type of contract is implied on the conduct of the parties. There are certain requirements that must be met before a court will find that this type of contract exists. These requirements are:

- The plaintiff gave services or property to the defendant.
- The plaintiff expected compensation for the property or services. In other words the property or services were not gifts.
- Even though the defendant could have refused to accept the property or services given by the plaintiff, he or she did not.

5. ***Objective Theory of Contracts*** applies to both express and implied-in-fact contracts - It does not matter whether or not the contract is express or implied-in-fact; the court will still apply the reasonable person standard. This means, would a reasonable person conclude that the words and conduct of the parties as well a surrounding circumstances were enough to demonstrate that the parties intended to create a contract? Subjective intent is irrelevant as it is the objective intent based on the reasonable person standard that will be examined.
6. ***Quasi-contracts*** - The term quasi-contract is an equitable one and is also known as implied-in-law contract. The Court will create a contract even though there is not an actual contract between the parties, if the plaintiff provided goods or services to the defendant without compensation. Further reinforcement for the creation of a quasi-contract exists when it is shown that it would be unjust not to require the defendant to pay for the benefit received.
7. ***Formal contracts*** - A formal contract is one requiring a special method or form to create it. Some examples of formal contracts are contracts under a state's wax seal, a recognizance for example in the form of a bond, negotiable instruments as per the Uniform Commercial Code, and letters of credit which are also governed by the Uniform Commercial Code.
8. ***Informal contracts*** - All contracts that do not require a special form or method to create are considered informal contracts.
9. ***Valid contract*** - A valid contract is one that meets all of the required elements to establish a contract.
10. ***Void contract*** - A void contract is one that does not have any legal affect.
11. ***Voidable contract*** - A voidable contract is one that enables one party to avoid his or her contractual obligations. Examples of where this situation may exist absent certain exceptions are contracts entered into by minors, insane individuals, intoxicated persons, those acting under undue influence, duress, or fraud and where there is a mutual mistake.
12. Unenforceable contract -_If there is a legal defense to the enforcement of the contract, the contract is unenforceable. An example of this would by if a writing such as the case with the purchase of real estate is required to be in writing as per the Statute of Frauds.
13. Executed contract -_If both parties have performed their required obligations under the contract, the contract is said to be executed.
14. Executory contract -_If only one side has fully performed his or her obligations of the contract, the contract is said to be executory.

- Equity Court and Contracts - The equity courts of England developed a set of rules whose foundation was premised on fairness, moral rights, and equality. Equity principles were applied when the remedy at law was not adequate or in the interest of fairness, equitable principle had to be applied.

- Importance of the Uniform Computer Information Transactions Act (UCITA) - This act targets a majority of the legal issues that are faced when conducting e-commerce over the Internet. Since a majority of the states have adopted some or all of the act, it is anticipated to become the foundation for the creation and enforcement of cyberspace licenses and contracts.

- Importance of The United Nations Convention on Contracts for the International Sale of Goods - The CISG is important because it incorporates rules from all of the prominent legal systems. It is substantially similar to the Uniform Commercial Code. This is another reason that Americans conducting overseas business should be familiar with its provisions.

Refresh Your Memory

The following exercise will enable you to refresh your memory on the rules and principles presented to you in this chapter. Read each question twice and place your answer in the blanks provided. Review the chapter material for any question you miss or are unable to remember.

1. Give the definition of a contract? ____
____

2. What are the two parties to a contract often referred to as? The ________________ and the ____________.

3. What are the four basic elements of a contract? (1) ____________, (2) ______________, (3) ____________ ______________, and a (4) ____________ ____________.

4. What are two defenses to the enforcement of a contract? (1) __________________ of __________________ and (2) __________________ and __________________.

5. List three sources of contract law. (1) ____________________________, (2) ________________________, and (3) ________________________.

6. Explain what a bilateral contract is ______________________________________
____

7. Give the definition of a unilateral contract. ______________________________________
____

8. An actual contract may be either __________________ or __________________.

9. Contracts that are stated in oral or written words are known as ____________ contracts.

10. The intent to enter into an implied-in-fact or express contract is judged by the ____________ ____________________ standard.

Critical Thought Exercise

Ricky Boggs, a 27-year-old country singer was severely injured in an automobile accident. Boggs was airlifted by Bishop County Air Ambulance to Bishop Trauma Center for surgery and treatment. Boggs slipped into a coma and after seven weeks was transported to Bishop County Extended Care Hospital. Boggs remained in the hospital for fourteen months before he died without ever having regained consciousness. The total charges assessed by Bishop County for the care of Boggs exceeded $370,000.00. After he died, Bishop County sued the Boggs estate to recover the expenses of the air ambulance, trauma treatment, surgery, hospital stay, and extended care.

Was there a contract between Bishop County and Boggs? If so, how much can Bishop County recover from the estate?

Answer. ____

____

____

____

____

____

____

____

____

____

____

____

____

____

____

Practice Quiz

True/False:

1. ___ The Restatement (Second) of Contract is law that does not take precedence over the common law of contracts. [p 171]

2. ___ Under the objective theory of contracts, the subjective intent of either party who enters into a contract does not play an important role in determining the true intentions of the parties. [p 174]

3. ___ Every contract involves at least two parties. [p 172]

4. ___ Consideration is defined as bargained-for exchange that is legally sufficient. [p 172]

5. ___ The contract is bilateral if the offeror's offer can be accepted only by the offeree's promise of acceptance. [p 175]

6. ___ If there is an ambiguity as to whether a contract is bilateral or unilateral, it will be presumed to be a unilateral contract. [p 175]

7. ___ The theory of quasi-contract applies to actual contracts between two parties. [p 177]

8. ___ The Uniform Commercial Code usually does not take precedence over the common law of contracts. [p 173]

9. ___ If a contract is required to be in writing under the Statute of Frauds but it is not, the contract is unenforceable because of the legal defense to enforcement of the contract. [p 173]

10. ___ A contract is voidable where at least one party has the option to avoid his or her contractual obligations. [p 178]

11. ___ A void contract is one that meets all of the essential elements to establish a contract. [p 178]

12. ___ An executed contract is one that has not been fully performed on both sides. [p 179]

Multiple Choice:

13. The four basic requirements to have an enforceable contract are [p 172]
    a. duty, breach, causation, and damages.
    b. bilateral, unilateral, executed and executory.
    c. agreement, consideration, capacity, and lawful object.
    d. offeror, offeree, offer and acceptance.

14. A bilateral contract is [p 175]
    a. a promise for performance.
    b. a promise for money.
    c. a promise for a promise.
    d. a promise for an offer.

15. Two types of defenses that may be raised to the enforcement of a contract are [p 172]
    a. writing and form and genuineness of assent.
    b. uniform commercial code and common law of contracts.
    c. contributory negligence and assumption of the risk.
    d. unilateral and bilateral promise.

16. A contract to commit a crime is [p 178]
    a. valid.
    b. void.
    c. voidable.
    d. informal.

17. The Uniform Computer Information Transaction Act will be useful in acting as [p 175]
    a. a quasi-contract.
    b. the reasonable person standard.
    c. the basis for establishing legally sufficient consideration.
    d. the basis for the creation and enforcement of cyberspace contracts and licenses.

18. An oral agreement to purchase a neighbor's gardening tools is an example of [p 176]
    a. an implied-in-fact contract.
    b. an express contract.
    c. an executory contract.
    d. a void contract.

Short Answer:

19. What does the equitable doctrine of quasi-contract allow a court to do? [p 172] ____

____

20. Formal contracts require ______________________________. [p 178]

21. Differentiate between a void and a voidable contract? [p 178] ____

____

22. A contract implied by law to prevent unjust enrichment is a ____________________. [p 177]

23. The United Nations Convention on Contracts for the International Sales of Goods (CISG) applies to contracts for ______________________________. [p 180]

24. If Kate tells her son Tony that she will give him everything she owns if he loves her the rest of her life, would a valid contract exist between the two? [p 172] ____

____

25. Jan Ruiz, a business owner says to Mary Munoz, a decorator, "If you promise to wallpaper my waiting room by December 1, I will pay you $600.00." Mary promises to do so. What type of contract has been created? [p 175] ____

26. Dr. Holly Craus says to James Dole, a contractor, "If you promise to have the extra rooms to my office built and ready to see patients by April 9, I will pay you $25,000." What type of contract may have been created? [p 175] ____

____

27. Which act is expected to become the basis for the creation and enforcement of cyberspace contracts and licenses? [p 175] ____

28. What type of contract is formed where Gio says to Paul, "I will give you $10,000 if you help my friend Clyde murder his wife Bonnie? [p 178] ____

____

29. Why is the Uniform Commercial Code important to the law of contracts? [p 173] ____

____

30. Why was the Uniform Computer Information Transactions Act developed? [p 175] ____

____

31. If Ellen has painted Max's entire house except for the front door, may Max revoke his offer to pay Ellen for painting his house? [p 172] ____

____

Chapter 9

AGREEMENT AND CONSIDERATION

Chapter Overview

As you will recall in Chapter 9, you learned about the different types of contracts as well as the requirements for contract formation. This chapter expands upon the requirement of agreement. You will learn what constitutes a valid offer as well as the various ways that an offer can be terminated. Offers such as rewards, advertisements, auctions and counteroffers are also discussed. Additionally, you will learn many ways that an acceptance can be effectuated with special attention being paid to the mailbox rule. Further, you will have an in depth understanding of what is meant by consideration as it pertains to the law of contracts. The material provided in this chapter will enable you to analyze promises that are not supported by consideration, as well as enforceable promises that are lacking consideration.

Objectives

Upon completion of the exercises in this chapter, you should be able to:

1. Give the definition of an offer and acceptance.
2. List the requirements of an offer.
3. Discuss the requirements of special offers such as rewards, advertisements and auctions.
4. Discuss what a counteroffer is as well as its impact.
5. Discuss the various ways an offer may be terminated.
6. Describe what the mailbox rule is and how it is applied.
7. Define consideration.
8. Explain the meaning of legal value.
9. Define and identify bargained-for-exchange
10. Describe when promises lacking consideration are enforceable
11. Define an accord and satisfaction and the effect it has on the original contract.
12. Discuss the doctrine of promissory estoppel.

Practical Application

You should be able to recognize whether or not a valid offer has been made and whether or not the essential terms are included within it. You should also be able to know if an offer has been properly terminated or if the mailbox rule applies. Finally, with your basic knowledge, you should be able to draft a simple offer by utilizing the information contained in this chapter.

You should be able to recognize whether there is sufficient consideration in a contractual situation to become part of the basis of the bargain between the parties. You should also be able to recognize what type of consideration is being given. Further, if consideration is lacking, you should be able to determine whether it will or will not be enforceable.

Helpful Hints

Each chapter, especially in the area of contracts builds on one another. As such, it is vital that you understand the information given in each chapter and know how to apply it to given fact situations. Your initial analysis of a potential contract should begin with the offer. You should use a mental checklist of what is required to establish a valid offer. If one of the elements is missing, then ask yourself whether there is a rule of law that may apply to satisfy that missing element. Next, you should determine whether or not you are examining a special offer such as a reward, an advertisement, auction or counteroffer. Once again, quickly review your mental checklist on any special rules that may apply to these types of offers. Before you proceed any further, look at the facts and determine whether or not the offer has been terminated. Next, has there been an acceptance to the offer you have analyzed? If so, you need to address the issue of whether the acceptance was proper. Examine whether the offer specified a means of acceptance, the time for acceptance, method of communication and the mailbox rule. Additionally, it will be very beneficial to you to break down the definition of consideration into several parts as well as give an example for each. The Study Tips section that follows gives easy to remember lists of what is required for the aspects of this chapter.

Study Tips

Offer

Definition as per Section 24 of Restatement (Second) of Contracts: "The manifestation of willingness to enter into a bargain, so made as to justify another person in understanding that his assent to that bargain is invited and will conclude it."

Requirements

- The offeror must objectively intend to be held to the offer. Remember objective intent is gauged against a reasonable person in the same or similar circumstances.
    a. Were mere preliminary negotiations going on between the parties? If the offeror is asking a question as opposed to making a statement of intent to bargain, it is probably an invitation to make an offer and not indicative of the offeror's present intent to contract.
    b. Was the offer made in anger, jest or undue excitement? If any of these exist, the objective intent is missing and the offer cannot result in a valid contract.
    c. Offers made as an expression of opinion are not enforceable promises.
- The offer's terms must be definite or reasonably certain.
    a. Were the terms clear so that the offeree was able to accept or reject the terms of the offer?
    b. Did the offer contain an identification of the parties, identification of the subject matter, the consideration to be paid and the time for performance? If the answer is yes, then the offer will probably be considered definite and certain.
    c. Were there any implied terms?
        Common Law: If any of the terms were missing, the offer would fail.
        Modern Law: There is more leniency, as the court will supply a missing term if a reasonable term can be implied, such as for price and time or performance.
- The offer has to be communicated to the offeree. Without communication, there can be no acceptance.

Special Types of Offers

Advertisements
- These are treated as invitations to make an offer.
- The exception to it being an invitation is if the offer is definite or specific that it is obvious that the advertiser had the present intend to be bound by the advertisement, then it will be considered to be an offer.

Rewards
- An offer to pay a reward is an offer to form a unilateral contract.
- The two requirements to accept a reward are that the offeree had knowledge of the reward before completing the requested act and he or she performed the requested act.

Auctions
- Usually a seller uses an auctioneer to offer to sell his or her goods.
- Auctions are with reserve as they are usually considered an invitation to make an offer. The seller can withdraw his or her goods from the sale and refuse the highest bid.
- Note, that if the auction is without reserve, the seller must accept the highest bid and cannot take his or her goods back.

Termination of an Offer By the Parties

An offer may be terminated by the parties by revoking the offer, rejecting the offer or by a counteroffer made by the offeree. These three means of terminating an offer are discussed below.

Revocation of an offer by the offeror
- At common law, the offeror could revoke his or her offer any time before the offeree accepted.
- The revocation may be express or implied by the offeror or a third party.
- The majority of states rule that the revocation is not effective until it is received.
- Revocation of an offer made to the public may be revoked by communicating in the same way that the offer was made for the same length of time.
- Prevention of revocation by the offeror is accomplished through an option contract. The offeree usually pays the offeror money to keep the offer open for an agreed-upon period of time. During this period of time the offeror agrees not to sell the subject matter of the offer to anyone else. Keep in mind that death or incompetency does not terminate the option contract unless it was a personal service contract.

Rejection of an offer by the offeree
- The rejection may be express or implied by the offeree's conduct.
- The rejection is not effective until it is received.
- An acceptance by the offeree after the offeree has rejected the offer is construed as a counteroffer.

Counteroffer by the offeree
- It terminates the original offer.
- It creates a new offer that the original offeror is now free to accept or reject.

Termination of the Offer by Operation of Law

An offer may be terminated by operation of law in several situations. It can be terminated by destruction of the subject matter or by death or incompetency of the offeror or offeree, by a supervening illegality or by lapse of time.

Destruction of the Subject Matter

- The offer is terminated if the subject matter of the offer is destroyed through no fault of either party before the offer is accepted.
- An example of this would be if a boat that was listed for sale sank and was unable to be recovered, the offer would automatically terminate

Death or Incompetency of the Offeror or Offeree

- Death of either the offeror or offeree terminates the offer.
- Incompetency of the offeror or offeree terminates the offer.
- Notice of the death or incompetency is not a requirement.
- Death or incompetency will not terminate an option contract unless it was a personal service contract.

Supervening Illegality

- If the object of the offer is made illegal before the offer is accepted, the offer terminates. For example, if a bog frog becomes an endangered species after an offer is made for its sale to pet stores, but before the pet stores accept, the offer is terminated.
- Many times statutes are enacted that make the object of the offer illegal.

Lapse of Time

- The offer sometimes limits the time in which it can be accepted.
- The time begins to run from the time it is actually received by the offeree and extends until the stated time period ends.
- If no time is stated in the offer, then the offer terminates within a "reasonable time" and on a case-by-case basis.
- If an offer is made over the telephone or face to face, then the offer usually terminates after the conversation.

Acceptance

Defined: Simply stated, an acceptance is an outward manifestation of assent to be bound by the terms of the offer as assessed by the reasonable person standard.

Basic Facts about Acceptance

- Only the offeree can accept the offer to create a contract.
- If an offer is made to more than one person, each person has the power to accept the offer.
- If an acceptance is made by one party, it terminates the offer as to the other individuals to whom the offer was made.
- If a joint offer has been made, the offer must be accepted jointly.

Mirror Image Rule

- This rule states that the offeree must accept the offeror's terms. The acceptance must be unequivocal.
- Grumbling acceptances do form contracts.
- Acceptances however that add conditions to them are not unequivocal and thus fail.

Silence as Acceptance

- The general rule is that silence is not held to be an acceptance despite the offeror stating it is.
- There are several exceptions to the general rule.

a. Where the offeree by his words intended his silence to mean acceptance.
b. A signed agreement by the offeree allowing continued delivery until notice was given. For example, if Sid continued to buy crafts from a monthly craft club then his silence would indicate acceptance until he notifies the craft club that he wants to discontinue his membership.
c. Prior course of dealings by the parties where silence is construed as an acceptance.
d. The offeree accepts the benefit of goods or services given by the offeror even though the offeree had the opportunity to reject the services or goods.

Time and Method of Acceptance

Mailbox Rule

- This rule is also known as the acceptance-upon-dispatch rule.
- Acceptance is effective when it is placed in the mailbox, or dispatched, even if it gets lost along the way.
- The rule does not apply if a rejection is sent first and then an acceptance is mailed.
- The acceptance has to be properly dispatched. In other words, it has to be properly addressed, packaged and have proper postage applied. Under common law, if the acceptance wasn't properly dispatched, it wasn't effective unless received by the offeror.

Mode of Acceptance

- The usual rule is that the offeree must accept by an authorized mode of communication.
- The offer can state how it is to be accepted. This is called express authorization.
  Note: If the offeree uses a different means to communicate his or her acceptance instead of the means stipulated to be the parties, then the acceptance is ineffective.
- Implied authorization may apply where it is customary in similar transactions between the parties, or prior dealings or usage of trade. Implied authorization will be allowed "by any medium reasonable in the circumstances." Section 30 of the Restatement Second.

Importance of the Comity Principle

This ethical rule states that each nation will respect the other nations' laws. It is usually applied in cases of concurrent jurisdiction and where the foreign law is different from the country where the case is being brought. Its purpose is to develop respect for the laws of other nations.

Enforceability of Computer Shrinkwrap Licenses

A recent issue before the courts involved whether licenses and contracts that are shrinkwrapped inside software boxes and computer equipment boxes are enforceable against purchasers. The courts have held that they are enforceable as the "accept-or-return" portion of the agreements inside of the shrinkwrap sufficiently protected the consumers or potential licensees against goods they did not want to accept as they were still allowed to return the goods under the contract.

Consideration

- Defined: "Something of legal value."
  Examples: money, property, forbearance of a right, the provision of services or anything else of legal value
- Presumption: A written contract is presumed to be supported by consideration.

- Two requirements for consideration
  1. Something of legal value must be given, and
  2. There must be a bargained-for exchange.

  Elaboration of the two requirements:
  - **Legal Value** is established if the promisee suffers a legal detriment or the promisor receives a legal benefit.
  - **Bargained-for exchange** refers to the exchange that parties engage in that leads to an enforceable contract. Gift promises and gratuitous promises by themselves are not enforceable, however if the promissee offers to do something in exchange for either of these two types of promises, then consideration is established.

Output Contracts

The seller agrees to sell all of its production to one buyer.

Requirements Contracts

The buyer contracts to purchase all of the requirements for an item from a single seller.

Nominal Consideration

This type of consideration is minimal in light of the subject matter of the contract. As such it is not considered legally sufficient in states that recognize the "shock the conscience of the court" standard for determining the adequacy of the consideration.
Example: "I will give you $1.00 for your ocean front home." One dollar is hardly adequate for an oceanfront home and in most states would "shock the conscience of the court."

Best Efforts Clause

This clause usually states that one or both of the parties will use their best efforts to achieve the objective of the contract. It's important to remember that the courts have held that imposition of the duty to use best efforts is sufficient consideration to make a contract enforceable.

Contracts that Lack Consideration

- **Illegal Consideration**
  A contract based on illegal consideration is void. A promise to refrain from doing an illegal act will not be enforceable as illegal consideration is part of the bargained-for exchange.

  Example: "If you pay me $5,000, I will not damage your brand new car!"

- **Illusory Promises**
  If the parties enter into a contract, but one or both of them choose not to perform, then consideration will be lacking.
  Example: Fred says to Jim, "I will paint your garage if I feel like it."

- **Moral Obligations**
  The general rule regarding moral obligations is that they lack consideration.
  The minority rule however allows for the enforcement of moral obligations.
  Example: Deathbed promises or contracts based on affection and love are promises based upon moral obligations.

- **Preexisting Duty**
  If a person promises to perform an act or do something he or she is already under an bligation to do, then the promise is unenforceable because no new consideration has been given. In other words, the individual had a preexisting duty.
  Exception: If a party encounters substantial unforeseen difficulties while performing his or her contractual duties and the parties modify their contract to accommodate these difficulties, no new consideration is necessary.

- **Past Consideration**
  When a party to a contract promises to compensate another for work that has been performed in the past, then the situation involving past consideration exists. A contract must be supported by new consideration in order to be binding.

Settlement of Claims Involving Accord and Satisfaction

- **Accord**
  An accord is an agreement where both parties agree to accept something different in satisfaction of the original contract
- **Satisfaction**
  Simply stated, this is the performance of the accord.

Promissory Estoppel

The purpose of promissory estoppel is to give a remedy to a person who has justifiably relied upon another's promise, but that person takes back his or her promise. Further, because there is no agreement or consideration, the recipient of the promise cannot sue based on breach of contract. This doctrine estops the promisor from revoking his or her promise and thereby prevents unjust enrichment by the promisor. An injustice would occur if the promise were not enforced.

Refresh Your Memory

The following exercise will enable you to refresh your memory on the rules and principles presented to you in this chapter. Read each question twice and place your answer in the blanks provided. Review the chapter material for any question you miss or are unable to remember.

1. An ________________ is the manifestation by two or more individuals of the substance of a contract. [p 205]

2. If June says to Monica, "I will give you ten dollars to wash my car." Who is the offeree in this example? [p 205] ______________
3. The offeror must ______________ intend to be bound by the terms of the offer. [p 205]

4. The terms of the offer must be definite or ______________ ______________. [p 205]

5. Which theory is used in determining whether the parties intended to enter into a contract? The ______________ ______________ of contracts. [p 205]

6. If Homer asked Ernie, "Would you be interested in selling your car to me?" Would this be a valid offer? [p 206] ____

7. Under the modern law of contracts, which two terms of an offer may be implied? [p 207] ______________ and ______________ ________ ______________

8. ______________ are usually viewed as invitations to make an offer. [p 208]

9. What type of auction provides that the seller must accept the highest bid and cannot withdraw the goods from sale? An ______________________________ [p 209]

10. An offer is terminated if the offeree ______________ it. [p 210]

11. A ______________________ by the offeree terminates the offeror's offer and creates a new offer at the same time. [p 211]

12. The offer terminates by operation of law if the ______________ ______________ of the offer is destroyed through no fault of either party before its acceptance. [p 212]

13. The offeree's acceptance must be ______________________. [p 213]

14. Under the mailbox rule, acceptance is effective upon ______________________. [p 215]

15. Usually an offeree must accept an offer by an ______________________ means of communication. [p 215]

16. Implied authorization may be inferred from ______________________________ ____. [p 216]

17. Why is an opinion not an enforceable promise? [p 206] ______________________ ____

18. Only the ______________ has the power to accept an offer and create a contract. [p 213]

Critical Thought Exercise

Gus Vincent sent invitations to a number of potential buyers to submit bids for the mineral rights to his 2,000-acre parcel in upstate New York on the outskirts of the City of Hudson. Seven bids were received, including the highest bid from International Mining and Cement Company, LTD. (IMC). Vincent then decided to hold onto the land for a few more years and never responded to any of the bidders. IMC claimed that a contract had been formed by submission of its winning bid and sued Vincent for breach of contract.

Did a contract exist?

Answer. ____

____

____

____

____

____

____

____

____

____

____

____

____

____

____

____

____

Practice Quiz

True/False:

1. ___ The objective theory of contracts is used to determine whether there was an intent to enter a contract. [p 205]

2. ___ A valid contract may result from preliminary negotiations. [p 205]

3. ___ The owner of the Z store shouts in frustration, "For even $50,000, I'd sell the whole business along with its company cars!" This statement will not be considered a valid offer. [p 206]

4. ___ Under modern law, the court will not imply terms in a contract. [p 207]

5. ___ An offer may be accepted even though it has not been communicated. [p 207]

6. ___ Generally speaking, price and time of performance can be implied even if these terms are not present. [p 207]

7. ___ An advertisement is considered an offer if it is so definite or specific that it is obvious that the advertiser has the present intent to be bound by the terms of the ad. [p 205]

8. ___ An auction with reserve is not considered an invitation to make an offer. [p 209]

9. ___ A majority of states do not require receipt of an offeror's revocation in order to be effective. [p 210]

10. ___ Rejection of an offer is effective upon receipt. [p 210]

11. ___ A counteroffer by the offeree doesn't terminate the original offer, as it is considered to be a mere inquiry. [p 211]

12. ___ If a snowmobile being purchased by Sam is destroyed after Jan makes the offer but before Sid accepts the offer is terminated. [p 212]

13. ___ The offeror may accept his or her own offer. [p 213]

14. ___ Generally speaking, a grumbling acceptance is a valid, legal acceptance. [p 213]

15. ___ Silence may also be considered an acceptance if the offeree has demonstrated that silence means assent. [p 214]

16. ___ Under the mailbox rule, acceptance is effective upon receipt. [p 215]

17. ___ An offeree must accept an offer by an authorized means of communication. [p 216]

18. ___ Unilateral contracts may only be accepted by the offeree's performance. [p 213]

19. ___ Implied authorization cannot be implied from prior transactions between the parties. [p 216]

20. ___ The comity principle is a rule that states nations will respect the laws of other nations. [p 216]

Multiple Choice:

21. Sam Brown stated to Mary Powers, "I will buy your house for $350,000." His statement was [p 206]
    a. a valid offer.
    b. a preliminary question.
    c. an opinion.
    d. a bilateral contract.

22. A car dealer tells his customer that he feels the car she is interested in buying is the best car on his lot and will probably give her a lifetime of happiness. If the customer buys the car and immediately has problems, the customer may [p 206]
    a. enforce the car dealer's promise.
    b. return the car for her money back.
    c. not enforce the promise.
    d. none of the above

23. To be considered a valid offer, the communication must contain [p 207]
    a. an offer, acceptance and consideration.
    b. protection against potential breach.
    c. the parties, consideration, time for performance and identification of the subject matter.

d. a provision against communications made in jest or anger.

24. In order to be entitled to collect on an offer to pay a reward, the offeree must [p 209]
    a. return the lost property or capture the criminal.
    b. offer the goods for sale through an auctioneer.
    c. let the offeror know that he or she is there to collect the reward.
    d. have knowledge of the reward before completing the requested act and perform the requested act.

25. Under common law, an offeror could revoke his or her offer [p 210]
    a. any time prior to its acceptance by the offeree.
    b. once a counteroffer has been made by the offeree.
    c. upon dispatch into a U.S. mailbox.
    d. by an authorized means of communication.

26. Two ways to terminate an offer by operation of law are [p 212]
    a. by rejection and revocation.
    b. death or incompetency of the offeror or offeree.
    c. rewards and auctions.
    d. intoxication and incapacity.

27. The ABC Corporation mailed an offer of employment to Ernest. The offer stated that acceptance of the job was to be by certified mail. Ernest was so elated about the idea of working for the ABC Corporation, that he flew to the city ABC was locate in and hand delivered his acceptance within the time stated in the offer. Has a contract been formed between ABC and Ernest? [p 216]
    a. No, because Ernest used an unauthorized means of communication to give his acceptance.
    b. Yes, as an offeree may accept an offer by an unauthorized means of communication.
    c. No, because the Restatement (Second) of Contracts permits implied authorization by "any medium reasonable in the circumstances."
    d. Yes, because adherence to the comity principle requires that ABC respect the law that Ernest is applying

28. In order for an offer to be effective, which elements must be established? [p 205]
    a. The offeror must objectively intend to be bound by the offer.
    b. The terms of the offer must be definite and reasonably certain.
    c. The offer must be communicated to the offeree.
    d. All of the above.

29. Implied authorization for acceptance of an offer may be [p 216]
    a. inferred by properly addressing and packaging and dispatching the acceptance.
    b. expressly stating that acceptance is not effective until received.
    c. inferred from prior dealings, trade usage, or what is customary from similar transactions.
    d. by stipulation that acceptance must be by specified means.

30. Mrs. Sweet, the President of Sweetest Things Corporation, puts an offer to sell the packaging division in writing to Mr. Baker but does not send it. Thereafter, Mrs. Baker stops in to visit Mrs. Sweet and notices the written offer on Mrs. Sweet's desk. She then goes home and tells Mr. Baker about the offer. Can Mr. Baker accept the offer to buy the packaging division of the Sweetest Things Corporation? [p 207]

a. Yes, as Mrs. Baker was acting as a proxy for Mr. Baker.
b. No, as Mrs. Baker did not tell Mr. Baker all of the particulars of the offer.
c. Yes, as a wife, Mrs. Baker steps into the shoes of her husband and may convey the message to Mr. Baker.
d. No, because Mrs. Sweet never communicated the offer to Mr. Baker and therefore there is no offer to be accepted.

Short Answer:

31. The statement, "I will purchase your mountain bike for $350.00" is a valid offer because it ______________________________. [p 206]

32. Hilda and Mildred are having a fun dinner together complete with wine and laughter. Hilda in a hysterical fit of laughter tells Mildred, "Since you are my funniest friend, I'll sell you my California farm for $30,000." Has Hilda made a valid offer to Mildred? [p 206]

____

____

33. If Tom, a tractor salesperson places an advertisement in a local circular that reads, "like new, 2002, Edwards Co. tractor, serial no. 3478942, $6,200." Is this an offer? [p 208]

____

34. Sean accidentally leaves his grandfather's top hat in a fancy restaurant he was dining at. He places an ad in the Bradley News Gazette stating, "$500.00 reward for the return of an old, black top hat left in Patrano's Italian Restaurant on March 15, 2003, at approximately 8 p.m. Call 911-555-1212. Dawn, who has not seen the offer, finds Sean's top hat and also notes that there is a phone number on a tag inside of it. She telephone's Sean and determines that she has found his top hat. Dawn's friend Sally thereafter tells Dawn that there is a reward for finding the hat as she had seen the ad in the paper and recognized that the number in the newspaper is the same as the number inside of the hat. Is Dawn entitled to the reward money? [p 209]

____

____

35. What type of auction is considered to be an invitation to make an offer? [p 209] ________

____

36. If Marcia places an ad in the Sunset News Press offering a reward for her lost cat Barney and she lets the ad run for five weeks, what must she do to revoke the ad? [p 210]

____

____

____

37. If Sue says to Julius, "I think $3,500. is too high for your old truck. I will pay you $2,500 instead." What is the effect of Sue's statement? [p 211] ______________________________

____

38. What is the result if a flood from a broken pipe destroys the bolts of silk fabric Martha was intending to buy? [p 212] ______________________________

____

39. If Omar decides to sell Jane his motor home for $60,000, provided she decides by May 1, and Omar is adjudged insane before Jane makes her decision, what is the effect of Omar's insanity? [p 212]

40. Acceptance is defined as [p 213]

41. A bilateral contract may be accepted by [p 213]

42. What does the mirror image rule require? [p 213]

43. What is an option contract? [p 213]

44. What happens if a person waits too long to accept an offer? [p 213]

45. Why is silence usually not considered an acceptance even if the offeror states that it is? [p 214]

46. Under the common law, what was the effect of an acceptance that was not properly dispatched? [p 215]

47. What is another name for an offer that stipulates that acceptance must be by a specified means of communication? [p 216]

48. The statement, "I will buy your dining room set for $5,000" is a valid offer because [p 206]

49. If the price term is missing from an offer, when can it be implied? [p 207]

50. What is the effect of a supervening illegality on an offer? [p 212]

Chapter 10

CAPACITY AND LEGALITY

Chapter Overview

This chapter's main focus concerns the capacity to enter into contracts as well as the lawfulness of certain contracts. You will learn about the obligations minors, intoxicated and insane individuals have under contracts that they enter into. Additionally, contracts that are contrary to statutes or those that are unconscionable are also explored in this chapter/

Objectives

Upon completion of the exercises contained in this chapter, you should be able to:

1. Describe and recognize situations where the infancy doctrine applies.
2. Describe legal insanity and explain its impact on contractual capacity.
3. Recognize and explain illegal contracts that are contrary to statutes.
4. Explain what a covenant not to compete is and recognize when they are lawful.
5. Explain the use for exculpatory clauses and explain when they are lawful.
6. Describe what an unconscionable contract is and when it is unlawful.

Practical Application

You should be able to determine whether an incapacitated individual will be responsible for what they contract for. Further, you should be able to determine whether the rules of law regarding the infancy doctrine, legal insanity and intoxication will have an impact on any contracts that you may enter into. Additionally you should be able to determine whether covenants not to compete as well as any exculpatory clauses are lawful based on the knowledge you should have obtained. Finally, your knowledge should enable you to determine whether or not a contract may be unconscionable, void or voidable.

Helpful Hints

This chapter lends itself toward simple organization based on who may be involved in a contractual situation as well as what type of clause the parties are concerned with. The rules are very straightforward in this chapter and simple to learn. It is very beneficial to explore the critical legal thinking cases at the end of the chapter in your text as well as answer the critical thought exercise contained herein. The more exposure you have to situations involving capacity and legality, the easier and more recognizable these issues will become for you.

Study Tips

You should start your studying of this chapter by learning that the general presumption is that the law presumes that parties that enter into a contract have the capacity to do the same.

Next, you should examine the contractual situation for any potential capacity issues. These usually involve minors, intoxicated or insane individuals.

Minors

- Who is considered to be a minor?
  Common law: Females under 18 years of age and Males under 21 years of age
  Most states have statutes specifying the age of majority
  Most prevalent age of majority is 18 years old for males and females.
  Any age below the statutory age of majority is called the period of minority.

- Infancy Doctrine - This gives minors the right to disaffirm most contracts they have entered into with adults. It serves as a minor's protection against unscrupulous adults who may want to take advantage of a minor. It is an objective standard.
  - A minor may choose whether or not to enforce the contract. If both parties are minors, both parties have the right to cancel the contract.
  - A minor cannot disaffirm as to part of the contract and affirm as to another part of the contract.

- Disaffirmance
  - A minor in may disaffirm a contract in writing, orally or by conduct.
  - No formalities are needed.
  - It must be done prior to reaching the age of majority or a reasonable time thereafter. Reasonable is assessed on a case-by-case basis.

Restoration and Restitution

If either party has not performed the contract, the minor only needs to disaffirm the contract. If the minor has given consideration to the competent party before disaffirming, the competent party must place the minor in the status quo. In other words, he or she must give the minor back his or her money to make him or her whole again. This is also known as the *competent party's duty of restitution.*

Minor's duty of restoration

Upon disaffirmance of the contract, the minor must return the goods to the adult, even if the goods are lost, destroyed, consumed or have depreciated in value.

Minor's duty of restitution

In a majority of states, the minor will be required to put the adult in status quo upon disaffirming the contract if the minor was intentionally or grossly negligent in his or her conduct thereby causing the adult's property to lose value. Some states require the minor to make restitution of the reasonable value of the item when disaffirming any contract.

Minor's misrepresentation of age

- At common law the minor would still be able to disaffirm the contract despite the misrepresentation.
- Modernly most states hold the minor must place the adult in the status quo if he or she disaffirms the contract and hence would owe the duties of restoration and restitution to the adult.

Ratification

- Simply define: To accept.
- How is ratification accomplished? Ratification may be expressed, impliedly or by conduct.
- Rule of law: A minor may ratify a contract before reaching the age of majority or a reasonable time thereafter. If disaffirmance does not occur in this time frame, it is considered accepted.

Contracts that are Enforceable Against Minors

- Minors are required to pay for the necessaries of life that they contract for.
- Examples of necessaries: food, clothing, tools of the trade, medical services, education.
- Note that the minor is required to pay the reasonable value of the services or goods.
- Also, statutes exist that make minors liable for certain contracts. Examples of some of these special types of contracts as per the statutes include, child support, education, medical, surgical and pregnancy cares to name a few.

Parents' Liability for Their Children's Contracts

- If the parents have not sufficiently provided for their children's necessaries of life, then they are liable for their children's contracts.
- Exception: If a minor becomes emancipated by voluntarily leaving home and living apart from his or her parents and can support him or herself, then the parents have no duty to support their child. This is looked at on a case-by-case basis.

Mentally Incompetent Persons

- In order for a person to be relieved of his or her duties under a contract, the law mandates that the person have been legally insane at the time he or she entered into the contract.

- Legal insanity defined: Legal insanity is determined by using the *objective cognitive understanding test* which involves determining whether the person was incapable of understanding or comprehending the nature of the transaction.

- The following do not qualify as insanity: delusions, light psychological or emotional problems or weakness of intellect.

- Impact of being found insane: If an individual is adjudged insane, the contract is void.

- Impact of being insane, but not adjudged insane: The contract is voidable by the insane person. The other party does not have the option to avoid the contract unless that party doesn't have the contractual capacity either.

- The other party must put the insane party back to the status quo. The sane party must also be placed back to the status quo if he or she was unaware of the other party's insane condition.

- Liability of insane people: Under a quasi-contract, insane individuals are liable for the reasonable value for the necessaries of life that they receive.

Intoxicated Individuals

- General rule: Contracts entered into be intoxicated individuals are voidable by that person. Intoxication may be by alcohol or drugs.

- The contract is voidable only if the person was so intoxicated that he or she was incapable of understanding or comprehending the nature of the transaction. Note, that some states will only allow the person to disaffirm the contract if he or she was forced to become intoxicated.

- Impact of disaffirming the contract based on intoxication: The intoxicated one must be returned to the status quo. Also, the intoxicated person must return the consideration under the contract thereby making restitution to the other party and returning him or her to the staus quo.

- Liability of intoxicated individuals: These individuals are liable in quasi-contract to pay the reasonable value for the necessaries that they receive.

Illegality

- The object of a contract must be lawful. If the object is illegal, then the contract is void and unenforceable.

- Illegal contracts

    - **Usury laws**- These laws set an upper limit on the annual rate that can be charged on certain loans. They are enacted to protect borrowers from loan sharks. Consequences for violating these laws include criminal and civil penalties.

    - **Gambling Statutes**- All states have some sort of regulation or prohibition concerning gambling,
    - **Lotteries, wagering and games of chance**. Consequences for violating these laws also include criminal and civil penalties.

    - **Sabbath Laws**- These are also known as blue laws or Sunday laws. They prohibit or limit the carrying on of certain secular activities on Sundays. Only certain states enact these laws.

    - **Contracts to commit a crime**- These are void. However, if the object of the contract became illegal after the contract was entered into because of a governmental statute, both parties no longer have to perform under the contract.

- **Licensing Statutes** – All states require that certain occupations and professions be licensed in order to practice. There are two types of statutes to be aware of, regulatory and revenue-raising statutes. The regulatory statutes concern those that protect the public. For example, an unlicensed doctor may not collect payment for services that a regulatory statute requires a licensed person to provide. The revenue-raising statutes are made to raise money for the government. Their purpose is to gather revenue. Protecting the public is not a consideration with this type of statute.

Contracts contrary to Public Policy

- If the contract has a negative impact on society or impacts public safety or welfare, it is void.

- Example: Immoral contracts may be against public policy, such as a contract that requests sexual favors. Societal beliefs and practices are used as a guide in determining what immoral conduct is.

- Exculpatory Clauses - An exculpatory clause relieves one or both parties from tort liability under a contract. This type of clause can relieve a party from ordinary negligence but not be used in cases of gross negligence, intentional torts, fraud, or willful conduct. Courts do not condone exculpatory clauses unless the parties have equal bargaining power.

- Covenants Not to Compete - These types of ancillary contracts are lawful if reasonableness can be demonstrated based on the line of business protected, the duration of the restriction and the geographical area that is being protected. The court can refuse to enforce it or alter it to make it reasonable if there is a need.

- Effect of Illegality - Generally speaking one cannot enforce an illegal contract. However, there are exceptions to every rule, including this one. Those that may enforce an illegal contract include innocent persons who justifiably relied on the law or fact making the contract illegal or, persons who were induced to enter into a contract to name just a few.

- Unconscionable Contracts - Some contracts are so unfair that they are unjust. The public policy based doctrine of unconscionablility allows the courts to refuse to enforce the contract, refuse to enforce the unconscionable clause but enforce the rest of the contract or limit the application of any unconscionable clause in order to avoid an unconscionable result.

- Requirements to Demonstrate a Contract is Unconscionable
    - The parties possessed severely unequal bargaining power.
    - The dominant party unreasonably used its unequal bargaining power to obtain unfair contract terms.
    - The subservient party had no reasonable alternative

Refresh Your Memory

The following exercise will enable you to refresh your memory on the rules and principles presented to you in this chapter. Read each question twice and place your answer in the blanks provided. Review the chapter material for any question you miss or are unable to remember.

1. The law presumes that the parties to a contract have the requisite contractual ___________ to enter into the contract.

2. Any age below the statutory age is called the ______________ of ______________.

3. The infancy doctrine is an ______________ standard whereby the court will not inquire into an individual's knowledge, sophistication or experience.

4. Under the infancy doctrine, the contract is ____________________ by the minor.

5. If both parties to the contract are minors, both parties have the right to ______________ the contract.

6. A minor can expressly disaffirm a contract ____________, in ______________, or by the minor's ______________.

7. Minors who misrepresent their age must place the adult in __________ _____ if they disaffirm the contract.

8. To ratify means to _____________.

9. Why are licensing statutes enacted? ____
____

10. Contracts that have a negative impact on society or interfere with public safety and welfare are ______________.

Critical Thought Exercise

You manage a small bicycle shop and sell a very good product, with some bikes costing $2,000. A young man comes into your store and wants to buy a mountain bike for $1,200. He has the cash. You are very happy to sell it to him. He tells you that he is an ambitious high school student who is taking classes at the local university and needs a bicycle that is capable of handling the large hills between the high school and college so that he can make it to class.

Two years later, the young man comes into the shop and tells you that yesterday was his 18th birthday and after drinking a great deal of alcohol, he rode his bike down the Cuesta Grade and crashed into a Ford Expedition. He hands you a piece of bent frame and states that this is all that was left of the bicycle when he went back to the accident scene this morning. He asks for his $1,200 back as he now "desires to undue the contract."

Will you agree to the full refund? Why or why not?

Answer. ____
____
____
____
____
____

Practice Quiz

True/False:

1. ___ Unconscionable contracts are enforceable. [p 217]

2. ___ Minors do not always have the maturity and experience they need to enter into contracts with adults. [p 206]

3. ___ The law does recognize the infancy doctrine. [p 206]

4. ___ Contracts for the necessities of life are exempt from the infancy doctrine. [p 209]

5. ___ If both parties are minors when entering into a contract, only one party may disaffirm the contract. [p 207]

6. ___ The infancy doctrine is an objective standard in most states. [p 206]

7. ___ A minor may not affirm one part of the contract and disaffirm another part. [p 207]

8. ___ A minor may disaffirm a contract if neither party has performed and the minor's contract is executory. [p 207]

9. ___ The competent party to a contract must return the minor to status quo if the minor transferred consideration, money, property or other valuables to the competent party before disaffirming the contract. [p 207]

10. ___ A minor is not required to put the adult in status quo upon disaffirmance of the contract if the minor's intentional or grossly negligent conduct caused the loss of value to the adult's property. [p 207]

11. ___ To ratify is another term for affirm. [p 208]

12. ___ A minor's ratification may be accomplished by express, oral or written words or implied from the minor's conduct. [p 208]

13. ___ Minors are obligated to pay for the necessaries of life that they contract for. [p 209]

14. ___ Minors are not responsible for such things as shelter, clothing, food, or medical services. [p 209]

15. ___ Parents do not owe a legal duty to provide food, clothing, shelter and other necessaries of life for their minor children. [p 209]

Multiple Choice:

16. Parents owe a legal duty to their children to provide [p 209]
    a. a good post secondary education so that they can get a good job.
    b. a place to live until they get married.
    c. food, clothing, shelter and other necessaries of life.
    d. tools of the trade for the occupation they are interested in.

17. People who are suffering from substantial mental incapacity will be protected from having contracts enforced against them because [p 209]
    a. they may have emotional problems rendering them legally insane.
    b. they may have been intoxicated.
    c. they may be delusional when entering into the contracts.
    d. they may not understand the consequences of their actions in entering into a contract.

18. Any contract entered into by a person who has been adjudged insane is [p 210]
    a. valid.
    b. void.
    c. voidable.
    d. enforceable.

19. A person who has contracted with an insane person must place that insane person [p 210]
    a. in status quo if the contract is void or voided by the insane person.
    b. in pari delicto with the competent party to the contract.
    c. in counseling to help him or her out.
    d. in status quo if the contract is void or voided by the sane person.

20. Most states hold with regard to intoxication that a contract is voidable only if the person [p 210]
    a. was so intoxicated when he or she entered into the contract that he or she was aware of how many drinks he or she had consumed.
    b. was so intoxicated that a subjective individual would be able to validate the nature of his or her transaction.
    c. was so intoxicated that he or she could not remember where he or she was.
    d. was so intoxicated that he or she was incapable of understanding or comprehending the nature of the transaction.

21. The amount of drugs or alcohol that is necessary to be consumed for an individual to be considered legally intoxicated to disaffirm contracts [p 210]
    a. is usually two or more alcoholic beverages.
    b. is a reasonable amount.

c. varies from case to case.
d. none of the above.

22. An individual who disaffirms a contract using intoxication as his or her basis must [p 211]
    a. be awarded punitive damages against the server of alcohol or drugs.
    b. be returned to status quo.
    c. understand or comprehend the nature of the transaction.
    d. pass a breathalyzer test.

Short Answer:

23. Explain what a covenant not to compete? [p 216] ______________________________
____
____
____

24. A contract that is so oppressive or manifestly unfair that it would be unjust to enforce it is known as an ____________________ ____________________. [p 218]

25. A doctrine that gives minors the right to affirm or disaffirm a contract entered into with an adult is ______________ ____________________. [p 206]

26. The act of a minor to rescind a contract under the infancy doctrine is known as ________________________. [p 207]

27. The minor's __________, ____________________ and status in life are what are looked at in determining what are necessaries as they pertain to contracts the minor has entered into. [p 206]

28. What is emancipation? [p 209] ______________________________________
____

29. Under most state laws, contracts entered into by certain intoxicated individuals are __________________. [p 210]

30. An immoral contract is ____
____. [p 241]

____

Chapter 11
REALITY OF CONSENT AND WRITING

Chapter Overview

The preceding chapters have discussed the requirements for creation of a contract as well as agreement, capacity and consideration. Even though an individual may consent to a contract, if his or her assent is not genuine, it may make the contract unenforceable. The issues that this chapter focuses on are in the areas of mistake, misrepresentation, duress and undue influence.

Objectives

Upon completion of the exercises in this chapter, you should be able to:

1. Give an explanation of genuineness of assent.
2. Give an explanation on how mutual mistake of fact excuses performance.
3. Differentiate between physical and economic duress.
4. Explain undue influence and its applicability to contracts
5. Describe the contracts that must satisfy the Statute of Frauds.
6. Discuss the impact of the failure to adhere to the Statute of Frauds.
7. Discuss the sale of goods and the need to satisfy the Statute of Frauds.
8. Explain parol evidence and its exceptions.
9. Discuss the writing requirements for international contracts.

Practical Application

You should be able to recognize whether a mistake as it applies to a contractual situation is a unilateral or a mutual mistake along with the particulars for each. Additionally, you should be able to decide whether or not a fraudulent misrepresentation or the more difficult types of fraud exist and the remedies that are available for the same. Finally you should be able to understand the impact of both physical and economic duress as well as undue influence upon a contractual situation. The information in this chapter will be particularly useful to you in developing a sense of what is genuine assent.

Further, you will be able to determine which documents comprise a contract. Additionally, you should be able to recognize when the Statute of Frauds applies to certain situations as well as whether or not the writing requirement can be satisfied in the absence of a writing. Finally, you should be able to determine whether there are any issues regarding parol evidence and if any exceptions exist.

Helpful Hints

The five main areas you should be familiar with are broken down into easy to remember sections in the Study Tips section. Since differentiating between the different types of fraud can be confusing, it is important that you gain exposure to as many cases and examples as possible. The exercises provided for this chapter will help to enhance the exercises given at the end of the chapter in your text.

Study Tips

Genuineness in General

Keep in mind you are studying the areas of mistake, misrepresentation, duress and undue influence. These areas impact whether or not a party's assent to a contract is genuine or whether other factors influenced his or her consent to enter into the contract in the first place.

Assent

The facts you should know are:

- It must be present to have an enforceable contract.
- It may be accomplished by express words or conduct.
- A special situation exists with click-wrap licenses.
  a. The Uniform Commercial Code provides that "a contract for the sale of goods may be made in any manner sufficient to show agreement, including conduct by both parties that recognizes the contract's existence."
  b. Under the new Uniform Information Transaction Act, "a licensee is bound by the terms of the license if the licensee manifests assent before or during the party's initial use of or access to the licensor's software."

Mistake

Mistakes occur when one or both of the parties have an incorrect belief about the subject matter, value or some other area of the contract.

Two types of mistake

- Unilateral mistake – This is where one party is mistaken about a material fact concerning the subject matter of the contract.

  1. General rule regarding unilateral mistakes: The mistaken party usually will not be allowed to rescind the contract.

  2. Exceptions to the general rule include:
     - If one party is mistaken and the other party knew or should have known about the mistake, then the mistake is treated like a mutual mistake and rescission is allowed.
     - If a unilateral mistake is made because of a clerical or mathematical error and is not because of gross negligence.
     - The gravity of the mistake makes enforcing the contract unconscionable.

- Mutual mistakes – A mistake made by both parties concerning a material fact that is important to the subject matter of the contract.

    1. General rule regarding mutual mistakes: Either party may rescind the contract if there has been a mutual mistake of a past or existing material fact.

What is considered to be a material fact?

There are several explanations for this question.
First, anything that is significant to the subject matter of the contract.

An ambiguity may also qualify as a mutual mistake of material fact.
An ambiguity is where there is confusion as to the meaning of a word or term in the contract.

Two types of mutual mistakes:

- Mutual mistake of fact – The contract may be rescinded because there has bee no meeting of the minds between the parties as the subject matter is in dispute.

- Mutual mistake of value – The contract remains enforceable because the subject matter is not in dispute and the parties are only mistaken at to the value.

Fraudulent Misrepresentation

The mnemonic you utilized in chapter 4 is also applicable here. The mnemonic is MISJD
M - Misrepresentation of a material fact that was false in nature
I - Intentionally made to the innocent party
S - Scienter (knowledge) of the statement's falsity by the wrongdoer
J - Justifiable reliance on the false statement by the innocent party
D - Damages were suffered by the injured party

Fraudulent misrepresentation as an inducement to enter into a contract – The innocent party's assent is not genuine and the contract is voidable. The remedies that are available are rescission and restitution or enforce the contract and sue for damages.

There are *five types of fraud* you need to become familiar with.
1) **Fraud in the Inception** (also known as fraud in the factum) - The person is deceived on what he or she is signing. The contract is void.
2) **Fraud in the Inducement** – The person knows what he or she is signing, but has been fraudulently induced to enter into the contract. The contract is voidable by the innocent party.
3) **Fraud by Concealment** – Where one party specifically conceals a material fact from the other party.
4) **Silence as Misrepresentation** – One need not divulge all facts to the other party, however, if the nondisclosure would cause death or bodily injury or there is a fiduciary relationship or federal or state statutes require that a fact be disclosed, then fraud may be implied.
5) **Misrepresentation of Law** – The general rule is that this is not actionable as fraud. However, if one party to the contract is a professional who should know what the law is and

still intentionally misrepresents the law to a less knowledgeable party, this will be enough to allow rescission of the contract.

Innocent Misrepresentation

This occurs when a party makes a statement of fact that he or she honestly believes is true even though it is not. The injured party may rescind the contract but may not seek damages. This type of misrepresentation is sometimes treated like a mutual mistake.

Duress

There are two types, both of which involve threatening to do a wrongful act unless the other party enters into a contract.

1. Duress via physical harm or extortion or to bring or not drop a criminal lawsuit is the first type. Note, the threat to bring or not drop a civil lawsuit is not duress, unless it's a frivolous suit.
2. Economic duress is the second type, which occurs when one party refuses to continue performing his or her duties unless the other party pays more money and enters into a second contract. The innocent party must show that her or she had no choice but to pay the extra money and succumb to the threat. Economic duress is also known as business compulsion.

Undue Influence

Rescission based on undue influence is allowed if it can be shown that a fiduciary or confidential relationship existed between the parties and the dominant party unduly used his or her influence to persuade the servient party to enter into a contract. This contract is voidable.

Statute of Frauds

General Information

Certain kinds of contracts must be in writing in order to memorialize the significant terms and prevent misunderstanding or fabrications, otherwise known as fraud. The mnemonic given below will help give you an easy way to remember which contracts are required to be in writing. The information that follows the mnemonic is organized in the same order as the mnemonic to provide you with an organized learning method.

Mr. Dibbles Places Many Fancy Real Estate Ads.

Mr.	–	Contracts in consideration of Marriage
Dibbles	–	Debt of another
Places	–	Part Performance
Many	–	Must be performed within one year
Fancy	–	For goods $500 or more
Real Estate	–	Transfers of ownership interests in Real Estate such as mortgages, leases
Ads	–	Agency contracts

Contracts in Consideration of Marriage

These types of contracts must be in writing for the most obvious reason, to determine ownership of property and assist in determining benefits and property distribution upon death or dissolution of the same. Also it is important for income tax purposes to know exactly who is a dependent if filing jointly.

Debt of Another

A collateral or guaranty contract occurs where one person agrees to answer for the debts or duties of another individual.

Part Performance

This involves the situation where there is an oral contract for the sale of land or other transfer of interest in real property and there is some sort of partial performance. In order for the partial performance to act as an exception to the Statute of Frauds, many courts require that the purchaser either take possession of the property and pay part of the purchase price or make valuable improvements on the land. If part performance can be shown, the oral contract will be ordered to be specifically performed in order to prevent an injustice.

Must be Performed Within One Year

If a contract cannot be performed by its own terms within one year, it must be in writing. If it can be performed within one year, the contract can be oral.

For Goods $500 or More

The Uniform Commercial Code requires contracts for the sale of goods that cost $500 or more to be in writing in order to be enforceable. Modifications that cause the goods to escalate in price to $500 or more will also need to be in writing.

Real Estate

Contracts that transfer an ownership interest in land must be in writing. This includes mortgages, leases, life estates, and most easements.

Real property includes the land, its buildings, trees, soil, minerals, timber, plants, crops, and permanently affixed things to the buildings (fixtures).

Agency Contracts

Agent's contracts to sell real estate must be in writing under the ***equal dignity rule***.

Electronic Contracts and the Writing Requirement of the Statute of Frauds

- The Electronic Signature in Global and National Commerce Act put electronic contracts on the same level as paper contracts.
- Electronic agreements meet the Statute of Frauds writing requirement.
- The act provides for record retention requirements.

Promissory Estoppel

- Promissory estoppel is also known as equitable estoppel.
- It is an exception to the Statute of Frauds
- It involves an oral promise that is enforceable if three conditions are met.
    1. The promise induces action or forbearance of action by another.
    2. The reliance on the oral promise was foreseeable, and
    3. Injustice can be avoided only by enforcing the oral promise.
- The effect of this doctrine is to estop the promissor from raising the Statute of Frauds as a defense.

Sufficiency of the Writing

Things you should know:

- A contract does not have to be drafted by a lawyer.
- A contract does not have to be formally typed to be binding.
- A contract can be a letter, telegram, invoice, sales receipts, checks and even handwritings on scraps of paper.
- The contract must be signed by the party to be charged.
- A signature can be a nickname, initial, a symbol, and even the letter 'X'. Also, modernly, a
- Fax may also constitute a signature even though it's a document by electronic means, if the party trying to enforce the contract can demonstrate that the obligation was intentionally incurred.

Japan's Use of a Signature in a Writing

- In Japan, they use a stamp with a set of characters on the end of it. This is called hanko.
- In China it is called chop.
- Hankos and chops are registered with the government.
- The signatures can be made of gold, wood, plastic, ivory, jade or agate.
- The use of hankos and chops are debated. Some say they promote fraud. Others value the rich tradition and feel it will remain in tact.

Integration of Several Writings

An entire writing does not have to be in one single document in order to be enforceable. Several writings can be combined or *integrated* to form a single written contract. Integration may be accomplished by expressly referring to it in one document that refers to and incorporates another document in it. This is known as *incorporation by reference.*

Interpreting Contract Words and Terms

- The parties may explain the words and terms used in the contract.
- Some contracts contain a glossary that defines the terms and used in a contract.
- If the words and terms are not defined, the courts will interpret using the following standard.
- Ordinary words- given the meaning as stated in the dictionary.
- Technical words – given their technical meaning.
- Specific terms qualify general terms.
- Typed words prevail over preprinted words.
- Handwritten words prevail over preprinted and typed.
- If an ambiguity exists, it will be resolved against the party who drafted the contract.
- If both parties are in the same sort of trade, then the words used in the trade will be given their meaning as per trade usage.
- Interpretation will be to advance the object of the contract.

Parol Evidence Rule

- Parol means word.
- Any words outside of the four corners of the contract are called parol evidence.
- The parol evidence rule states that if a written contract is a complete and final expression of the parties' agreement, any prior oral or written statements that alter, contradict, or are in addition to the terms of the written contract Are inadmissible in any court proceeding concerning the contract.

Refresh Your Memory

The following exercise will enable you to refresh your memory on the rules and principles presented to you in this chapter. Read each question twice and place your answer in the blanks provided. Review the chapter material for any question you miss or are unable to remember.

1. What are the two types of mistake? ____________________ and ____________________

2. What is meant by the term rescission? ____

3. When only one party is mistaken about a material fact regarding the subject matter of the contract, this is known as a ____________________ mistake.

4. What is a mutual mistake of fact? ______________________________
____

5. If Ken telephones the manager of Your Home Town Electronics store and asks how much the smallest high density television he sells is and the manager replies, "Fourteen twenty." Thereafter Ken says, "Put my name on one as I can't pass up a bargain like that!" Ken arrives at the store ready to pay fourteen dollars and twenty cents for the small high-density television set at which point the manager laughs hysterically and says, "Buddy you must be joking! The smallest set we have costs one thousand four hundred twenty dollars!" If Ken tries to enforce the contract he claims has been formed against Your Home Town Electronics store, what would Home Town's best defense be? ____________________
____
____

6. If Bart Brown, a contractor tells Mary Morris a homeowner that he will not finish her room addition on her home unless she agrees to pay him an additional $10,000 and Mary feels pressured to give him the additional compensation, this may be construed as __________ __________.

7. A threat to bring or drop a civil lawsuit will not be considered duress unless __________
____.

8. Undue influence happens when one person takes advantage of another person's __________, __________, or __________ weakness and unduly persuades that person to enter into a contract.

9. All states have enacted a __________ of __________ that requires certain types of contracts be in writing.

10. What type of contract is not enforceable by either party under the Statute of Frauds? an ____________________ contract.

11. Any contract that transfers an ownership interest ___ _____ must be in writing under the Statute of Frauds.

12. Give three examples of real property as it pertains to the Statute of Frauds.
__________, ____________________, ____________________

13. Which rule helps to prevent disputes about contract terms that might occur toward the end of a long-term contract? The _____ _____ rule.

14. At what price do contracts for the sale of goods have to be in writing? ____________

15. How does the doctrine of promissory estoppel apply to oral land sale contracts? ________
____

Critical Thought Exercise

At Rip-Off Motors, an exotic used car dealership, you are the general manager and Slick is your dishonest salesman. Slick told a potential customer, Dupe, that the Porsche he was interested in purchasing had been driven only 25,000 in four years and had never been in an accident. Dupe hired Grease, a mechanic, to appraise the condition of the car. Grease said that the car probably had at least 75,000 miles on it and probably had been in an accident. In spite of this information, Dupe still thought the car would be a good buy for the price, which was still lower than a Porsche with 75,000 miles. Dupe bought the car and it immediately developed numerous mechanical problems which would cost over $10,000 to repair. Dupe has now come back to Rip-Off Motors and is seeking to have you rescind the contract on the basis of Slick's fraudulent misrepresentations of the car's condition. If you rescind the contract, it will cause the dealership to lose over $13,000.

Write a letter to either:

A) Dupe, if you are refusing to rescind the contract, or

B) Mr. Big, the owner of Rip-Off Motors, if you intend to rescind the contract and suffer the loss.

Explain the reasons for your decision, citing authority for your action.

Answer. ____

____

____

____

____

____

____

____

____

____

____

____

Practice Quiz

True/False:

1. ___ The courts make distinguish between a mutual mistake of value and a mutual mistake of fact. [p 226]

2. ___ Either party may rescind a contract if there has been a mutual mistake of past or existing mistake of fact. [p 226]

3. ___ If Brandon asks his mother to take him to the store to buy a new mouse and she takes him to the pet store when he wanted to go to the electronics store for a computer mouse, any contract between the two of them may not be rescinded as there has not been a mutual mistake of fact. [p 226]

4. ___ Fraud in the inception is not the same as fraud in the inducement. [p 228]

5. ___ If Chad fails to tell Cory about the wobbly frame on a bike he just bought from him and William loses control of the steering on his first ride resulting in a broken leg and collar bone, William may bring suit under the theory of silence as misrepresentation. [p 228]

6. ___ John calls Funco Inc. to inquire about one of their arcade games and is told that it costs thirty- two fifty. Thereafter John tells the representative of Funco, "That's a great price. Put my name on it and I'll be right there to pick it up. Upon arrival he is told that the game costs three thousand two hundred and fifty dollars. Despite this fact, John will be able to purchase the arcade game for thirty-two dollars and fifty cents. [p 226]

7. ___ A misrepresentation of law will be allowed as a ground for rescission of a contract even if one of the parties to a contract is a professional who should know what the law is and intentionally misrepresents the law to a less knowledgeable contracting party. [p 228]

8. ___ The innocent party to a contract may not rescind the contract based on fraud and obtain restitution or enforce the contract and sue for damages. [p 228]

9. ___ Justifiable reliance will be found in a cause of action for fraud even if the innocent party did not know that the misrepresentation was false. [p 229]

10. ___ An intentional misrepresentation occurs when someone consciously induces another to rely and act on a misrepresentation. [p 227]

11. ___ Fraudulent misrepresentation is not the same as fraud. [p 227]

12. ___ A party's assent to a contract needs to be genuine. [p 227]

13. ___ Intent in a cause of action based on fraud may be inferred from the circumstances. [p 228]

14. ___ The signature of the person enforcing the contract is not necessary when enforcing a contract. [p 236]

15. ___ The placing of several documents in a tube may indicate integration. [p 236]

16. ___ Attaching several documents together by a staple is an example of integration. [p 236]

17. ___ The Uniform Commercial Code does allow several writings to be integrated to form a single document. . [p 236]

18. ___ A contract must be in writing, contain the essential terms and need not be drafted by a lawyer in order to be binding. [p 236]

19. ___ In Japan individuals use their hand written signatures to sign legal documents. [p 238]

20. ___ Handwritten words prevail over preprinted and typed words in a contract. [p 237]

Multiple Choice:

21. If an innocent misrepresentation has been made, what type of action may the innocent party bring? [p 227]
    a. An action for fraudulent misrepresentation.
    b. An action for specific performance.
    c. An action based on undue influence.
    d. An action for rescission of the contract without damages.

22. If Walter threatens to bring a criminal lawsuit against Joshua if Joshua doesn't sign a fencing contract giving Walter the job, this would constitute [p 258]
    a. a misunderstanding between the parties.
    b. duress.
    c. undue influence over Joshua.
    d. mutual mistake of fact.

23. If a unilateral mistake happens because of a mathematical or clerical error that is not the result of gross negligence, a contract between the parties will [p 253]
    a. be enforced.
    b. be deemed unconscionable.
    c. not be enforced.
    d. rewritten to reflect the correct mathematical amount.

24. An innocent party's assent to a contract is not genuine when [p 227]
    a. the innocent party has made a unilateral mistake.
    b. a fraudulent misrepresentation is used to induce the innocent party to enter into the contract.
    c. the innocent party knew that the misrepresentation was false or so extravagant to be obviously false.
    d. the innocent party has participated in the fraudulent misrepresentation.

25. A clause in a contract that stipulates that it is the complete integration and the exclusive expression of the parties agreement is known as a [p 238]
    a. promissory estoppel clause.
    b. marital clajuse.
    c. incorporation by reference claue.
    d. merger clause.

26. Real property as it pertains to the Statute of Frauds includes [p 231]
    a. timber, crops., fixtures, soil and buildings.
    b. stocks, bonds, money and certificates.
    c. timber, inoperable automobiles, plants and minerals.
    d. fixtures, crops, and farm equipment.

27. Which aspect of the Statute of Frauds is intended to prevent disputes about contract terms that may otherwise occur toward the end of a long-term contract? [p 233]
    a. the part performance exception
    b. the guaranty contract rule
    c. the one year rule

d. goods for $500 or more

28. A collateral guaranty contract happens where [p 234]
    a. contracts for the sale of goods $500 or more are present.
    b. one person agrees to answer for the debts or duties of another person.
    c. electronic commerce agreements are a second means of enforcement to contracts.
    d. the most recent agreement of the parties is integrated with the former contract thereby guaranteeing its enforcement.

29. Jane and John entere into a contract for the purchase of Jane's computer, with delivery set for December 15. Upon signing the contract, John discovers that a price has not been set. Which rule would best assist the parties for enforcing the contract? [p 238]
    a. the Kelly Blue Book rule
    b. the promissory estoppel rule
    c. the parol evidence rule
    d. the equal dignity rule

30. Cameron expressly grants to Jennifer the right to use his land from her land to the boat dock that is adjacent to the end of his property. If Cameron decides that Jennifer cannot use his land to get to the boat dock. what must Jennifer show in order to enforce the right to use Cameron's land? [p 231-232]
    a. that an easement was created
    b. that she was given a right to use Cameron's land
    c. that the right to use Cameron's land was in writing
    d. all of the above

Short Answer:

31. What are the three situations when a unilateral contract will not be enforced? [p 225]

____

____

____

32. What are the elements necessary for proving fraudulent misrepresentation? [p 227]

____

____

____

33. What is the measure of damages in a cause of action for fraud? [p 227] ____________

____

34. What is meant by the term undue influence? [p 230] ____________________

____

35. When one party takes specific action to hide a material fact from another party, this is known as ______________________________________. [p 228]

36. Briefly define the meaning of fixtures as they pertain to real estate. [p 231] _________

____

37. What type of contract has been formed if Stephanie agrees to pay Sally's debt to Visa? [p 233] ______________________________

38. If Bert decides to sell his golf cart to Maria for $900.00., what will be required? [p 234] ______________________________

39. What is the rule that says that agent's contracts to sell property covered by the Statute of Frauds must be in writing to be enforceable? [p 232] ______________________________

40. Explain why telegrams that are not signed may still be enforceable. [p 237] ______________________________

Chapter 12
THIRD-PARTY RIGHTS AND DISCHARGE

Chapter Overview

This chapter examines third party rights under other individual's contracts, more specifically assignees and intended third-party beneficiaries. Additionally it explores conditions to performance and the various ways of discharging the duty of performance. The delegation of contractual duties by mutual agreement, impossibility of performance and operation of law are also discussed.

Objectives

Upon completion of the exercises contained in this chapter, you should be able to:

1. Define the meaning of assignment as it pertains to contracts.
2. Discuss what contracts are assignable.
3. Define the meaning of delegation of duties and discuss the parties' liability in a delegation.
4. Define an intended beneficiary and discuss his or her rights under a contract.
5. Define a covenant.
6. Discuss the impact of objective impossibility on a contract.
7. Discuss the meaning of commercial impracticability and when it applies.
8. Discuss the various ways that contracts are discharged by operation of law.

Practical Application

Upon mastering the concepts in this chapter, you should be able to recognize whether or not a contract may be assigned or delegated and any liabilities that may have been incurred as a result of the delegation. Further, you will be able to determine if a third party to a contract has any rights as a beneficiary to the contract. Finally, you should be able to analyze questions and real life situations concerning the various ways a contract may be discharged by law.

Helpful Hints

Since it is often difficult keeping the parties straight in contracts involving more than two parties, it is helpful to diagram the transaction either in box form as is displayed within your text, or by use of a triangle or any other means that may be useful to you. It is also especially helpful to imagine yourself as the person being given an assignment or right, delegation or duty. If you substitute yourself into the question or hypothetical, the concepts begin to become clear. Do not get burdened by the titles assignee, assignor, delagatee, delegator, or obligor and obligee. It is much easier to learn the concept behind the titles first and then the titles and who is doing what and its impact will become second nature to you.

Study Tips

It is very important that you become familiar with the terminology expressed in this chapter as it can become confusing.

Vocabulary

Privity of Contract – The state of two specified parties being in contract.

Obligor –The party who owes the duty of performance.
Obligee – The party owed a right under a contract.
Assignor – This is the obligee in disguise as he or she is transferring his or her right under a contract.
Assignee – The party to whom the right has been transferred.
Anti-delegation clause – A clause that prohibits the delegation of duties under the contract. The courts will enforce this clause.
An assignment and a delegation – Where both the rights and duties are transferred under the contract.

Assignment

The transfer of contractual rights by the obligee to another party. No formalities are necessary, however, words to express the intent of the assignor are carefully examined. Words such as transfer, give and convey have been used to express intent in an assignment.

Rights that may not be assigned include:

- Personal service contracts are not assignable.
  Exception: A professional athletics contract with a clause that permits the contract to be assigned.

- Assignment of Future Rights- The general rule is that a person may not assign a currently non- existing right that he or she is expecting in the future.

- Contracts Where Assignment Would Materially Alter the Risk of the Obligor – A classic example would be assigning your homeowner's insurance to a friend of yours who cannot afford it.

- Assignment of Legal Actions – An individual may not assign the right to sue, however, he or she may assign the right to the judgment once it is procured.

Effect of an Assignment

The assignee stands in the shoes of the assignor. The assignor is entitled to performance by the obligor. The assignment extinguishes all rights of the assignor against the obligor.

The assignee must notify the obligor about the assignment and the performance by the obligor must be given to the assignee. If there is no notice given to the obligor, he or she can continue performing under the contract to the assignor. The assignees only recourse is to sue the assignor for damages.

Rules used for Successive Assignments

- The American Rule (New York Rule) – The majority of states use this rule, which states that the first assignment in time prevails regardless of notice.

- The English rule – This rule states that the first to give notice prevails.

- The Possession of Tangible Token Rule - Under either the American or English rule, if the assignor makes a successive assignment of a contract right that is represented by a tangible token, such as a savings passbook, stock certificate etc, the first assignee who receives delivery of the tangible token prevails over subsequent assignees.

If the obligor knows of the assignment but continues to perform to the assignor, the assignee can due the obligor for payment. He or she will also have to pay to the assignor and to the assignee. Further he or she may sue the assignor for damages.

Anti-assignment and Approval Clauses

- The anti-assignment clause prohibits the assignment of rights under the contract.
- An approval clause is one in which the obligor must approve any assignment.

Delegation of Duties

- A transfer of contractual duties by the obligor to another party for performance.
- Delegator – The obligor who transferred his or her duty.
- Delagatee – The party to whom the duty has been transferred.

Duties that May Not be Delegated Include:

- Personal service contracts that require the discretion, expertise and the exercise of personal skills.
- Contract whose performance would materially vary if the obligor's duties were delegated.

Effect of Delegation of Duties:

- The delegator remains legally liable for the performance of the contract, thereby being subjected to a lawsuit if the delegatee does not perform properly.

- The delegate's liability depends on if there has been a declaration of duties or an assumption of duties. If the word assumption or a similar term is contained in the delegation, then there has been an assumption of duties.

- Compare though, if a delegatee has not assumed the duties under the contract, then this is called a declaration of duties. In the case of a declaration of duties, the delegatee is not obligated to the obligee for nonperformance, and the obligee can only sue the delegator.

Third-Party Beneficiaries

- Third parties who claim rights under contracts are either intended or incidental. The intended beneficiaries are either donee or creditor beneficiaries.

- Intended:
  Donee beneficiary contract – A contract, which confers a benefit, or gift on an intended third party.
  Donee- The third party to whom the benefit is conferred.
  Creditor beneficiary contract – A contract where a debtor has borrowed money from a creditor to buy an item. The debtor enters into an agreement to pay the creditor back with interest. The debtor thereafter sells the item to another individual before the loan is paid off. The new buy then promises the debtor that he or she will pay the balance of the loan amount to the creditor.
  Creditor- The party that becomes a beneficiary under the new debtor's contract with another party.

- Incidental beneficiary:
  An incidental beneficiary is one who is incidentally benefited by other people's contracts

Covenants and Conditions

- Covenant – An unconditional promise to perform.
- Nonperformance of a covenant equals a breach of contract giving the other party the right to sue.

- Condition – A conditional promise is not as definite as a covenant.

- Types of conditions:

  1. Condition precedent – The occurrence or nonoccurrence of an event before a party is obligated to perform under the contract.

     Example: Condition precedent based on satisfaction. There are two tests to determine whether this unique form of condition precedent has been met. They are:

The personal satisfaction test – This is a subjective test whereby the person is to act in good faith in matters involving personal taste and comfort.

The reasonable person test – This is an objective test that is used to judge contracts involving mechanical fitness and most commercial transactions. This is used when a third person is involved who is used to judge another's work.

Time of performance as a condition precedent:
If a party is not jeopardized by a delay, this will be considered a minor breach. If *"time is of the essence,"* performance by the stated time is an express condition. This will be considered a breach of contract if performance is not rendered by the start date.

2. Condition Subsequent
This condition exists when a contract provides that the occurrence or nonoccurrence of a certain event automatically excuses the performance of an existing duty to perform.
In the Restatement (Second) of Contracts, there is no distinction between a condition precedent and a condition subsequent.

3. Concurrent Conditions
This condition occurs when both parties render performance at the same time.

4. Implied Conditions
Any of the above conditions may be considered to be express or implied in nature. A condition is implied from the situation surrounding the contract and the parties' conduct.

Discharge of Performance

- There are three ways to discharge a party's duty under a contract. They are by mutual agreement of the parties, by impossibility of performance, or by operation of law.

- **Discharge by agreement** is accomplished by:

1. Mutual rescission – The parties to a contract can mutually agree to discharge or end their contractual duties.
2. Substituted contract – The parties can enter into a new contract that revokes and discharges a prior contract.
3. Novation – This agreement substitutes a new party for one of the original contracting parties. All three must be in unison regarding the substitution.

4. Accord and Satisfaction – The settlement of a contract dispute where the parties accept something different than originally agreed upon and performance of the same. If an accord is not satisfied when it is due, the injured party may enforce either the accord or the original agreement.

- **Discharge by Impossibility**
  - Discharge by impossibility occurs under the following circumstances:

  - Impossibility of Performance
    This excuse of nonperformance is excused if the contract becomes objectively impossible to perform.
  - Examples:
    Death of a promissory in a personal service contract.
    Destruction of the subject matter prior to performance.
    A supervening illegality makes performance of the contract illegal.

  - Commercial Impracticability
    This excuse of nonperformance indicates that if an extreme or unexpected development or expense makes it impractical for the promissory to perform, then this excuse may be recognized.

  - Frustration of Purpose
    If the object or benefit of the contract is made worthless to the promisor and both parties knew what the purpose was, and the act that frustrated the purpose was reasonably unforeseeable, then
    This doctrine will excuse the performance of commercial obligations.

  - Force Majeure Clauses
    These type of clauses are where the parties agree in their contract as to the events that will excuse nonperformance of the contract. These typical force majeure clause excuses nonperformance
    caused by natural disasters. Modernly labor strikes, and shortages of materials excuse performance by way of a force majeure clause.

Discharge by Operation of Law

The legal rules that discharge parties from performing their duties under their contracts are as follows:

- Statute of Limitations – The statutory frame in which to bring a lawsuit. The U.C.C. indicates that four years is the time frame to bring a cause of action based on breach of contract.

- Bankruptcy- If the debtor's assets are inadequate to pay all of the creditors' claims, then the debtor receives a discharge of the unpaid debts and is relieved of liability to pay the discharged debts.

- Alteration of Contract –This occurs when a party to the contract intentionally alters the contract 's material terms such as price or quantity. The innocent party may discharge the contract or enforce it on its original or modified terms.

Refresh Your Memory

The following exercise will enable you to refresh your memory on the rules and principles presented to you in this chapter. Read each question twice and place your answer in the blanks provided. Review the chapter material for any question you miss or are unable to remember.

1. The state of two specified parties being in contract is known as _______________ of _______________.

2. Explain what an assignment is. ____.

3. What is the obligee's role under the contract?____

____

4. What is the obligor's role under the contract? ____

____

5. Joseph cannot assign his expected right to receive inheritance from his living grandmother because ____.

6. Edna assigns her homeowner's insurance to Betty, as Betty cannot get insurance. What is the effect of this assignment? ____

7. If an obligor does not want to deal with or render performance to an unknown third party, what type of clause may he or she use? ____

8. Explain what an approval clause is. ____

____

9. A transfer of contractual duties by the obligor to another party for performance is a _______________________________.

10. The original creditor who becomes a beneficiary under the debtor's new contract with another party is a _______________ _______________.

Critical Thought Exercise

The Rocky Mountain Plumbing Company (RMP), which you manage, is very successful and has an excellent reputation. Your business is known for its fairness, prompt performance and superior work. After a severe earthquake that measured 7.4 on the Richter scale, billions of dollars worth of pipe damage occurred to hundreds of structures within the area serviced by your company. RMP has signed several huge contracts to repair or replace plumbing for government buildings, hospitals, and three hotels owned by Alexis. Each of these contracts will be for $800,000 or more.

You are uncertain if RMP will be able to meet the deadlines set in the contracts as the urgency of the work needing to be done to so many buildings might call for more time.

You have the option of assigning some of the work to Bob's Plumbing, a far less reputable company, or making other arrangements with the county, the hospital district, and Alexis. You are afraid that if you inform people that RMP is unable to perform the contracts on time, it may lose the contracts along with the huge profits they will bring.

Your partners share your skepticism about meeting the deadlines and want to hire Bob's Plumbing immediately without mentioning it to any of the parties involved.

RMP's partners request that you draft a memorandum advising them of the options and risks involved with each option.

Answer. ____

Practice Quiz

True/False:

1. ___ The unconditional assignment of a contract right extinguishes all the assignor's rights, including right to sue the obligor directly for nonperformance. [p 284]

2. ___ The assignee has a duty to notify the obligor of the assignment nor about to whom performance must be rendered. [p 246]

3. ___ Mandy hires Dr. Saran, a plastic surgeon to give her a new nose. Thereafter Dr. Saran delegates his contract with Mandy to Dr. Foiler, another plastic surgeon. This is not acceptable delegation of duties. [p 250]

4. ___ If a delegatee does not perform his or her duties under a delegation, then the obligee can only sue the obligor-delegator. [p 250]

5. ___ A declaration of duties is present when the delegatee has not yet assumed the duties under a contract. [p 250]

6. ___ When there has been a transfer of both rights and duties under a contract, an assignment as well as delegation has occurred under the contract. [p 251]

7. ___ When a person enters into a contract with the intent to confer a benefit or a gift on an intended third party, the contract is called a donee beneficiary contract. [p 251]

8. ___ In a creditor beneficiary situation, the creditor is the new intended creditor beneficiary to a second contract. [p 252]

9. ___ When the parties to a contract unintentionally benefit a third party, this third party is referred to as a donee beneficiary. [p 253]

10. ___ A covenant is an unconditional promise to perform. [p 254]

11. ___ Commercial impracticability does not excuse performance under a contract if an unforeseeable event make impractical for the promisor to perform. [p 258]

12. ___ The Uniform Commercial Code provides that the statute of limitations for a breach of a sales or lease contract is one year after the cause of action accrues. [p 259]

Multiple Choice:

13. Which two exceptions allow third parties to acquire rights under other parties' contracts? [p 246]
    a. A majeure clause and an approval clause
    b. An assignment and a discharge of duties
    c. An assignment and a third-party beneficiary contract
    d. An assignment and a conveyance of personal or real property

14. An obligee who transfers the right to receive performance is called [p 246]
    a. a delegator.
    b. an assignor.
    c. a delegatee.
    d. a lessor.

15. An assignee is [p 246]
    a. the party who transfers the right to receive performance.
    b. the party who transfers the right to suspend performance.
    c. the party to whom the right has been transferred.
    d. the party to whom the right has been delegated.

17. Tom's Tourist Shop is located on the beach next to where a new high-rise hotel is going in. There is supposed to be sixteen floors to the hotel, however, Charter Construction Company decides to stop building at the thirteenth floor. Since the beginning of the project, the owner of Tom's has noticed a definite increase in business. He knows that once the hotel is complete, his profits will escalate due to the patrons staying at the hotel. Tom decides to bring a cause of action against the Charter Construction Company for breach of contract as he is claiming that his tourist shop was a beneficiary of the hotel and Charter Construction Company contract. What will be the probable result? [p 253]
    a. Tom will win because his shop is a donee beneficiary under the hotel and Charter Construction Company.
    b. Tom will lose, as his shop is merely an incidental beneficiary as his business unintentionally benefited from the contract just by being located next to the new hotel.
    c. Tom will win because if it were not for Tom, the area surrounding the hotel would be unappealing to tourists.
    d. Tom will lose because he did not give notice of the benefit to Charter Construction.

Short Answer:

18. The transfer of contractual rights is called an [p 246] ____________________.

19. Can Julie transfer her sailboat insurance to her roommate Liz? Be sure to include why or why not. [p 247] ____________________

20. Who is an assignee entitled to receive performance from? [p 248] ____________________

21. Which rule states that the first assignment in time prevails? [p 260] ____________________

22. What are the three ways that a party's duty of performance may be discharged? [p 256]
____
____

23. Give examples of terms or words that may indicate that the assignor intends to transfer a contract right. [p 247] ____________________

24. Alice is suing Roger for injuries she sustained when his tractor plowed into the back of her small sports car she was driving. She is tired of all of the delays in getting the case to trial and assigns her legal action to her best friend Stephanie. What is the effect of Alice's assignment? [p 247] ____________________

25. What is the effect of an unconditional assignment of a contract right? [p 285] ____________________
____

26. Which rule regarding assignments provides that the first assignee to give notice to the obligor prevails? [p 249] ____________________

27. If Sid assigns his savings passbook to Marla and then assigns the same savings passbook to Claude but delivers the actual passbook to Claude, who is entitled to the savings account and why? [p 249] ____________________
____

Chapter 13
REMEDIES FOR BREACH of TRADITIONAL AND ONLINE CONTRACTS

Chapter Overview

This chapter differentiates between the types of performance in a contract as well as the consequences for the same. Additionally, it clearly explains the various types of legal damages as well as equitable remedies that are available for breach of contract. The torts associated with contracts along with the consequences of punitive damages are also explored. Finally, with technology becoming so much a part of our daily lives, Internet contracts and the breach of the same are also discussed.

Objectives

Upon completion of the exercises in this chapter, you should be able to:

1. Discuss complete performance in relation to discharging contractual duties.
2. Explain inferior performance as well as material breach of contract.
3. Explain and differentiate between compensatory, consequential and nominal damages.
4. Discuss the equitable remedies of injunction, quasi-contract and specific performance.
5. Explain the torts that are associated with contracts.
6. Explain breach as it applies to Internet contracts.

Practical Application

Upon learning the objectives in this chapter, you should be able to determine whether a minor or material breach has occurred in a contract as well as what remedies, legal or equitable may be available for the breach. Further, you will have a better understanding of what is necessary in order to seek the equitable remedies of specific performance, injunction and quasi-contract. Additionally, you will be able to recognize the torts that sometimes accompany contracts and whether punitive damages may be an option. Finally, you will have a better understanding of breach as it applies to Internet contracts.

Helpful Hints

It is important that you learn the terminology associated with this chapter in order to know which types of remedies apply to certain situations. Some mnemonics for the equitable remedies of injunction as well as specific performance have been provided for you to assist you in committing what is required for these equitable remedies to memory. The material will be easier to grasp if you list and learn the legal remedies separately from the equitable remedies.

Study Tips

You should begin your study of remedies recognizing that there are three levels of performance of a contract. Each level of performance as well as what is meant by it is given below.

Level 1 – Complete Performance

Complete performance happens when a party to a contract gives performance exactly as outlined in the parties contract. If the contract is fully formed, it is said to be executed. Also, be aware
that a contracting party's unconditional and absolute offer to perform will also discharge a party's obligations under the contract.

Level 2- Substantial Performance

Substantial performance happens when a party to a contract gives performance that only has a Little bit left to do before it will be considered completely performed. The non-breaching party has several options available to him or her. He or she can convince the breaching party to lift his or her performance to completion of the contract. Or, he or she may deduct whatever it costs to repair the defect from the contract price and give the remaining amount under the contract to the breaching party. Finally, if the breaching party has been paid, the innocent party may sue the breaching party to recover the cost of repair.

Level 3 - Inferior Performance: Material Breach

A material breach happens when a party gives inferior performance of his or her contractual obligations so much so that it destroys or impairs the purpose of the contract. The courts will examine each case individually to determine whether the breach is a minor or material breach. The non-breaching party may rescind the contract and seek restitution of any monies paid under the contract is there has been a material breach. A material breach allows the non-breaching party from further performance. Another option for the non-breaching party is to sue for breach of contract and ask for damages.

What About Anticipatory Repudiation?

Anticipatory repudiation happens when one party lets the other party know in advance that either he or she will not perform or may not perform the contractual duties when they come due. The repudiator may expressly state this or his or her conduct may show it. The non-breaching party's obligations are discharged immediately and he or she may sue for breach of contract immediately without waiting for performance to become due.

Damages

The next section categorizes the legal remedies for you, otherwise known as damages. You should be familiar with the differences between compensatory, consequential, liquidated and nominal damages as well as the requirement for mitigation of the same.

- **Compensatory Damages**
  Purpose- to compensate a non-breaching party for the loss of the bargain.
  These were designed to "make the person whole again."
  The court determines how much will be awarded based upon the type of contract involved.

- **Types of contracts and the compensatory damages for the same:**

Sale of Goods - The measure of compensatory damages for a breach of sales contract is the difference between the contract price and the market price at the time and place of delivery of the goods.

Construction Contracts- The amount of compensatory damages available for breach depends upon the status of the construction project itself. In other words, it depends on the stage of completion that the project is in when the breach happens. The contractor may recover the profits that he or she might have made on the contract if the owner breaches before the construction begins.

Employment Contracts –Recovery based on an employer breaching equals lost wages or salary as compensatory damages. If however the employee breaches, the employer can recover the costs of hiring a new employee plus any salary increase to pay the replacement.

- **Consequential Damages**
  These types of damages are foreseeable damages that happen because of circumstances not related to the contract itself. In order to recover consequential damages, the breaching party must be aware or have reason to know that the breach will cause special damages to the other party.

- **Liquidated Damages**
  Sometimes the parties to a contract agree in advance as to the amount of damages that will be payable in the event of a breach. This is known as liquidated damages. In order for this type of damages to be enforced, it must be shown that the actual damages are difficult or impracticable to determine and the liquidated amount must be reasonable in the circumstances. This is an exclusive remedy regardless of what the actual damages later are assessed as being.

  CAVEAT – A liquidated damages clause is looked upon as a penalty if the actual damages are clearly able to be determined in advance and if the liquidated damages are unconscionable or excessive. When a liquidated damages clause is viewed as a penalty, it is unenforceable.

- **Nominal Damages**
  These damages are awarded based on principle and are usually a very small amount. No real financial loss is suffered when a party brings a suit based upon principle.

Mitigation of Damages

The law places a duty on the non-breaching party to avoid and reduce the resulting damages. This is referred to as mitigating the damages. A party's duty of mitigation will be based on the type of contract involved.

Enforcement of Remedies

Once a judgment has been rendered, an attempt to collect it is made. If the breaching party fails to satisfy the judgment, then the court may issue a Writ of Attachment or Issue a Writ of Garnishment.

- Writ of Attachment – The writ orders the sheriff to seize the breaching party's property that he or she has in his or her possession and to sell the property to satisfy the judgment. Not all property can be sold depending on the applicable state exemptions.

- Writ of Garnishment- Wages, bank account and other property owned by the breaching party that Is being handled by a third party, such as a bank must be paid to the non-breaching party. There are limitations on the amount of wages or salary that can be garnished as per federal and state laws,

Rescission and Restitution as Remedies

- Rescission – This is an action to undo a contract where there has been a material breach of contract due to fraud, duress, undue influence or mistake. The parties must make restitution of the consideration they received under the contract if they are going to rescind it. In other words, they must return the goods, property, money or other consideration that was received from the other property. Notice of the rescission is a requirement.

Equitable Remedies

If the remedy at law is not adequate, then the equitable remedies of specific performance, quasi-contract and injunction and reformation may be available so that an injustice may be prevented.

- Specific Performance - This is a discretionary remedy the courts may award if the subject matter is unique and a service contract is not involved. The following mnemonic is a practical application memory device you may use when analyzing whether specific performance applies.

  Cathy Always Eats Much Candy During Easter

  C - Was there a **contract** for unique goods or land between the parties?
  A - The remedy at law was not **adequate.**
  E - The contract may only be **enforced** by this remedy.
  M - The remedy is **mutual**; both the buyer and seller may ask for it.
  C - All **conditions** have been satisfied by the party asking for the remedy.
  D - A discussion of any **defenses** is also brought to light.
  E - A reminder that this is an **equitable** remedy.

- Reformation - This is an equitable remedy that allows the court to rewrite the parties' contract to reflect their true intentions.

- Quasi Contract - This equitable remedy is an implied-in-law contract often referred to as quasi-meruit. Under this remedy, a party may receive compensation even though there is not an actual enforceable contract due to a failure of the Statute of Frauds or lack of consideration, etc. The reasonable value of materials or service is the recovery that is available in order to prevent unjust enrichment.

- Injunction - An injunction is an equitable remedy that prohibits a person from doing a certain act. The following mnemonic is a practical application memory device that you may use in determining whether an injunction may be sought.

  Ted Always Enjoys Potatoes and Ham at Dinner

  T - Usually a **tort** is involved which must first be proven.
  A - The remedy at law was not **adequate**.
  E - The tortuous conduct may only be **enforced** by this remedy.
  P - There is a **property** right involved.
  H - A **hardship** will be suffered if this remedy is not enforced.
  D - A discussion of **defenses** is shown if they apply.

Torts Associated With Contracts

If a party demonstrates that a contract-related tort has occurred, tort damages will also be available to a party. These include compensation for pain and suffering, emotional damages, possible punitive damages and personal injury. The torts in this area include interference with contractual relations and breach of implied covenant of good faith and fair dealing.

- Intentional Interference with Contractual Relations - This occurs when a third party induces a contracting party to breach the contract with another party. Note that a third party will not be held to have induced a breach if the breach already existed between the original parties.

- Breach of Implied Covenant of Good Faith and Fair Dealing - This is implied in certain types of contracts whereby the parties are held to act in "good faith" and deal fairly in also aspects in obtaining the contract's objective. This tort is sometimes called the tort of bad faith.

Punitive Damages

These are usually not recoverable for breach of contract. Nonetheless, if certain tortuous conduct such as fraud, or intentional conduct is associated with the nonperformance of a contract, punitive damages in addition to actual damages may be awarded to punish the defendant. Other purposes of punitive damages are to prevent similar conduct from happening in the future and to set an example for other individuals.

Refresh Your Memory

The following exercise will enable you to refresh your memory on the rules and principles presented to you in this chapter. Read each question twice and place your answer in the blanks provided. Review the chapter material for any question you miss or are unable to remember.

1. Explain the three levels of performance of a contract? ______________________________
____

2. Explain the equitable remedies available for breach of contract? ____________________
____

3. What duty does a contracting party owe if a contractual duty has not been discharged or excused? ____

4. Give an explanation of an executed contract. ______________________________________
____

5. What type of breach has occurred when there has been substantial performance of one of the parties duties under the contract? ____________________

6. When it has been determined that there has been a material breach of contract, what type of performance had been rendered? ______________________ performance.

7. When there has been a material breach, the non-breaching party may __________________ the contract.

8. __________________________ damages help to compensate a non-breaching party for the loss of the bargain.

9. The compensatory damages for a breach of contract involving the sale of goods is _______
____

10. What damages are available to an employee when an employer has breached his or her employment contract?
____

Critical Thought Exercise

The Cheersville Fire Department (CFD) entered into a written contract on 2-17-02 with American Emergency Truck Co. (AET) for the purchase of a $290,000.00 ladder/pump truck. The contract set forth a delivery date of September 1, 2002 as insisted upon by CFD. According to CFD Chief Sam Miller, their 1932 pumper truck was not going to last beyond that date and time was of the essence. On August 1, 2002, the CFD truck died and was not able to be repaired. The Cheersville Town Council voted to wait until the new truck arrived on September 1, 2002 instead or renting another old truck from Friendsville Fire District. On August 15, 2002, AET notified CFD that the truck would not be ready for delivery until October 1, 2002. The Town Council again decided to wait without renting another truck. Cheersville notified AET that its truck was out of service and the new truck was desperately needed by September 1, 2002. On September 15, 2002, a major fire damaged the Cheersville School. The fire started in the kitchen and could have easily been controlled with normal fire fighting equipment. The damage to the school was estimated to be approximately $2,800,000.

AET denies any liability. The truck was delivered by AET on October 5, 2002. You are on the Cheersville Town Council and have been assigned the task of drafting a memorandum for the council detailing the following:

1. Whether Cheersville has grounds to sue American Emergency Truck.
2. What damages would be recoverable from AET.
3. What defenses AET may assert.

Answer. ____

Practice Quiz

True/False:

1. ___ Monetary damages are not available for breach of contract. [p 270]

2. ___ Equitable remedies are premised on the idea of monetary compensation. [p 275]

3. ___ A material breach of contract does not occur when performance deviates only slightly from complete performance. [p 268]

4. ___ Compensatory damages help defer costs associated with a breach of contract, as they compensate a non-breaching party for the loss of the bargain. [p 270]

5. ___ The standard measure of damages for a breach of sales contract involving goods is the difference between the contract price and the market price. [p 271]

6. ___ If an employee breaches an employment contract, the employer can recover the costs to hire a new employee, but must absorb any increase in salary paid to the replacement. [p 271]

7. ___ A liquidated damages clause may act as a penalty if there were actual damages that could have been assessed in advance. [p 273]

8. ___ Nominal damages may be awarded in amounts up to but not exceeding $125,000. [p 274]

9. ___ To mitigate means to avoid or reduce. [p 271]

10. ___ The court may not issue a Writ of Attachment in order to assist in the collection of a judgment. [p 274]

11. ___ The remedy of rescission is unavailable if there has been fraud, undue influence or mistake involved with regard to the parties' contract. [p 274]

12. ___ A party may not seek the remedy of specific performance for all contracts he or she is having difficulty enforcing. [p 276]

13. ___ Specific performance of personal service contracts is usually granted. [p 276]

14. ___ An equitable doctrine that allows the court to rewrite the parties contract to reflect their true intentions is known as reformation. [p 276]

15. ___ A party may seek damages for a breach of the tort of bad faith. [p 279]

Multiple Choice

16. Suppose Manny Musolf contracts with The Snowy Construction Company to have Snowy build a recreation building for $20 million. The architectural plans indicate that installation of special insulation that is four times that of normal is required for this building, as it will be located in northern Rhode Island. Snowy constructs the building according to specification except that Snowy forgets to put in the insulation. It will cost five million dollars to blow in proper insulation, and will lose them time that they have already promised to give to other jobs. What may Manny sue Snowy for if Snowy does not elevate its level of performance under the contract? [p 267]
    a. Manny may deduct the cost to have the building repaired (insulated) from the contract price and remit the difference to Snowy.
    b. Nothing, as Snowy did the best they could under the winter conditions.
    c. Manny may sue for the cost of standard insulation if Snowy has substantially performed.
    d. None of the above.

17. Where there is anticipatory repudiation in a contract, the non-breaching party's obligation under the contract [p 268]
    a. is partially fulfilled
    b. remains in tact
    c. is discharged immediately
    d. is rescinded

18. Suppose Mogul Bear's Fun Land enters into a written contract to employ a manager for five years at a salary of $4,000 per month. However, before work is to begin, the manager is informed that he or she will not be needed after all. Thereafter, the manager finds another job, but it pays only $2,000 per month. How much will the manager be able to recover from Mogul Bear's Fun Land if a law suit is brought? [p 270]
    a. Nothing, as the manager "assumed the risk" of job loss when he or she agreed to word for Mogul Bear's Fun Land.
    b. liquidated damages
    c. Nominal damages, as it was an at will contract
    d. $120,000.

19. Patsy asked her daughter Ellie to leave her job and move from Wisconsin to come and take care of her in Arizona for two years when Patsy would be moving into an assisted living facility. In exchange for Ellie doing this, Patsy orally told Ellie that she would sign the deed over to the lovely 3,000 square foot home. Ellie quit her well paying job, loaded a moving van and moved in with Patsy into her Arizona home. Ellie had a lot of spare time on her hands, so she painted all of the interior walls of the house and hired a contractor to add on a large family room as well as add a built-in swimming pool. Two years passed very quickly and Patsy has decided to stay in her new and improved home. She refuses to sign the deed to the home over to Ellie. If Ellie sues Patsy, which theory would give her the greatest chance at getting the Arizona home? [p 277]
    a. One based on quasi contract
    b. One based on rescission
    c. One based on injunction
    d. One based on reformation

20. Hillside Resort contracted to buy a piece of ice resurfacing equipment from The Zamboni Company for $80,000, however the equipment never gets delivered. Hillside decides to purchase the equipment from another seller, but must do so at $100,000 due to an increase in the market price. What may Hillside recover? [p 271]
    a. $20,000.
    b. $180,000.
    c. Nothing, as inflation is implied in contracts involving goods.
    d. $65,000.

21. The Random Engineering Corporation has hired Lisa Sharpe as a robotics engineer to design housekeeper robots. Lisa contracted with Random to give her an initial annual income of $132,000 plus benefits. Additionally, if she can design a microchip to place in the robot which will enable it to garden as well, Random will give Lisa a percentage of the profits and a twelve percent salary increase. Lisa works for Random for two months and Random decides to downsize and use engineers who have been employed with them for twenty or more years to design the housekeeper/gardener robots. Lisa is told she will need to find another place to work. If Lisa brings a lawsuit against Random based on breach of her employment contract, what does she need to do in order to mitigate her damages? [p 271]
    a. She will need to gather as much information about Random as possible.
    b. She will need to try to find comparable, substitute employment.
    c. She will need to beg to be given a second chance, as she is the best person for the job.
    d. She will need to ask for specific performance based upon her skills and experience.

22. If the liquidated damages are excessive or unconscionable and the actual damages are clearly able to be determined in advance, the liquidated damages clause will be considered to be [p 273]
    a. an adhesion clause.
    b. enforceable.
    c. a penalty.
    d. compensation for a breach of contract.

23. In order to obtain an injunction, the requesting party must show that he or she [p 276]
    a. will suffer irreparable harm unless the injunction is issued.
    b. deserves the injunction more than the other party.
    c. requires recovery of compensation even though no enforceable contract exists.
    d. needs the contract to be rewritten to reflect the true intentions of the parties.

24. In order to recover for the tort of intentional interference with contract relations, what must be shown? [p 277]
    a. The third party had knowledge of a valid enforceable contract between contracting parties.
    b. A valid, enforceable contract between the contracting parties existed.
    c. The third party induced one of the parties to breach the contract.
    d. All of the above.

Short Answer:

25. Which writ orders the sheriff to seize property in the possession of the breaching party that he or she owns, and to sell the property at auction to satisfy the judgment? [p 274] ______

____

26. When will punitive damages be awarded in a contract situation? [p 277]______________

____

27. What must the parties do in order to rescind a contract? ________________________

____[p 274]

28. When are equitable remedies available? ______________________________________
[p 275]

29. Give examples of what restitution consists of. [p 275] ____________________

____

30. What may the court do if a judgment is entered against a breaching party and the breaching party refuses to pay it? [p 274] ____

____

31. What is a Writ of Garnishment? [p 274] ______________________________

____

32. What is one purpose that an equitable remedy might have? [p 275] ______________

____

____

33. What is an injunction? [p 276] ____
____

34. What is the function of the equitable remedy called specific performance?
____. [p 276]

Chapter 14
FORMATION OF SALES AND LEASE CONTRACTS

Chapter Overview

This chapter focuses on the formation of sales and lease contracts and the requirements for the same. Also, the requirements and exceptions as they pertain to modification, the Statute of Frauds, and parol evidence are explored.

Objectives

Upon completion of the exercises in this chapter, you should be able to:

1. Explain what sales contracts are governed by Article 2 of the UCC.
2. Explain lease contracts as governed by Article 2A of the UCC.
3. Be able to apply the principles of good faith and reasonableness as per the UCC
4. Discuss how sales and lease contracts are formed.
5. Explain the UCC's firm offer rule.
6. Explain the UCC's additional terms rule and how to apply it to the "battle of the forms"
7. Discuss the UCC's written confirmation rule

Practical Application

You should be able to determine what is necessary as well as acceptable to form a valid sales or lease contract. Further, your studies should provide you with the knowledge you need to modify, explain or validate either of these types of contracts should the need arise.

Helpful Hints

It is important to remember that basic contract principles also apply to sales and lease contracts, so, in essence, you are not learning all new material. By reviewing the elements of basic contract formation, and adding to it, you will have a better chance at retaining the information. As you study this chapter, keep in mind the Uniform Commercial Code's leniency in forming sales and lease contracts. As a reminder, when you are analyzing a fact situation or a contract, it is advisable to read and analyze each line separately so that you do not miss any potential issues.

Study Tips

This chapter primarily focuses on Article 2 (Sales) and Article 2A (Leases) of the Uniform Commercial Code. It is easiest to study this chapter if you learn the basic scope of each of these articles. Article 2 involves transactions in goods whereas Article 2A involves consumer and finance leases.

Article 2 (Sales)

- You must learn what a sale is. A sale is the passing of title from a seller to a buyer for a price.

- Next, what are goods? Goods are tangible things that are movable at their identification. Be careful in this area, as there are some things that are not considered to be goods. These include money, intangible items, bonds, patents, stocks and land. Another caveat, things that are severable from the land can be goods.

Services are not covered under Article 2, however, when there is a mixed sale of both goods and services, if the goods dominate the transaction, then Article 2 does in fact apply. Each case involving a mixed sale is examined individually.

Article 2 applies to all sales regardless of a person's status of being or not being a merchant in the transaction. Note though that some sections of Article 2 apply only to merchants as well as expressed the special rules of duty placed upon merchants.

Article 2A (Leases)

- This article applies to personal property leases, which also involves the formation, performance and default of leases.

- What is a lease? A lease is the conveyance of the right to the possession and use of the named goods for a set time period in return for certain consideration.

- What are the parties to a lease? The lessor who is the person who transfers the right of possession and use of the goods under the lease and the lessee who obtains the right to possession and use of goods under a lease.

- What is a finance lease? This involves three parties, the lessor, the lessee, and the vendor (supplier). Here the lessor is not a manufacturer or supplier of goods, but still acquires title to the goods or the right to use and possess in connection with the lease terms.

Formation of Both Sales and Lease Contracts

As with other contracts, both sales and lease contracts require an offer, acceptance and consideration in order to be properly formed.

Offer

At common law, all necessary terms needed to be in place.
Modernly under the UCC, if a term is left open, the courts will apply the following rules:

Open Terms- The court will look at the parties' intent to make a contract and then determine if there is a reasonably certain basis for giving an appropriate remedy. When open terms are allowed to be read into the contract, this is referred to as gap-filling rules.

Open Price term
If a price in a contract is missing, the court will imply a "reasonable price" at the time of delivery.

Open Payment Term
In the absence of an agreement on payment terms, payment is due at the time and place where the buyer is to receive the goods.

Open Delivery Term
If there is no agreed upon place of delivery, then delivery is to take place at the seller's place of business.

Open Time Term
The contract must be performed within a reasonable time if there is no provision in the parties contract for a set specified time of performance.

Open Assortment Term
This occurs when the buyer is given the option of choosing the goods from an assortment of goods.

Acceptance

At common law and under the UCC, a contract is created when the buyer or lesee sends his or her acceptance to the offeror, not upon receipt.

Acceptance may be accomplished in any manner and by any reasonable medium of acceptance. If a buyer makes an offer, then the seller's acceptance is signified by either the seller's prompt promise to ship or his or her prompt shipment of conforming or nonconforming goods.

Acceptance of the goods by the buyer occurs if after the buyer has a reasonable opportunity to accept the goods, either indicates that the goods are conforming, or signifies that he or she will keep the goods regardless of their nonconformity or if he or she fails to reject the goods within a reasonable period of time after delivery of the goods.

Accommodation Shipment is Not an Acceptance- A shipment of nonconforming goods is not considered an acceptance if the seller seasonably notifies the buyer that the shipment is being offered as an accommodation to the buyer. An accommodation shipment is considered a counter offer from the seller to the buyer.

Importance of the Mirror Image Rule- At common law, an offeree's acceptance had to mirror the Image of the offer. If additional terms were included, it was considered a counteroffer. The UCC However has given flexibility to this rule.

If one or both parties are ***nonmerchants***, any additional terms become ***proposed additions*** to the contract. The proposed additions do not terminate the offer nor does it constitute a counteroffer. If the offeree's proposed additions are accepted by the offeror, they become part of the contract.

If both parties are ***merchants,*** the additional terms become part of the contract unless the acceptance is expressly conditional on assent to the terms of the offer or the additional terms materially alter the terms of the original contract or the offeror notifies the offeree that he or she is rejecting the additional terms.

Consideration

Consideration is also required in the formation of sales and lease contracts.
However, unlike common law, the UCC indicates that modification of sales and lease contracts do not require consideration, but, they do require the element of ***good faith.***
Statute of Frauds

Goods costing $500 or more and lease payments of $1,000 or more must be in writing. The agreement must be signed by the party to be charged.

Exceptions to the Statute of Frauds – These sale and lease situations do not have to meet the writing requirement of the Statute of Frauds:

Specially Manufactured Goods
Admissions in Pleadings or Court
Part Acceptance

Important Note: If both parties are merchants and one of the parties to the oral contract sends written confirmation within a reasonable time after entering into the contract and the other merchant does not object to the contract within ten days of his or her receipt of the confirmation, then the Statute of Frauds is satisfied.

Modification Required to be in Writing
If the parties state that the modification must be in writing, then it has to be. However, in general, an oral modification is sufficient if it does not violate the Statute of Frauds.

Parol Evidence

A rule that states that a written contract is the complete and final expression of the party's agreement.

Any prior or contemporaneous oral or written statements to the contract may not be introduced to alter or contradict or add to the written contract.

Exceptions to the parol evidence rule:
When the contract's express terms are unclear, the court may consider the course of performance, course of dealing and usage of trade as outside sources to clarify the terms of the parties' agreement.

Refresh Your Memory

The following exercise will enable you to refresh your memory on the rules and principles presented to you in this chapter. Read each question twice and place your answer in the blanks provided. Review the chapter material for any question you miss or are unable to remember.

1. What is Article 2A of the Uniform Commercial Code mainly concerned with? ____________________________

2. What is a lease? ____________________________

3. How may an offer for a contract for the sale or lease of goods be formed? ____________________________

4. What price will the Uniform Commercial Code affix to a good if none is stated? ____________________________

5. Explain the type of acceptance permissible under the Uniform Commercial Code. ____________________________

6. If one or both parties to a sales contract are both nonmerchants, any additional terms would be considered ______________ ______________ to the contract.

7. According to the Statute of Frauds, what types of sales and lease contracts need to be in writing? ____________________________

8. Part of the ______________ ______________ rule states that "when a sales or lease contract is evidenced by a writing that is intended to be a final expression of the parties' agreement … the terms of the writing may not be contradicted by evidence…"

9. What three situations involving a sales or lease contract will still warrant their enforcement despite the fact that they are not in writing as per the Statute of Frauds? ____________________________

10. What is one of the functions of the Federal Trade Commission Act? ____________________________

Critical Thought Exercise

Apex Mattress Company, for whom you are the vice-president of material acquisition, entered into an oral agreement with Davis Wool Ranch (DWR), a wool supplier, in which DWR agreed to sell Apex 800 bundles of wool, each weighing 350 pounds. Shortly after your conversation with Dan Davis of DWR, you sent Davis an e-mail confirming the terms of the oral contract. Davis did not respond to the e-mail or offer any objection to the terms stated in the e-mail. When the delivery date arrived four months later, you contacted DWR to finalize the delivery terms. DWR stated that there was no agreement and DWR had sold the 800 bundles to Fluffy-Air Mattress because the price of wool had doubled on the open market since the date of the oral agreement. The board of directors of Apex requests that you inform them of your position in regards to bringing suit against DWR and the likelihood that Apex will prevail.

Write a memo to the board setting forth your position and authority for your conclusion.

Answer. ____________________________

Practice Quiz

True/False:

1. ___ A lessee is the individual who transfers the right of use and possession of goods under a lease. [p 289]

2. ___ Goods are tangible things that are mobile at the time of their identification to the contract. [p 287]

3. ___ Stocks, bonds, patents and money are intangible goods. [p 287]

4. ___ Article 2 of the U.C.C. governs such things as equipment, computers and other transactions in goods. [p 287]

5. ___ Under the UCC, an agreement sufficient to constitute a contract for the sale or lease of goods may be found even if the moment of its making is undetermined. [p 287]

6. ___ Under a finance lease, the lessor selects, manufactures or supplies the goods. [p 289]

7. ___ Sale and lease contracts require only an offer and acceptance to be binding. [p 293]

8. ___ The UCC is very strict with open contract terms. [p 291]

9. ___ Under the UCC rules, a court will fill in gaps if terms are missing. [p 291]

10. ___ A seller or buyer who reserves the right to fix a price must do so in bad faith. [p 291]

11. ___ If Jon, a seller and Nathan, a buyer do not agree on payment terms, payment is due at the time and place Nathan receives the goods. [p 291]

12. ___ When goods are to be shipped but the shipper is not named, the buyer is obligated to make the shipping arrangements. [p 291]

13. ___ The firm offer rule states that a merchant who offers to buy, sell, or lease goods and gives a separate signed, written assurance that the offer will be held open cannot revoke the offer for the time state, or if no time is stated, for a reasonable time, not to exceed three months. [p 291]

14. ___ Generally speaking, contracts for specially manufactured goods need to be in writing. [p 294]]

15. ___ If an oral modification brings a contract within the Statute of Frauds, then it must be in writing in order to be enforceable. [p 294]

Multiple Choice:

16. Goods for $500 or more and lease payments of $1,000 or more must [p 293]
    a. be insured.
    b. be in writing.
    c. be inspected.
    d. all of the above.

17. Goods that are severable from real estate include [p 287]
    a. stocks, patents, bonds.
    b. money, coins.
    c. dental services and legal services.
    d. minerals, structures, and growing crops.

18. Which of the following properly defines what a merchant is? [p 288]
    a. A person who deals in the good of the kind involved in the transaction.
    b. A person by his or her occupation holds him or herself out as having knowledge or skill peculiar to the good involved in the transaction.
    c. answer a only.
    d. answers a and b.

19. Article 2 applies to [p 383]
    a. merchants.
    b. nonmerchants.
    c. sales contracts.
    d. all of the above.

20. How may the Statute of Frauds requirement be met if both parties to a lease or sales contract are merchants? [p 294]
    a. One of the parties to the oral agreement sends a written confirmation within a reasonable time after contracting and the other party does not give written notice of an objection within 10 days of receiving the confirmation.
    b. One of the parties may send an oral confirmation.
    c. One of the parties to the oral agreement may send a written confirmation.

d. One of the parties may have his or her agent or broker send an oral confirmation.

21. Suppose Joey's Hardware store contracts to purchase 1,000 wrenches from Ed's Wholesale Hardware Supply Co. The contract is silent as to the assortment of sizes of wrenches. What must Joey's Hardware do when choosing the sizes of wrenches from Ed's stock? [p 291]
    a. make the selection in good faith and within limits set by commercial reasonableness
    b. ask that the contract guarantee more choices for future transactions
    c. request document of title regardless of whether the goods chosen are actually received
    d. pay for what is chosen and ask that the contract thereafter be cancelled

22. Which of the following does not apply to the firm offer rule? [p 292]
    a. The rule applies to merchants.
    b. A merchant must give a written and signed assurance on a separate form that the offer will be held open.
    c. A merchant cannot revoke the offer for the time stated.
    d. The maximum amount of time permitted under this rule is six months.

23. Both the common law and the UCC state that a contract is created when [p 292]
    a. the lessor sends an acceptance to the lessee.
    b. the lessee receives the acceptance from the lessor.
    c. the offeree sends an acceptance to the offeror.
    d. the offeror sends an acceptance to the lessee or buyer.

24. Julie, a buyer offers to purchase 400 pairs of purple gloves from Debbie, a seller. The seller's purple gloves are temporarily out of stock. Debbie sends Julie 400 pairs of red gloves and notifies her that the gloves are being sent as an accommodation. What may Julie do under the circumstances?
    a. not respond to Debbie's substitution of goods.
    b. accept or reject Debbie's counteroffer
    c. She has no choice but to accept the different colored gloves, as the product type remained the same.
    d. none of the above

25. Norman, a veterinarian contracts to purchase dog treats for his patients' owners to purchase from the Eat Right Dog Food Company. Eat Right delivers byproduct dog treats to Norman's office. Norman rejects the dog treats and demands delivery of all natural treats that are specifically formulated for natural digestion. If Norman and Eat Right had prior dealings, what would be the parties primary source of interpretation of the parties agreement? [p 295]
    a. usage of trade
    b. course of performance
    c. the express terms of the parties contract
    d. the usage of the term dog treats in their prior dealings

Short Answer:

26. What does the lessee acquire under a lease? [p 289] ______________________________
____

27. Explain what a finance lease is. [p 289] ______________________________

28. What is meant by gap filling rules? [p 291] ____
____

29. The maximum amount of time permitted under the firm offer rule is ____ ______. [p 291]

30. Modification of a sales or lease contract must be made in ________ ________. [p 293]

31. What is a sale that involves both the provision of a good and a service called? [p 287] ____
____

32. The _____________ _____________ ________ is a comprehensive statutory scheme that includes laws that cover most aspects of contract transactions. [p 286]

33. Define the term goods as it applies to contracts. [p 287]

34. State the mirror image rule. [p 295]

35. What type of contract is offered to a buyer as a replacement for the original replacement when the original shipment cannot be filled? [p 293]

Chapter 15

PERFORMANCE OF SALES AND LEASE CONTRACTS

Chapter Overview

This chapter provides a clear understanding of sales and destination contracts as well as risk of loss and the passage of title to goods. Additionally, it provides a good understanding of sales on approval and how it differs between a sale or return. Further emphasis is placed on insurable interest in goods, good faith purchasers for value and the rules that were created to prevent fraud in bulk transfers of goods.

Objectives

Upon completion of the exercises in this chapter, you should be able to:

1. Explain the difference between a shipment and destination contract and when title passes.
2. Explain the different shipment and delivery terms.
3. Identify who bears the risk of loss when goods are damaged or lost in shipment.
4. Differentiate between a sale on approval and a sale or return.
5. Determine who bears the risk of loss when goods are stolen and resold.
6. Explain the meaning of a good faith purchaser for value.

Practical Application

You should be able to determine what type of contract has been formed as you analyze the shipping terms. Additionally you should be able to determine who bears the risk of loss in situations involving damaged, lost or stolen and resold goods. You will have gained a better familiarity with the laws involving consignments, as well as laws that will assist you in protecting against fraud with bulk transfers of goods.

Helpful Hints

As you peruse the material in this chapter, it is helpful to keep in mind who is receiving the most benefit with regard to the type of contract the parties are entering into. If you remember that the seller begins with the letter "s" and usually will want a shipment (also begins with the letter "s") contract as the carrier that the goods are placed on will then bare the risk of loss. Further, that a buyer will want the contract to be a destination contract as the seller will bare the risk of loss up until the time that the buyer receives the goods.

The remaining rules in this chapter are fairly easy to learn and have been categorized in an order that will make sense as you apply each to any given fact situation. One of the easiest ways to analyze facts in this area is to ask the following questions in the following order.

1) Who are the parties?
2) Have the goods been identified to the contract?
3) Do the parties have a shipment or a destination contract?
4) Who bears the risk of loss in light of the type of contract that exists?
5) What if anything has happened to the goods?
6) Are there any third parties involved?
7) If so, what is their capacity or role in the facts?
8) Are there any special rules of law that apply?

Study Tips

Identification

This can occur at any time and in any manner.
If no time is specified, then the UCC will state when it occurs.
Already existing goods are identified at the contract's inception.
Goods that are part of a bulk shipment are identified when specific merchandise is separated or tagged.

Shipment contract

Creation is accomplished in one of two ways:
1) by using the term shipment contract or
2) using delivery terms such as F.O.B., F.A.S., C.I.F. or C.& F

This requires the seller to ship and deliver goods to the buyer via a common carrier.
Proper shipping arrangements are required.
Title passes to the buyer at the time and place of shipment.
Risk of loss passes to the buyer when conforming goods are delivered to the carrier.

Destination contract

Creation is accomplished in one of two ways:
1) by using the term destination contract or
2) using delivery terms such as: F.O.B. *place of destination,* ex-ship, or no-arrival, no-sale contract

This requires the seller to deliver the goods to buyers place of business or another specified destination.
The seller is also required to replace any goods lost in transit.
Title passes when the seller tenders delivery of the goods at the specified destination.
Risk of loss does not pass until the goods are tendered at the specified destination.

Special Situation Involving Goods That Are Not Moved

Where goods are not required to be moved by the seller, passage of title is dependent upon whether or not document of title is required to be given to the buyer.

If the Seller is a Merchant –Risk of loss does not pass until the goods are received.
If the Seller is a Nonmerchant – Risk of loss occurs when there is a *tender of delivery* of the goods.

Sale on Approval

A sale does not occur unless the buyer accepts the goods.
The situation presents itself when a merchant allows a buyer to take the goods home for a specified period of time to determine if it meets the customer's needs.

Acceptance is shown by:
1) expressly accepting the goods
2) failing to notify the seller of buyer's rejection
3) use of the goods inconsistently with the purpose of the trial

Risk of loss and title stay with the seller and do not pass until the buyer accepts the goods.
Goods are not subject to buyer's creditor's claims until buyer accepts them.

Sale or Return

The seller delivers the goods to the buyer letting the buyer know that he or she may return them if they are not used or resold within a stated period of time.

If the buyer doesn't return them within a reasonable time, the goods are considered sold.

Risk of loss and title pass when the buyer takes possession of the goods.
Buyer's creditors may make claims against the buyer while the goods are in the buyer's possession.

Risk of Loss Involving Breach of Contract Situations

Seller in Breach

Breach occurs when the seller tenders nonconforming goods to the buyer.
If the buyer has the right to reject the goods, the *risk of loss* stays with the seller until the nonconformity or defect is cured or the buyer accepts the non-conforming goods.

Buyer in Breach

Breach occurs where the buyer refuses to take delivery of conforming goods. Also, if the buyer repudiates the contract or otherwise breaches the contract.
The *risk of loss* rests on the buyer for a commercially reasonable time.
Buyer is liable for any loss in excess of insurance covered by the seller.

Risk of Loss in Lease Contracts

The parties may agree who will bear the risk of loss if the goods are lost or destroyed.

If there is no provision, the UCC states that in an ordinary lease, the *risk of loss* stays with the lessor. If it is a finance lease, then the *risk of loss* passes to the lessee. [UCC 2A-219]

If tender of delivery of goods fails to conform to the lease contract, the *risk of loss* stays with the lessor or supplier until acceptance or cure. [UCC 2A-220(1)(a)].

Sales by Nonowners

This category involves individuals who sell goods that they do not have good title to.

Void Title and Lease: Stolen Goods

Where the buyer purchases goods from a thief, title to the goods does not pass and the lessee does not require any leasehold interest in the goods.

The real owner of the goods may reclaim the goods from the buyer or lessee. Title is void.

Voidable Title: Sales or Lease of Goods to Good Faith Purchasers for Value

A seller has voidable title to goods if the goods were obtained by fraud, dishonored check, or impersonation of another person.

An individual with voidable title may transfer good title to goods to a good faith purchaser for value or a good faith subsequent lessee.

Note, a good faith purchaser for value is one who pays consideration or rent for the goods to one he or she honestly believes has good title to those goods. The real owner cannot reclaim the goods from this type of purchaser.

Entrustment Rule

If an owner entrusts the possession of his or her goods to a merchant who deals in the particular type of goods, the merchant may transfer all rights to *a buyer in the ordinary course of business.* The real owner cannot reclaim the goods from this type of buyer.

Article 6 of Bulk Sales

The rules under Article 6 of the UCC established rules that were made to prevent fraud when there is a bulk transfer of goods. This often happens when assets to a business are sold. The owner transfers a major part of the business's merchandise, inventory, equipment or material not in the ordinary course of business.

Requirements for a Bulk Transfer:

1) Seller is to give buyer a list of all of the business's creditors.
2) The buyer is to notify all of the listed creditors at least 10 days prior to taking possession of or paying for the goods. The buyer is not responsible or liable for creditors that are not listed.

If the requirements are met, then the buyer receives title to the goods free of all of seller's creditor's claims. If the requirements are not met, then the buyer takes possession subject to the seller's creditor's claims for six months after the date of possession.

Refresh Your Memory

The following exercise will enable you to refresh your memory on the rules and principles presented to you in this chapter. Read each question twice and place your answer in the blanks provided. Review the chapter material for any question you miss or are unable to remember.

1. Goods that are part of a larger mass of goods are identified when ______________________________
____.

2. Future goods are those that are not ______________________________.

3. Excluding crops and unborn children, future goods are identified when the goods are ______________, ______________, or otherwise designated by the seller or lessor as the goods referred to in the parties contract.

4. A ______________ contract requires the seller to ship goods to the buyer via a common carrier.

5. A ______________ contract requires the seller to deliver the goods either to the buyer's place of business or to another destination set forth in the sales contract.

6. A shipment contract requires the seller to ship goods ______________ to the contract via a ______________.

7. A destination contract requires the seller to ______________ conforming goods to a specific destination.

8. What types of terms signify a destination contract? ______________________________
____

9. Who bears the risk of loss if the goods are stolen or destroyed after the contract date and before the buyer picks up the goods from the seller who is a merchant? ______________________________
____

10. When do nonmerchant sellers pass the risk of loss to the buyer? ______________________________
____

Critical Thought Exercise

Bristol Physical Therapy (BPT) contracted with Summit Pools, Inc. for the purchase of a "fully installed portable therapy whirlpool" for the sum of $14,000. The price included all labor and parts but the order form was not itemized. The freight carrier hired by the manufacturer delivered the pool to the parking lot just outside the building occupied by BPT. A receptionist for BPT signed the delivery invoice and immediately called Summit Pools. When the installation crew for Summit Pools arrived five days later to install the whirlpool, it was gone.

In this situation, had the risk of loss of the whirlpool passed from Summit Pools to BPT?

Answer: ______________________________
____
____
____
____
____
____
____
____

____

____

____

Practice Quiz

True/False:

1. ___ The Uniform Commercial Code does not have any impact on the time of when the identification of goods occurs. [p 302]

2. ___ The buyer or lessee retains the risk of loss of the goods until the goods are identified to the contract. [p 303]

3. ___ Goods such as unborn young animals and crops to be harvested can be identified to a contract. [p 303]

4. ___ Once the goods exist and are identified, the seller may not pass title to the buyer. [p 303]

5. ___ The time and place of passage of title will be different regardless if a document of title is required. [p 303]

6. ___ The UCC places the risk of loss to goods on the party who has title to the goods. [p 303]

7. ___ The UCC is reluctant to allow the parties to a sales contract too much leniency in determining who will bear the risk of loss if the goods subject to the contract are lost or destroyed. [p 304]

8. ___ Sales contracts are recognized as being destination contracts rather than shipment contracts. [p 305]

9. ___ The delivery terms to a contract do not dictate the risk of loss of goods while they are being transported. [p 305]

10. ___ Marla's Magnificent Creations, a large Oklahoma clothing manufacturer places the term, F.O.B. Atlanta when shipping an order of clothes to Tamara's Boutique in Atlanta, Georgia. Marla's will not bear the expense and risk of loss until Tamara's Boutique has the goods tendered upon it. [p 305]

11. ___ In a consignment situation, the consignee delivers goods to a consignor to sell. [p 307]

12. ___ A buyer does not breach a sales contract if he or she refuses to take delivery of conforming goods. [p 308]

13. ___ Betty purchases goods from Slick, a thief who has stolen them. Betty does not acquire title to these goods. However, Slick has a leasehold interest in the goods. [p 310]

14. ___ A good faith purchaser or lessee for value is someone who pays sufficient consideration or rent for goods to the person he or she honestly believes has good title to those goods. [p 310]

15. ___ Article 6 of the UCC provides for efficient ways in transferring large lots of goods. [p 312]

Multiple Choice

16. Future goods that are in existence are identified when [p 303]
    a. they are conceived or have yet to be harvested.
    b. they are shipped, marked or otherwise designated by the seller or lessor.
    c. they are part of a larger mass of goods.
    d. it is mandated that they be identified.

17. A buyer orders 5,000 toy racecars that light up when pushed along a flat surface. The contract between the parties was a shipment contract. Further, the cars that were shipped were plain racecars that did not have the light up feature. The toy cars are smashed flat while in transit. Who will bear the risk of loss in this situation? [p 303]
    a. The buyer will as it is a shipment contract passing the risk of loss to the buyer.
    b. The buyer will as he or she did not purchase insurance to cover potential loss.
    c. The seller will as he or she did not ship conforming goods.
    d. Both the buyer and seller are responsible due to the nature of their transaction.

18. Jacob wants to purchase insurance to protect against financial loss in case the goods that he sells are damaged, destroyed, lost or stolen. He is told that he must have an insurable interest in the goods. What does this mean? [p 309]
    a. He must have a valid driver's license with no convictions against him.
    b. He must retain title or have a security interest in the goods.
    c. He must sell the goods to a good faith purchaser for value.
    d. He must not have an insurable interest at the same time as the buyer.

19. If Joe steals an entire shipment of computers that are owned by Computer City and resells them to Computer Land who does not know that they are stolen, Computer City may reclaim the goods from Computer Land because [p 310]
    a. it found out where the goods were located.
    b. Computer Land was a good faith purchaser for value.
    c. as a seller with an insurable interest in the computers, Computer City is protected.
    d. Joe had no title in the goods and title was not transferred to Computer Land.

20. A person to whom a lease interest can be transferred from a person with voidable title is [p 310]
    a. a good faith purchaser for value.
    b. a lessee.
    c. an insured interested party.
    d. a good faith subsequent lessee.

21. A buyer orders 500 musical teapots from a seller. The contract is a shipment contract. The seller ships nonconforming teapots that will not play music when the water becomes heated. The goods are destroyed in transit. Who bears the risk of loss? [p 308]
    a. the seller
    b. the buyer
    c. both share the risk of loss equally
    d. the teapot maker

22. In a sale or return contract, when does the risk of loss and title to the goods pass to the buyer? [p 307]
    a. The risk of loss never passes
    b. The risk of loss passes when the seller takes possession.
    c. The risk of loss passes when the buyer takes possession of the goods.
    d. None of the above

23. When do non-merchant sellers pass the risk of loss to buyers? [p 306]
    a. upon acceptance by the buyer.
    b. upon tender of delivery of goods
    c. upon presentation of the document of title
    d. all of the above

24. Which of the following does not indicate the acceptance of goods? [p 307]
    a. A buyer expressly states acceptance of goods.
    b. A buyer fails to notify the seller of rejection of the goods within the agreed-upon trial period.
    c. A buyer inconsistently uses the goods with the purpose of the trial.
    d. A buyer rejects the goods.

25. When does title pass if the goods named in the sales contract are located at a warehouse? [p 303]
    a. Title passes at the inception of the sales contract.
    b. Title passes after the buyer's check has cleared the seller's account.
    c. Title may not pass until the goods are removed from the warehouse.
    d. Title passes when the seller delivers a warehouse receipt representing the goods to the buyer.

Short Answer:

26. In a shipment contract, the _________ bears the risk of loss during transportation. [p 303]

27. In a destination contract, the risk of loss does not pass until the goods are tendered to the buyer at a ___________________ ___________________. [p 303]

28. The shipping term C.I.F. stands for ____________, _____________, and ___________, which are costs that the seller is responsible for. [p 305]

29. The shipping term F.A.S. requires the seller to deliver and tender the goods ___________________ ____. [p 305]

30. When does a sale on approval occur? [p 307] ____ ____

31. A seller breaches a sales contract if he or she tenders __________________ goods. [p 308]

32. In the case of an ordinary lease, the risk of loss is kept by the _______________. [p 309]

33. If the goods are so nonconforming that the buyer has the right to reject them, the risk of loss remains on the seller until the defect or nonconformity is cured, or the buyer __________________ ____. [p 309]

34. A holder of goods who is not a seller or a buyer is a _______________________________. [p 306]

35. In a sale on approval, the risk of loss remains with the ______________________________. [p 307]

Chapter 16
REMEDIES FOR BREACH OF SALES AND LEASE CONTRACTS

Chapter Overview

The Uniform Commercial Code provides several remedies to an injured party based on a breach of a sales or lease contract. This chapter explores the prelitigation as well as litigation remedies available to an injured party. Additionally, the performance of obligations and options of the remedies that are available for breach of sales and lease contracts are also examined.

Objectives

Upon completion of the exercises in this chapter, you should be able to:

1. Describe the seller's and lessor's obligations under a contract.
2. Discuss the "perfect tender rule."
3. Describe the buyer's and lessee's obligations under a contract.
4. Discuss what remedies are available to a seller and lessor if a buyer or lessee breaches the contract.
5. Discuss what remedies are available to a buyer or lessee if a seller or lessor breaches the contract.
6. Discuss agreements and additional terms that could affect the remedies available to a buyer or seller under a contract.

Practical Application

This chapter should enable you to know what types of obligations are expected of you as a buyer or a seller. Additionally it will solidify the remedies that are available to you in the event of a breach of a sales or lease contract if you are a buyer and lessee or a seller and lessor.

Helpful Hints

As with many of the chapters involving the area of contracts, it is helpful to organize your studying around the parties as well as the concepts that pertain to those parties. In this chapter, you are studying the buyer and seller's obligations as well as the remedies available in the event of a breach by the buyer or seller. As such, the study tips section has been created to enable you to learn what each parties obligations are as well as what remedies are available to each of them in the event of a breach.

Study Tips

Seller and Lessor's Obligations

Basic obligation – The seller must tender delivery in accordance with his or her contract terms with the buyer.

Tender of Delivery – There are a few things to remember about this topic:

1) Tender of delivery refers to conforming goods.
2) Seller must give the buyer reasonable notice of the delivery and delivery must be at a reasonable hour and goods must be kept for a reasonable time.
3) Goods must be delivered in one single delivery unless the parties agree to another arrangement.

Place of Delivery –The contract may state where delivery is to take place.

1) The contract may state that the buyer will pick up the goods.
2) If nothing is stated in the contract, the UCC will dictate this term.
3) If no carrier is involved, then delivery is at the seller's or lessor's business.
4) If the parties know the goods are located in another location, then that is the place of delivery.
5) If a carrier is involved, it will depend on if the contract is a shipment or a destination contract.
   a. If it is a *shipment* contract, the seller must deliver the goods to the carrier, obtain proper contract documentation and give the buyer notice.
   b. If it is a *destination* contract, the seller is required to deliver the Goods to the buyer's place of business or wherever is designated in the parties' contract. Delivery must be at a reasonable time and in a reasonable manner accompanied with proper notice and documents of title.

Perfect Tender Rule – The seller is under a duty to deliver conforming goods to the buyer.

1) If tender is not perfect, the buyer may:
   a. reject the whole shipment
   b. accept the whole shipment
   c. reject part and accept part of the shipment
2) The parties may also agree to limit the application of the perfect tender rule by doing so in their written contract.
3) If a carrier is involved, the UCC mandates a commercially Reasonable substitute be used if the agreed upon manner of delivery fails or becomes unavailable.

4) If nonconforming goods are delivered, the UCC gives the Seller the chance to cure the defective delivery if the time For performance has not expired or the lessor gives the

Buyer notice that he or she will make a conforming delivery within the time frame stated in the parties' contract.

Installment contract- One that requires or authorizes the good s to be accepted or delivered in separate lots.

1) The UCC alters the perfect tender rule by allowing the buyer to reject the entire shipment if the noncomformity substantially impairs the entire contract.
2) The court will view installment contracts on a case-by-case basis.

Destruction of Goods – If the destruction of goods is not the fault of either party and the goods have been identified to the contract, the contract will be void. but, if the goods are partially destroyed, the buyer may then inspect and partially accept the goods or treat it as void. If the buyer opts to accept, compensation will be adjusted accordingly.

Good Faith and Reasonableness – These two principles rule the performance of lease and sales contracts. These principles apply to both the buyer and the seller.

Seller's and Lessor's Remedies

The seller and lessors have several remedies available if the buyer or lessee breaches the contract. These remedies are as follows:

Right to Withhold Delivery – Delivery of the goods may be withheld if the seller is in possession of the goods when the buyer or lessee is in breach. If there has been a partial delivery of the goods when the breach occurs, then the seller or lessor may withhold delivery of the remaining part of the goods. A buyer or lessee's insolvency will also justify a seller or lessor's withholding of delivery of the goods under the contract.

Right To Stop Delivery of Goods in Transit –Goods are in transit when they are in the carrier's bailee's possession. If a buyer is discovered to be insolvent while the goods are in transit, the seller may stop the goods while in transit.
If the buyer or lessee repudiates the contract, delivery can be withheld only if it is a carload, a planeload or a truckload. Notice to the carrier or bailee is required.

The seller must hold the goods for the buyer after the delivery has been stopped. If the seller resells the goods, the amount received must be credited against the judgment procured against the buyer.

Right to Recover Damages for Breach of Contract – A cause of action to recover damages caused by the breach of contract may be brought where the buyer or lessee repudiates a sales or lease contract or wrongfully rejects tendered goods.

The measure of damages is the difference between the contract price and the market price at the time and place where the goods were delivered plus incidental damages. If this does not place the seller in a position as though the contract was performed, the seller may recover lost profits that would have resulted from full performance plus an allowance for reasonable overhead and incidental damages.

<u>Right to Cancel the Contract</u> – The seller or lessor may cancel the contract if the buyer or lessee breaches the contract by revoking acceptance of the goods, rejects the contract or fails to pay for the goods or repudiates all or any part of the contract. The cancellation may apply to the entire contract or to only the affected goods.

Effect of the cancellation- The seller or lesser who notifies the buyer or lessee of the cancellation is discharged from any further obligations under the contract, and he or she may also seek damages against the buyer or lessee for the breach.

<u>Right to Reclaim Goods</u> – Reclamation refers to a seller or lessor's right to demand the return of goods from the buyer or lessee under certain situations.

Where the buyer is insolvent – Seller has 10 days to demand the return of the goods.

Where the buyer has misrepresented his or her solvency in writing three months before delivery or presents a check that is later dishonored, reclamation may occur at any time.

Requirements of reclamation include:

Written notice to the buyer or lessee
Refraining from self-help if the buyer refuses.
Use of legal proceedings must be instituted.

<u>Right to Dispose of Goods</u> – If the buyer or lessee breaches or repudiates before the seller or lessor disposes of the goods, then the seller may release or resell goods and recover damages from the buyer or lessee.

Disposition of the goods must be in good faith and in a commercially reasonable manner. Disposition may be as a unit or in parcels and publicly or privately. Notice must also be given.

Damages incurred as a result of disposition are measured by the disposition price and the contract price. Incidental damages may also be recovered.

Unfinished Goods- If a sales or lease contract is breached or repudiated before the goods are finished the seller can:

1) stop manufacturing of the goods and resell them for scrap or salvage value or
2) complete the goods and resell, release or otherwise dispose of them.
3) recover damages from the buyer or lessee.

<u>Right to Recover the Purchase Price or Rent</u> – The UCC allows a seller to sue the buyer for the purchase price or rent as provided in the parties sale or lease contract. This remedy is available when:

1) The buyer or lessee accepts the goods but does not pay for them when the rent is due.
2) The buyer or lessee breaches the contract after the goods have been identified to the contract and the seller or lessor cannot dispose of or sell the goods.
3) The goods are damaged or lost after the risk of loss passes to the buyer or lessee.

Buyer and Lesee's Obligations

Basic obligation—If properr tender of delivery is made to the buyer (lessee), the buyer is then obligated to accept and pay for the goods as per the parties' contract or as mandated by the UCC in the event that there is no contract.

Right of Inspection – Buyer has the right to inspect goods that are tendered, delivered or identified to the contract.

1) If the goods are shipped, inspection will be at the time the goods arrive. If the goods are nonconforming, buyer may reject the goods and not pay for them.
2) Parties may agree as to time, place and manner of inspection. If there Is no agreement, then it must be at a reasonable time, place and manner. Reasonableness is determined by common usage of trade, prior course dealings, etc. If the goods conform to the contract, buyer pays for the inspection. If the goods are nonconforming, the seller pays for the inspection.
3) C.O.D. deliveries are not subject to buyer inspection until the buyer pays for the goods.

Payment of the Goods – Goods that are accepted must be paid for when the goods are delivered even if the delivery place is the same as the place where the goods are shipped.

1) Goods paid for on credit have a credit period that begins to run from the time that the goods are shipped.
2) Goods may be paid for using any acceptable method of payment unless The agreed upon terms involve cash only. If cash is all that a seller will accept from the buyer, then the buyer must be given extra time to procure the cash.
3) Payment by check is conditioned on the check being honored

Assurance of Performance – If one party has reasonable grounds to believe that the other party either will not or cannot perform his or her contractual obligations, The other party may demand assurance for performance in writing. Also, the aggrieved party may suspend his or her own performance if it is commercially practicable to do so until the assurance is forthcoming from the potential wrongdoer.

Anticipatory Repudiation – The repudiation of a lease or sales contract by one of the parties before the date set for performance.

1) Simple wavering of performance does not equate to anticipatory Repudiation.
2) The aggrieved party may:
   a. await performance for a commercially reasonable time or
   b. treat the contract as breached at the time of the anticipatory repudiation
   c. both remedies allow the aggrieved party to suspend performance.
3) An anticipatory repudiation may be retracted before the aggrieved parties performance is due if the aggrieved party has not:
   a. cancelled the contract or
   b. materially changed his or her position or
   c. otherwise stated that the repudiation is viewed as final.

   Repudiation may be made by any method as long as the intent to perform the contract is clearly expressed.

Buyer and Lessee's Remedies

The buyer or lessee also has many remedies available to him or her upon the breach of a sales or lease contract by the seller or lessor. These remedies are as follows:

Right to Reject Nonconforming Goods or Improperly Tendered Goods – If tender of delivery fails, the buyer may

1) reject the whole,
2) accept the whole or
3) accept any commercial unit and reject the rest.

Note, a buyer who rejects nonconforming goods must identify the defects that are able to be determined by a reasonable inspection. Rejection must be within a reasonable time after delivery and in a reasonable manner. The buyer must also hold the goods for a reasonable period of time.

Right to Recover Goods from an Insolvent Seller or Lessor – If the buyer makes a partial payment to the seller and the seller or lessor becomes insolvent within tend days of the first payment, the buyer or lessee may recover the goods from the seller or lessor. This is called capture.

Right to Obtain Specific Performance – When the remedy at law is inadequate and the goods are unique, the buyer or lessee may ask for specific performance of the sales or lease contract.

Right to Cover – The buyer or lessee may cover if the seller or lessor fails to make delivery of goods or repudiates the contract or the buyer or lessee rightfully rejects the goods or justifiably revokes their acceptance. Renting or purchasing substitute goods accomplish covering.

Right to Replevy Goods – A buyer or lessee may recover scarce goods wrongfully withheld by a seller or lessor by demonstrating that he or she was unable to cover or the attempts to cover will not come to fruition. This remedy is only available as to goods identified to the lease or sales contract.

Right to Cancel the Contract –Failure to deliver conforming goods , repudiation of the contract by the seller, rightful rejection of the goods, or justifiable revocation of goods that were accepted all may enable the buyer to cancel with respect to the affected goods or the whole contract if the breach is material in nature.

Right to Recover Damages for No delivery or Repudiation – The buyer or lessee may recover damages that equate to the difference between the contract price and the market price, along with incidental and consequential damages, less expenses saved if a seller or lessor fails to deliver the goods or repudiates the sales or lease contract.

Right to Recover Damages for Accepted Nonconforming Goods – A buyer may seek to recover damages from any loss as a result of the nonconforming goods accepted from the seller. Incidental damages as well as consequential damages may also be recovered. The buyer must give notice of the nonconformity to the seller within a reasonable time of when the breach should have been discovered.

Statute of Limitations- Under the UCC, an action for breach of any written or oral sales or lease contract must be within four years. The parties can agree to a one-year statute of limitations.

Agreements Affecting Remedies

Preestablished damages - These are called liquidated damages, which act as a substitute for actual damages.

Consequential damages for the breach of sales or lease contract may be excluded or limited unless it would be unconscionable to do so.

Refresh Your Memory

The following exercise will enable you to refresh your memory on the rules and principles presented to you in this chapter. Read each question twice and place your answer in the blanks provided. Review the chapter material for any question you miss or are unable to remember.

1. What are the remedies designed to do for the aggrieved party? ______________________
____

2. The failure of a party to perform an obligation in a sales or least contract is known as ______________________.

3. What is the seller's or lessor's basic obligation under a sales or lease contract? __________
____

4. If the parties have no agreement respecting the time, place and manner of delivery, tender must be made at a __________________ hour and the goods must __________________ ______________________.

5. A pre-established substitute for actual damages is ________________ damages.

6. In noncarrier cases, the place of delivery is the ________________________________.

7 A sales contract that requires the seller to deliver the goods to the buyer's place of business or other specified location is a ______________________ contract.

8. The UCC gives a seller or lessor who delivers nonconforming goods a chance to ________ the nonconformity.

9. If John, a party to a contract has reasonable grounds to believe that Sophie, the other party will not perform her contractual obligations, an _____________ _______________ of due performance may be demanded in writing.

10. A buyer or lessee may ______________ goods from a seller or lessor who is wrongfully withholding them.

Critical Thought Exercise

Sanco Corporation agreed to sell two seven-ton diesel forklifts to Agro-Star, Inc., for $250,000, with an option to purchase four more at $500,000. The forklifts were to be installed in a produce cooling warehouse according to specific design and performance standards. Sanco did not deliver and Agro-Star covered by purchasing different forklifts from Power Arm Lifts for $200,000, plus an additional $300,000 for testing and development by Power Arm Lifts. Agro-Star also bought the four additional lifts that they needed from Power Arm Lifts for $350,000. At trial, Agro-Star is awarded $250,000, the difference between Sanco's price for the first two forklifts and the cost of the first two Power Arm forklifts.

As an officer in Sanco Corporation, you must decide whether to pay the judgment or pay an additional $20,000 in attorney's fees and appeal the judgment. Will you authorize the appeal? Why? Is it fair for Sanco to receive the benefit of a bargain struck by Agro-Star when they covered?

Answer. ____

Practice Quiz

True/False:

1. ___ If Eb's Furniture Store calls Charlene Jones at 2:00a.m. to let her know the delivery truck will be at her home in 30 minutes, Charlene does not have to allow Eb to tender delivery of the goods. [p 318]

2. ___ If goods are delivered in lots, payment is calculated by the entire delivery. [p 318]

3. ___ If a seller or lessor does not have a place of business, then the place of delivery is the warehouse where the goods are kept. [p 318]

4. ___ Under a shipment contract, one thing that the seller must do is put the goods in the buyer's possession and contract for the safe and proper transportation of the goods. [p 319]

5. ___ In a destination contract, delivery of the goods is to be tendered at the seller's place of business or other location designated in the sales contract. [p 319]

6. ___ A contract is void if identified goods to a lease or sales contract are totally destroyed through no fault of either party before the risk of loss passes to the buyer or lessee. [p 321]

7. ___ The parties' prior course of dealing, common usage of trade and the overall circumstances are not considered by the court looks at in determining reasonableness with respect to the buyer's right to inspection. [p 322]

8. ___ Buyers who agree to C.O.D. deliveries are not entitled to inspect the goods before paying for them. [p 322]

9. ___ Payment is usually due from a buyer where and when the goods are delivered even if the place of delivery is the same place of shipment. [p 322]

10. ___ The repudiation of a sales or lease contract by one of the parties after the date set for performance is known as anticipatory repudiation. [p 331]

11. ___ A buyer contracts to purchase 2,500 tires from a tire manufacturer with delivery set for May 1 and partial payment due March 1. In February the buyer learns that automobile sales have decreased by 38% and assembly line workers have been laid off in the small plant that he would need the tires in. The tire manufacturer contacts the buyer and wants a written demand for adequate assurance on February 18. The buyer fails to give adequate assurance of performance. The tire manufacturer has no recourse and must need not wait until March 1 when partial payment is due before it can do anything. [p 332]

12. ___ Delivery of goods may be withheld if the seller or lesser is in possession of them when the buyer or lessee breaches the contract. [p 324]

Multiple Choice

13. The perfect tender rule is altered when [p 319]
    a. the parties to the sales or lease contract agree to limit the effect of the rule.
    b. the buyer or lessee rejects the whole shipment of goods.
    c. the buyer or lessee rejects part of the shipment of goods.
    d. the buyer or lessee accepts the entire shipment of goods.

14. Rachel contracted for a crystal chandelier from Phoebe, a crystal dealer. Phoebe agrees to deliver the chandelier to Rachel's home. The truck delivering the chandelier breaks down and the chandelier is stolen while the delivery driver has walked away trying to find help. What effect does the theft of the chandelier have on the parties' agreement? [p 321]
    a. The risk of loss had already passed to Rachel and she is responsible for payment.
    b. The risk of loss remains with Rachel, but, she can get her insurance to cover the damage.
    c. The risk of loss is shared between both parties as the situation involved a thief which requires both parties to share the cost of the damages.
    d. The risk of loss had not yet passed to Rachel and as such, the contract is voided and she does not have to pay for the chandelier.

15. If Jaclyn's Fine Vases begins manufacture of 50 vases all of which have a sculpted form of sea life on them and the buyer, a tourist shop on the ocean goes out of business before the goods are finished, Jaclyn, the seller may choose to [p 325]
    a. open up the buyer's business and try to sell the vases herself.
    b. stop manufacturing the goods and resell them for scrap or salvage value.
    c. use self-help in reclaiming what is due her under the parties' agreement.
    d. obtain an injunction against the buyer to prevent him or her from contracting with her again.

16. A buyer enters into a sales contract to purchase a rare pink diamond ring with a platinum band for $1.3 million. When the buyer tenders payment, the seller refuses to sell the rare ring to the buyer. What type of action may the buyer bring in order to get the ring? [p 329]
    a. The buyer may bring an action for damages.
    b. The buyer is out of luck and will have to find another jeweler.
    c. The buyer may bring an equity action to obtain a decree of specific performance from the court ordering the seller to sell the ring to the buyer.
    d. The buyer may bring an action in tort for embezzlement.

17. A buyer or lessor who rightfully covers may sue the seller or lessor to recover [p 329]
    a. the difference between the cost of cover and the contract price or rent.
    b. incidental damages.
    c. consequential damages less expenses saved.
    d. all of the above.

18. The measure of damages a buyer or lessor may recover for a seller or lessor's failure to deliver the goods is [p 330]
    a. an equitable decree of specific performance.
    b. the difference between the contract price and the market price at the time the buyer or

lessee learned of the breach.
c. the difference between the market price and the contract price at the time the buyer or lessee learned of the breach.
d. a set amount that is preestablished by using a liquidated damages clause.

19. The UCC provides that if goods identified in a sales or lease contract are totally destroyed without the fault of either party before the risk of loss passes to the buyer or the lessee, the contract is [p 321]
   a. void.
   b. voidable.
   c. valid.
   d. all of the above

20. A buyer contracts to buy a red and purple striped, fully loaded corvette for $33,000. When the seller tenders delivery, the buyer refuses to accept the corvette or pay for it. The seller in good faith, and in a commercially reasonable manner, resells the corvette to a third party for $29,000. Incidental expenses of $400 are incurred on the resale. What can the seller recover from the original buyer? [p 325]
   a. Nothing, as the seller ultimately sold the corvette.
   b. $33,400.
   c. $4,400.
   d. $29,400.

21. What recourse does a buyer or lessee have against a seller or lessor who is wrongfully withholding goods that were identified in the parties sale or lease contract? [p 329]
   a. The buyer may ask for an injunction.
   b. The buyer may ask for cancellation of the contract
   c. The buyer may bring an action for replevin to recover the goods from the seller.
   d. none of the above.

22. If a seller or lessor fails to deliver goods or repudiates the sales or lease contract, what is the measure of damages that the buyer or lessee may recover? [p 330]
   a. The buyer may recover the contract price.
   b. The buyer may recover the difference between the contract price and the market price at the time the buyer or lessee learned of the breach.
   c. The buyer may recover incidental and consequential damages, less expenses saved.
   d. Both b and c.

Short Answer

23. The buyer may reject the goods if a _____________ delay or the seller's causes loss failure to make a proper contract for the shipment of goods or properly _________________ the buyer of the shipment. [p 328]

24. Explain what an installment contract is. [p 321] ______________________________

____

25. What do the initials C.O.D. stand for when used as part of a shipment form? [p 322]

____

____

26. If a buyer pays for goods by check, payment is conditional upon ____________________ ________________________ when it is presented to the bank for payment. [p 323]

27. What is a commercial unit? [p 323] ____

28. List at least two things must occur in order for a revocation by the buyer to be effective. [p 324] ____
____

29. When may an adequate assurance of due performance be demanded of one party by the other party? [p 331] ____

30. A seller or lessor who discovers that the buyer or lessee is insolvent before the goods are delivered may refuse to deliver as promised unless ________________________________ ____. [p 324]

31. What is the measure of damages a seller or lessor may recover when disposing of goods? [p 325] ____

32. What is reclamation? [p 325] ____

Chapter 17
E-COMMERCE, DOMAIN NAMES, AND INTERNET LAW

Chapter Overview

The evolution of the Internet as well as the vast amount of information available to users all over the world has given rise to several legal issues. This chapter discusses Web businesses and the operation of the same as well as registration of domain names. Further, it explores the roles of the Uniform Electronic Transactions Act as well as the Computer Information Transactions Act in e-commerce. Other additional laws concerning the creation, transfer and enforcement of e-commerce and informational licensing contracts are also discussed.

Objectives

Upon completion of the exercises in this chapter, you should be able to:

1. Explain how freedom of speech applies to the Internet using the rationale expressed in the case of *Reno v. American Civil Liberties Union.*
2. Explain the procedure for procuring Internet domain names.
3. Discuss what a license is and the parties to a licensing agreement.
4. Explain the provisions of the Federal Electronics Signature Act for e-commerce.
5. Discuss the importance of the Uniform Computer Information Transactions Act (UCITA)
6. Discuss the process of arbitration involving Internet domain name disputes.

Practical Application

You will have a clearer understanding of the various electronic and computer information acts that apply to the Internet as well as web businesses. Also, you will have a better understanding of e-commerce created licensing contracts as well as what necessary steps you may need to take if confronted with an Internet domain name dispute.

Helpful Hints

Since this chapter involves technology and the Internet, it would be very helpful for you to familiarize yourself with the technical terminology associated with the Information Age of today. Additionally, it is imperative that you learn the acts that protect as well as guide your conduct on the Internet in order to responsibly do business with the world. By learning the various acts, you will have a better understanding of what is expected of you as well as what you should expect of transactions on the Web.

Study Tips

There are two acts that were promulgated to provide a uniform and comprehensive set of rules involving for software and information licenses and contracts concerning computer information transactions. These acts are the Uniform Electronic Transaction Act and the Uniform Computer Information Transaction Act. However, prior to discussing these and other important acts associated with technology and business, you must get a firm grasp of the basic technological vocabulary.

Basic Vocabulary and Terminology

Internet – a collection of millions of computers that enable a network of electronic connections to exist between computers.

Electronic mail otherwise referred to as **e-mail** – Written communication between individuals whose computer is connected to the Internet.

Electronic communication – This involves any writing, images, sound, data, transfer of signals or any intelligence that is communicated electronically.

World Wide Web- The connection between millions of computers that enforces a standard set of rules for exchanging information referred to as Hypertext Transfer Protocol (HTTP).

Computer formatting – This refers to the use of common code languages such as Java and Hypertext Markup Language (HTML).

Web site- A combination of Web pages stored on various servers throughout the world.

Domain name – This identifies and differentiates one web site from another. Suffixes, or endings that are often used are *com* for commercial use, *org* for organizations, *edu* for educational institutions and *net* for networks.

Internet Corporation for Assigned Names and Numbers (ICANN) – This is an organization whose job is to regulate the issuance of domain names on the Internet.

Licensor- The party who owns the informational rights or the intellectual property and obligates Him or herself to transfer rights in the property or information to the licensee.

Licensee- The party who is given limited rights in or access to the informational rights or intellectual property.

License- This grants the contractual rights that are expressly stated in the license and the right to use any informational rights within the licensor's control that are necessary to exercise the expressly described rights. [UCITA Sec.307]

Exclusive License- This license gives the licensee exclusive rights in the information as described in the license for a specified period of time.

Licensing Agreement – A very detailed agreement between licensor and licensee that sets forth the terms of their agreement concerning the uses granted with respect to the intellectual property and informational rights.

Title to Copy – This is established by the license as the licensor may reserve title to the copy or the copy can transfer to the licensee.

Authenticate – This means executing an electronic symbol, sound or message linked to a record or signing the contract.

Uniform Dispute Resolution Policy – This policy mandates that all ICANN registered domain name users agree to utilize this dispute resolution policy as part of their accreditation.

Various Acts that Protect and Guide Internet Transactions

The Electronic Communications Privacy Act (ECPA)

- It is a crime to intercept "electronic communication" at any stage of its delivery.
- There are exceptions to the ECPA that allow access to the electronic communications without being in violation of the act. They are:
- The individual providing the service. An example would be your boss accessing information from your work computer.
- Government and law enforcement agencies that are investigating suspicious illegal activity are allowed if a valid search warrant is in place.
- Violation of the ECPA include criminal and civil penalties.

Anticybersquatting Consumer Protection Act

- The act was promulgated to oust cybersquatters who register Internet domain names of famous people and companies thereby holding them hostage for ransom payments from the famous individual or company.
- Two Requirements for this act:

  The name has to be famous. Trademarked names qualify, as do nontrademarked names of famous personalities.

  The domain name was registered in bad faith. Bad faith can be shown by considering the degree of resemblance between the holder's name and the famous individuals name, whether services and goods are being sold under the names, and the number of Internet domain names of famous individuals and companies that have been acquired by the holder.

Uniform Computer Information Transaction Act (UCITA)

- This act provides an exhaustive set of uniform rules that sets the standard for performance, and enforcement of computer information transactions. This act creates contract law for the licensing of information technology rights. For purposes of this act, a computer information transaction is an agreement to create, transfer, or license computer information or informational rights. [UCITA Sec.102 (a)(11)]. A state makes UCITA law by way of a state statute. Further, federal law preempts UCITA.

- Consumers are benefited by this act if they make an electronic error in contracting. UCITA provides that consumers are not bound if they learn of the error and tell the other party. Further, the consumer must not derive any benefit from the information. Also, the consumer must deliver all copies of the information to the third party or destroy the information as per the third party's instruction and the consumer must pay all shipping and processing costs of the other party.

- UCITA provides for the limitation of remedies for a breach of contract. They may be limited to return of copies and repayment of the licensing fee or to just the repair and replacement of the nonconforming copies. These limitations are enforceable unless they are found to be unconscionable.

<u>The Uniform Electronic Transactions Act (UETA)</u>

- This act was developed to create uniform laws for electronic signatures and electronic records. The purpose was to put electronic signatures and records on the same plane as written signatures and contracts. UETA only applies to electronic transactions between parties. Two main provisions are elaborated on within the act. First, UETA finds that an electronic record is sufficient for a contract as well as for purposes of the Statute of Frauds. Next, UETA acknowledges an electronic signature by giving it the same equivalence as a written signature. If the electronic signature requires notarization and witnessing; UETA finds this has been satisfied provided that all the necessary information regarding the notarization, acknowledgment, etc. are included.

- A state must adopt the act as its own statute in order for UETA to become law.

<u>The Electronic Signature in Global and National Commerce Act</u>

- This federal statute's purpose was to provide electronic commerce with the same credence as written contracts in the United States. As such, it recognizes an e-signature, or electronic signature as being validated in one of three ways. First, by something the signatory knows, such as the answer to a personal question. Second, by something the person has that stores personal information. Finally, by the use of a digitally calibrated device that recognizes fingerprints or parts of the eye. This technology is known as biometrics.

- This act also provides that electronic contracts satisfy the writing requirements of the Statute of Frauds. Further, record retention requirements are fulfilled by electronically stored records.

- This federal act preempts state law with the exception of state enacted e-signature provisions as per the UETA.

- There is a problem area with this act and that is that some countries have developed their own electronic commerce statutes that are different from those in the United States. Therefore, conflicts could arise without a global solution regarding contracts.

<u>How does an individual or business get a domain name?</u>

Step 1 - Determine whether anyone else owns the name.

You may search the databases of InterNIC or Network Solutions, which lists domain names that have been registered.

Step 2 - The registration form must be completed which by the way may be done online.

Step 3 - Submit the proper registration fee.

Formation of an Online Contract

- An online contract is much like that of a written one in that the same elements of offer, acceptance and consideration must be satisfied.
- If an electronic offer elicits an electronic acceptance, then an electronic contract is formed upon receipt of that acceptance. Changing the terms of the contract when accepting a conditional offer does not create a contract under UCITA.
- If the transaction involves merchants, any proposed terms become part of the contract unless they are objected to or if they are material alterations, then no contract is formed. If one party is a merchant and the other one is not, any proposed changes by way of the acceptance will be viewed as a counteroffer.
- The Statute of Frauds does not apply to contracts covered under the Uniform Computer Information Technology Act.
- Tender of Performance amounts to the offering of complete performance.

Risk of loss of the copy – Risk of loss passes to the licensee upon receipt of the copy if it is not delivered by carrier or delivered electronically.

Risk of loss in a designated delivery contract – The risk remains with the licensor until tendered to the designated destination. Otherwise, the risk of loss is placed with the carrier when the licenses are transferred to the carrier.

Acceptance of a copy – This occurs when the licensee through conduct signifies that there was conforming tender, keeps a copy despite the nonconformity or commingles the information with other information, receives a significant benefit from nonreturnable copy or uses the copy inconsistently with the licensor's ownership of the copy.

Excuse of Performance –A delay in performance under a license agreement due to impracticability will not constitute a breach if the requirements of UCITA are met. The party must reasonably notify the other party of the delay.

What types of warranties attach to a license of informational rights?

- Warranties of noninterference and noninfringement - A licensor warrant that no third person holds any claim or interest that would interfere with the licensor's use or enjoyment of the information.

- Express Warranty – Any affirmation of fact or promise made by the licensor about the software's quality or information. Statements of opinion do not constitute an express warranty.
- Implied Warranty of Merchantability of the Computer Program –_The computer program is fit for the ordinary purpose for which the program was going to be used.

- Implied Warranty of Informational Content – This warranty implies that there is no inaccuracy in the content of the information caused by the failure of the merchant to perform with reasonable care.
- Implied Warranty of Fitness for a Particular Purpose-When a licensee relies on the licensor's skill or judgment to select or furnish suitable information for which the computer information is required by the licensee, then the implied warranty of fitness for a particular purpose applies.

General Disclaimers of Warranties – UCITA permits disclaimers of all implied warranties with phrases like "as is." The language and disclaimers must be conspicuous.

Electronic Self-Help
If the licensee does not pay the license fee, the licensor can give at least a 15 day notice and activate a disabling bug that is embedded in the software or information that will prevent further access to the same. Proper notice to enable the licensee to make lawful adjustment must be made. Self-help is not available if it causes or results in public health or safety issues or personal injury.

Breach of License Agreements

- Licensee's refusal of defective tender – The licensee may refuse the defective tender, accept the tender or accept any commercially reasonable units and refuse the rest.
- Licensee's revocation of acceptance- The licensee may revoke his or her acceptance if he or she could not have reasonably discovered the nonconformity at the time of acceptance or the nonconformity was discovered upon acceptance and the licensor agreed to cure the defect but it was not reasonably cured.

Adequate assurance of performance – This is akin to anticipatory repudiation whereby an aggrieved party may suspend performance if he or she has reasonable grounds to believe that the performance from the other party is not going to be forthcoming. The aggrieved party may demand adequate assurance of performance within a specified time frame.

Remedies

A party cannot recover more than once for the same loss, nor may it be more than the loss caused by the breach.

- Cancellation – The ending of a contract by a contracting party upon the material breach of contract by the other party.

- Licensor's damages – The licensor may sue a licensee who is in breach and seek monetary damages caused by the breach.

- Licensor's right to cure – Under UCITA, a licensor may cure a breach if the time for performance under the contract has not expired, or if it has expired, the licensor had reasonable grounds to feel that the performance would be acceptable and would cure within a reasonable time. Also, if the licensor making a conforming performance before cancellation by the licensee.

- Licensee's Damages – Damages depend on the facts of the situation. The licensee may cover or recover the value of the performance. Remember cover means engaging in a commercially reasonable substitute transaction.

- Licenssee can get Specific Performance – If this remedy was agreed to in the parties' contract, or if the performance that was agreed upon was unique, then it will be available to the parties.

- Limitation of Remedies –The parties may limit which remedies are available in the event of a breach. Limitation of remedies is enforceable unless they are unconscionable.

Refresh Your Memory

The following exercise will enable you to refresh your memory on the rules and principles presented to you in this chapter. Read each question twice and place your answer in the blanks provided. Review the chapter material for any question you miss or are unable to remember.

1. What is the Internet? ____
____

2. Define e-mail. ____
____

3. Which act makes it a crime to intercept an "electronic communication" at any stage of its delivery? ____

4. A ______________ ______________ is a unique name that signifies an individual's or a company's Web site.

5. What is the purpose of the Anticybersquatting Consumer Protection Act? The purpose is to ____.

6. Who is responsible for regulating the issuance of domain names on the Internet? ________
____

7. What is the arbitration procedure for challenging cybersquatting called? ______________
____

8. What is a license? ____

9. Who are the parties to a license? The ________________ and the ________________

10. Which act establishes a uniform and exhaustive set of rules the rule the creation, performance and enforcement of computer information transactions? ________________
____

Critical Thought Exercise

The James Co. of New York has been in the business of retail chocolate and confection sales since 1923. As the Internet has developed, James has commenced doing business by e-mail. Mrs. Dubyah communicates with James by numerous e-mails, negotiating the sale of 300 one-pound chocolate Easter eggs. They agree that the price will be $18 per egg and they will be shipped for arrival in Maryland 10 days before Easter. James produces the eggs and ships them in a timely manner. At the last minute, Mrs. Dubyah decides to order her Easter gifts from another company. When the shipment arrives in Maryland, Mrs. Dubyah wants to reject the shipment and order her eggs from her friend in Oklahoma. As the business secretary for Mrs. Dubyah, you are responsible for advising Mrs. Dubyah on business matters and executing her contracts as instructed.

Write a brief memorandum to Mrs. Dubyah, explaining to her your position on whether she can rely upon the Statute of Frauds as a defense to a damages claim by James Co. and whether the shipment should be accepted.

Answer. ____

____

____

____

____

____

____

____

____

____

____

____

Practice Quiz

True/False:

1. ___ Domain names can not be registered. [p 346]

2. ___ Electronic contracts do meet the Statute of Frauds requirements. [p 344]

3. ___ The license does not govern a licensee's right to possess, control and use a copy of the licensed software. [p 349]

4. ___ The Internet Corporation for Assigned names is responsible for regulating the issuance of domain names on the Internet. [p 346]

5. ___ Mary has entered into an electronic contract with Watson for the purchase of Watson's motorcycle. Mary authenticates the contract by using an electronic symbol. Mary's means of authentication will be sufficient to constitute a signing. [p 345]

6. ___ Electronic agents usually do not have the ability to evaluate and accept counteroffers or to make counteroffers. [p 349]

7. ___ The Uniform Dispute Resolution Policy does not make arbitration of domain name disputes optional. [p 343]

8. ___ A transaction that is provided for by the UCITA is exempt from the Statute of Frauds. [p 345]

9. ___ One of the benefits of the Electronic Signature in Global and National Commerce Act is that the act does not provide for verification of digital signatures. [p 345]

10. ___ The implied warranty of informational content warrants that there is inaccuracy in the informational content caused by the merchant's failure to perform with reasonable care. [p 351]

11. ___ The warranty that the computer program is fit for the ordinary purposes for which the computer program is used is called the implied warranty of merchantability of the computer program. [p 351]

12. ___ Under UCITA, if a licensing agreement is breached, the statute of limitations is open ended due to the electronic nature of the transaction. [p 352]

Multiple Choice:

13. Which of the following is one of the most widely used means of communication over the Internet? [p 356]
    a. Licensing agreements
    b. Electronic mail
    c. Chat rooms
    d. None of the above

14. What was the court's opinion regarding the Communications Decency Act and the freedom of speech in the case of *Reno v. American Civil Liberties Union?* [p 342]
    a. The act is effective in allowing freedom of speech.
    b. The act is vague and has a chilling effect on free speech.
    c. The act is specific and protects our children from sexually oriented speech.
    d. The act appropriately protects all that are concerned.

15. Who is the owner of intellectual property or informational rights who transfers rights in the property or information to the license? [p 349]
    a. The licensee
    b. The licensor
    c. The obligor
    d. The obligee

16. This procedure is used to verify electronic authentication and to find errors or modifications in electronic authentication by using codes, algorithms, encryption and other means. [p 345]
    a. Arbitration
    b. Dispute resolution
    c. Attribution procedure
    d. Hypertext investigation

17. If a license agreement requires the licensor to deliver a copy to a particular destination, who bears the risk of loss? [p 354]
    a. The licensee
    b. The Internet Service Provider
    c. The state in which the agreement was enacted
    d. The licensor

18. Which of the following established a uniform comprehensive set of rules to govern the creation, performance, and enforcement of computer information transactions? [p 348]
    a. the Uniform Computer Information Transactions Act
    b. the express warranty
    c. the Federal Electronics Signatures Act
    d. all of the above

19. Which of the following is a function of InterNIC? [p346]
    a. to establish an extension for U.S. Web sites
    b. to establish a uniform international code among nations using the Internet
    c. to maintain a "Whois" database that contains the domain names that have been registered.
    d. to enable organizations unrestricted global name recognition

20. Which of the following may result in an express warranty? [p 351]
    a. advertising
    b. samples or models
    c. description of information
    d. all of the above

21. When is cancellation of a contract effective? [p 353]
    a. when the breaching party notifies the canceling party of the cancellation
    b. when the canceling party notifies the breaching party of the cancellation
    c. when it is obvious that the contract must be canceled due to a material breach of a contract
    d. none of the above

22. What may a licensor recover for a licensee's failure to accept or complete performance of a contract? [p 353]
    a. lost wages
    b. unemployment insurance
    c. discretionary damages
    d. lost profits

Short Answer:

23. What type of remedies are provided for by the Electronic Communications Privacy Act? [p 356] ______________________________

24. Who is the party who is granted limited rights or access to intellectual property or informational rights? [p 357] ______________________________
____

25. What is an access contract? [p 357] ______________________________

26. Which act permits a court to issue cease-and-desist orders and injunctions and to award monetary damages against anyone who has registered a domain name of a famous name in bad faith? [p 357] ______________________________
____

27. What is an express warranty? [p 351] ______________________________
____

28. What is a licensor liable for if he or she uses electronic self-help improperly? [p 355]
____

29. When may specific performance be obtained under UTICA? [p 355] ______________________________
____

30. What does the term cover mean? [p 355] ______________________________
____

31. What may an aggrieved party do if he or she thinks that prior to the performance date the other party might not deliver performance when do? [p 352] ______________________________
____

32. What may a licensee to whom a defective tender of copy has been made do? [p 352]
____

Chapter 18

WARRANTIES AND PRODUCT LIABILITY

Chapter Overview

This chapter discusses the multiple tort principles that are available to injured parties as a result of defectively made products. The causes of action that are available include negligence, misrepresentation, and strict liability. Many individuals including purchasers, users, lessees and even innocent bystanders who are injured by a defective product may seek recovery under the legal theory called products liability. This chapter will help you understand how manufactures, sellers, lessors and others involved with the defective product may be held liable for the injuries caused to others who were injured by the product.

Objectives

When you have completed the exercises in this chapter, you should be able to:

1. Differentiate between the different legal theories surrounding product liability.
2. Discuss what strict liability is.
3. Determine which parties may be held liable for injuries that are a result of a defective product.
4. Compare and contrast the difference between a manufacture, design and packaging defect.
5. Compare and contrast defects associated with a failure to warn and a failure to provide sufficient instructions.
6. Recognize and be able to state applicable defenses in product liability lawsuits.
7. Differentiate between contributory and comparative negligence.

Practical Application

You should be able to identify the different types of legal theories as well as their elements when establishing a basis for a product liability lawsuit. Additionally you should be able to identify the proper party to assess liability against, identify and apply potential defenses and be familiar with the types of damages that are available.

Helpful Hints

This chapter is not only a good chapter for reviewing the concepts of negligence and misrepresentation that you learned in the last chapter, but it is also one that you can utilize to build upon your knowledge of torts. It is important to learn the duties that are owed by those who manufacture as well as sell or lease products that are defectively made so that you will be able to select the appropriate cause of action to bring against the proper party. In the Study Tips section that follows, the necessary elements for the causes of action in a product liability
lawsuit as well as the proper parties whom suit should be brought against are listed under the same. By studying the causes of action in this manner, it will assist you in committing the entire concept of liability to memory.

Study Tips

Negligence

In order to be successful in a negligence action based on products liability, the plaintiff must first establish that a duty was owed and thereafter breached by the defendant. There are several types of duties that are owed, any of which can be breached alone or in combination with the others. These duties as well as who owes the duty (which is listed in parenthesis) include:

✓ the duty to assemble the product safely. (the manufacturer)
✓ the duty to properly design the product. (the manufacturer)
✓ the duty to inspect or test the product. (the manufacturer)
✓ the duty to properly package the product. (the manufacturer)
✓ the duty to warn of any dangerous propensities that the product may have. (the manufacturer and possibly the retailer and/or wholesaler)

Of course a breach of any of these duties gives rise to a negligence cause of action of which the plaintiff must demonstrate that the defendant was the actual as well as proximate cause of his or her injuries. The interesting part of this aspect is that there may be more than one defendant who is being sued for negligence, and as such, each may assert that the other was a supervening act that breaks the chain of proximate causation thereby making he or she the indirect cause of the plaintiff's injuries.

✓ The plaintiff will have a difficult time in proving a negligence cause of action based upon product liability as it is often a challenge determining who was negligent. Any one of the parties that suit will be brought against could have caused the plaintiff's injuries. The potential parties in a negligence cause of action may include the manufacturer, the retailer, a possible wholesaler, and maybe even a repairperson. Any one of these parties could singly or together have caused the plaintiff's injuries.

Misrepresentation

A plaintiff bringing a lawsuit based on misrepresentation will do so because of the fraud associated with the quality of the product. Only those who relied on the misrepresentation and thereafter suffered injury may bring a cause of action under this tort.

✓ Though misrepresentation is not the most common cause of action of which to base a product liability action on, it can be utilized if the plaintiff shows the seller or lessor made a misrepresentation concerning the product's quality or did not reveal a defect in the product. Manufacturers, sellers and lessors are potential defendants for this type of cause of action.

Strict Liability

The basis behind strict liability is to impose liability regardless of whose fault it is. As you learned in the previous chapter, strict liability is often imposed when a defendant is engaged in an ultrahazardous activity. Strict liability is also imposed upon lessors and sellers who are in the business of leasing and selling products. Casual sellers are exempt from the facet of being in the business of leasing and selling products. A casual seller is someone who is not a merchant.

✓ Be careful as strict liability involves products and not services. If the situation involves both, the court will look at the prevalent element in order to determine whether or not strict liability applies.

✓ Who may be liable under a strict liability theory?

All manufacturers, distributors, wholesalers, retailers, lessors, manufacturers of sub-components may be held strictly liable for the injuries caused by the product. Note that if one or more of the parties in the chain of distribution are held liable in a strict liability lawsuit, the parties may seek indemnification by bringing a separate cause of action against the negligent party.

✓ Special notation concerning entrepreneur liability for a defective product - Entrepreneurs may avoid the concern of being named in a product liability lawsuit by taking the cautionary measure of purchasing a products liability insurance policy. This will help minimize or eliminate the costs associated with such a lawsuit. Note that any amount of damages above and beyond what the policy covers will be the responsibility of the business.

✓ Elements in a Strict Liability cause of action
First , a defect must be shown. Several types of defects exist.

Manufacturing defect – A failure on the manufacturer' part to properly assemble, test or check the product's quality.

Design defect – This defect involves the application of a risk-utility analysis. The court will weigh the gravity of the danger from the design, the likelihood that injury will result from the design and the availability as well as expense of producing a safer different design against the utility of the design. The crashworthiness doctrine falls under this category of defect, as the court have held that automobile manufacturers have a duty when designing automobiles to take into account the possibility of a second collision from within the automobile. A failure to protect occupants from foreseeable dangers may result in a lawsuit based upon strict liability.

Packaging defect – A manufacturer has a duty to design and provide safe packages for their products so that they are either tamperproof or indicate if they have been tampered with. This type of defect has particular application in the pharmaceutical industry.

Failure to warn is viewed as a defect – Manufacturers as well as sellers have a duty to warn users about the dangerous aspects. The warning must be clear and conspicuous on the product. A failure to warn may subject those in the chain of distribution to a lawsuit based on strict liability.

Miscellaneous defects – There are other defects that can give rise to a strict liability cause of action, included of which are the failure to safely assemble a product, failure to provide adequate instructions for the safe use or assembly of a product, failure to adequately test a product or select proper component parts or materials, and failure to properly certify the product.

✓ Defenses to a Product Liability Lawsuit
There are many ***defenses*** that may have applicability in a product liability lawsuit.

Supervening Event- No liability exists if the product is materially altered or modified after it leaves the sellers possession and the modification or alteration causes the injury.

Generally Known Dangers – If a product is generally known to be dangerous and a seller fails to warn of this, then liability may attach. However, placing a safety feature on a generally known dangerous product may assist in limiting or absolving liability.

Government Contractor Defense – A Government contract must show that the government provided precise specifications for the product and the contract did in fact conform to those specifications. Further that the government was warned by the contractor of any known product defects or dangers.

Assumption of the Risk – Even though a defendant may utilize this defense by showing that the plaintiff knew and appreciated the risk involved and voluntarily assumed the risk, this defense is not widely used.

Misuse of Product – The main aspect the defendant must prove is that the plaintiff has abnormally misused the product and that such misuse was unforeseeable. If the misuse was foreseeable, the seller of the product will remain liable.

Statute of Limitations and Repose – A failure to bring a cause of action within the allowed time frame will relieve the defendant of liability. Many jurisdictions state that the statute of limitations begins to run when the plaintiff suffers an injury. Other states feel this is unfair to the seller and have created statutes of repose that limit the liability a seller has by setting a time frame in terms of years from when the product was initially sold.

Contributory and Comparative Negligence – If a person is found to have been negligent in contributing to his or her own injuries, this will not prevent him or her from recovering in a strict liability cause of action as it would under an ordinary negligence cause of action. Further, the courts have also applied the defense of comparative negligence thereby apportioning the damages based upon the negligence of each of the parties.

✓ Damages in a strict liability action include
- personal injury with some jurisdictions limiting the dollar amount of the award.
- property damage, which is recoverable in most jurisdictions.
- lost income which is recoverable in some jurisdictions.
- punitive damages are recoverable if the plaintiff can show that the defendant intentionally injured him or her or acted maliciously for his or her safety.

✓ Compare to Product Liability in Japan
- Japan has very few product liability cases. The reasons for the lack of cases are given below.
- The plaintiff must show that the company was negligent.
- Japan does not recognize the doctrine of strict liability.
- Japan does not allow the use of discovery in order to strengthen and build one's case.
- Losers and winners of a lawsuit must both pay a percentage of the requested damages as well as court fees, and therefore the damage requests are low.
- Japanese court granted awards are small and punitive damages are not available.

Refresh Your Memory

The following exercise will enable you to refresh your memory on the rules and principles presented to you in this chapter. Read each question twice and place your answer in the blanks provided. Review the chapter material for any question you miss or are unable to remember.

1. All parties in the _______ of __________________ of a defective product are strictly liable for injuries caused by the product.

2. Who may be sued under the doctrine of strict liability in tort? ______________________________
____

3. When examining a design defect, the court will apply the _______ ________ analysis.

4. What doctrine says that automobile manufacturers are under a duty to design automobiles to take into account the possibility of a second collision? ______________________________

5. When won't sellers of inherently dangerous products be held liable for failure to warn?
____

6. What is used to determine whether or not the defense of product misuse is effective?
____

7. What effect does a supervening event have with regard to a product liability action? ____________
____

8. What type of defect exists if a drug manufacturer fails to place its product in a childproof container?
____

9. What type of defect exists if a manufacturer constructs a toy with removable parts that are eventually swallowed by five-year old Tommy Toodles? ______________________________

10. In a strict liability cause of action, what must an injured party show with regard to the product that caused his or her injury? ______________________________

Critical Thought Exercise

Bruce Owens bought a Chevrolet Suburban from General Motors Corp. (GMC). Four years later, Owens crashed into the rear of another car while commuting to work. The speed of Owens' vehicle at the time of the crash was estimated to be less than 35 miles per hour. A properly functioning seatbelt will restrain the driver from impacting the steering wheel and the windshield during a crash at 40 miles per hour. During the crash, the seatbelt that Owens was properly wearing broke away from its anchor, causing Owens to be thrust against the steering wheel and into the windshield. Owens received a fractured skull, broken ribs, and a fractured left ankle. Owens sued GMC, Chevrolet, and the dealership that sold the vehicle to him. Owens claimed in his suit that because the seat belt broke, the defendants were strictly liable for his injuries. Investigation determined that the seatbelt anchor was both inadequate to sustain the forces involved in restraining a person during a crash, and had been installed in a manner that increased the likelihood of failure during a crash.

Are the defendants strictly liable to Owens?

Answer. ____
____
____
____
____
____

Practice Quiz

True/False

1. ___ If a person is injured by a defective product, her or she may not bring a cause of action for negligence against the negligent party. [p 369]

2. ___ Since most respectable manufacturers, sellers and lessors often purposefully misrepresent the quality of their products, misrepresentation is used very often as a basis for a product liability lawsuit. [p 368]

3. ___ Most states have not adopted the doctrine of strict liability in tort as a foundation for product liability actions. [p 369]

4. ___ Strict liability, like negligence does require the injured person to prove that the defendant breached his or her duty of care. [p 369]

5. ___ If Ronnie's Rafts fails to provide a booklet regarding the safe use or assembly of its products, Rhonda Rapids may bring a strict liability cause of action against Ronnie's Rafts for failure to provide adequate instructions, if she is injured. [p 375]

6. ___ Everyone in the chain of distribution of a defective product may be held strictly liable for the injuries caused by the product. [p 370]

7. ___ There does not have to be privity of contract between the plaintiff and the defendant in a strict liability cause of action. [p 371]

8. ___ Bystanders are not afforded the protection of strict liability. [p 371]

9. ___ A plaintiff may recover property damage in a strict liability action. [p 366]

10. ___ A defendant who is not negligent but who has to pay a strict liability judgment can bring a separate action against the negligent party in the chain of distribution. [p 370]

11. ___ Economic loss such as lost income is never recoverable in strict liability actions. [p 370]

12. ___ For strict liability purposes, the term user includes but is not limited to guests, employees and even persons who passively enjoy the benefits of the product in question. [p 371]

Multiple Choice:

13. Which of the following best describes a Japanese product liability action? [p 379]
    a. Discovery is often easy.
    b. Court awards are often higher than American product liability awards.
    c. Japan's product liability action mirrors the United States doctrine of strict liability.
    d. Regardless of winning or losing, the claimants must pay a percentage of any kind of damages requested as court fees

14. Under the doctrine of comparative negligence, a plaintiff who is contributorily negligent for his or her injuries is responsible for [p 378]
    a. a small share of the damages.
    b. a proportional share of the damages.
    c. only the property damage that may have resulted.
    d. replacement of part of the product.

15. Punitive damages are usually allowed in a strict liability action if the plaintiff can prove that [p 371]
    a. jurisdictions have judicially or statutorily extended the protection of strict liability to bystanders.
    b. property damage is recoverable in most jurisdictions.
    c. the defendant either intentionally injured him or her or acted with reckless disregard of his or her safety.
    d. sellers and lessors are liable to the ultimate user or consumer.

16. Which of the following would not be considered a defect in manufacture? [p 372]
    a. A failure to properly assemble a product.
    b. A failure to place a product in tamperproof packaging.
    c. A failure to properly test a product.
    d. A failure to adequately check the quality of the product.

17. A manufacturer that makes a defective product and thereafter discovers the defect must [p 377]
    a. notify users and purchasers of the defect and correct the defect.
    b. know and appreciate the risk and voluntarily assume the risk.
    c. file a complaint in accordance with its state's statute of limitations.
    d. prove that the plaintiff has abnormally misused the product.

18. Which doctrine establishes a duty of an automobile manufacturer to design an automobile to account for the possibility of harm from a person's body striking something inside the automobile in case of a car accident? [p 374]
    a. The collision doctrine
    b. The doctrine of res ipsa loquitur
    c. The negligence per se doctrine
    d. The crashworthiness doctrine

19. Who may be able to recover for his or her injuries as a result of a product's defect? [p 371]
    a. Sellers, lessors and manufacturers

b. Purchasers, lessees, users or bystanders
c. Anyone who witnesses the defect causing the injuries
d. All of the above

20. Drug manufacturers owe a duty to [p 375]
    a. place their products on shelves out of a child's reach.
    b. provide nicely packaged containers for their drugs.
    c. properly design easy to swallow pills.
    d. place their products in containers that cannot be opened by children.

Short Answer:

21. _____________ ___________ is the liability of manufacturers, sellers, lessors, and others for injuries caused by a defective product. [p 362]

22. The defense of _______________ ____________ bars an injured plaintiff from recovering from the defendant in a negligence action. [p 378]

23. The doctrine of comparative negligence says that a plaintiff who is contibutorily negligent for his or her injuries is responsible for a _________________ of the damages. [p 378]

24. The doctrine of ___________ ___________ in tort is a basis for product liability actions. [p 370]

25. When a manufacturer fails to adequately check the quality of the product, this is considered to be a defect in _________________. [p 107]

26. A __________-_________analysis involves weighing the gravity of the danger posed by a product's design against the utility of the product. [p 373]

27. If an automobile manufacturer fails to design an automobile to protect the passengers from foreseeable dangers caused by a second collision, the ______________ and the ______________ are subjected to a lawsuit based on strict liability. [p 374]

28. If a manufacturer of Get Well Quick drugs places its tablets into bottles that a child could easily twist the cap off of, it may have breached the duty to provide ___________ ______________ for its products. [p 375]

29. If Peter leases a boat and the front end is too weighted from the materials used to construct it thereby causing it to sink its first time in the water, Peter may utilize ____________________ ______________ laws in order to recover for the design defect. [p 375]

30. A ___________ and ____________ warning placed on the product protects those in the chain of distribution from strict liability. [p 380]

31. If a computer manufacturer fails to place instructions on how to put together its brand of computer, and a buyer gets injured from overloading the system due to an improperly installed plug, the consumer may claim that the product defect was the manufacturer's __________ to ___________ ___________ _____________. [p 375]

32. The defense that acknowledges that certain products are inherently dangerous and are known to the general population to be so is known as _____________ _______________ _________________.
[p 376]

Chapter 19
CREATION AND TRANSFER OF NEGOTIABLE INSTRUMENTS

Chapter Overview

This chapter focuses on the different types of negotiable instruments as well as their creation and the transfer of the same. Additional attention is given to nonnegotiable contracts, transfer of negotiable instruments by assignment and negotiation, as well as the various types of indorsements.

Objectives

Upon completion of the exercises in this chapter, you should be able to:

1. Differentiate between a negotiable and a nonnegotiable instrument.
2. Discuss drafts and checks as well as name the parties to these instruments.
3. Explain promissory notes and certificates of deposit as well as name the parties to these
4. Explain the difference between instruments payable to order and payable to bearer.
5. Discuss the process for indorsing and transferring negotiable instruments.
6. Differentiate between blank and special indorsements.
7. Discuss and apply the imposter rule and the fictitious payee rule.

Practical Application

This chapter will enable you to have a better understanding of negotiable instruments and their importance in conducting your personal as well as business affairs. Further, it will give you the tools that you need in the creation of a negotiable instrument. You will also obtain invaluable knowledge with regard to the different types of indorsements as well as requirements and restrictions for each.

Helpful Hints

Since this chapter involves one form or another of a negotiable instrument, the chance of you having used one or more of these instruments in your lifetime is great. If you keep in mind what you have used or are familiar with in terms of commercial paper, this chapter will be very understandable for you. The best approach is a simple approach. As with other chapters that have had confusing names for the parties involved, it is best to keep the parties separated on a sheet of paper to be able to view how they differ. The more you expose yourself to hypotheticals in this area, the easier the material becomes. Also, if you imagine yourself in one or more of the party's positions, it becomes easier.

Study Tips

Negotiable Instruments

Importance: Commercial paper aids in conducting personal and business affairs.

Three functions:
Negotiable instruments act as a substitute for money. An example is a check.
Negotiable instruments may also act as a credit device.
Negotiable instruments also may serve as a record-keeping device for preparing tax returns, etc.

Types of Negotiable Instruments

Draft – A three-party instrument that is an unconditional written order by one party that orders a second party to pay money to the third party. The parties involved are the drawer, the drawee and the payee. Note that the drawee is also known as the acceptor because of his or her obligation to pay the payee instead of the drawer.

Drawer – The customer who writes (draws) the check.
Drawee – The financial institution upon which the check is written.
Payee – The party to whom the check is written.

Promissory Note – An unconditional written promise by one party to pay money to another party.

Maker – This is the borrower who makes the promise to pay.
Payee – This is the lender to whom the promise is made.

Collateral – Sometimes the lender needs security known as collateral is needed when a promissory note is made.

Examples of promissory notes: Mortgage notes which are notes that are secured by real estate.
Collateral notes are notes that are secured by personal property.

Certificates of Deposit – A specially created note that is created upon a depositor depositing Monies at a financial institution in exchange for the institution's promise to pay the deposited amount back with an agreed upon amount of interest after a set period of time.

Creation of a Negotiable Instrument

In order to create a negotiable instrument in compliance with UCC 3-104(a), the following must be present and must appear on the face of the instrument:

It must be in writing. – This involves permanency and the writing must be portable.

It must be signed by the maker or drawer. – The UCC is broad with this requirement. Symbols, typed, printed, lithographed, rubber-stamped or other mechanical signatures are allowed.

It must be an unconditional promise or order to pay. – Mere debt acknowledgement is not sufficient for this requirement.
It must state a fixed amount of money. – The principal amount of the instrument has to be on the face of the instrument. Note, money is a "medium of exchange authorized or adopted by a foreign or domestic government as part of its currency." [UCC 1-201(24)]

It must not require any undertaking in addition to the payment of money.

It must be payable on demand or at a definite time. – Payable on demand instruments are created by language such as "payable on sight," or "payable on demand." Checks are an example of payable on demand instruments. Payable at a definite time are called time instruments.

It must be payable to order or to bearer.

Nonnegotiable Contracts

If a promise or order to pay does not meet the requirements discussed under negotiable instruments, then it is a nonnegotiable contract. A nonnegotiable contract is enforceable under contract law.

Transfer by Assignment or Negotiation

After issuance, negotiable instruments may be transferred to subsequent parties either by negotiation or assignment. The transferees rights will depend on how the transfer was effectuated. There are two main types:

Transfer by Assignment – It transfers contract rights of the assignor (transferor) to the assignee (transferee). An assignment results when there has been a transfer of a nonnegotiable instrument.

Transfer by Negotiation - Negotiation is defined as the transfer of a negotiable instrument by a person other than the issuer.

Indorsements

Defined – The signature of a signer (not the maker, drawer or acceptor) that is put on an instrument to negotiate it to another person. The signature may be by itself, state an individual to whom the instrument is to be paid or be with other words.

Indorser – The one who indorses the instrument.
Indorsee – The payee named in the instrument.

Types of Indorsements

Blank– No indorsee is given and it creates bearer paper.

Special indorsement – It contains the indorser's signature and it indicates the person to whom the indorser intends the instrument to be payable to. Special indorsements create order paper, which are preferred over bearer paper.

Unqualified indorsement – "An indorsement whereby the indorser promises to pay the holder or any subsequent indorser the amount of the instrument if the maker, drawer, or acceptor defaults on it."

Qualified indorsement – "Indorsements that disclaim or limit liability on the instrument." Note that there is no guarantee d payment of the instrument by the qualified indorser if the maker, drawer, or acceptor defaults on the instrument. These types of indorsements are often used by individuals signing instruments in the capacity as a representative.

Nonrestrictive indorsement- This is an indorsement without conditions or instructions attached to the payment of the funds.

Restrictive indorsement – An indorsement with an instruction from the indorser.
There are two restrictive indorsements you should be familiar with as provided for under UCC 3-206.

> Indorsement for Deposit or Collection – This is an indorsement that establishes the indorsee The indorser's collecting agent. For example: "for deposit only."
>
> Indorsement in Trust- An indorsement for the benefit or use of the indorser or another individual.

Misspelled or Wrong Name

If the payee or indorsee name is misspelled, the payee or indorsee in the negotiable instrument may indorse the instrument in the misspelled name, the correct name or both.

Multiple Payees or Indorsees

If more than one person are listed as indorsees or payees on a negotiable instrument and are listed jointly, both indorsements are needed to negotiate the instrument. Example: Payable to Joe and Jan Smith requires both Joe and Jan's signature.

If the instrument indicates that one or the other may negotiate the instrument, then each person's signature is sufficient to negotiate the instrument. Example: Payable to Ann or Mark Jones would allow either Ann or Mark signature.

If a *Virgule* (which is a slash mark) is used, then the negotiable instrument may be paid in the alternative. Example: Maile Price/Winnie Simms indicates that either person may individually negotiate the instrument.

Forged Instrument

The general rule is that unauthorized indorsements are inoperative as the indorsement of the person who signed it. The loss is born by the party accepting the forged instrument. There are two exceptions, the imposter rule and the fictitious payee rule.

Imposter rule -The drawer or maker is liable on the instrument to any person who in good faith pays the instrument or takes it for value or for collection.

The fictitious payee rule – A drawer or maker is liable on an unauthorized or forged indorsement of a fictitious payee rule.

Refresh Your Memory

The following exercise will enable you to refresh your memory on the rules and principles presented to you in this chapter. Read each question twice and place your answer in the blanks provided. Review the chapter material for any question you miss or are unable to remember.

1. ___________________ is the person who issues a draft.

2. ___________________ is a person to whom the check is made payable to.

3. The financial institution where the drawer's checking account is located is the ______________________.

4. To be negotiable, an instrument must have a promise or order to pay a fixed ____________ ______________________.

5. Under the UCC, money is defined as ____ ____.

6. Instruments that are payable on demand are called _____________ _________________.

7. An__________________________ clause allows the date of maturity of an instrument to be extended to some time later on.

8. If a promise or order to pay does not meet the UCC requirements of negotiability, it is a __________________________ ___________________.

9. What is the transfer of a negotiable instrument by an individual other than the issuer called? ___________________________

10. An ________________________ is the signature of a signer that is placed on an instrument to negotiate it to another person.

Critical Thought Exercise

The Gold Coast Investment Group (IG) is building a large office building that it is financing itself through its banking arm, Gold Coast Bank (GCB). When payments for the final phase of the building come due, GC issues checks to the contractors with a condition on the front of the check that states:

"This instrument valid only after a permit to occupy the building is granted by all governmental agencies from which a permit is mandatory."

Ace Construction deposits the check with its bank, First City Bank. The occupancy permits are not issued by the city or county entities where the building is located. When presented with the checks by First City Bank, GCB refuses to honor them.

Ace Construction then brings suit against First City Bank, GCB, and IG.

Should GCB be compelled to pay the checks presented to it by First City Bank on behalf of Ace Construction? Was it ethical for IG to place a condition upon the negotiation of the instrument?

Answer. ____

____

____

____

____

____

____

____

____

____

____

____

____

____

____

____

____

Practice Quiz

True/False:

1. ___ An check is not a substitute for money. [p.386]

2. ___ The drawee need not be obligated to pay the drawer money before the drawer can order the drawee to pay this money to the payee. [p.387]

3. ___ The drawee of a check is not the financial institution where the drawer has his or her account. [p. 388]

4. ___ The party who makes the promise to pay is not the payee. [p. 387]

5. ___ Examples of collateral that may be used as security against repayment of a note to a lender include cars, homes or other property. [p.389]

6. ___ A maker is not the party to whom the promissory note is made payable which is usually the lender. [p.389]

7. ___ A maker is the financial institution that issues the certificate of deposit. [p.390]

8. ___ A writing on Kleenex meets the permanence aspect of the writing requirement of negotiable instruments. [p.391]

9. ___ A promise to pay that is indented in a steel girder would not qualify as a negotiable instrument because the girder is freely transferable in commerce. [p.391]

10. ___ The drawer or maker is liable on the instrument regardless if his or her signature appears on it. [p.391]

11. ___ A negotiable instrument has to contain a promise or order to pay a fixed amount of money. [p. 393]

12. ___ The value of an instrument cannot be determined with certainty by having a fixed amount. [p.393]

13. ___ After issuance of a negotiable instrument, it may not be transferred to a subsequent party. [p.397]

14. ___ An assignment cannot take place when a nonnegotiable contract has been transferred. [p.397]

15. ___ The transfer of a negotiable instrument by an issuer is known as negotiation. [p.397]

Multiple Choice:

16. Negotiable instruments serve which function [p.391]
    a. as a substitute for money.
    b. as a credit device.
    c. as a record keeping device.
    d. all of the above.

17. A drawer of a draft is the [p. 390]
    a. person to whom the check is made payable.
    b. person who issues the draft.
    c. person to whom the draft is made payable.
    d. person who owes money to the drawer.

18. To qualify as a negotiable instrument under the UCC, the writing must [p.391]
    a. contain an unconditional promise to pay.
    b. contain an unconditional order to pay.
    c. contain an unconditional promise or order to pay.
    d. none of the above.

19. A promise or order to pay may include [p.392]
    a. authorization or power to protect collateral.
    b. a vague amount.
    c. a conditional promise to perform.
    d. an immobile writing.

20. Stewart draws a check payable to the order of Kurt. Kurt indorses the check and negotiates it to Martha. When Martha presents the check for payment, there are insufficient funds in Stewart's account to pay the check. If Kurt is an unqualified indorser and is liable on the check, who may Kurt recover against? [p.400]
    a. Martha
    b. Henry
    c. Martha's daughter
    d. Stewart

21. An instrument that is not payable to a specific payee or indorsee is [p 397]
    a. order paper
    b. bearer paper
    c. stationary paper
    d. electronic paper

22. The purpose of a prepayment clause is [p 395]
    a. to permit the maker to pay the amount due before the due date of the instrument.
    b. to permit the maker to pay the amount due after the due date of the instrument.
    c. to permit the maker to waive one of his or her payments.
    d. all of the above

23. Which of the following is not true with regard to variable interest rate loans? [p 394]
    a. These loans tie the interest rate to some set measure.
    b. The interest changes during the life of the loan.
    c. Interest may not be stated in an instrument as a fixed or variable amount of money.
    d. Many lending institutions offer variable interest rate loans.

24. An extension clause is [p 395]
    a. a clause that permits the maker to pay the amount due prior to the due date of the instrument.
    b. a clause that allows the payee or holder to accelerate payment of the principal amount of the instrument, plus accrued interest, upon the happening of an event.
    c. a clause that allows the borrower extra time to secure financing.
    d. a clause that allows the date of maturity of an instrument to be extended to some time in the future.

25. Nonrestrictive indorsements do not have [p 401]
    a. restrictions placed on them.
    b. any instructions or conditions attached to the payment of funds.
    c. subsequent indorsers in place of qualified indorsers.
    d. any negotiability attached to them.

Short Answer:

26. Negotiable instruments include such things as ______________________________. [p.387]

27. Merchants and consumers often use negotiable instruments as a substitute for ____________________________. [p.386]

28. Ellen owes Grace $100. Grace writes out a draft ordering Ellen to pay the $100 to Bart. Ellen agrees to this change of obligation and accepts the draft. Grace is the drawer and Bart is the ______________________________. [p.389]

29. A ______________________________ is an unconditional written promise by one party to pay money to another party. [p.388]

30. A _______________________note is one that is payable at a specific time. [p.389]

31. A _____________ _____________ is one in which the note is payable on demand. [p 389]

32. The party who makes the promise to pay is known as the maker of the note or the ______________________________________. [p.389]

33. The party to whom the promise to pay is made is the payee of a note or the ___________ ___________________. [p.389]

34. _________________ and __________________ are two elements that must be present in order to establish the writing requirement of a negotiable instrument. [p 391]

35. List three requirements that must be on the face of an instrument in order to be considered a negotiable instrument. [p 391] ____
____

Chapter 20
HOLDER IN DUE COURSE AND LIABILITY

Chapter Overview

In the previous chapter, you learned about the various types of negotiable instruments as well as their creation and the ability to transfer the same. This chapter expands on the concept of commercial paper being a substitute for money by exploring the liability of parties on negotiable instruments, as well as the requisites that must be satisfied in order to be deemed a holder in due course. Further, you will learn the defenses that can be raised against the imposition of liability as well as what is involved in discharging liability.

Objectives

Upon completion of the exercises in this chapter, you should be able to:

1. Explain the meaning of a holder and a holder in due course.
2. Discuss the signature liability of makers, drawers, drawees, acceptors and accommodation parties.
3. Discuss transfer warranties as well as the liability of parties for breaching them.
4. Recognize real defenses that can be asserted against a holder in due course.
5. Explain the Federal Trade Commission rule that prohibits the holder in due course rule in consumer transactions.

Practical Application

This chapter will provide you with the understanding that you need to determine if you are a holder in due course of negotiable instruments. Further, you will be aware of any defenses that you may be able to assert, as well as what is involved in discharging liability.

Helpful Hints

Since this chapter lays out a list of requirements that are necessary to be a holder in due course as well as requirements for each of the elements contained within the basic definition, it is especially helpful to make use of lists. To facilitate your studies in this area, the study tips section has been organized so that you will be able to easily refer to the lists when analyzing the case studies or hypotheticals presented to you.

Study Tips

Holder	*versus*	Holder in Due Course
Defined: A person in possession of instrument An instrument that is payable to bearer notice or an identified person who is in possession of an instrument payable to person.		Defined: A holder who takes an for value, in good faith, and without that is defective or is overdue.

Requisites for being a Holder in Due Course

The individual must be a holder of a negotiable instrument that was taken:

1. **for value** (as elaborated on in UCC 3-303)
   a. if the holder performs the agreed-upon promise.
   b. acquires a security interest or lien on the instrument.
   c. takes the instrument in payment of or as security for an antecedent claim.
   d. Gives a negotiable instrument as payment
   e. Gives an irrevocable obligation as payment.

2. **in good faith**
   a. means honesty in fact.
   b. Honesty is a subjective test as judged by the circumstances.
   c. Good faith only applies to the holder.

3. **without notice of defect**
   a. means that a person cannot be a holder in due course is he or she knows that the instrument is defective in any way.
   b. Defect can be construed as
      1. it being overdue.
      2. it has been dishonored.
      3. it contains an unauthorized signature or has been altered (the red light doctrine).
      4. there is a defense against it.

4. **Other important information**
   a. A holder may not be a holder in due course if at the time of negotiation to the holder, It was forged or altered casting doubt on its authentication.
   b. Payees usually are not considered to be holders in due course because of their knowledge of claims or defenses against the instrument.
   c. Signature liability involves identifying those who are obligated to pay on the negotiable instrument. The signature's location on the instrument gives a clue as to the signer's capacity. The general presumption is that the signature is that of the **indorser.**
      1. Defined- any word, symbol, mark in lieu of written signature that is handwritten, typed, stamped, etc. and adopted or executed by a party to authenticate the writing.
      2. Agent's signature – An individual may sign the negotiable instrument him or herself or authorize an agent to do so. The represented person is the principal. No formal appointment is needed.
      3. Unauthorized Signature – This is a signature made by a purported agent without authority from the alleged principal. The purported agent is liable to any individual who in good faith pays the instrument or takes it for value. The alleged principal is liable if he or she ratifies the unauthorized signature.

liable if he or she ratifies the unauthorized signature.

5. **Primary Liability**
   a. Makers of certificates of deposits and promissory notes have what is known as primary liability. The maker unconditionally promises to render the amount stipulated in the note when it is due.
   b. No party is primarily liable when a draft or check is issued since these instruments are merely an order to pay.

6. **Secondary Liability**
   a. Secondary liability attaches to the drawers of checks and drafts and unqualified indorsers of negotiable instruments.
   b. This is easy to remember, as it's similar to a guarantor of a simple contract.
   c. The drawer is obligated to pay if it is an unaccepted draft or check that is dishonored by the drawee or acceptor.
   d. Requirements for Secondary Liability
      1. The instrument must be properly presented for payment.
      2. The instrument is dishonored.
      3. Notice of the dishonor is given in a timely manner to the person who is to be secondarily liable on the instrument.

7. **Accommodation Party**
   a. Defined- A party who signs an instrument and lends his or her credit (and name) to another party to the instrument.
   b. Special notations:
      1. Guarantee of Payment- The accommodation party who signs an instrument is basically guaranteeing payment and is primarily liable on the instrument.
      2. Guarantee of Collection – This arises where the accommodation party guarantees collection rather than payment. Requirement of payment arises only if:
         a. execution of judgment against the other party has been returned unsatisfied,
         b. the other party is in an insolvency proceeding or is insolvent,
         c. the other party is unable to be served with process, or
         d. it is otherwise obvious that payment cannot be received from the other party. [UCC3-419(d)]

Warranty Liability of Parties

Basic information – Warranty liability is placed upon a transferor irrespective of whether the Transferor signed the instrument or not.

Two types of implied warranties:

1. Transfer of warranties – As defined in your main text, "Any passage of an instrument other than its issuance and presentment for payment is consider a **transfer.**" There are five warranties that are made when a person transfers a negotiable instrument for consideration. They are:
   a. The transfer of good title to the instrument or authorization to obtain acceptance or payment on behalf of one who does have good title.
   b. All signatures are authentic or authorized.
   c. The instrument has not been altered materially.
   d. No defenses of any party are applicable against the transferor.

e. The transferor is unaware of any insolvency proceeding against the maker, the acceptor, or the drawer of an unaccepted instrument.
f. **Special notation** – Instruments other than checks may disclaim transfer warranties with the use of an indorsement such as "without recourse" [UCC3-416 (c)]

2. Presentment Warranties – As defined in your main text, "Any person who presents a draft or check for payment or acceptance makes the following warranties to a drawee or acceptor who pays or accepts the instrument in good faith [UCC 3-417(a)]:
   a. The presenter has good title to the instrument or is authorized to obtain payment or acceptance of the person who has good title.
   b. The material has not been materially altered.
   c. The presenter has no knowledge that the signature of the maker or drawer is unauthorized.

Defenses

There are real and personal defenses that arise from the underlying transaction concerning the creation of negotiable instruments.

Real defenses	versus	Personal defenses
These can be raised against both holders and holders in due course If one of these defenses is proven, neither holder nor holder in due course can recover on the instrument.		These can be raised against enforcement of a negotiable instrument by an ordinary holder.
Minority Extreme duress Mental incapacity Illegality Discharge in bankruptcy Fraud in the Inception Forgery Material alteration		Breach of Contract Fraud in the Inducement Other Personal Defenses - mental illness - illegality of a contract - ordinary duress or undue influence UCC3-305(a)(ii) -discharge of an instrument by payment or cancellation [UCC 3-602 and 3-604]

FTC Elimination of Holder in Due Course Status Concerning Consumer Credit Transactions

The rule puts the holder of due course of a consumer credit contract on the same level as an assignee of a simple contract. The result is the holder of due course of a consumer credit instrument is subject to all of the defenses and claims of the consumer.

This rule applies to consumer credit transactions that includes a promissory note, the buyer signs an installment sales contract that contains a waiver of defenses clause, and the seller arranges consumer financing with a third-party lender.

Discharge

There are several rules that are specified by the UCC on when and how certain parties are discharged from liability on negotiable instruments. The three main ways that will relieve the Parties from liability are:

- By payment of the instrument
- By cancellation
    - by any manner or
    - by destroying or mutilating a negotiable instrument with the intent of getting rid of the obligation.
- By impairment of the right of recourse which is accomplished by
    - releasing an obligor from liability or
    - surrendering collateral without the consent of the parties who would benefit by it.

Refresh Your Memory

The following exercise will enable you to refresh your memory on the rules and principles presented to you in this chapter. Read each question twice and place your answer in the blanks provided. Review the chapter material for any question you miss or are unable to remember.

1. A person in possession of an instrument that is payable to an identified person or a bearer in possession of an instrument payable to that person is a ________________.

2. A holder who takes an instrument for value, in good faith, and without notice that is defective or is overdue is a _________ in ________________ __________________.

3. Suppose Monica draws a check "payable to the order of Greg Wallace" and delivers the check to Greg. Greg indorses the check and gives it as a gift to his son. Can Greg's son qualify as a holder in due course? ____
____

4. Steve, a thief steals a negotiable instrument and transfers it to Cindy. Cindy is unaware that the instrument is stolen. Since Cindy meets the good faith test, she will qualify as a
_________________ _____ ______ ___________.

5. A person cannot qualify as a holder in due course if he or she has _____________ that the instrument is defective in certain ways.

6. An instrument that is payable on demand is known as a ___________ _____________.

7. When an instrument has been presented for payment and payment has been refused, it is
______________________________.

8. A person who has been authorized to sign a negotiable instrument on behalf of another person is an ________________________.

9. A ________________________ is a person who authorizes an agent to sign a negotiable instrument on his or her behalf.

10. An __________________________ signature is one that is made by a purported agent without authority from the purported principal.

Critical Thought Exercise

Betty Smith made out a check to George Bell of Bell Plumbing for $1,500 as a partial payment for plumbing renovation of her kitchen. When it was time for Bell to begin his work, he did not appear, nor could Ms. Smith locate him. Smith immediately ordered her bank to stop payment on the check. Bell had already cashed the check at Redi-Cash. When the check was returned to Redi-Cash marked "payment stopped by account holder," Redi-Cash was contacted by an attorney for Smith who informed Redi-Cash that the plumber did not have a license and that engaging in a contracting trade without a license was a crime. Therefore the contract was void and his client would not honor the check.

As manager of Redi-Cash, will you commence suit against Smith to collect the amount of the check?

Answer. ____

Practice Quiz

True/False:

1. ___ If Samantha is in possession of a negotiable instrument that is drawn, issued or indorsed to her, or to bearer, or in blank, she may not be a holder. [p 414]

2. ___ Under the UCC, value has been given if the holder gives a revocable obligation as payment. [p.414]

3. ___ Good faith applies to only the holder. [p 416]

4. ___ A holder cannot qualify as a holder in due course if he or she has notice that the instrument contains an unauthorized signature. [p 417]

5. ___ Signature liability refers to an individual's contractual liability on a negotiable instrument and whether or not his or her signature appears on it. [p 417]

6. ___ The location of a signature on the instrument cannot determine the signer's capacity. [p 418]

7. ___ The signature on a negotiable instrument can be by word, mark, symbol or name. [p 477]

8. ___ When a person authorizes a representative to sign an instrument on his or her behalf, the representative is the agent. [p 418]

9. ___ A signature made by a purported agent without authority from a purported principal is an unauthorized signature. [p 419]

10. ___ The makers of promissory notes and certificates of deposit have secondary liability for the instrument. [p 419]

11. ___ It is not a requirement that the negotiable instrument be dishonored before imposing secondary liability on it. [p 480]

12. ___ The two types of implied warranties are transfer warranties and presentment warranties. [p 423]

Multiple Choice:

13. A holder is [p 414]
    a. a person who takes an instrument for value and in good faith.
    b. a person who takes without notice that it is defective or overdue.
    c. a person in possession of an instrument that is payable to bearer or an identified person who is in possession of an instrument payable to that person.
    d. a person who takes a negotiable instrument free of all claims and most defenses.

14. If Megan promises to perform but has not done so yet and there has been no value given, Megan is not a [p 414]
    a. holder in due course.
    b. third-party beneficiary.
    c. holder without value.
    d. None of the above.

15. If a time instrument is not paid on its expressed date, then it [p 416]
    a. becomes effective.
    b. becomes overdue and is defective as to its payment.
    c. is payable on demand.
    d. can be made payable according to business practices.

16. Hugo draws a check on Coast Bank "payable to the order of Lamar Huff." When Lamar presents the check for payment, Coast Bank refuses to pay it. Lamar can collect the amount of the check from Hugo because Hugo is [p 420]
    a. the maker.
    b. the drawee.
    c. the person who ratified the check.
    d. the drawer.

17. A demand for acceptance or payment of an instrument made upon the maker, acceptor, drawee, or other payor by or on behalf of the holder is referred to as [p 421]
    a. a notice of dishonor.
    b. an unqualified indorser.
    c. the red light doctrine.
    d. presentment.

18. An authorized agent's personal liability on an instrument he or she signs on behalf of a principal depends on [p 418]
    a. the agent's signature.
    b. information disclosed in the signature.
    c. the unauthorized signature of an unauthorized signer.
    d. none of the above

19. An indorsement that states "without recourse" disclaims [p 423]
    a. the transfer warranties.
    b. negotiable instrument originally issued.
    c. secondary liability
    d. primary liability

20. Which of the following may give rise to a defense against the payment of a negotiable instrument? [p 424]
    a. extreme duress
    b. discharge in bankruptcy
    c. forgery
    d. all of the above

21. Which of the following is true with regard to a holder in due course? [p 428]
    a. He or she takes a negotiable instrument free of all claims.
    b. Most defenses can be asserted against the transferor.
    c. A holder in due course can acquire greater rights than a transferor.
    d. all of the above

22. The party who signs an instrument for the purpose of lending his or her name to another party to the instrument is the [p 422]
    a. guarantor of collection.
    b. ethical party
    c. accommodation party
    d. none of the above

Short Answer:

23. _____________ defenses may be asserted against a holder in due course. [p 424]

24. A demand instrument is one that is ____________________________ [p 416]

25. An instrument that sets a definite date for payment of that instrument is known as _________________________________ [p 416]

26. What is the liability for unqualified indorsers of negotiable instruments that they indorse? [p 420] __________________

27. Indorsers who indorse instruments "without recourse" or similar language that disclaims liability are referred to as _______________________________________ indorsers. [p 420]

28. Any passage of an instrument other than its issuance and presentment for payment is known as a __________________ [p 423]

29. Mental incompetency is a ________________ defense that can be raised against holders in due course. [p 425]

30. Breach of contract is a _________________ defense that can be raised against enforcement of a negotiable instrument by an ordinary holder. [p 426]

31. When is an instrument dishonored? [p.421] ______________________________________ ____ ______

32. An accommodation party is a party who signs ____________________________________ ____. [p 422]

Chapter 21
CHECKS AND DIGITAL BANKING

Chapter Overview

This chapter is primarily concerned with checks, the most common form of negotiable instrument. In this chapter you will learn about several different kinds of checks as well as the process involved regarding payment and collection of checks through the banking system. Additionally, this chapter explores the duties as well as liabilities of banks and other parties in the collection process along with electronic fund transfers.

Objectives

Upon completion of the exercises in this chapter, you should be able to:

1. Differentiate between a cashier's check, certified and traveler's checks.
2. Explain the system of processing and collecting checks through the banking system.
3. Recognize when a bank participates in a wrongful dishonor of a check.
4. Explain the liability of parties when a check has been altered.
5. Discuss the requisites of the Expedited Funds Availability Act.
6. Explain the electronic fund transfer system
7. Explain the term wire transfer and discuss the main provisions of Article4A of the Uniform Commercial Code.

Practical Application

Since almost everyone will have the opportunity to either have a checking account or purchase one of the various types of checks, this chapter will prove to be an invaluable resource to those who study it. It will provide insight into the banking procedures involving payment and collection of checks as well as assist you in knowing what the banks' duties and other parties' duties and liabilities are in the collection process. Further, you will gain useful information concerning electronic fund transfers.

Helpful Hints

This chapter will be relatively easy for most individuals to learn, since much of what is presented has already been experienced in most individuals' everyday personal and business affairs. There may be a few terms that you recognize by definition but not by term that you will want to review a little more carefully. Examples of these types of terms include but are not limited to such words as stale checks, incomplete checks, deferred posting, provisional posting, etc. This chapter's high applicability makes it a very interesting learning experience.

Study Tips

Checks

Explained: A substitute for money and also a record-keeping device.
Special Notation: They do not serve a credit function.

The Banking Relationship:

The customer is the creditor.
The bank is the debtor.
A principal-agent relationship may also be formed whereby the customer is the principal ordering the bank to collect or pay on the check. The bank in turn is the agent that is obligated to follow the customer as principal's order.

The Basics of Banking:

Ordinary checks — When a customer goes to a bank, fills out the proper forms along with a signature card, followed by a deposit, the bank issues checks to him or her. Thereafter, the customer uses the checks for his or her purchases. The checks are presented to the bank and paid provided the drawer's signature matches the signature card.

Parties to a check — Drawer – This is the customer with a checking account.
Drawee - This is the bank (or payor) at which the check is drawn.
Payee – The one to whom the check is written.

Indorsement — This refers to the holder or payee signing the back of the check. The payee is the indorser and the person to whom the check is indorsed is the indorsee.

Point-of-Sale Terminals — The customer's account is immediately debited for the amount of the purchase by using a bank issued debit card to make a purchase.

Direct Deposits And Withdrawals — The customer's bank and the payee's bank must belong to the same clearinghouse in order to provide the service of paying recurring payments and recurring deposits.

Pay-by-Internet — Customers may pay bills from their account using their PIN number and account number, the amount of the bill to be paid, and the account number of the payee.

Special Checks: — Bank checks are special checks. There are certified checks, cashier's checks, and traveler's checks.

Certified checks – With this type of check, the bank agrees in advance to accept the check when it is presented for payment and pay the check out of funds set aside from the customer's account. These types of checks are payable at any time from when they are issued. The bank writes or stamps the word ***certified*** across the face of an ordinary check thereby certifying it. The date, amount being certified and the individual certifying the check also are placed on the check. Payment may not be stopped on a certified check.

Cashier's check – This is a bank-issued check where the customer has paid the bank the amount of the check and a fee. The bank guarantees the payment of the check. The bank acts as the drawer and the drawee with the holder as payee. The bank debits its own account when the check is presented.

Traveler's checks – This type of check is a two-party instrument where the bank who issues it is both the drawer and the drawee. An interesting notation about this type of check is that it has two signature lines, one for the purchaser to sign when he or she purchases the checks and the other for the purchaser to sign when he or she uses the check for purchases. This type of check is especially popular among travelers as it serves as a safe substitute for cash, as it is not negotiable until it is signed a second time.

Honoring Checks — The customer of a bank agrees to keep sufficient funds in the account to cover any checks written. If the customer keeps his or her end of this implied agreement, the bank is under a duty to honor the check and charge the customer (or drawer's) account for whatever amount(s) the check(s) were written for.

Stale Checks — A stale check is one that has been outstanding for more than six months. Under UCC 4-404, the bank is not obligated to pay on a stale check. If the bank does pay it, it may also in good faith charge the drawer's account.

Incomplete Checks — If a drawer fails to provide information on a check, the holder may complete the information and the bank may charge the customer's account the amount of the completed amount. The exception to this is if the bank receives notice that the completion was improper.

Death or Incompetence of A Drawer — Checks may be paid against the accounts of deceased customers on or prior to the date of death for 10 days after the date of death. With regard to incompetent customers, the checks may be paid against their accounts until the bank has actual knowledge of the condition and has had a reasonable chance to act on the information given.

Stop Payment Order — This is an order by a drawer of a check to the payor bank not to pay or certify a check. It may be accomplished orally or in writing, however, if it is oral, the order is good for only fourteen days. If it is in writing, the order is good for six months, and may be renewed in writing for additional six months periods.

Overdrafts — If a customer does not have sufficient funds in his or her account to cover the amount, the payor bank may either dishonor the check or honor the check and create an overdraft in the drawer's account. In the event of a dishonor, the payor bank notifies the drawer of the dishonor and returns the check to the holder marked insufficient funds. If the holder resubmits the check and there still are insufficient funds in the customer's account, then the holder may seek recourse against the drawer.

Wrongful dishonor When the bank fails to honor a check where there are sufficient funds in the drawer's account to pay a properly payable check, it is liable for wrongful dishonor. The bank is liable to the drawer for damages that were proximately caused by the dishonor along with consequential damages and damages that may have resulted from criminal prosecution.

Forged and Altered Checks:

Forged signature of the drawer: The bank is under a duty to verify the drawer's signature by matching the signature on the check with that of the signature card on file at the bank.

Impact of a forged signature – The instrument is inoperative. The bank cannot charge the customer's account if it pays a check over a forged signature. The bank's recourse is against the party who presented the check provided he or she was not aware of the unauthorized signature. The forger is liable on the check if he or she can be found.

Altered checks: An unauthorized change in the check that modifies a legal obligation of a party is an altered check. The check may be dishonored by the bank if it discovers the alteration. If an altered check is paid by the bank, the bank may charge the drawer's account for the original tenor (amount) of the check, but not the altered amount.

The warranty of presentment applies here especially if there has been an alteration in a chain of collection. Each party in the chain may collect from the preceding transferor based on a breach of this warranty.

The Collection Process: The collection process is ruled by Article 4 of the UCC. When an individual receives a check, he or she may go to the drawer's bank or to his or her own bank (known as the **depository bank**). The depository bank must present the check to the payor bank for collection. Banks not classified as a payor or depository bank are **intermediary banks.**

The Federal Reserve System The Federal Reserve System helps banks to collect on checks. Member banks may submit paid checks to the Federal Reserve Bank for payment. Member banks pay the federal reserve to debit and credit their accounts and to show collection and payment of checks.

Deferred Posting

Deferred posting applies to all banks. This refers to a daily cutoff for posting checks or deposits. Weekends and holidays do not count as business days unless all of the banks functions are carried on as usual on those days.

Provisional Credits

"When a collecting bank gives credit to a check in the collection process prior to its final settlement. Provisional credits may be reversed if the check does not "clear."

Final Settlement

A check is deemed finally settled if the payor bank pays the check in cash, settles for the check without having the right to revoke the settlement or fails to dishonor the check within certain time periods. UCC 4-215(a)

If the drawer and holder have accounts at the same bank, then the check is called an **"on us"** item. The check is considered paid if the bank fails to dishonor the check by business on the second banking day following the receipt of the check.

If the drawer and holder have accounts at different banks, the check is an **"on them"** item. Each bank must take action prior to its **midnight deadline** following the banking day it received an "on them" check for collection. UCC 4-104(a)(10)

A deposit of money becomes available for withdrawal at the opening of the next banking day following the deposit. UCC 4-215 (a)

Four Legals that Prevent Payment of a Check

1. Receipt of notice of customer's death, bankruptcy and adjudication of incompentcy.
2. Receipt of court order freezing the customer's account.
3. Receipt of a stop payment order from the drawer.
4. The payor bank's exercise of its right of setoff against the customer's account.

Failure to Examine Bank Statements in A Timely Manner

Generally banks send monthly statements to their customers. If this does not occur, banks must provide adequate information to allow the customer to be aware of which checks were paid and when and for what amount. If the checks are not given back to the customer, then the bank must keep the checks or copies for seven years.

Customer's duty - To examine the statements promptly and with reasonable care. If an error or forgery is present, the customer must promptly notify the bank.

Liability of Collecting Banks for Their Own negligence

The collecting bank owes a duty to use ordinary care in presenting and sending a check for collection. A bank is liable only for losses caused by its own negligence. UCC 4-202

Commercial Wire Transfers

A commercial wire transfer involves the transferring of money over one or both of the two main wire systems, the Federal Reserve wire transfer network and the New York Clearing House Interbank Payments System.

Article 4A of the UCC governs wholesale wire transfers. It only applies to commercial electronic fund transfers.

Security procedures that are commercially reasonable should be established.

Refresh Your Memory

The following exercise will enable you to refresh your memory on the rules and principles presented to you in this chapter. Read each question twice and place your answer in the blanks provided. Review the chapter material for any question you miss or are unable to remember.

1. A ____________________ relationship is formed upon making a deposit into a bank.

2. What types of rules and principles does Article 4 of the UCC regulate? ________________ ____

3. Which article of the UCC establishes rules that regulate the creation and collection of and liability for wire transfers? ________________________________

4. Explain the meaning of a check. ______________________________________

5. The payee is the ____________________ and the person to whom the check is indorsed is the ____________________________.

6. The bank on which the check is drawn is the ____________________________.

7. Give three examples of bank checks. ______________________________________, ________________________________, and ________________________________.

8. When is a check considered to be certified? ________________________________
____

9. Individuals usually purchase these types of checks to use as a safe substitute for cash while on vacation or other trips. ____________________ __________________

10. Which act regulates consumer electronic fund transfers? The ______________ ________
____________________ Act

Critical Thought Exercise

Dave Austin of Austin Imports is an antique dealer who often makes purchases without sufficient funds in his account because he must often act quickly to purchase a one-of-a-kind item before another dealer can take advantage of a very profitable sale price. Austin often postdates checks for the purchases of furniture, art, rugs and other items that he resells. Austin has a very good relationship with Everglades Bank in Miami, where his main studio is located. The operations officer of Everglades Bank knows that Austin uses postdated checks for purchases approximately 50-75 times per year out of a total of 1,200 checks written on his account.

When the operations officer at Everglades Bank took a position with another bank, four postdated checks totaling $58,000 were negotiated before the written date, causing 47 other checks to be dishonored.

If Austin sues Everglades Bank to recover incidental and consequential damages for wrongful dishonor, will he prevail?

Answer. ____
____
____
____
____
____
____
____
____
____
____

Practice Quiz

True/False:

1. ___ Checks can act as a substitute for money but cannot serve as a credit function. [p 437]

2. ___ It is necessary that a traveler's check be signed a second time. [p 441]

3. ___ The bank need not pay on a stale check if it has been outstanding for more than six months. [p 442]

4. ___ Checks may be paid against the accounts of deceased customers. [p 442]

5. ___ If Joanne does not have enough money in her account when a properly presented check is presented for payment, the bank may honor the check and create an overdraft in Joanne's account. [p 444]

6. ___ Under the Forged Signature Act, a bank is required to verifiy signatures involving customers who have banked with them for more than ten years. [p 445]

7. ___ If a payor bank pays on an altered check, it can charge the drawer's account of the original tenor but not the altered amount. [p 445]

8. ___ A depository bank is the bank where the payee or holder has an account. [p 446]

9. ___ An intermediary bank is neither the depository bank and other banks in the collection process. [p 446]

10. ___ Under the deferred posting rule, banks are allowed to fix an afternoon hour as a cutoff for the purpose of processing items. [p 446]

11. ___ An "on us" item refers to the fact that both the drawer and the payee or holder have accounts at different banks. [p 447]

12. ___ Article 4A applies only to commercial electronic fund transfers. [p 450]

13. ___ Depository banks often let their customers withdraw their funds before the final settlement of account. [p 447]

14. ___ Purchasers of traveler's checks do not have an account at the issuing bank. [p 451]

15. ___ If a bank fails to pay electronic fund transfer when there are sufficient funds in the customer's account to do so, the bank will not be liable for wrongful dishonor. [p 452]

Multiple Choice:

16. In order for a bank to provide the service of paying recurring payments and crediting recurring deposits, which of the following is necessary? [p 439]
    a. The customer's bank and the payee's bank must belong to the same clearinghouse.
    b. The customer must have a computer to pay his or her bills on the Internet.
    c. The customer must qualify for a debit card at the bank that holds his or her money.
    d. None of the above.

17. Which of the following is a type of check where a bank agrees in advance to accept the check when it is presented for payment? [p 439]
    a. A point-of-sale terminal check
    b. A traveler's check

c. An automatic withdrawal check
d. A certified check

18. A stale check is one that [p 442]
a. has been left on the counter for a week.
b. has been presented for payment of a drawer's properly drawn check by the drawee bank.
c. has the risk of loss of an incomplete item on the drawer.
d. has been outstanding for more than six months.

19. What type of duty does a customer owe when determining if any payment was unauthorized due to alteration of a check or forged signature? [p 446]
a. The customer does not owe any duty whatsoever.
b. The customer owes a duty to change banks.
c. The customer owes a duty to promptly examine the statements and determine if payment was unauthorized.
d. The customer owes a duty to apprise the bank of its duty.

20. A check is finally paid when the payor bank [p 447]
a. pays the check in cash.
b. settles for the check without having a right to revoke the settlement.
c. fails to dishonor the check within certain statutory time periods.
d. all of the above.

21. What is the banking term that refers to a depositor physically presenting a check for payment at the payor bank? [p 448]
a. the four legals
b. presentment across the counter
c. on them item
d. the midnight deadline

22. What type of duty does the collecting bank owe when presenting and sending a check for collection? [p 449]
a. duty to use ordinary care
b. duty to use minimal care
c. duty to use intermediate care
d. duty to use strict care

23. In the creditor-debtor relationship involving the customer and the financial institution, who is the creditor? [p 450]
a. the financial institution
b. the Visa organization
c. the customer
d. the debtor

24. In the principal-agent relationship involving the customer and the financial institution, who is the agent? [p 450]
a. the customer
b. the principal
c. the debtor
d. the financial institution

25. Bank checks include which of the following: [p 451]
    a. certified checks
    b. traveller's checks
    c. cashier's checks
    d. all of the above

26. How long is a written stop-payment order binding for? [p 452]
    a. only fourteen days
    b. for six months and may be renewed for additional six-month periods
    c. for forty-eight hours
    d. none of the above

Short Answer:

27. Describe the bank process of certification. [p 439] ____________________

____

28. What will the bank who is obligated on a cashier's check be held liable for? [p 440]

____

29. If a check is dishonored because of insufficient funds, it is said to have ______________. [p 444]

30. A check with a forged drawer's signature is called a __________ ______________. [p 445]

31. What is meant by presentment across the counter? [p 448] ____________________

____

32. When is the process of posting considered to be complete? [p 449] ______________

____

33. If Kurt wants to write a post-dated check to Mona, what must he do to accomplish this under the rules of UCC 4-401(c)? [p 443] ______________________________

____

34. Wanda, a customer of Mississippi Bank and Trust passes away on January 1. What is the rule regarding the length of time that her bank may pay or certify checks drawn on her account? [p 443] ____

35. The amount of money a drawer owes a bank after it has paid a check despite insufficient funds in the drawer's account is known as an ________________________. [p 444]

36. An order by a drawer of a check to the payor bank to not pay or certify a check is a ______________________________________. [p 443]

Chapter 22
CREDIT, SECURED TRANSACTIONS, AND SURETY AGREEMENTS

Chapter Overview

This chapter examines the rights of creditors and debtors under federal and state consumer protection laws. In this chapter, you will explore the repercussions of noncompliance with the recording statutes, as well as the foreclosure process in real estate. Further, you will learn about deficiency judgments, lender liability and the difference between a surety and a guaranty arrangement. Finally, this chapter gives a good explanation of attachment, garnishment and execution as well as the difference between a composition agreement and an assignment for the benefit of creditors.

Objectives

Upon completion of the exercises in this chapter, you should be able to:

1. Explain unsecured credit verses secured credit.
2. Discuss mortgages and deeds of trust.
3. Explain the repercussions of noncompliance with recording statutes.
4. Explain what a deficiency judgment is and discuss the effects of an antidifficiency statute.
5. Discuss a secured transaction in personal property and the scope of Article 9 of the UCC.
6. Discuss lender liability.
7. Explain material person's liens.
8. Discuss the difference between a surety and guaranty arrangement.

Practical Application

This chapter will provide you with greater insight about the various types of credit along with security interests in real and personal property. Further, you will gain a better understanding of the available remedies associated with personal property transactions. Also, you will have a broader base of knowledge concerning surety and guaranty arrangements as well as remedies associated with the collection of debts.

Helpful Hints

Many items are purchased on credit. The best way to approach this chapter is by differentiating between the main terms such as secured verses unsecured credit, real verses personal property, and surety arrangement verses a guaranty arrangement. Once you have a grasp of these main terms, the remedies that are available become easier to understand and learn. The exercises that follow, as well as the critical thinking exercises located at the end of the chapter in your main text, are very helpful in solidifying the concepts you should be familiar with.

Study Tips

Basic vocabulary

Debtor – The borrower in a credit transaction.
Creditor – The lender in a credit transaction.

Types of credit:
Unsecured – Credit that does not need any collateral to protect the debt.
Secured – Credit that does need collateral to secure the payment of the loan.

Deficiency judgment – When a debtor has insufficient collateral to cover the debt, the court will issue an order allowing the creditor to recover other property or income from the defaulting debtor.

Personal property – This involves tangible property such as furniture, automobiles, and jewelry, and intangible property such as intellectual property, and securities.

Vocabulary relating to Real Property

Mortgage – A property owner borrows money from a creditor who thereafter uses a deed as a means of security (collateral) to secure the repayment of the loan.

Mortgagor – This is the owner-debtor in a mortgage transaction.

Mortgagee – This is the creditor in a transaction involving a mortgage.

Note- A legal instrument that is proof of the borrower's debt to the lender.
Deed of Trust – A legal instrument that evinces the creditor's security interest in the debtor's property that is pledged as collateral.

Land Sales Contract – The transfer and sale of real property in accordance with a land sales contract whereby the owner of the real property agrees to sell the property to a buyer, who assents to pay the asking price to the owner-seller over a stated, agreed period of time. The loan is termed as ***"carrying the paper."*** If the purchaser defaults, the seller may claim a forfeiture and retake possession of the property. The right of redemption is allowed in many states.

Recording Statute – Law that requires the mortgage or deed of trust to be recorded in the county recorder's office of the county where the real property is located.

Material Person's Lien – When an individual provides contracting or a service toward improvement of real property, their investments are protected by statutory law that allow them to file a material person's lien (also referred to as a mechanic's lien) against the improved real property.

Vocabulary relating to Third Person Liability on a Debt

Surety arrangement – A situation where a third party promises to be primarily liable with the borrower for the payment of the borrower's debt.

Surety- This is the third person who agrees to be liable in a surety arrangement and in essence acts as a co-debtor and is often called an accommodation party or a co-signer.

Guaranty arrangement – A situation where a third party promises to be secondarily liable for the payment of another's debt.

Guarantor – This is the third person who agrees to be liable in a guaranty arrangement.

Defenses of a Surety or Guarantor

A surety or guarantor may utilize the same defenses as the principal debtor against the creditor. Possible defenses include fraudulent inducement to enter into the guaranty agreement or surety, duress and the guarantor's or surety's own bankruptcy or incapacity.

Remedies

Foreclosure – A legal procedure whereby the mortgagee can declare the entire debt due and payable if a debtor defaults on his or her loan.

Deficiency judgments – As stated above, some states allow a mortgagee to bring a separate legal action to recover a deficiency from the mortgagor.

Antideficiency statute – Many states prohibit deficiency judgments on mortgages, especially those involving residential property.

Right of Redemption – Many state laws follow the common law, which gives the mortgagor the right to redeem his or her real property after default and before foreclosure. The mortgagor must pay the entire debt including principal, interest, and other costs bore by the mortgagee as a result of the mortgagor's default. The mortgagor will obtain title free and clear upon redeeming the property. ***Note,*** a majority of states allow any party holding an interest in the property may redeem the property during the redemption period.

Collection Remedies

Attachment – This remedy involves a prejudgment order allowing the seizure of the debtor's property while the lawsuit is pending.

Execution – This remedy concerns a postjudgment court order allowing seizure of the debtor's property that is in possession of the debtor.

Garnishment – This is also a postjudgment court order. However it allows the seizure of the debtor's property that is in the possession of third parties.

Title III of the Consumer Credit Protection Act - This law protects debtors who are subject to a writ of garnishment to keep the greater of seventy-five percent of their weekly disposable earnings (after taxes) or an amount equivalent to thirty hours of work paid at federal minimum wage.

Refresh Your Memory

The following exercise will enable you to refresh your memory on the rules and principles presented to you in this chapter. Read each question twice and place your answer in the blanks provided. Review the chapter material for any question you miss or are unable to remember.

1. What are the two basis from which credit may be extended? ________________ and ____________________

2. If Bob is not required to have any security to protect the payment of a debt to Fine Lamps, Inc., then it may be said that Bob has ____________________________________ credit.

3. When a creditor brings a lawsuit against a debtor to recover on a loan what the collateral cannot satisfy, the lawsuit is for recovery of a _________________ _________________.

4. Give at least two examples of personal property that are tangible and two examples that are intangible. ___________________, ___________________, ___________________, and ____________________.

5. What is an artisan's or mechanic's lien? ____

6. What is a mortgage? ____

7. Carrie signs a piece of paper that indicates her debt to United Bank. What is this piece of paper called? It is called a ___________________________________.

8. What is a legal instrument that gives a creditor a security interest in the debtor's property that is pledged as collateral called? It is called a _______________ of _____________.

9. What requires the mortgage or deed of trust to be documented in a county office where real property is located? ____________________ ____________________

10. Edna fails to pay her monthly mortgage payment on the ranch she is purchasing from California Savings and Loan. What legal procedure may California Savings and Loan bring against Edna? ____

Critical Thought Exercise

Steve and Bonnie West purchased an old Victorian home outside St. Louis and planned on renovating it and selling it for a profit before moving onto another renovation project. Bonnie's brother, Doug Nixon did most of the major work on the house and hired trades people to assist in areas that are beyond his expertise. Nixon hired Summit Roofing to replace the old shake roof with a fire resistant composite product that matched the house in color and style. The cost of the new roof is $17,400, including all labor and materials. Steve and Bonnie pay Doug $86,500 for the entire project. Doug failed to pay Summit Roofing and absconded with all the funds.

Steve and Bonnie West entered into a real estate purchase agreement with Lucy Rogers to purchase the home for $515,000. The contract between West and Rogers states that the property is free of all encumbrances and escrow will close in 30 days.

Summit Roofing filed a mechanics lean against the property. The West's demanded that Summit Roofing seek payment from Doug Nixon. Summit Roofing gave notice that it was going to foreclose against the property to recover the $17,400 owed to it.

What action should Steve and Bonnie West take to ensure that the sale to Rogers will not be thwarted?

Answer. ____

Practice Quiz

True/False:

1. ___ A mechanic's lien becomes the security for the payment of improvements. [p 463]

2. ___ The right of redemption prohibits the mortgagor from paying the full amount of the debt which includes principle, interest and other costs. [p 462]

3. ___ A deed of trust gives the creditor a security interest in the owner-debtor's real property. [p 476]

4. ___ A surety arrangement involves a third person who agrees to be liable in a guaranty arrangement. [p 473]

5. ___ A surety is a third person who does not agree to be liable in a surety arrangement. [p 473]

6. ___ In a guaranty arrangement, the debtor is secondarily liable for the debt of the debtor. [p 474]

7. ___ Samson purchases a riding lawnmower on credit and Gloria acts as the surety for the debt. Thereafter, both Samson and Gloria discover that the gearshift is defective. Both Samson and Gloria may assert the defect as a defense to liability. [p 474]

8. ___ An attachment is a prejudgment order permitting seizure of the debtor's property while litigation is still pending. [p 474]

9. ___ Automobiles, furniture and jewelry are examples of real property. [p 464]

10. ___ Real estate owners can create security interests in their property. [p 460]

11. ___ In some states a deed of trust may be used in place of a mortgage. [p 461]

12. ___ Under a power of sale, the procedure need not be contained in the mortgage or deed of trust. [p 462]

13. ___ Several states provide a statutory procedure that must be adhered to foreclose on a land sales contract. [p 462]

14. ___ Felix, a contractor files a mechanics' lien against Virginia for laying brick around Virginia's home. Felix may use the improvements as security for payment on the services and materials. [p 463]

15. ___ The general time frame to foreclose on a lien is anywhere from six months to two years from the date that the lien is filed. [p 463]

Multiple Choice:

16. A person's ownership interest in real property is usually detailed in writing in [p 461]
    a. a foreclosure.
    b. a deed.
    c. a lien.
    d. a letter.

17. An improperly recorded mortgage or deed of trust is not effective against [p 461]
    a. debtors.
    b. subsequent purchasers of real property.
    c. mortgagor.
    d. the original mortgagee.

18. The benefits of a statutory procedure of foreclosing on a land sale contract include [p 462]
    a. the fact that it is a simpler way to foreclose.
    b. the fact that it is less time consuming.
    c. the fact that it is less expensive than foreclosure on a mortgage or deed of trust.
    d. all of the above.

19. A writ of attachment is [p 475]
    a. a court order that states that the debtor must pay the creditor an amount equal to 30 hours of work paid at federal minimum wage.
    b. a court order that directs the sheriff to seize the debtor's property and authorizes a judicial sale of the property.
    c. a prejudgment order allowing seizure of the debtor's property while litigation is pending.
    d. a court order stating that property such as tools of the trade, homestead exemption and clothing are exempt from being levied upon.

20. The Consumer Credit Protection Act provides that debtors may [p 475]
    a. have their wages garnished up to 75 percent of their weekly disposable earnings after taxes.
    b. have their wages garnished up to 30 hours of work paid at federal minimum wage.
    c. retain up to 75 percent of their weekly disposable earnings or an amount equal to 30 hours of work paid at federal minimum wage, which ever is greater of the two.
    d. protect debtors from the garnishment of any wages whatsoever.

21. What type of procedure allows a mortgagee to declare an entire property based debt to be due and payable immediately? [p 462]
    a. deficiency judgment procedure
    b. foreclosure
    c. right of redemption
    d. all of the above

22. In a secured transaction, who is the secured party? [p 463]
    a. the debtor
    b. the redeemer
    c. the seller or lender
    d. none of the above

23. Article 9 of the UCC does not apply to which of the following transactions? [p 464]
    a. real estate mortgages
    b. artisan's liens
    c. judicial liens
    d. all of the above

24. What is meant by after-acquired property? [p 466]
    a. property that the debtor acquires after the security agreement is executed
    b. property that the debtor acquires before the security agreement is executed
    c. property that the debtor acquires during the security agreement
    d. none of the above

25. What is the most common method of perfecting a creditor's security interest in a debtor's collateral? [p 467]
    a. by filing a writ of attachment
    b. by filing a lawsuit
    c. by filing a perfection of attachment
    d. by filing a financing statement

Short Answer:

26. What purpose does collateral have? [p 460] ____

____

27. What legal option is available to a mortgagor who has defaulted on a loan but has not yet been foreclosed upon? [p 462] ____

____

28. What types of real property interests are sold using a land sale contract? [p 469] ________

____

29. What must a creditor do in order to obtain a writ of attachment? [p 475] ____________

____

30. In a writ of execution, who are the proceeds from the debtor's property used for? [p 479]

____

____

31. What is involved with a foreclosure by power of sale? [p 462] ____________________

____

32. A surety is called an accommodation party or a ________________________. [p 473]

33. Explain what role a guarantor plays with regard to a debtor's debt. [p 474] ___________

____

34. Explain a deficiency judgment. [p 472] ____

____

35. The defenses that the principal debtor has against the creditor may also be asserted by a ____. [p 474]

Chapter 23
BANKRUPTCY AND REORGANIZATION

Chapter Overview

This chapter explores Chapter 7 liquidation bankruptcy as well as Chapter 13 consumer debt adjustment bankruptcy and Chapter 11 business reorganization bankruptcy. Individual debtors as well as businesses often find that they are unable to be responsible for the debts that they have incurred, and as such must rely on the federal bankruptcy laws to free them from their obligations for past debts. You will become more familiar with the procedure involved in filing for bankruptcy as well as creditors' rights, the order of priority for paying creditors, the meaning of an automatic stay in bankruptcy, and voidable transfers and preferential payments.

Objectives

Upon completion of the exercises contained in this chapter, you should be able to:

1. Discuss the procedure for filing for bankruptcy.
2. Explain what is involved in a Chapter 7 liquidation bankruptcy.
4. Explain the meaning of an automatic stay in bankruptcy.
5. Explain business reorganization as it pertains to a Chapter 11 bankruptcy.
6. Discuss a Chapter 13 consumer debt adjustment bankruptcy.

Practical Application

You should be able to better understand the main purpose of bankruptcy law as well as be familiar with the different types of bankruptcies. Additionally, you will have a clearer understanding of the impact of bankruptcy as well as which creditors take priority with regard to payment of the same.

Helpful Hints

The concepts in this chapter are easier to learn if you keep it simple by learning each of the three types of bankruptcies separately. The study tips section that follows gives you background information, procedures and little nuances that may be important to know for each kind of bankruptcy. As you will notice, under each type of bankruptcy has main points that you should become familiar. The most important terms are boldly printed.

Study Tips

Two Important Facets of Bankruptcy Law:

There are two preliminary aspects of bankruptcy that you should keep in mind. The first is that the law of bankruptcy is federally governed. Secondly, the main purpose of bankruptcy is to free the debtor from cumbersome debts.

Chapter 7 Liquidation Bankruptcy

This is the most common type of bankruptcy and is also referred to as a ***straight bankruptcy***. The debtor's nonexempt property is sold to obtain case and then the money is distributed to the debtor's creditors. Debts that are not paid are then discharged.

The procedure to file and maintain a Chapter 7 bankruptcy includes the ***filing of a petition*** by either the debtor (a voluntary petition) or by one or more creditors (an involuntary petition). When a voluntary or involuntary petition is filed, this is known as an ***order for relief***. After the order for relief, the court must call a ***meeting of the creditors*** wherein the debtor is questioned by his or her creditors without a judge being present. At this meeting, a ***permanent trustee*** is elected to be the legal representative of the debtor's estate. The trustee has many duties which include but are not limited to setting aside exempt property, looking into the debtor's finances, investigating the proof of claims and making reports to the debtor, his or her creditor's and the court concerning the estate's administration.

An ***automatic stay*** goes into effect upon the filing of an involuntary or voluntary petition. The effect of an automatic stay is that it suspends creditors' actions against the debtor or the debtor's property. It should also be noted that a debtor may have an injunction issued against its creditors for activity that is not covered in the automatic stay. However, a creditor does have some recourse against a bankrupt debtor. The secured creditor may seek a ***relief from stay*** in cases where the property is depreciating.

The bankruptcy ***estate*** involves all of the debtor's legal and equitable interests in all types of property, including community property from the onset of a Chapter 7 bankruptcy proceeding. If the debtor obtains property after he or she files his or her petition, this property usually is not considered to be part of the estate. However, there are certain exceptions, which include but are not limited to inheritance, divorce settlements, and the like if obtained within 180 days of the filing of the petition.

Exempt property may be kept by the debtor. The Federal exemptions are given on p.549 of your main text. Some state laws also provide for exemptions which are broad in scope. Some states require that the debtor choose between federal or state exemptions or adhere to the state laws.

Distribution of nonexempt property has to be distributed to the debtor's unsecured and secured creditors. The secured creditors take priority over the unsecured creditors. After the property has been distributed to satisfy the claims that are allowed, then the debtor is no longer responsible for the remaining unpaid claims. Only individuals may be given a ***discharge.***

Nondischargeable debts are those that are not dischargeable in bankruptcy. Some examples are alimony, child support and certain fines payable to federal, local and state authorities. Other examples may be found on page 554 of your main text.

Chapter 11 Reorganization Bankruptcy

Under this type of bankruptcy, the court assists the debtor in reorganizing his or her financial affairs. Individuals, corporations, nonincorporated associations, railroads and partnerships are able to utilize this type of bankruptcy. Corporations use Chapter 11 bankruptcies the most.

A unique feature about this type of bankruptcy is that the debtor is left to run his or her business while the reorganization proceeding is taking place. The debtor is referred to as a ***debtor-in-possession.*** The debtor-in-possession has the authority to enter into contracts and operate the business accordingly.

The debtor has a right to file a ***plan of reorganization*** within 120 days of the ***order for relief***. The reorganization plan describes the debtor's proposed new capital structure that indicates the different classes of claims and interests. The creditors and equity holders must be given a court approved ***disclosure statement.***

The court must ***confirm*** the debtor's plan for reorganization in order for it to become effective. Confirmation may be accomplished by giving the different classes of creditors the chance to accept or reject the plan. The court looks at whether the plan is in the best interests of each class of claims, if the plan is feasible, if at least one class has accepted the plan and whether or not each class of claims and interests is nonimpaired. Confirmation may also be achieved using the ***cram down method.*** Under this method, the plan has to be fair and equitable to the impaired class. Remember, the impaired class can be forced to take part in the plan of reorganization.

The debtor is given a ***discharge*** of all claims that were not a part of the plan of reorganization.

Chapter 13 Consumer Debt Adjustment

Under this plan, the court may oversee the debtor's plan for installment payments of his or her unpaid debts. Chapter 13 is beneficial to both the debtor as well as creditor. The debtor's costs are less under this type of proceeding as well as the fact that he or she may keep more property than is exempt under Chapter 7. The creditors are able to elicit a greater amount of the debts that are owing to them.

The debtor must file a ***petition*** claiming that he or she is insolvent or not able to pay his or her debts when they are due. A debtor may ask for more time (an ***extension***) to pay his or her debts or ask for a ***composition*** which reduces his or her debts. Subsequent to the filing of the petition, the debtor has to give the court a ***list*** of his or her creditors, liabilities and assets. Then there is a ***meeting of creditors*** where the debtor must be present. A ***trustee*** is then ***appointed*** to confirm the plan.

As with a Chapter 7 filing, once a debtor files a petition under Chapter 13, an ***automatic stay*** is in place regarding liquidation bankruptcy proceedings, creditors' judicial and nonjudicial actions and creditors' collection activities. The automatic stay is not applicable concerning business debts.

The debtor must file a ***plan of payment*** within 15 days of filing his or her petition. The plan may not go beyond three years, however, the court may grant a five-year period plan. The debtor must make payments within 30 days of filing his or her plan. If a debtor's circumstances change, then his or her plan may be ***modified.***

As with a Chapter 11 bankruptcy, the plan must also be ***confirmed*** under a Chapter 13 bankruptcy.

When the debtor has made all payments under the plan, the court will ***discharge*** the debtor from all unpaid debts. Most debts are dischargeable except for such things as child support, alimony and trustee fees. The court will grant a ***hardship discharge*** if there are unforeseeable circumstances, or the unsecured creditors have been given an amount equal to what they would have received under a Chapter 7 liquidation proceeding or it is not feasible to modify the plan.

Refresh Your Memory

The following exercise will enable you to refresh your memory on the rules and principles presented to you in this chapter. Read each question twice and place your answer in the blanks provided. Review the chapter material for any question you miss or are unable to remember.

1. Give examples of noncore proceedings involving the debtor.______________________
____

2. Since federal bankruptcy law discharges the debtor from cumbersome debts, it is in essence giving the debtor a _____________ _______________ by relieving them from legal responsibility for past debts.

3. Which type of bankruptcy is referred to as a straight bankruptcy? __________________
____

4. Once a debtor's nonexempt property is sold for cash, the money is given to the creditors, and any unpaid debts are ____________________________.

5. The debtor begins a Chapter 7 bankruptcy by filing a ____________________.

6. What type of petition is filed by the debtor's creditors that states that the debtor is not paying his or her debts as they become due? ________________________________
____.

7. What does the filing of a voluntary petition or an unchallenged involuntary petition designate? ____

8. After an order for relief is granted, then the court calls a ___________________________
____.

9. When is a permanent trustee elected? _________________________________

10. What must unsecured creditors file that states the amount of their claims against the debtor?
____

Critical Thought Exercise

Nancy Mills attended two different institutions of higher learning. She received educational loans totaling $22, 480. After graduation, Mills was employed, but her monthly take-home pay was less than 1200. The monthly expenses for herself and her four children were approximately $1650. Mill's husband had abandoned the family and provided no financial support. Mills received no public assistance and had no possibility to increase her income. A neighbor paid her telephone, water, and gas bills for the two months prior to filing a petition in bankruptcy. Mills also had substantial medical bills and had not been well for months. In her bankruptcy petition, Mills sought to discharge her educational loans.

Are the educational loans owed by Mills dischargeable in bankruptcy? Why was the Bankruptcy Code amended to generally prohibit the discharge of student loans?

Answer. ____

____

____

____

____

____

____

____

____

____

____

____

____

____

Practice Quiz

True/False:

1. ___ Federal bankruptcy law serves the main purpose of obligating the debtor to make good on his or her debts. [p 485]

2. ___ There is a set time frame for filing a proof of claim in a Chapter 7 bankruptcy. [p 487]

3. ___ There is a bankruptcy estate upon the commencement of a Chapter 7 proceeding. [p 487]

4. ___ Property obtained after filing a Chapter 7 petition does not become part of the bankruptcy estate. [p 487]

5. ___ Dividends, rents and interest payments are not considered property of the bankruptcy estate. [p 487]

6. ___ States that have Homestead Declarations as an exemption require that the debtor file this document after the bankruptcy. [p 488]

7. ___ A debtor's use of a preferential lien is a way of demonstrating a debtor's favoritism toward certain unsecured creditors. [p 490]

8. ___ The court may not void preferential liens that are made to relatives, partners, partnerships, officers and directors of corporations or anyone else with a relationship to the debtor. [p 490]

9. ___ The Bankruptcy Code allows the court to void fraudulent transfers of property if the transfers occurred within one year of the filing of the petition in bankruptcy. [p 489]

10. ___ Once the property is distributed to satisfy any allowed claims, any existing unpaid claims will not be discharged and the debtor is still responsible for them. [p 493]

11. ___ Wilson files for a Chapter 7 bankruptcy and has several unsecured creditors, with the Handy Dandy Tool Co. being one of them. Wilson owes Handy Dandy $1,500, but his Bankruptcy estate has only enough to pay all of his unsecured creditors .05 on the dollar. Handy Dandy will receive $75.00 from Wilson's estate and may thereafter collect the unpaid balance from Wilson in a separate lawsuit. [p 493]

12. ___ A creditor such as one who is owed alimony may not participate in the distribution of the bankruptcy estate. [p 492]

13. ___ A party who has no interest may file an objection to the discharge of a debt. [p 494]

14. ___ A bankruptcy may be revoked if the discharge is obtained through the fraud of the debtor. [p 494]

15. ___ Creditors may involuntarily file a Chapter 11 petition or the debtor may voluntarily file the petition him/herself. [p 493]

Multiple Choice:

16. A voluntary petition for bankruptcy must include which of the following? [p 486]
    a. A list of secured and unsecured creditors
    b. A list of the property owned by the debtor, including exempt property
    c. A statement of the debtor's financial affairs as well as the debtor's income and expenses
    d. All of the above.

17. A permanent trustee is [p 486]
    a. required to set aside exempt property.
    b. required to separate secured and unsecured property.
    c. required to take immediate possession of the debtor's property.
    d. elected at the first meeting of the creditors

18. If a debtor's equity in property exceeds the exemption limits, a trustee may [p 491]

a. liquidate the property to realize the excess value for the bankruptcy estate.
b. sell the home and not distribute the excess to the debtor's creditors.
c. require the debtor to file a declaration of Homestead after the bankruptcy.
d. none of the above.

19. Since a secured creditor's claim takes priority over unsecured creditor's claims, what may the secured creditor do with regard to the debt that is owed? [p 491]
a. Foreclose on the collateral and use the proceeds to satisfy the debt.
b. Allow the trustee to keep the collateral, dispose of it at a sale and give the proceeds to him or her.
c. Accept the collateral in full satisfaction of the debt.
d. All of the above.

20. Once a plan of reorganization is confirmed, the debtor is [p 498]
a. granted a discharge of all claims not included in the plan.
b. not granted a discharge of all claims not included in the plan.
c. not considered bankrupt.
d. free to incur more debt using his or her same creditors.

21. Which of the following tests are included in the acceptance method with regard to a Chapter 11 bankruptcy? [p 497]
a. The plan must be in the best interests of each class of claims and interests.
b. The plan must be feasible in terms of the debtor surviving as an ongoing concern.
c. At least each class of claims must vote to accept the plan.
d. all of the above.

22. A Chapter 13 petition for bankruptcy is also referred to as what? [p 498]
a. a corporation's easy way out
b. The Debtor's Reform Act
c. consumer debt adjustment
d. the discharge of all claims

23. What is an advantage of filing under Chapter 13? [p 499]
a. It avoids the stigma of Chapter 7 liquidation.
b. It is less expensive than a Chapter 7 proceeding.
c. More property may be retained than is exempt under Chapter 7
d. All of the above

24. When filing a Chapter 13 petition, what is meant when the debtor states that he or she desires a composition? [p 499]
a. It means that the debtor wants a longer period of time for him or her to pay whatever debts are owed.
b. It means that that the debtor wants a provision for a reduction of debts.
c. It means that the debtor wants to provide an explanation via a writing so that the court will exonerate him or her from any and all debts.
d. None of the above.

25. What is meant by the term hardship discharge? [p 501]
a. A discharge given to the debtor even if he or she does not complete the payments called for in the plan.
b. A discharge given to "family farmers."

c. A discharge granted for foreseeable circumstances that were the fault of the debtor.
d. A discharge from all paid debts that weren't covered by the plan.

Short Answer:

26. Allowing creditor claims and confirming plans of reorganization are examples of ________ ____ that bankruptcy judges decide. [p 484]

27. Personal injury, divorce and other civil proceedings that are resolved in federal or state court are considered to be ____. [p 484]

28. The term, "a fresh start" refers to what in terms of the debtor. [p.485]
____
____

29. Give the most familiar type of bankruptcy? [p 485] ____________________

30. What does Chapter 7 Bankruptcy involve? [p 485] ____________________
____

31. Describe what a petition is, as it applies to bankruptcy? [p 486]
____
____

32. How many creditors must sign the petition if a debtor has more than 12 creditors? [p 486]
____

33. Which bankruptcy meeting is the judge prohibited from attending? [p 486]
____

34. What may a secured creditor whose claims exceed the value of the debtor's collateral do? [p 487] ____

35. List three examples of property that is exempt from bankruptcy. [p 488] ____________
____

Chapter 24
AGENCY

Chapter Overview

This chapter will provide you with a thorough understanding of agency including the important role that it plays in the business world, as well as the creation and termination of the same. Additionally you will become familiar with the three most common types of employment relationships and how to differentiate between them.

Objectives

Upon completion of the exercises contained in this chapter, you should be able to:

1. Discuss what an agency is.
2. Recognize and define a principal-independent contractor relationship.
3. Discuss a principal's liability for the actions of independent contractors.
4. Discuss the creation of an express agency verses and implied agency.
5. Discuss the duties that the principal owes to the agent and the agent owes to the principal.
6. Discuss the various ways an agency may be terminated by the acts of the parties.
7. Discuss how an agency is terminated by operation of law.
8. Discuss who should be notified upon the termination of an agency.

Practical Application

You will learn how the different types of agencies are created as well as terminated. You will also be able to recognize an irrevocable agency and whether or not there has been a wrongful termination of an agency contract. Further, you will know the difference between the three main types of employment relationships and the liabilities associated with each. This chapter will be especially useful to anyone in business, because agencies are an essential part of any successful business.

Helpful Hints

Since most of us have been or will be in some sort of employment relationship in our lifetime, this chapter is very easy to apply to either our past employment experiences or our future endeavors. Many of us have been agents and have not realized that fact. You will find this chapter easier to learn if you place yourself in the shoes of the situation you are trying to learn about. Additionally, if you familiarize yourself with the basic terminology given in the Study Tips section that follows, the concepts will become easier and clearer for you to understand.

Study Tips

Basic Terminology

Agency: Section 1(1) of the Restatement Second of Agency defines agency as "a fiduciary relationship which results from the manifestation of consent by one person to another that the other shall act in his behalf and subject to his control, and consent by the other so to act."

Principal – A party who employs another individual to act on his or her behalf.

Agent – A party who agrees to act on behalf of another.

Employer-employee relationship – An association that results when an employer hires an employee to perform some type of physical service.

Principal-agent relationship – A relationship whereby an employee is hired and given the authority to act and enter into contracts on the employer's behalf.

Independent contractor – A person or business who is not an employee but who is hired by a principal to perform a certain task on his behalf. This person is not controlled by the principal with regard to the performance of the task that he or she is employed to do.

At-will employee – An employee without an employment contract.

Express Agency – An express agreement between a principal and agent thereby agreeing to enter into an agency agreement with one another.

Exclusive agency contract – A distinct contract between the principal and agent whereby the principal agrees not to employ any agent other than the exclusive agent.

Power of Attorney – An agency agreement that expressly gives an agent the authority to sign legal documents on the principal's behalf. The agent in this situation is referred to as an Attorney-in-fact.

Implied Agency- An agency that is inferred from the parties' conduct and where there has not been an express creation of an agency between the principal and the agent.

Apparent Agency – An agency that the principal creates that appears to exist but really does not exist.

Agency by Ratification – An agency that is created by a principal ratifying an agency that is created by an unauthorized act such as the misrepresentation of oneself as another's agent when in fact he or she is not an agent at all.

Wrongful Termination – A violation of the terms of the agency contract thereby resulting in the termination of the agency contract.
Revocation of Authority – The termination of an agency contract by a principal.

Renunciation of Authority – The termination of an agency contract by an agent.

Strategic Alliance – An agreement between two or more businesses from different countries to accomplish a certain purpose or function.

Agency Basics

Capacity – If an individual has the capacity to enter into a contract, then he or she can appoint an agent to act on his or her behalf.

Purpose – The agency must be formed for a lawful purpose.

Three types of employment relationships:

- Employer-Employee Relationship – Where an employer hires an employee to perform some sort of physical service.

- Principal-Agent Relationship– Where an employer hires an employee and gives the employee power to act and enter into contracts on his or her behalf.

- Principal-Independent Contractor Relationship– Persons and businesses who are hired to perform certain tasks on behalf of the principal. The ***degree of control*** that an employer has over an agent is the determining factor on whether one is an employee or an independent contractor. Other considerations include but are not limited to: ***The duration of the agent's employment by the principal, the degree of skill required to complete the task, whether the principal provides the equipment and tools needed in the work, etc.***

Agency Formation

There are four ways that an agency may be formed. They are expressly, impliedly, apparently and by ratification.

- **Express Agency** – This is the most common type of agency wherein an agent and a principal expressly agree to enter into an agency agreement with one another. It may be oral or in writing. An example of an express agency is a ***power of attorney.*** The power of attorney may be ***general*** thereby giving broad powers to the agent to act in any matters on the principal's behalf or it may be ***special*** giving limited powers as provided for in the parties' agreement. ***Incidental authority*** is implied authority to act in emergency situations and other contingent circumstances in order to protect the principal's property and rights.

- **Implied Agency** – An agency that is created by the parties' conduct. The implied authority of the agent may be given by custom in the industry, the agent's position or the prior dealing between the parties. There cannot be a conflict between the express and implied authority.

- **Apparent Agency** – An agency by estoppel (or apparent agency) is created when a principal gives the appearance of an agency that in reality does not exist. Upon creation of this type of agency, the principal is bound to contract entered into by the apparent agent while acting within the parameters of the apparent agency.

- **Agency by Ratification** – An agency that is a result of a principal ratifying an unauthorized act by another who represents him or herself as another's agent when the reality is that he or she is not the principal's agent.

The Agent's Duties

The agent's duties are presented in the parties' agency agreement or implied by law.
An easy mnemonic to remember the agent's duties is: L̲oyal P̲ercy's A̲ccounting is N̲oteworthy.

L̲oyalty – The agent owes a duty to be faithful to the principal. The following are examples of breaches of loyalty:

- An agent is prohibited from **undisclosed self-dealing** with the principal.
- An agent may not **usurp an opportunity** that belongs to the principal unless upon consideration the principal has rejected it.
- An agent may **not compete** with the principal during the agency relationship.
- An agent may not **misuse confidential information** regarding the principal' affairs.
- An agent may not act for two or more different principals in the same transaction as this is a **dual agency**. The parties may agree to it though.

P̲erformance – The agent owes a **duty to perform** the lawful duties stated in the parties' contract. Additionally the agent must meet the standard of reasonable care, skill and diligence that is implied in all contracts.

Beware, an agent that presents himself or herself as having higher than average skills will be held to a higher standard of performance. For example, a physician who contends that he or she is a plastic surgeon specialist will be held to a reasonable specialist in plastic surgery standard.

A̲ccountability – The agent owes a **duty to keep an accurate accounting** of all transactions performed on behalf of the principal. This means that the agent must keep records of all money that has been spent and all money that has been received during the duration of the agency.

The principal's separate account must be maintained by the agent and the principal's property must be used in an authorized manner.

N̲otification – The agent owes a **duty of notification** to the principal if the agent learns information that is important to the principal. It is assumed that the principal knows most information that the agent knows. This is called **imputed knowledge.**

The Principal's Duties

The principal's duties may also be stated in the parties' contract or implied by law.
An easy mnemonic to remember the principal's duties is: C̲onnie **R̲**emembers the **I̲n̲**dian C̲oin.

Compensation – The principal owes a **duty to compensate** an agent for the services he or she has provided. If the compensation is not stated in the parties' agreement, then compensation will be based on custom or what is the reasonable value for the agent's services.

Reimbursement – The principal owes a **duty to reimburse** the agent for all expenses the agent has expended from his or her own money if the expenses were authorized and within the scope of the agency and necessary to discharge the agent's duties in carrying out the agency.

Indemnification – The principal owes a **duty to indemnify** the agent for any losses that the agent may suffer due to the principal's misconduct.

Cooperation – The principal owes a **duty to cooperate** with and help the agent in the performance of the agent's duties and the goal of the agency.

Contract Liability to Third Parties

Basic Information: If an agent is authorized by the principal to enter into a contract with a third party, then the principal is liable on the contract. In order to determine liability, the classification of the agency must be examined.

Agency Classifications: There are three types of agency classifications. They are the fully disclosed agency, the partially disclosed agency and the undisclosed agency.

- **Fully Disclosed** – The third party knows who the agent is acting on behalf of. The principal is liable in a fully disclosed agency situation. However, the agent will also be held liable if he or she guarantees that the principal will perform the contract.

- **Partially Disclosed** – The agent's status is disclosed but the principal's identity is undisclosed. Both the principal and agent are liable on a third-party contract. If the agent is made to pay, he or she may seek indemnification from the principal.

- **Undisclosed** – If a third party does not know about the agency or the principal's identity, then an undisclosed agency exists. The principal as well as the agent are liable on a contract with a third party as the agent's nondisclosure makes him a principal to the contract. However, the agent may seek indemnification from the principal if he or she is made to pay on the contract.

Agent Exceeding the Scope of Authority

- An agent who enters into a contract with a third party has in essence warranted that he or she has the authority to do so. However, the principal will not be liable on the contract where the agent has exceeded his or her authority on the contract unless the principal **ratifies** the contract.

Tort Liability to Third Parties

The principal and agent are personally responsible for their own tortious conduct. However, the principal is liable for the agent's conduct if he or she was acting within the scope of his or her authority. The agent though is only liable for the torts of the principal if he or she directly or indirectly participates in or abets and aids the conduct of the principal. The factors that are examined in determining whether an agent's conduct was within the scope of his or her employment include:

- Did the principal request or authorize the agent's act?
- Was the principal's purpose being advanced by the agent when the act occurred?
- Was the agent employed to perform the act that he or she completed?
- Was the act accomplished during the time that the time of employment authorized by the principal.

Misrepresentation

- As you may recall, this tort is also referred to as **fraud** or **deceit**.
- The principal is liable for the misrepresentation of the agent if it is made during the scope of his or her employment.
- The third party may rescind the contract with the principal and recover any consideration paid or affirm the contract and recover damages.

Negligence

Liability for negligence is based on the doctrine of **respondeat superior** which assesses liability based on the employment relationship between the princiapal and agent not on any fault of the principal. However there are some situations where liability is not clear.

- **Frolic and Detour** – This refers to the situation where an agent performs a personal errand while performing a job for the principal. Negligent acts in this situation are viewed on a case-by-case basis. The court will examine if the detour is minor or substantial.

- **The Coming and Going Rule** – Under common law, a principal is not held liable for injuries caused by employees and agents who are on their way to or from work. This rule holds true regardless if the principal provided the transportation.

- **Dual-Purpose Mission** – This situation refers to when the agent is doing something for him or herself and for the principal. The majority rule holds that both the principal and agent are liable if an injury occurs while the agent is on this sort of mission.

Intentional Torts

If the intentional tort occurs outside of the principal's scope of business, the principal is not liable. The doctrine of vicarious liability applies though in the situation where the agent or employee commits an intentional tort in the scope of his or her employment. The **Motivation Test** and the **Work-Related Test** are applied to determine if the torts were committed within the scope of the agent's employment.

- **The Motivation Test** – If the agent's motivation in performing the intentional tort was the principal's business, then the principal is liable for any injury caused by the tort.

- **The Work-Related Test** – If the intentional tort was performed during a work-related time or space, the principle is liable for any injuries caused by the intentional torts. The motivation of the agent is not considered in the use of this test.

Independent Contractor

As you may recall from the previous chapter, the degree of control that an employer has over an agent is the most important factor in determining whether someone is an employee or an independent contractor. Additional factors include but are not limited to:

- The amount of skill needed to finish the task.
- Whether the principal provides the equipment and tools used in the job.
- Whether payment is by time or by the job.
- Whether the employer controls the means and manner of completing the job.

Liability for Independent Contractor Torts

The general rule is that a principal is not liable for the torts of its independent contractors. However, there are some **exceptions**. They are:

- **Non-delegable duties** – A principal may not avoid liability by delegating non-delegable duties.
- **Special risks** – Principals may not avoid strict liability for dangerous activities by assigning them to independent contractors.
- **Negligence in the Selection of an Independent Contractor** – The hiring of an unqualified or knowingly dangerous person who injures someone while on the job will cause the principal to be held liable for such negligent selection of this type of independent contractor.

Termination of an Agency and Employment Contract

An agency contract may be terminated by an act of the parties or by operation of law. There are four ways to terminate an agency relationship by the actions of the parties.

- **Mutual Agreement** – The parties may mutually agree to terminate their agreement.
- **Lapse of Time** – The agency agreement will end after a certain period of time passes.
- **Purpose Achieved** – The agency ends when the purpose of the agreement is accomplished.
- **Occurrence of a Specified Event** – The agency ends when a specified event in the parties' agreement happens.

There are six ways to terminate an agency relationship by operation of law.

- **Death** – The death of either the agent or principal ends the agency relationship.

- **Insanity** – Insanity of either party ends the agency relationship.
- **Bankruptcy** – If the principal is found bankrupt, the agency is terminated. However, an agent's bankruptcy usually does not end the agency.
- **Impossibility** – The agency ends if circumstances make the agency impossible. The following have been recognized under this method of termination:
  - **Loss or destruction of the subject matter of the agency**
  - **Loss of a required qualification** – For example, a private physician loses his or her license.
  - **A change in the law** – If the agency contains a provision that becomes illegal, the agency contract will end.
- **Changed circumstances** – If there are changed circumstances that lead the agent to determine that the original instructions he or she received from the principal no longer apply, then the agency will be terminated.
- **War** – War between the agent and principal's country terminates the agency.

Irrevocable Agencies – These are referred to as agencies coupled with an interest. This type of agency is not ended by death or incapacity of either party and only terminates upon performance of the agent's obligations. It is irrevocable and created for the agent's benefit.

Wrongful Termination of an Agency or Employment Contract – If the principal's or agent's termination of an agency contract breaches the agency contract, then the termination may be considered to be wrongful.

Revocation of Authority – When a principal ends an agency agreement, he or she is terminating the agency agreement by revocation of authority.

Renunciation of Authority – When an agent ends an agency agreement, it is called a renunciation of authority.

Refresh Your Memory

The following exercise will give you the opportunity to refresh your memory of the principles given to you in this chapter. Read the question twice and place your answer in the blanks provided. If you do not remember, go to the next question, and come back to the one you did not answer.

1. A ____________________ is a party who employs another individual to act on his or her behalf.

2. An ____________ is an individual who agrees to act on behalf of another.

3. List the three types of employment relationships? ____________________________
____

4. What are some of the characteristics of an independent contractor? _______________
____

5. What is the most common type of agency? ________________________________

6. A ________________ of ______________ is a formal type of agency agreement that is used to empower an agent to sign legal documents.

7. Explain what an apparent agency is?

____

____

8. If no termination date is stated, when does an agency terminate? ________________

____

9. Give three ways to terminate an agency by operation of law. ____________________

____

10. If the __________________ is declared bankrupt, the agency relationship is ended.

Critical Thought Exercise

Dave Polk was a self-employed handyman, doing business under the name Polk Speedy-Fix. From 1994-2001, Polk performed maintenance and repair work for numerous people in Sun City West, Arizona, including Frank and Martha Hamilton. Polk did landscape maintenance, cactus trimming, painting, plumbing, and carpentry. Polk completed a job in May 2001 for the Hamilton's wherein he replaced a toilet and vanity. Polk was then hired to trim a 30-foot tall palm tree in the Hamilton's side yard. Polk was paid $20 per hour for his previous jobs by the Hamiltons. Polk was to receive the same rate of pay for trimming the palm tree.

When Polk arrived to trim the palm tree, Mr. Hamilton told him he wanted it trimmed to a height that was approximately the same as the house, along with trimming back the fronds so that they were at least five feet from the homes of both the Hamiltons and their neighbors. Polk took out several saws and two ladders from his repair van. Polk also borrowed a tree trimming saw and a rope from the Hamiltons. When his ladder was unable to reach the top areas of the tree, Polk climbed the tree. Polk fell from the palm tree when the rope broke and he received severe injuries to his back, pelvis, and internal organs. At age 32, he was totally unable to work.

Polk sued the Hamiltons to recover for his injuries, claiming that he was working as an employee at the time of his injuries and was therefore entitled to workers' compensation protection from the Hamiltons. The Hamiltons argued that Polk was an independent contractor.

Was Polk an employee of the Hamiltons or an independent contractor?

Answer. ____

____

____

____

____

____

____

____

____

____

____

Practice Quiz

True/False:

1. ___ The principal is the party who is hired by another person to act on his or her behalf. [p 509]

2. ___ Insane persons and minors generally may not appoint agents regardless of capacity. [p 509]

3. ___ An employer-employee relationship exists when an employer hires an employee to perform some form of physical service. [p 510]

4. ___ A beanie baby assembly person is an employee of the Ty corporation because he or she performs a mental task. [p 510]

5. ___ A principal may not give an independent contractor the authority to enter into contracts. [p 527]

6. ___ Express agency contracts can be either oral or written. [p 510]

7. ___ Another name for an apparent agency is an agency by estoppel. [p 512]

8. ___ A principal is not prevented from denying the agency relationship exist when the apparent agency is established. [p 512]

9. ___ Parties to an agency contract may agree to terminate their agreement. [p 523]

10. ___ Changed circumstances are enough to terminate an agency. [p 525]

11. ___ The death of either the agent or the principal will not end the agency relationship. [p 525]

12. ___ The agency relationship is terminated if the agent is found to be bankrupt. [p 525]

13. ___ When an agent terminates an agency, it is called a renunciation of authority. [p 525]

14. ___ An agency can only be formed to accomplish a lawful purpose. [p 509]

15. ___ The relationship whereby an employer employs an employee and gives that employee the authority to act and enter into contracts on his or her behalf is a principal-agent relationship. [p 510]

Multiple Choice:

16. A party who employs another individual to act on his or her behalf is called a(n) [p 509]
    a. agent.
    b. independent contractor.
    c. principal.
    d. vice-principal.

17. A principal-agent relationship is formed when [p 510]
    a. a person or business who is not an employee is hired to perform a certain task on the principal's behalf.
    b. an employer hires an employee and grants that employee authority to act and enter into contracts on his or her behalf.
    c. a principal authorizes an independent contractor to enter into contracts.
    d. the principal exerts a large degree of control over the employee.

18. What is the most significant factor in determining whether someone is an employee or an independent contractor? [p 510]
    a. Whether the employee can act and enter into contracts on behalf of the principal.
    b. Whether the president of a corporation has the authority to enter into major contracts on the corporation's behalf.
    c. Whether the principal and agent expressly agree to enter into an agency agreement with one another.
    d. The degree of control that the employer has over the agent.

19. What is the most used common law exception to the employment at-will doctrine? [p 526]
    a. The public policy exception which states that an employee cannot be discharged if such discharge violates public policy.
    b. The implied-in-fact contract which is developed by the conduct of the parties.
    c. Title VII and other federal and state antidiscrimination laws that prohibit employers from engaging in discrimination.
    d. The environmental protection laws.

20. Authority that is derived from the conduct of the parties, custom and usage of trade, or act that is incidental to carrying out the agent's duties is [p 513]
    a. express authority.
    b. retroactive authority.
    c. obvious authority.
    d. implied authority.

21. Which of the following is true with regard to an apparent agency? [512]
    a. The principal creates the appearance of a non-existing agency.
    b. The principal is estopped from denying the agency relationship.
    c. The principal's actions, not the agent's actions create an apparent agency.
    d. all of the above

22. An agency by ratification occurs when [p 513]
    a. The principal creates the appearance of an agency that in actuality does not exist.
    b. The principal and agent enter into an expressly stated agency agreement.
    c. A person misrepresents himself or herself as another's agent when he or she is not and the person accepts the unauthorized act.
    d. none of the above

23. Which of the following is considered part of an agent's duty of performance? [p 514]
    a. The agent is to perform the lawful duties as set forth in the contract.
    b. The agent is to meet the standards of reasonable care in all contracts.
    c. The agent is to meet the standards of skill and diligence implicit in all contracts.
    d. all of the above

24. Which of the following is not true with regard to an agent's misuse of confidential information? [p 517]
    a. The agent must not disclose any confidential information about the principal's affairs.
    b. The agent is prohibited from using general information, knowledge, or experience acquired during the course of the agency.
    c. The agent may not misuse business plans, technological innovations, customer lists or trade secrets.
    d. All of the above statements are false.

25. What may the court consider in determining whether an agent's conduct occurred within the scope of his or her employment? [p 519]
    a. Was it the kind of act that the agent was employed to perform?
    b. Was the agent advancing the principal's purpose when the act occurred?
    c. Did the act occur substantially within the location of employment authorized by the employer?
    d. All of the above

Short Answer:

26. Agency agreements that are formed for illegal purposes are void and against ____________ ______________. [p 509]

27. When does the employer-employee relationship exist? [p 510] ______________________
____

28. A great deal of control over and individual may indicate that what type of relationship exists? [p 527] ____

29. Whose actions create an apparent agency? [p 512] ____________________________

30. Give three ways that the parties may terminate an agency relationship. [p 523] ________
____

31. Give at least two ways that an agency relationship may terminate where a situation presents itself and thereby makes its fulfillment impossible. [p 525] ____________________
____

32. When an agent terminates an agency, it is referred to as a [p 525] ________________
____

33.. When will a principal be liable for the tortuous conduct of an independent contractor? [p 528] ____

34. What effect does the agent's actions after the principal dies have on the principal's estate? [p 525] ____

35. What does constructive notice of the termination of an agency usually consist of? [p 524]
____

Chapter 25
SOLE PROPRIETORSHIPS AND PARTNERSHIPS

Chapter Overview

This chapter is primarily focused on the role of the entrepreneur and sole proprietorships in business. You will learn the advantages as well as disadvantages for operating a business as a sole proprietorship. Additionally you will become aware of the liabilities that a sole proprietor may face. You will also learn about the various types of partnerships, their formation and the liability associated with them.

Objectives

Upon completion of the exercises in this chapter, you should be able to:

1. Discuss the role of entrepreneurs in beginning and operating businesses.
2. State the different entrepreneurial forms of conducting business.
3. Explain the meaning of sole proprietorship.
4. Discuss formation of the sole proprietorship.
5. Explain the meaning of d.b.a.
6. Compare and explain the advantages and disadvantages of operating a business as a sole proprietorship.
7. Discuss the liability of the sole proprietor.
8. Explain how to conduct international business using direct export and import sales.

Practical Application

This chapter will enable you to be more aware of the positive and concerning aspects of operating a business as a sole proprietorship. You will have a greater understanding of the magnitude of the liability associated with conducting business in this manner as well. Further, you will have a hint of the ways in which you may consider conducting international business should the opportunities arise.

Helpful Hints

Since the information contained in this chapter primarily focuses on the single topic of entrepreneurs and sole proprietorship, the principles are quickly committed to memory.
The Study Tips section has been organized in much the same way as the chapter in your text has been presented. Since the information is so concisely written, the concepts will be easy to grasp.

Study Tips

When studying this chapter, it is best to commit the definition of an entrepreneur to memory as well as be familiar with the fact that there are various choices in which to operate an entrepreneur's business organization. As you know, the primary emphasis of this chapter is on the sole proprietorship and partnerships, however, you will learn about the other forms of business that are mentioned in the chapters that follow.

Entrepreneur

An individual who creates and operates a new business.

Ways in which to operate a business organization include:

- sole proprietorship
- general partnership
- limited partnership
- corporation
- limited liability company
- franchise
- joint venture

Basic Information

Sole proprietorships are the simplest form of business organization as well as most common form in the United States. A sole proprietorship is not a distinct legal entity.

Advantages

1. Easy to form and relatively inexpensive.
2. The owner can make all management decisions, including hiring and firing.
3. The owner has the right to all profits of the business.
4. It is easily transferred or sold without anyone else's approval.

Disadvantages

1. Access to capital is limited to personal funds plus any loans the proprietor can obtain.
2. The sole proprietor is held responsible for the business's contracts and torts he/she or any of his or her employees employees commit in the course of employment.

Creation

No state or federal formalities are required.
Some local governments may require that a sole proprietor obtain a license to do business within the city.

Operation of a Sole Proprietorship

A sole proprietorship may conduct itself under the name of the sole proprietor or a trade name.

If a trade name is chosen, it is commonly referred to as **d.b.a. (*doing business as*)**. Also, if a d.b.a. is used, most states necessitate the filing of a **fictitious business name statement**. This statement gives the name and address of the applicant, address of the business and the trade name. Publication of the notice of the trade name is often required.

Personal Liability of Sole Proprietors

- If the sole proprietorship fails, the owner will lose his or her entire contribution of capital.
- The sole proprietor has unlimited personal liability, thereby subjecting his or her personal assets to creditors claims.

Partnerships - Formation

Forming a partnership is akin to laying the foundation of a house and having a blueprint to build the house from. A partnership agreement is like a blueprint, in that it sets forth the terms of the parties' agreement, which includes but is not limited to the following:

- the name of the firm and names of the partners.
- the main partnership office as well as nature and scope of the business.
- the monetary contributions each partner is to be making.
- the distribution of profits and losses among the partners.
- the partners management duties.
- limitations on the partners' authority to bind the partnership.

Partnerships may be **expressly** formed or **impliedly** formed. There is no necessity to file a partnership's agreement in most states. However, a select few require a general partnership to file **certificates of partnership** with the proper government agency. Partnerships are viewed as **separate legal entities** that can hold title to real and personal property.

General Partnership Requirements

There are four requirements in order to be considered a general partnership. They are:

1. It must be an association of two or more persons.
   a. All partners must be in agreement of each participating co-partner.
   b. Person includes natural persons, partnerships, associations and corporations.
2. These persons must be carrying on a business.
   a. Co-ownership such as joint tenancy, tenancy by the entireties, and tenancy in common qualify.
   b. A series of transactions conducted over a period of time.
3. These individuals must be operating as co-owners.
   a. Essential to form a partnership.
   b. Co-ownership is evaluated based on the sharing of business profits and management responsibility.
4. The business must be for profit or have a profit motive.

General partners are personally liable for the obligations as well as debts incurred by the partnership.

Uniform Partnership Act (UPA)

The Uniform Partnership Act requirements is like the building code requirements of a house in that it is codified partnership law that has been adopted by 48 states. The Uniform Partnership Act details laws concerning formation, operation and dissolution of basic partnerships.

Property Rights of the Partnership and the Partners

Property rights of the partnership are like fixtures in a home in that all property brought into the partnership on account of the partnership is considered partnership property. A written record of all partnership property should be kept. If a partner dies, the partnership property passes to the remaining partners. However, the value of the deceased partner's share in the partnership passes to his or her heirs. A partner's interest in a partnership is his or her share of the profits and surplus of the partnership.

Partner's Rights

Like roommates or family members in a home, all partners have equal rights in the management of the partnership business. Each partner has a vote. The partners' unanimous consent is required for assignment of the partnership property for creditors' benefit as well as the disposal of the goodwill of the business. There are other issues that require a unanimous vote, which can be found on p. 621 of your text.

Right to an Accounting

Instead of being allowed to sue one another, partners may bring an **action for an accounting** against the other partners.

Refresh Your Memory

The following exercise will enable you to refresh your memory on the rules and principles presented to you in this chapter. Read each question twice and place your answer in the blanks provided. Review the chapter material for any question you miss or are unable to remember.

1. Explain the term entrepreneur?

   ____

   ____

2. What are three major forms of business organizations. ____________________

   ____

3. A ______________________________ is the most basic form of business organization.

4. Give at least two advantages of operating a business as a sole proprietorship. __________

   ____

5. One of the disadvantages of operating a sole proprietorship is____________________

   ____

   ____

6. The formalities that are required to create a sole proprietorship are ________________
____

7. What do the initials d.b.a. stand for? ________________________________

8. If a business is operating under a fictitious business name, what must it file? __________
____

9. In a sole proprietorship ____________________________ bears the risk of loss.

10. Creditors can satisfy the claims they have against a sole proprietor from ____________
____

Critical Thought Exercise

Larry and Diane Ortiz own and operate Maria's Restaurant in Houston, Texas. As husband and wife, they operate the restaurant as a sole proprietorship. As part of the advertising plan for Maria's, they participate in several 2-for-1 dinner coupon books and school fundraiser sticker books. An average of 15 2-for-1 coupons are redeemed each week. After Larry Ortiz is struck with a serious illness, the restaurant is sold to Bob Nelson. Nelson files the proper fictitious business name statement with the county and city clerk. The sale of the restaurant did not include the assignment of any contracts entered into prior to the sale by Larry and Diane Ortiz.

After Nelson remodels the restaurant, he reopens it with a Grand Reopening advertising campaign. Signs stating, "New Owners" are posted at the restaurant and the same notice is in each advertisement. When Nelson refuses to honor the 2-for-1 coupons, 24 plaintiffs file suit against Maria's Restaurant and Bob Nelson for breach of contract and fraud.

Is Bob Nelson liable because he failed to honor coupons for Maria's Restaurant?

Answer. ____

Practice Quiz

True/False

1. ___ An entrepreneur may operate a new business only by himself. [p 537]

2. ___ One of the major forms of business organization is a limited liability company. [p 538]

3. ___ The extent of an individual's personal liability should be a factor in determining which form of business organization is best. [p 537]

4. ___ In a sole proprietorship, there is a separate entity. [p 538]

5. ___ One of the disadvantages to operating a business as a sole proprietorship is the legal responsibility for the contracts and torts of the business. [p 539]

6. ___ The sole proprietor is responsible for the business's contracts and torts that he or she or any of his or her employees commit during the course of employment. [p 539]

7. ___ The least common form of business organization in the United States is the sole proprietorship. [p 539]

8. ___ The initials d.b.a. stand for doing business as. [p 539]

9. ___ It is not necessary to procure a license to operate a sole proprietorship with the city. [p 539]

10. ___ If a form of business organization has not been chosen, then it will operate by default as a corporation. [p 539]

11. ___ A sole proprietorship may not operate under a trade name or under the name of the sole proprietor. [p 539]

12. ___ A fictitious business name statement needs to contain the name of the applicant, as the trade name is sufficient for identification of the business. [p 541]

13. ___ The rights and duties in a partnership are established in the partnership agreement and by law. [p 541]

14. ___ An agreement to share losses of a business indicates that the business may be a partnership [p 542]

15. ___ A partner may be held liable for torts as well as breaches of trust even if he or she did not participate in the commission of the act. [p 544]

Multiple Choice:

16. What is the general rule regarding the individual liability of limited partners for the obligations or conduct of the partnership? [p 551]
    a. The limited partners are not liable beyond the amount of their capital contribution.
    b. The limited partners are liable regardless of their capital contribution.
    c. The limited partners are liable up to one third of their initial capital contribution.
    d. The limited partners are not liable regardless of their capital contribution.

17. In many states the use of the Limited Liability Partnership is restricted to [p 552]
    a. nonprofessionals
    b. corporations
    c. professionals
    d. None of the above.

18. Which of the following is true with regard to the dissolution of a partnership? [p 547]
    a. A partner has the power to withdraw and dissolve the partnership at any time.
    b. Notice of dissolution must be given to certain third parties.
    c. A partner is liable for damages caused by a wrongful dissolution of the partnership.
    d. all of the above

19. The term tenant in partnership refers to what as it pertains to the death of a partner? [p 549]
    a. It refers to the remaining tenant's position on their joint office space.
    b. It refers to the vestment of deceased partner's right in specific partnership property in the remaining partner or partners.
    c. It refers to the limited use of the partnership for business ventures.
    d. It doesn't refer to anything specific other than the capacity to be in a partnership.

20. Which of the following does the Revised Uniform Limited Partnership Act (RULPA) allow? [p 549]
    a. It permits a corporation to be the sole general partner of a limited partnership.
    b. It requires a limited partnership to have one or more general partners and one or more limited partners.
    c. There are no upper limits on the number of general or limited partners allowed in a limited partnership.
    d. All of the above

21. In which situation would limited partners be individually liable for the debts, obligations and tortuous acts of the partnership? [p 551]
    a. When a limited partner participated in the management and control of the partnership.
    b. When there has been substantial compliance in good faith with the statutory requirements to create a limited partnership.
    c. Where the limited partner has not signed an enforceable personal guarantee that guarantees the performance of the limited partnership.
    d. None of the above

22. Which of the following is true with respect to a Limited Liability Partnership? [p 553]
    a. Articles of partnership need not be filed.

b. The Limited Liability Partnership law of the United States govern the operation of the LLP regardless of where it is organized.
c. The LLP is a domestic LLP in the state in which it is organized.
d. An LLP may not do business in other states.

23. What type of action do partners of a partnership have the right to bring against the other partners? [p 544]
    a. The partners may bring an action in law against the other partners.
    b. The partners may bring an action for an accounting against the other partners.
    c. The partners may bring an action for the right to vote against the other partners.
    d. The partners may bring an action for profit sharing against the other partners.

24. A partner who is made to pay more than his or her proportionate share of contract liability may seek what remedy from the partnership and from those partners who have not paid their share of the loss? [p 545]
    a. an injunction
    b. an order for specific performance
    c. a retrial
    d. indemnification

25. What is the trade-off in being classified as a limited partner? [p 551]
    a. The limited partner is only liable for the debts and obligations of the limited partnership up to his or her capital contribution.
    b. The limited partner gives up his or her right to participate in the control and management of the limited partnership.
    c. The limited partner is liable the same as a general partner would be.
    d. The limited partner can participate in management as compared to a general partner who can not.

Short Answer:

26. Give an example of a business that started with one individual as a sole proprietor and thereafter grew into a giant company. [p 538] ______________________________

27. An individual's choice of the type of business organization that he or she wants to operate as depends on several factors. Give at least two of these factors. [p 537] ______________
____

28. Sandy Simpkins wants to open her own craft store. She asks for your input regarding the formalities in forming a sole proprietorship. What will you tell her? [p 539] __________
____

29. If Ben Barnes conducts a business called Barnes Bikes, which of these two names is the trade name? [p 539] ____

30. What is another name for a fictitious business name statement? [p 539] ______________
____

31. The sole proprietor has ______________________________ personal liability. [p 539]

32. A sole proprietorship is not a separate legal ______________ from that of the person who owns it. [p 538]

33. If the Shiny Collectible Corporation desires to conduct business in other countries, the form that it chooses will depend on several factors. Give at least two of these factors. [p 542]
____

34. What do the initials UPA stand for? [p 541] ____________________
____

35. What was the goal of the UPA? [p 541] ______________________________
____

Chapter 26
FORMATION AND OPERATION OF DOMESTIC AND MULTINATIONAL CORPORATIONS

Chapter Overview

This chapter explores the formation as well as financing of corporations. Additionally, it explains the difference between publicly held and closely held corporations. Further it examines the various types of stock issues as well as the preferences associated with preferred stock. Other topics that are covered include promoters' liability, S Corporations, various issuances of stock as well as preferences that accompany preferred stock, rights of debenture and bondholders and the organization and operation of multinational corporations. Though a corporation is an unnatural being, it is one of the strongest as well as most important forms of business organization forms in business today.

Objectives

Upon completion of the exercises in this chapter, you should be able to:

1. Discuss the meaning and major characteristics of a corporation.
2. Discuss how a corporation is formed.
3. Differentiate between a publicly held corporation and a closely held corporation.
4. Explain what an S Corporation is and discuss its tax benefits.
5. Explain the meaning of common stock and differentiate between authorized, issued, treasury and outstanding shares.
6. Discuss the preferences that are connected with preferred stock.
7. Explain the organization and operation of multinational corporations.

Practical Application

You will have a better understanding of how a corporation is formed and operates. You will also be better aware of the benefits as well as concerns with operating a business as a corporation. Finally, you will have a better appreciation of the impact corporations have on business, the world and our every day lives.

Helpful Hints

Since there is a vast amount of information to learn in this chapter, organization is key to learning the various topics. A corporation is similar to raising a child, in that it starts out small without a name and eventually grows with the help of its family members into a fully functioning being. If you keep in mind that the different aspects of operating a business as a corporation all depend on one another, you will begin to see how the entire picture fits together. The most important key terms and concepts have been typed in bold in the Study Tips section that follows.

Study Tips

General Information

It is important to realize that corporations are **created according to the state laws** where it is incorporated. These laws are vital to a corporation's success as they regulate formation, operation and the dissolution of corporations. It is beneficial to learn the characteristics associated with a corporation as given below.

A corporation is considered to be **a legal person or legal entity** that is separate and distinct which include the following many interesting characteristics:

- A corporation is an artificial person that is state created.
- A corporation may bring a lawsuit or be sued.
- A corporation may enter into and enforce contracts, hold title to and transfer property.
- A corporation may be found civilly and criminally liable and may have fines assessed or its license revoked.

Other fascinating characteristics that may be attributed to corporations include:

- The shareholders have limited liability to the extent of their contributions.
- Corporate shares are freely transferable by the shareholder.
- Corporations have a perpetual existence if there is no duration stated in the corporation's articles of incorporation.
- Shareholders may voluntarily terminate the corporation's existence.
- Death, insanity or bankruptcy of a shareholder has no affect on a corporation's existence.
- The shareholders elect the directors who in turn appoint corporate officers to conduct the corporation's daily business.

Classifications of Corporations

Corporations are classified based on **location, purpose** or **owners**. Private corporations may be for **profit** or **non-profit**. Non-profit are created for charitable, educational, scientific or religious reasons. Note that non-profit corporations may not distribute any profit to their members, directors, or officers. **The Model Nonprofit Corporation Act** governs nonprofit corporations. **Government-owned** (or public) corporations are formed with a governmental or political reason in mind. **Private corporations** are created to carry on a privately owned business.

Publicly Held verses Closely Held Corporations

Publicly Held Corporations

These are generally large corporations with hundreds and even thousands of shareholders whose shares are **traded on organized securities markets**. Coca Cola and Bristol Myers are examples of publicly held corporations. An **important fact to know** about publicly held corporations is that the **shareholders seldom participate in** this type of corporation's **management**.

Closely Held Corporations

These are **relatively small** corporations whose **shares** are **held by** a few shareholders, mostly comprised of **family, friends and relatives**. An **important fact to know** and compare to publicly held corporations is that the **shareholders do participate in** a closely held corporation's **management.** Sometimes the shareholders attempt to prevent outsiders from becoming shareholders.

Professional Corporations

These are **formed by professionals**, such as dentists, doctors, lawyers, and accountants. The initials give a clue that it is a professional corporation. You may see the initials **P.C.** for Professional Corporation or **S.C.** for service corporation. This type of corporation is formed like other corporations and have many of the same traits. Its **professional members** are generally **not liable for** the **torts** committed **by** its **agents or employees.**

Domestic, Foreign and Alien Corporations

These terms should be somewhat familiar to you in light of the previous chapters, if you have had to study them.

Domestic corporation – A corporation in the state in which it was formed.

Foreign corporation – A corporation in any state or jurisdiction other than the one in which it was formed.

Alien corporation – A corporation that is incorporated in another country.

A corporation begins with promoter's activities

Now that you are familiar with the different types of corporations, let us study how a corporation begins. It begins with a promoter. **A promoter is an individual or individuals who organizes and starts the corporations**. Additionally he/she or they enter into contracts before the corporation is formed, find investors and sometimes subject themselves to liability as a result of all that is done.

Promoter's Liability

Promoters enter into contracts such as leases, sales contracts, property contracts, etc. Liability depends on the corporation keeping the following instances in mind.

- If the **corporation never** comes **into existence**, then the promoter is solely liable on the contract unless the third party exempts the promoter.
- If the **corporation is formed**, it is liable on the promoter's contract if it agrees to be bound to the contract as per a board of director's resolution.

- The promoter remains liable on the contract unless a **novation** is entered into. A novation is a three-party agreement wherein the corporation assumes the promoter's contract liability with the third party's consent. A novation has the effect of leaving the corporation solely liable on the promoter's contract.

Issues concerning incorporation procedures

An **incorporator** is the person or persons, partnerships or corporations that are responsible for the incorporation of the corporation.

The **articles of incorporation** also known as the corporate charter are the basic documents that must be file with and approved by the state in order to be officially incorporated. The **articles must contain:**

- the name of the corporation
- number of shares the corporation is authorized to issue
- address of the corporation's registered office
- agent for the corporation
- name and address of each incorporator
- duration, regulation of powers and corporate affairs
- the corporate purpose

Amendments to the articles of incorporation must be filed with the secretary of state after the shareholders approve them.

The organizers must:

- choose a name for the corporation
- the name must contain the words corporation, company, incorporated, limited or an abbreviation of any one of these
- the name cannot contain a word or phrase that states or implies that the corporation is organized for a purpose different than that in the articles of incorporation
- a trademark search should be conducted to make sure that the name is available for use
- a domain name search for purposes of Internet use should also be performed

A general purpose clause should be in a corporation's articles. Some corporations insert a limited purpose clause.

A registered agent must be identified along with a registered office. The purpose of the agent is to have someone be able to accept service of process on behalf of the corporation.

Corporate bylaws are a more exacting set of rules adopted by the board of directors. It contains provisions for managing the business and the affairs of the corporation. The bylaws may also be amended.

An organizational meeting of the first corporate directors must be held upon the filing of the articles of incorporation. The bylaws are adopted, officers elected and other business transacted at this initial meeting. Additional matters such as ratification of promoter's contracts, approving the form of stock certificates, etc are also discussed.

A corporate seal is a design affixed by a metal stamp containing the name and date of incorporation.

Corporate status begins when the articles of incorporation are filed. Upon the secretary of state's filing of the articles of incorporation, it is conclusive proof that the incorporators have satisfied all conditions of the incorporation. Note, failure to file the articles of incorporation is conclusive proof that the corporation does not exists.

S Corporation has been defined as those which elect to be taxed under Chapter S thereby avoiding double taxation. Note C corporations are all other corporations.

Financing the corporation – The sale of equity and debt securities is the most simple way to finance the operation of a corporation. **Equity securities** are stock which represent the ownership rights in the corporation in the form of **common stock** or **preferred stock.**

- **Common stock** - A kind of equity security that represents the residual value of the corporation. The creditors and preferred shareholders receive their interest first. There is no fixed maturity date. Common stockholders may vote on mergers, elect directors and receive dividends.
- **Par and no par value** – This refers to a value assigned to common shares. Par value is the lowest price that the shares may be issued. Most shares are no-par shares where no value is assigned to them.
- **Preferred stock** – This is a kind of equity security that is given preferences and rights over common stock. Holders of this type of stock are issued **preferred stock certificates.** The general rule with regard to voting is that this class of stock may not do so, unless there has been a merger or there has been a failure to pay a dividend.
- **Preferences of preferred stock include** dividend preference, liquidation preference, cumulative dividend right, cumulative preferred stock, the right to participate in profits participating preferred stock and convertible preferred stock.
- **Redeemable preferred stock (also termed callable preferred stock)** allows the corporation to buy back the preferred stock at a future date.

Authorized, Issued and Outstanding Shares

- **Authorized shares** are the number of shares that are provided for in the articles of incorporation.
- Authorized shares that have been sold are called **issued shares.**
- Repurchased shares are called **treasury shares.**
- Shares of stock that are in the shareholder hands are called **outstanding shares.**

Purchase of Stock and Corporate Debt

- **Consideration to be paid for shares** may include any property or benefit to the corporation as determined by the board of directors.
- **Stock Options and stock warrants** may be offered for sale. A **stock option** is generally given to **top-level managers.** It is the nontransferable right to purchase corporate stock at a set price during an option period. A **stock warrant** is an option that

is demonstrated by a **certificate** whereby the holder can exercise the warrant and buy the common stock at a state price during the warrant period. Warrants are both transferable and nontransferable.

- **Debt Securities** are securities that establish a debtor-creditor relationship in which the corporation borrows money from the investor to whom the debt security is issued.

- **Debenture** – A long-term unsecured debt instrument that is based on the corporation's general credit standing.

- **Bond** – A long-term debt security that is secured by some form of collateral.

- **Note** – A debt security with a maturity of five years or less.

- **Indenture agreement** – A contract between the corporation and the holder that contains the terms of the debt security.

Corporate Powers

A corporation has **express** and **implied powers**. Express powers may be found in the U.S. Constitution, state constitutions, federal statutes, articles of incorporations, bylaws and resolutions by the board of directors. Corporations may purchase, own, and lease real as well as personal property. They also may borrow money, incur liability, make donations and perform various other financial functions.

The **implied powers** of a corporation are those that **go beyond** the **express powers** and that allow a corporation to accomplish its corporate purpose.

Ultra Vires Act – This refers to a corporate act that goes beyond its express and implied powers. An injunction as well as damages and an action to enjoin the act or dissolve the corporation are the remedies available for the commission of an ultra vires act.

Dissolution and termination of corporations

There are three main ways to dissolve and terminate a corporation. One way is by **voluntary dissolution** which occurs upon recommendation of the board of directors and a majority vote of the shares entitled to vote. Another is by **administrative dissolution** which is an **involuntary dissolution** of a corporation that is order by the secretary of state to comply with certain procedures required by law. The third way is by **judicial dissolution** which occurs when a corporation is dissolved by a court proceeding initiated by the state.

Winding-Up, Liquidation and Termination

Winding-up and liquidation refers to the method which a dissolved corporation's assets are gathered, liquidated and then distributed to creditors, shareholders and other claimants.

Termination is the ending of the corporation that happens only after the winding-up of the corporate affairs, the liquidation of its assets and the distribution of the proceeds to the claimants.

Refresh Your Memory

The following exercise will enable you to refresh your memory on the rules and principles presented to you in this chapter. Read each question twice and place your answer in the blanks provided. Review the chapter material for any question you miss or are unable to remember.

1. Who is the person responsible for the organization as well as for starting the corporation?
____
____

2. Give three characteristics of a corporation. ______________________
____

3. How are private corporations classified? ______________________
____

4. What are local government corporations called? ______________________

5. What type of individuals form professional corporations? ______________________

6. What do the initials P.C. stand for when identifying a corporation? ______________
____

7. What do the initials S.C. stand for when identifying a corporation? ______________
____

8. What is a domestic corporation? ______________________
____

9. What is a foreign corporation? ______________________
____

10. What is an alien corporation? ______________________

Critical Thought Exercise

Gus Hill runs a successful sole proprietorship under the name "Custom Rides." Hill makes custom motorcycles that often sell for over $40,000 each. Hill decides to expand the business and make motorcycles that are more of a standard production. In order to do this, Hill decides to form a corporation and solicit investors through the sale of company stock. Hill contacts an attorney and requests that all of the paperwork necessary for the incorporation be prepared. To prepare for the expanded business that will be done by the corporation, Hill leases a large manufacturing building from LandCo for one year at $12,000 per month. Hill also signs a $175,000 contract with VanTolker Tool Co. for the purchase of equipment and an employment contract with Dirk Dodds, who was hired to serve as plant manager and chief financial officer. Dodds' contract stated that he understood that his $130,000 yearly salary would come from corporate income and that Hill had no ability to pay his salary.

The corporation is formed and all legal filings are complete. Custom Rides immediately begins making payments on all three contracts. Custom Rides, Inc. operates for eight months before poor sales make it unable to meet its financial obligations. Landco, Dodds, and VanTolker all file suit against Custom Rides, Inc. and Gus Hill personally to recover their contract damages.

Is Gus Hill personally liable for the contracts he signed on behalf of Custom Rides, Inc.?

Answer. ____

Practice Quiz

True/False:

1. ___ There is not a general federal corporation law governing the formation and operation of private corporations. [p 561]

2. ___ Members of professional corporations are not liable for the torts committed by its employees or agents. [p 563]

3. ___ Most corporations are publicaly owned. [p 563]

4. ___ A domestic corporation is in the state in which it does business. [p 566]

5. ___ An alien corporation is a corporation that is in another country. [p 566]

6. ___ The articles of incorporation must be prepared and filed as well as approved by the state before the corporation can be officially incorporated. [p 567]

7. ___ A corporation may be formed for any unlawful purpose. [p 569]

8. ___ An organizational meeting of the initial corporate directors is required. [p 570]

9. ___ One of the major advantages of doing business as an S corporation is that there is double taxation. [p 581]

10. ___ The secretary of state's filing of the articles of incorporation is conclusive proof of the existence of the corporation. [p 568]

11. ___ One class of preferred stock may not be given preferences over another class of preferred stock. [p 573]

12. ___ Stock options are often issued to attract executive talent to work for the corporation. [p 582]

13. ___ Stock Options are transferable. [p 582]

14. ___ A "C" Corporation must pay federal income tax at the corporate level. [p 572]

15. ___ There are not any requirements in becoming an S corporation. [p 572]

Multiple Choice:

16. Which type of corporation is formed for educational, scientific, charitable or religious purposes? [p 563]
    a. An S Corporation
    b. A public corporation
    c. A nonprofit corporation
    d. A publicly held corporation

17. Shares that are referred to as being authorized are [p 574]
    a. shares of stock that are in shareholder hands.
    b. the number of shares provided for in the articles of incorporation.
    c. shares of stock repurchased by the company itself.
    d. stock that permits the corporation to redeem the preferred stock at some future date.

18. An administrative dissolution of a corporation is [p 577]
    a. a dissolution recommended by the board of directors.
    b. an involuntary dissolution by a judicial proceeding.
    c. an involuntary dissolution that is ordered by the secretary of state.
    d. all of the above.

19. The ending of a corporation that happens after the winding-up of the corporation's affairs is known as [p 577]
    a. winding-up.
    b. judicial dissolution.

c. voluntary dissolution.
d. termination.

20. A corporation in the state in which it is formed is a(n) [p 566]
    a. domestic corporation.
    b. alien corporation.
    c. foreign corporation.
    d. promoter's corporation.

21. A corporation whose shares are owned by a few shareholders would most likely be [p 563]
    a. a closely held corporation.
    b. a publicly held corporation.
    c. a government-owned corporation
    d. All of the above

22. As a general rule, shareholders are liable [p 561]
    a. only to the extent of the debts of the corporation.
    b. only to the extent of their capital contributions.
    c. only to the extent of the assessments of fines or other sanctions.
    d. none of the above.

23. What are the most dominant form of business organization in the United States? [p 561]
    a. partnerships
    b. sole proprietorships
    c. joint ventures
    d. corporations

24. Who make policy decisions concerning the operation of the corporation? [p 562]
    a. the shareholders
    b. the consumers
    c. the board of directors
    d. all of the above

25. Which of the following is true with respect to common stock holders? [p 572]
    a. They have a right to elect directors.
    b. They have a right to vote on mergers.
    c. They receive dividends declared by the board of directors.
    d. All of the above

Short Answer:

26. A ________________ is the person or persons who organize and start the corporation. [p 564]

27. List three things that the articles of incorporation must include. [p 567] ________________
    ____

28. What must be filed upon approval of an amendment of the articles of incorporation by the shareholders? [p 568] ____

29. A registered agent is [p 569] ____

30. The failure to file articles of incorporation is conclusive proof of ____________________ ____. [p 568]

31. A person who owns common stock is a ________________________________. [p 572]

32. The term liquidation preference refers to [p 573] ________________________________ ____

33. Repurchased shares are often called ____________________________________. [p 574]

34. A ____________________ is a debt security with a maturity of five years or less. [p 575]

35. What is a stock warrant? [p 575] _____ ____

Chapter 27
CORPORATE DIRECTORS, OFFICERS, AND SHAREHOLDERS

Chapter Overview

The previous chapter explored the formation as well as various types of corporations and the characteristics associated with corporations. In this chapter, the rights, duties and liabilities of corporate shareholders, officers and directors are examined, with an emphasis on the differences in the roles and responsibilities of each.

Objectives

Upon completion of the exercises in this chapter, you should be able to:

1. Discuss the function of shareholder, directors, and officers in managing the affairs of the corporation.
2. Differentiate between straight and cumulative voting for directors.
3. Discuss the agency authority of officers to enter into contracts on behalf of the corporation.
4. Discuss a director's and officer's duty of care and the business judgment rule.
5. Explain the director's duty of loyalty and how it can be breached.
6. Explain what is meant by the corporate veil or alter ego doctrine.

Practical Application

Whether you are a shareholder, a director, officer or a corporate observer, this chapter will provide you with practical information regarding the internal management structure and its direct impact on one another. This knowledge will provide you with the ability to make educated decisions as may pertain to the basic decisions associated with the management of corporations.

Helpful Hints

Just as it takes a village to raise a child, it takes an entire management structure to mold and develop a corporation. If you keep this analogy in mind as you study the key players in its infrastructure, your learning of this area will be rewarding and insightful. Additionally, if you view the shareholders, directors and officers like a pyramid with each having different responsibilities that impact the other tiers, you will begin to better understand their importance in keeping the pyramid in tact in order to avoid corporate collapse. The most important key terms and concepts have been typed in bold in the Study Tips section that follows.

Study Tips

Shareholders

The shareholders hold a significant position in the corporate pyramid, as they are the **owners** of the corporation. They also **vote** on the directors and other important actions to be taken by the corporation, but cannot bind the corporation to any contract.

Shareholder Meetings

Annual shareholder meetings are held to take actions such as the election of director and independent auditors. Note: there are ***special shareholder meetings*** that may be conducted to evaluate and vote on significant or emergency issues. Examples include potential mergers, or amendments to the articles of incorporation. Attendance at a shareholder meeting may be by a **proxy,** which is another person who acts as an agent of the shareholder. Proxies must be in **writing** and they are **valid** for **11 months.**

As long as a majority of the shares entitled to vote are present, there will be a ***quorum*** to hold the meeting. An affirmative vote for elections other than the board of directors is required. However, the election of the directors may be by **straight voting** wherein each shareholder votes the number of shares he or she owns on candidates for the directors positions that are open. The method of **cumulative voting** may also be used in voting for the directors. This method entails a shareholder accumulating all of his or her votes and voting them all for one candidate or dividing his or her votes among many candidates. In essence, a shareholder may multiply the number of shares he or she owns by the number of directors to be elected and then vote the entire amount on a single candidate or apportion the product among contenders. This method is good for minority shareholders. ***Supramajority voting requirements*** can be made thereby requiring a greater than majority of shares to comprise a quorum or the shareholders' vote.

Voting Agreements – The two types of voting agreements to be concerned with are the voting trust and shareholder voting agreements. In a **voting trust** situation, the shareholders transfer their stock certificates to a trustee who is given the authority to vote the shares. In a **shareholder voting agreement,** two or more shareholders agree on how they will vote their shares.

Shareholder's Rights

Right to Transfer Shares

Shareholders have the right to transfer their shares **under Article 8 of the Uniform**

Commercial Code. There are certain restrictions however that the shareholders must be aware of. They concern the right of first refusal and what is known as a buy-and sell agreement. When shareholders do not want certain people to become owners of the corporation, they will often enter into an agreement with another shareholder to prevent new ownership.

The right of first refusal is an agreement that shareholders enter into which grants one another the right of first refusal to purchase shares they are going to sell. Compare this to a buy-and sell agreement whereby the shareholders are required to sell their shares to the other shareholders or the corporation at a price set in the agreement.

Shareholders also have preemptive rights

Preemptive rights give existing shareholders the option of subscribing to new shares being issued in proportion to their current ownership interest. These rights are usually found in the articles of incorporation.

Right to Receive Information and Inspect Books and Records

Shareholders have a right to be up to date about the financial affairs of the corporation and must be given an **annual financial statement.** Further, shareholders have an absolute **right to inspect** the articles of incorporation, bylaws, minutes, and so on within the past three years.

Shareholder Lawsuits

There are two types of lawsuits a shareholder may bring. The first is a **direct lawsuit** against the corporation. The second is a **derivative lawsuit** wherein the directors are empowered to bring an action on behalf of the corporation. If the corporation does not bring a lawsuit, the shareholders have the right to bring it on the corporation's behalf.

Directors

The board of directors makes policy decisions as well as employ the major officers for the corporation. They also make suggestions concerning actions implemented by the shareholders.

Selection of Directors

There are two types of directors, an **inside director** and an **outside director**. An inside director is a member of the board of directors who is also an officer of the corporation. An outside director is a member of the board of directors who is not an officer of the corporation.

The **number of directors** is stated in the articles of incorporation, but may be **as little as only one** individual. A **director's term** expires at the next annual shareholders' meeting following his or her election unless the terms are **staggered** so that only a part of the board of directors is up for election each year.

Vacancies and Removal of Directors

Death, illness and resignation are some of the reasons vacancies occur on the board of directors. The vacant position may be filled by the shareholders or the balance of directors. Also, directors may be removed, but only **for cause** and by a vote of the holders of a majority of the shares entitled to vote at the election.

Quorum and Voting Requirement

A quorum is the number of directors required to hold a board of directors' meeting or conduct business of the board.

Committees created by the Board of Directors

Directors may create committees of the board and give certain powers to those committees.

Examples of these committees include the executive committee, audit committee, nominating committee, compensation committee, investment committee, and litigation committee.

The **board may not** delegate the power to declare dividends, initiate actions the require shareholders' approval, appoint members to fill openings on the board, amend the bylaws, approve a merger plan that does not require shareholder approval or authorize the issuance of shares.

Compensation and Inspection

Directors may set their own compensation fee. Additionally, directors are required to have access to the books, records, facilities, premises as well as any other information concerning the corporation's formation.

Directors may pay dividends

Dividends are a distribution of profits of the corporation to the shareholders. Directors have the **discretionary power** to pay dividends. If a dividend is to be paid, a date is set prior to the actual payment date called the **record date**. Corporations may use extra shares of stock as a dividend. Stock dividends are paid in proportion to the ownership interests of shareholders.

Officers

Officers have the responsibility of managing the day-to-day operation of the corporation. They also act as agents and hire other officers and employees. The following officers exist in many corporations: president, one or more vice-presidents, a secretary and a treasurer.

Agency Authority of Officers

Officers have the express, implied and apparent authority to bind the corporation to contract.

Removal of Officers

The board of directors may remove any officer unless there is an employment contract to the contrary.

Liability of Corporate Directors and Officers

Directors and officers owe the **fiduciary duties of obedience, care and loyalty.** A director or officer must not intentionally or negligently act outside of their authority. If he or she does, he or she is personally responsible for any resulting damages caused to the corporation or its shareholders. The **duty of due** care involves an officer or directors obligation to discharge his or her duties in good faith and with the care of an ordinary prudent person in a like position would use, and in a manner that is in the best interests of the corporation. Examples of breaches a director or officer will be held personally liable for include the failure to make a reasonable investigation in a corporate matter, or the failure to regularly attend board meetings, or properly supervise a subordinate and failure to keep sufficiently informed of corporate affairs.

The Business Judgment Rule

A director or officer's duty of care is measured as of the time that he or she makes a decision.
Honest mistakes of judgment do not render the director or officer liable.

Reliance on Others

A director is not liable if information he or she relied upon is false, misleading or unreliable unless the director or officer has knowledge that would cause his or her reliance to be unwarranted.

Dissent to Director's Action

If an individual director dissents to an action taken by a majority of the board of directors, he or she must either resign or register his or her dissent by placing it in the meeting's minutes, filing a written dissent to the secretary or forwarding his or her dissent by registered mail to the secretary immediately following the meeting.

Duty of Loyalty

Officers and directors are to place their personal interest below that of the corporation and its shareholders. Breaches of this duty include the usurping of a corporate opportunity, self-dealing, competing with the corporation and disgorgement of secret profits.

Liability for Crimes

Officers, directors, employees and agents are personally liable for crimes that are committed while acting on behalf of the corporation. Punishment includes fines and imprisonment.

Liability of Shareholders

Shareholders have limited liability and are liable for the debts as well as obligations of the corporation only to the extent of their capital contribution. Note that a controlling shareholder has a fiduciary duty to monitor shareholders.

Corporate Entity Disregarded

If a corporation is used for improper purposes by a shareholder or many shareholders, the shareholder(s) may be personally liable for the obligations and debts of the corporation. When this is enforced, this is known as piercing the corporate veil. Piercing the veil occurs when a corporation has not been formed with sufficient capital, commingling of personal with corporate funds has transpired or there's been a failure to maintain books and hold meetings.

Refresh Your Memory

The following exercise will enable you to refresh your memory on the rules and principles presented to you in this chapter. Read each question twice and place your answer in the blanks provided. Review the chapter material for any question you miss or are unable to remember.

1. A written document that a shareholder signs authorizing another person to vote his or her shares at the shareholders' meetings in the event of a shareholder's absence is
______________________________________.

2. A ________________ is an exact date in the corporate bylaws that decides whether a shareholder may vote at a shareholder meeting.

3. If a majority of shares entitled to vote are represented at a meeting either by proxy or in person, there is a _________________to hold the meeting.

4. What is a voting trust?

____

5. When can an act that can be taken at a shareholders' meeting be taken without a meeting?

____

____

6. What rights give existing shareholders the option of subscribing to new shares being issued in proportion to their current ownership interest?

____

7. What right do shareholders have with respect to the books and records of the corporation?

____

8. A member of the board of directors who is also an officer of the corporation is an

____

____

9. A meeting brought by the board of directors to discuss new shares, merger proposals, hostile takeover attempts is a ____________________ meeting.

10. What is the main responsibility of the corporations' officers?

____

____

Critical Thought Exercise

Ned West was the sole shareholder and president of Westward Co., a corporation that ran truck stops along interstate highways. The corporation did not have its own bank accounts. All business was conducted through West's personal account. All supplies, payroll, debts, and purchases were handled through this one checking account. West also paid all of his personal expenses out of this account. All receipts from the truck stops were deposited into the same account. While the corporation was in business, no directors meetings were ever held. All decisions for the corporation were made solely by West.

For a four-year period, Westward Co. accumulated $187,455 in federal tax liabilities. The government is now seeking to collect the overdue tax payments directly from West. West argues that the government is ignoring his corporate entity.

Can the government pierce the corporate veil in this case and force West to incur personal liability for the taxes owed by Westward Co.?

Answer.

____

Practice Quiz

True/False:

1. ___ The rights of shareholders, directors and officers do not differ from one another. [p 588]

2. ___ A corporation can be held liable for the acts of its directors and officers as it is a legal entity. [p 588]

3. ___ A corporation's shareholders are not agents of the corporation and as such may not bind the corporation to any contracts. [p 588]

4. ___ It is not necessary for any class of shares of the corporation to have voting rights. [p 589]

5. ___ A shareholder can accumulate all of his or her votes and vote them all for one candidate. [p 590]

6. ___ The supramajority voting requirement is one in which the corporation's bylaws requires a lesser number of shares to constitute a quorum. [p 590]

7. ___ The board of directors of a corporation are responsible for formulating policy decisions affecting the management, supervision and control of the operation of the corporation. [p 594]

8. ___ An outside director is a member of the board of directors, but who is not an officer of the corporation. [p 595]

9. ___ An individual needs to have any special qualifications in order to be elected a director of a corporation. [p 595]

10. ___ The articles of incorporation can not require a greater than majority of directors to compose a quorum of the vote of the board. [p 595]

11. ___ Dividends are not automatically paid to shareholders. [p 592]

12. ___ A director or officer who breaches the duty of care is personally liable to the corporation and its shareholders for any damages caused by the breach. [p 600]

13. ___ Officers and directors are entitled to rely on information, statements and opinions presented by officers and employees of the corporation as they generally are not able to investigate every corporate matter. [p 602]

14. ___ Usurping a corporate opportunity is a violation of an officer's or a director's duty of care. [p 603]

15. ___ Officers and directors can engage in activities that compete with the corporation regardless if full disclosure is made and a majority of the disinterested directors or shareholders endorse the activity. [p 604]

Multiple Choice:

16. Alice and Harvey are on the Board of Directors of the Whizo Corporation. They want to create committees of the board and delegate certain powers to those committees. Which of the following would be the type of committee that Alice and Harvey may create? [p 597]
    a. The Compensation Committee
    b. The Regular Meeting Committee
    c. The Crime Committee
    d. None of the above

17. What officers do most corporations have? [p 598]
    a. President, vice-president, coordinator
    b. President, one or more vice presidents, secretary and treasurer
    c. President, vice-president, human resource director, treasurer
    d. President, vice-president, secretary and an agent

18. Which of the following expresses the duties that the officers and directors owe to the corporation and its shareholders? [p 600]
    a. Duty of obedience, duty to spend, duty of care
    b. Duty of loyalty, duty of care, duty to account properly
    c. Duty of loyalty, duty of care, duty of obedience
    d. Duty of loyalty, duty to make decisions, fiduciary duty

19. Under the business judgment rule, which choice states what the directors or officers are not

    liable for? [p 600]
    a. Usurping a corporate opportunity
    b. Self-dealing
    c. Honest mistakes of judgment
    d. Lending trade secrets to corporate competitors

20. Which situation best describes when the court will pierce the corporate veil? [p 593]
    a. When the corporation has been formed with thin capitalization.
    b. When there has been a commingling of personal and corporate assets.
    c. When there has been a failure to maintain corporate books and records.
    d. All of the above.

21. What must be in a corporation's written notice to its shareholders when calling the annual meeting? [p 588]
    a. place
    b. day
    c. time
    d. all of the above

22. Which of the following is not true with respect to preemptive rights? [p 591]
    a. These rights give existing shareholders the option of subscribing to new shares being issued in proportion to their current ownership interests.
    b. The purchase of shares based on preemptive rights can prevent a shareholder's interest from being diluted.
    c. Shareholders who do not exercise their preemptive rights may accumulate rights for the future when new shares become available for purchase.
    d. Shareholders are given a reasonable period of time to exercise their preemptive rights.

23. When may a shareholder bring a derivative lawsuit? [p 593]
    a. If the shareholder fairly and adequately represents the interests of the corporation.
    b. If the shareholder made a written demand on the corporation to take suitable actions.
    c. If the shareholder was a shareholder of the corporation at the time of the act complained of.
    e. All of the above

24. Which of the following is true with respect to constituency statutes? [p 595]
    a. Constituency statutes apply the strict principle that shareholders are the only "owners" of the corporation.
    b. Constituency statutes acknowledge the rights of a variety of participants, including lender, suppliers, and distributors.
    c. Constituency statutes allow directors to consider only the shareholders when making decisions.
    d. None of the above

25. Which of the following powers must be exercised by the board itself? [p 597]
    a. amending the bylaws
    b. recommend independent public accountants and supervise the audit of the corporation's financial records by the accountant
    c. invest and reinvest the funds of the corporation
    d. review and decide whether to pursue requests by shareholders for the corporation to sue persons who have allegedly harmed the corporation

Short Answer:

26. What type of meetings are held to elect directors? _____________ [p 588]

27. What is the right of first refusal as it pertains to stock? [p 591]

____

28. What does the annual financial statement that is provided to a corporation's shareholders contain? [p 592] ____

29. In order to reflect technology, what does the Revised Model Corporations Act provide with respect to directors' meetings? [p 596] ____________________________________

____

30. What type of liability are directors who vote for illegal dividends subject to? [p 600]

____

31. What is a stock dividend? [p 592]

____

32. Define the meaning of fiduciary duty. [p 600]

____

33. Tell what D &O insurance is and what its main purpose is. [p 602]

____

34. What does indemnification mean as it applies to the corporation? [p 602]

____

35. When an individual director opposes the action taken by the majority of the board of directors, this is known as [p 602]______________________________________.

Chapter 28
CORPORATE MERGERS AND ACQUISITIONS

Chapter Overview

Corporate change is obtained by controlling stockholder votes. Shareholder votes are solicited and voted by proxy. Persons who desire fundamental change in the direction or control of a company often engage in a proxy contest to win over shareholder votes. Another fundamental change may be made by acquiring another company. This may be through a friendly merger of consolidation or by a hostile tender offer. The target company may mount a defense to the takeover. This chapter focuses on all these possible fundamental changes that a corporation may go through.

Objectives

Upon completion of the exercises in this chapter, you should be able to:
1. Explain the process of soliciting proxies.
2. Understand when a shareholder can insert a proposal in proxy materials.
3. Explain the process involved in approving a merger or share exchange.
4. Define tender offer and describe poisons pills, white knight mergers, greenmail, and other defensive maneuvers to prevent hostile takeover.
5. Explain a tender offer.
6. Analyze the lawfulness of state antitakeover statutes.

Practical Application

For those businesspersons that obtain ownership interests incorporations or choose the corporation as their business form, obtaining or maintaining control of the company is often imperative. It is wise to understand how control of the company may be lost and what efforts can lawfully be made to thwart a proxy battle or hostile takeover.

Helpful Hints

In the corporate environment, mergers, acquisitions, proxy fights, and tender offers are realties that are effectuated only be adhering to the laws and regulations related to these processes and changes. The individual has a greater ability to control their financial stake in a corporation if they understand their rights and duties under the applicable laws. The exercises in this chapter will help you advance your understanding of this area of corporate law.

Study Tips

Before an individual can participate in corporate change and defend their investment, they must understand the major guiding principles and law that controls the areas of proxy fights, mergers, acquisitions, tender offers, and defenses to corporate takeovers. Understanding the following terms and principles is essential to meaningful participation in any of these corporate events. This short outline and glossary of terms is divided into subject areas.

Solicitation of Proxies

proxy voting – shareholders have the right to vote by proxy. A proxy is a means by which a shareholder authorizes another person to represent him or her and vote his or her shares at a shareholders' meeting. This is common in large corporations.

proxy card – a written document signed by a shareholder that authorizes another person to vote the shareholder's shares.

Section 14(a) – of the Securities Exchange Act of 1934 gives the SEC the authority to regulate the solicitation of proxies.

proxy statement – anyone soliciting proxies must prepare a proxy statement that fully describes (1) the matter for which the proxy is being solicited, (2) who is soliciting the proxy, and (3) any other pertinent information.

Section 14(a) prohibits misrepresentations or omissions of a material fact in proxy materials.

proxy contests – when shareholders oppose the actions of incumbent directors and management, they may challenge the management in a proxy contest in which both sides solicit proxies.

reimbursement of expenses – because proxy contests can be very expensive, the incumbent management can obtain reimbursement from the corporation if the contest concerns an issue of corporate policy. The dissenting group can get reimbursed only if it wins the proxy contest.

SEC's proxy rules – shareholders who own less than $5 million in stock of a company may communicate with other shareholders without filing proxy solicitation materials with the SEC. Companies seeking proxies must unbundle the propositions so that the shareholders can vote on each separate issue. Performance charts must be included in annual reports. Companies must provide tables in their annual reports that summarize executive compensation.

Mergers and Acquisitions

Mergers, consolidations, share exchanges, and sale of assets are friendly in nature. Both corporations have agreed to the combination of corporations or acquisition of assets.

merger – occurs when one corporation is absorbed into another corporation and ceases to exist. The corporation that continues is the surviving corporation. The other is the merged corporation. Shareholders of the merged corporation receive stock or securities of the surviving corporation.

consolidation – occurs when two or more corporations combine to form an entirely new corporation. Modernly, consolidations are a rarity.

share exchanges – when one corporation (parent corporation) acquires all the shares of another corporation (subsidiary corporation) and both corporations retain their separate legal existence.

required approvals for a merger – a merger requires (1) the recommendation of the board of directors of each corporation and (2) an affirmative vote of the majority of shares of each corporation that is entitled to vote.

articles of merger or share exchange – must be filed with the secretary of state. The secretary of state will then issue a certificate of merger or share exchange to the surviving corporation. If the parent corporation owns 90 percent of the subsidiary corporation, a **short-form merger** procedure may be followed. Approval of shareholders of neither corporation is required for short-form merger. All that is required is approval of the board of directors of the parent corporation.

sale or lease of assets – a corporation may sell, lease, or otherwise dispose of all or substantially all of its property. Such a sale requires (1) the recommendation of the board of directors and (2) an affirmative vote of the majority of the shares of the selling corporation that is entitled to vote.

Dissenting Shareholder Appraisal Rights

Shareholders who object to a proposed merger, share exchange, or sale or lease of all or substantially all of the property of a corporation have a right to have their shares valued by a court and receive cash payment of this value from the corporation.

Tender Offers

A tender offer is an offer that an acquirer (tender offeror) makes directly to a target corporation's shareholders in an effort to acquire the target corporation. The shareholders of the target make an individual decision about whether to sell to the tender offeror.

Williams Act – regulates tender offers.

leveraged buyout – the tender offeror uses loans to purchase the stock from the stockholders of the target corporation. These loans, called bridge loans, are usually paid back after assets of the target corporation are sold off. Another source of funds for the tender offeror is the sale of junk bonds, which are risky corporate bonds that pay a higher rate of interest. After the tender offer is completed, the acquiring company is saddled with huge debts. When it merges with the target corporation the resulting company's capital structure consists of a low amount of equity and huge amounts of debt.

tender offer rules:

1. offer cannot be closed before 20 days after the commencement of the tender offer
2. offer must be extended for 10 days if the tender offer increases the number of shares that it will take or the price it will pay

3. **fair price rule** stipulates that any increase in price paid for shares must be offered to all shareholders, even those who have already tendered their shares
4. **pro rata rule** requires that shares must be purchased on a pro rata basis if too many shares are tendered.

Section 14(e) of the Williams Act – prohibits fraudulent, deceptive, or manipulative practices in connection with tender offers.

Opposing a Tender Offer

The incumbent management of a target corporation may desire to oppose a tender offer. Management may engage in a variety of activities to impede or defeat the tender offer. Some of these include:

1. **Persuasion of shareholders** – media campaigns used to oppose the tender offer
2. **Delaying lawsuits** – suits filed alleging antitrust or securities violations to buy time
3. **Selling a crown jewel** – selling an asset that makes the target corporation less attractive
4. **White knight merger** – merger with friendly party that will leave target intact
5. **Pac-Man tender offer** – target makes tender offer for the tender offeror
6. **Adopting a poison pill** – strategy built into articles of incorporation, bylaws, contracts, or leases whereby large payouts or termination of contracts become effective if the corporation changes hands
7. **Issuing additional stock** – issuing more stock makes tender offeror buy more shares
8. **Creating Employee Stock Ownership Plan (ESOP)** – block of stock owned by employees is used to oppose acquirer in proxy fight
9. **Flip-over and flip-in rights plans** – allows stockholders to buy twice the value in stock to make company too expensive to buy
10. **Greenmail and standstill agreements** – target pays premium to get back shares from tender offeror

Business Judgment Rule

Fiduciary duty – the duty the directors of a corporation owe to act carefully and honestly when acting on behalf of the corporation

Business judgment rule – a rule that protects the decisions of the board of directors, who act on an informed basis, in good faith, and in the honest belief that the action taken was in the best interests of the corporation and its shareholders.

State Antitakeover Statutes

These are statutes that enacted by state legislatures that protect corporations incorporated in or doing business in the state from hostile takeovers. They are often challenged as being unconstitutional because they violate the Williams Act and the Commerce and Supremacy Clauses of the U.S. Constitution.

Exon-Florio Law

The Exon-Florio Law of 1988, as amended by the Byrd-Exon Amendment of 1992 mandates the President of the United States to suspend, prohibit, or dismantle the acquisition of U.S. businesses by foreign investors if there is credible evidence that the foreign investor might take action that threatens to impair the national security.

Refresh Your Memory

The following exercises will enable you to refresh your memory as to the key principles and concepts given to you in this chapter. Read each question carefully and put your answer in the blanks provided. Review the chapter material for any question you miss or are unable to remember.

1. A written document signed by a shareholder that authorizes another person to vote the shareholder's shares is known as a __________ __________.

2. Section _____ of the Securities Exchange Act of 1934 gives the SEC the authority to regulate the solicitation of _________.

3. When shareholders oppose the actions of incumbent directors and ____________, they may challenge the management in a _______ contest.

4. A ________________ corporation is one that continues after a merger.

5. When two or more corporations combine to form an entirely new corporation, a _____________________ occurs.

6. A share exchange occurs when a ________ corporation acquires all the shares of the _____________ corporation and both corporations retain their separate legal existence.

7. Articles or merger or share exchange must be filed with the ___________ ___ _______.

8. If the parent corporation owns 90 percent of the subsidiary corporation, a _______-______ merger procedure may be followed.

9. The __________ Act is an amendment to the Securities Exchange Act of 1934 that regulates ________ offers.

10. The _____ _______ rule stipulates that any increase in price paid for shares under a tender offer must be offered to all shareholders, even those who have already tendered their shares.

Critical Thought Exercise

Blue Cab Co. was merged into Atlantic Cab Corp., with Atlantic being the surviving corporation in the merger. Atlantic did not take over any of the cabs owned by Blue because they were old and in disrepair. Blue Cab was poorly run and owed over $600,000 to Valley Bank for cab purchases. Blue Cab also owed over $60,700 to Fleet Gas Co for fuel purchased by its employees. Blue Cab is owed $43,000 by Broadway Actors Transportation, Inc. (BAT) for limousine services rendered pursuant to a contract. Blue Cab has already commenced suit against BAT for breach of contract. Valley Bank and Fleet Gas brought a suit against Atlantic for payment of the debts. The board of directors of Atlantic refused to honor the debts of Blue Cab because the purpose in taking over Blue Cab was to eliminate a competitor. Atlantic had no desire to acquire the assets of Blue Cab. Co. Atlantic argued that it had never agreed to assume any debt owed by Blue Cab.

What is the effect of the merger and will Valley Bank and Fleet Gas be able to recover breach of contract damages from Atlantic? Can Atlantic maintain the suit against BAT?

Answer. ____

____

____

____

____

____

____

____

____

____

____

____

____

____

____

Sample Quiz

True/False

1. ___ A proxy is a means by which a shareholder votes his or her shares at the shareholders' meeting. [p 617]

2. ___ In order to act as a proxy, you must be an officer or director of the corporation whose shares are being voted by proxy. [p 724]

3. ___ The Securities Act of 1934 authorized the SEC to regulate the solicitation of proxies. [p 618]

4. ___ A proxy statement must contain information about who is soliciting the proxy and the number of proxies already solicited on the matter. [p 618]

5. ___ Management is not entitled to recover its proxy contest costs for all policy issue contests unless it wins. [p 618]

6. ___ In a merger, two corporations are combined, with both of the original corporations surviving. [p 621]

7. ___ In a share exchange, both corporations retain their separate legal existence. [p 621]

8. ___ In an ordinary merger, approval is needed by votes of both board of directors, as well as by the shareholders. [p 626]

9. ___ Shareholder appraisal rights may be exercised in mergers, consolidations, short-form mergers, and sales of substantially all the corporate assets not in the ordinary course of business. [p 623]

10. ___ Placing additional stock on the market increases the number of outstanding shares that the tender offeror must purchase in order to gain control of the target corporation. [p 626]

11. ___ Mergers with friendly parties that promise to leave the target corporation and/or its management in tact are known as white knight mergers. [p 626]

12. ___ Large severance payments received by top executives upon their departure from their employment at the corporation is known as a golden parachute. [p 627]

13. ___ State takeover statutes are aimed at permitting takeovers by hostile takeovers. [p 628]

14. ___ The pro rata rule stipulates that any increase in price paid for shares tendered must be offered to all shareholders, even those who have previously tendered their shares. [p 625]

15. ___ The fair price rule holds that the shares must be purchased on a pro rata basis if too many shares are tendered. [p 625]

Multiple Choice

16. Proxy solicitations are regulated by the Securities and Exchange Act of 1934 under [p 618]
    a. Section 10(b).
    b. Section 14(a).
    c. Section 14(e).
    d. Section 16(a).

18. A shareholder's proxy can be granted to [p 618]
    a. only another shareholder.
    b. officers only.
    c. officers or directors only.
    d. anyone.

18. What is required in order for a merger to use the short-form procedure? [p 622]
    a. There must be agreement by both boards of directors to use the short-form procedure.
    b. There must be an increase of less than 20 percent in the number of shares of voting stock of the surviving corporation.
    c. There must be ownership by the parent corporation of at least 90 percent of the shares of the subsidiary corporation before the merger.
    d. The SEC must approve the use of the short-form procedure.

19. In a typical situation, a shareholder is allowed to exercise a right of appraisal in conjunction with [p 622]
    a. regular mergers.
    b. short-form mergers.
    c. sale or lease of substantially all of the corporate assets.
    d. all of the above.

20. Jungle Corporation purchases a large bloc of shares in Harvest Corporation as its first step in an attempt to take over Harvest. The management of Harvest immediately purchases a similar size bloc of shares in Jungle and notifies it of Harvest's intent to take over Jungle. This defensive tactic is an example of [p 626]
    a. a flip-over plan.
    b. selling a crown jewel.
    c. adopting a poison pill.
    d. a Pac-Man tender offer.

21. Which rule protects the decisions of a board of directors that acts on an informed basis, in good faith, and in the honest belief that the action taken was in the best interests of the corporation and its shareholders? [p 626]
    a. the business judgment rule
    b. the fiduciary duty rule
    c. the duty of due care rule
    d. the employee stock ownership rule

22. What is meant by the term greenmail? [p 626]
    a. mail that is placed in a green envelope
    b. tactic that make the target corporation more expensive to the tender offeror
    c. Where the tender offor will agree to give up its tender offer and agree not to purchase any further shares if the target corporation agrees to buy back the stock at a premium over fair market value.
    e. none of the above.

23. An offer than an acquirer makes directly to a target corporation's shareholders in an attempt to acquire the target corporation or control of the target corporation is known as a [p 631]
    a. target offer
    b. tender offer
    c. fair value offer
    d. regular course of business offer

24. Which act regulates all tender offers, whether they are made with securities, cash, or other consideration? [p 624]
    a. The Tender Offer Act.
    b. The SEC Act

c. The Target Corporation Act
d. The Williams Act

25. An ordinary merger or share exchange requires [p 622]
 a. the recommendation of the board of directors of each corporation.
 b. an affirmative vote of the majority of shares of each corporation that is entitled to vote.
 c. compliance with RMBCA Section 11.03.
 d. all of the above

Short Answer

26. A proxy statement must contain [p 618] ______________________________

____

____

27. Section 14(a) of the Securities Exchange Act of 1934 prohibits [p 618] ______________________________

____

28. A dissenting group get reimbursement for its expenses associated with a proxy contest [p 618] ______________________________

____

29. Explain the term merger? [p 621]

____

____

____

30. Explain the concept of a share exchange. [p 621] ______________________________

____

____

31. What approvals are required for a regular merger? [p 622] ______________________________

____

____

32. When can corporations use the short-form merger procedure? [p 622] ______________________________

____

33. What is a tender offer. [p 624] ______________________________

____

34. What is required by the fair price rule? [p 625] ______________________________

____

35. What is required by the pro rata rule? [p 625] ______________________________

____

Chapter 29
LIMITED LIABILITY COMPANIES

Chapter Overview

The main focus of this chapter is the formation, operation and thorough explanation of the business entity called a limited liability company (LLC). A limited liability company is a hybrid company of sorts in that it has some of the desirable characteristics of general partnerships, corporations and limited corporations. The interesting fact about the LLC is that the owners are allowed to manage the business and yet have limited liability. Further, it is allowed to be taxed as a partnership. Since it does offer so many advantages, it is a very favorable way for new business entrepreneurs to begin their ventures.

Objectives

Upon completion of the exercises in this chapter, you should be able to:

1. Explain what comprises a limited liability company.
2. Explain the procedure for organizing a limited liability company.
3. Explain what is meant by the limited liability shield as it pertains to the limited liability company.
4. Differentiate between a member-managed limited liability company and a manager-managed limited liability company.
5. Decide and discuss when members and managers owe fiduciary duties of loyalty and care to the limited liability company.

Practical Application

You should be able to recognize the benefits from conducting a newly organized business in the form of a limited liability company. Your previous studies of partnerships will aide you in reaching a decision as to the form your own business may want to take. If you are not planning on operating a business, not only is this chapter useful for general information but, it will give you insight on the choices available as well as why a company may choose to function in this manner from a tax, liability and management perspective.

Helpful Hints

It is important to keep in mind that the Uniform Limited Liability Company Act is responsible for codifying the limited liability company law. Further, its primary goal is to establish a comprehensive limited liability company law that is uniform throughout the United

States. Since it is vital to this type of business, it is crucial to realize that it is your foundation toward learning this area of the law.

A limited liability company is much like a work of unique art that begins much like an ordinary piece of work, but develops into a creation that others would like to have too. As you go through the study tips section, keep in mind that as with all forms of business, a limited liability company will need to be organized with articles of organization, time limits set, capital contributions noted, its management set in place and of course the duties of those operating under the company umbrella. Using your imagination to compare the characteristics of the limited liability company to an artistic endeavor will help to make the material enjoyable as well as manageable to learn.

Study Tips

General Information For You to Remember

- It's important to remember that limited liability companies are created by **state law.**
- A large number of states have adopted the **Uniform Limited Liability Company Act** which sets forth the laws concerning formation, operation and termination of the LCC.
- A limited liability company is referred to as a LLC and is a **separate legal entity** separate from its members.
- Limited liability companies can sue or be sued, enter into or enforce contracts, transfer and hold title to property and be civilly as well as criminally liable under the law.
- Owners are called **members** and members usually are not personally liable to third parties for debts obligations and liabilities of an LLC beyond their capital contribution.
- Debts and obligations of the LLC are entirely those of the LLC.

Why do business as a LLC?

- If you were to **compare an LLC to and S Corporation**, you would learn that the S Corporations have several undesirable restrictions concerning who can be shareholders, how many shareholders and the percentage of stock that may be owned, whereas the LLC has none of these limitations.

- In **comparing an LLC to a general partnership**, members of the LLC have limited liability instead of personal liability for the obligations of the general partnership.

- Finally, in **viewing a LLC against a limited partnership**, the LLC allows all members to take part in management of the business with limited liability to its members. The limited partnership however requires at least one general partner who is personally liable for the partnership's obligations. Further, limited partners may not take part in the management of the business.

Lawful Purpose

A limited liability company may be organized for any lawful purpose. An example would be a real estate development company. Beware, an LLC cannot operate the practice of certain professions, such as doctors or lawyers. However, these professionals can conduct business as a limited liability partnership.

Organization

A LLC can conduct business in all states, but may only be registered in one. A LLC is usually organized in the state that it will be transacting most of its business in.

Choosing a Name for the LLC

- The name must have the words **"limited liability company"** or limited company or the abbreviations L.L.C. or LLC or LC.
- Trademark issues must be explored so as to not violate federal law.
- The issue of similar names must be explored to determine if use of the name chosen is even a viable option for the new LLC.
- If the name is available, it may be reserved for 120 days while the organization process of the LLC is being completed.

Filing the Articles of Organization

Articles of organization must be delivered to the secretary of state's office for filing. If the articles are in **proper form**, the articles will be filed. The articles must contain the name and address of the initial LLC office, the name and address of the initial agent for service of process, the name and address of each organizer and whether the LLC is a term LLC and if yes, then the specifics of the term must be stated. Additionally, the article s must state whether the LLC is to be manager-managed and the identity and address(es) of the manager(s). Finally, the articles must indicate whether the members will be personally liable for the debts and obligations of the LLC.

Duration

An LLC is either an at-will LLC or a term LLC. The term LLC states how long the LLC will exist. An at-will LLC does not state a term of duration.

Capital Contribution

A member's capital may consist of money, real property, personal property, intangible property, services performed, and so on. A member's death will not excuse a member's obligation to contribute, nor will disability or the inability to perform.

Agent for Service of Process

An agent for service of process of notices, demands, litigation or administrative proceedings is required by the ULLCA. Usually a lawyer fills this capacity, however, other individuals may do so as well.

Certificate of Interest

This act like a stock certificate as it indicates a member's ownership interest in the LLC.

Conversion of an Existing Business to an LLC

Many businesses convert to operate as a limited liability company. They do so to obtain tax benefits as well as utilize the limited liability benefit. In order to convert, ULLCA at section 902 requires that there be a statement of terms contained in an agreement of conversion, that the agreement be approved by all parties and owners concerned, and that the articles of organization be filed with the secretary of state indicating the prior business name and form of operation.

Foreign Limited Liability Company

An LLC that is organized in one state may transact business in a different state. An LLC is termed a domestic limited liability company in the state where it is organized and a foreign limited liability company in all other states it is transacting business in. A certificate of authority is required to conduct business in states that it is not organized in. An alien liability company is an LLC organized in a foreign country, but conducting business in the United States.

Operating a Limited Liability Company

There are a variety of rights, duties and rules that you need to be aware of as they pertain to the transacting of business by an LLC

- **Powers of an LLC** – An LLC has the same powers as an individual that are needed to conduct business or affairs of the LLC.

- **Operating Agreement** – Members of an LLC may enter into an operating agreement to regulate the affairs of the company and the conduct of its business.

- **Liability of the LLC** – Liability for loss or injury caused by a wrongful act or omission by a member, agent, etc within the ordinary course of business of the LLC will attach to the LLC.

- **Member-Managed and Manager Managed LLCs** – An LLC is considered member-managed unless it is deemed manager-managed in the articles of organization. In a member-managed LLC, all of the LLC member have agency authority to enter into contracts and bind the LLC. In a manger-managed LLC however, only designated managers have agency authority to enter into contracts and bind the LLC and they also have equal rights in the management of the LLC business. Note, that the contracts must be in the ordinary course of business or ones in which the LLC has authorized.

- **Dissolution and Winding Up** – A member may disassociate him or herself from the LLC by withdrawing from both a term and an at-will LLC. Wrongful disassociation from an at-will LLC occurs if the power to withdraw is absent from the operating agreement. Once a member is disassociated, he or she may not participate in the management of the LLC. Also, the member's duties of loyalty and care to the LLC end upon disassociation. Rightful disassociation requires the LLC's purchase of the disassociated member's distributional interest.

- **Notice of Disassociation** – An LLC may give constructive notice of a disassociating member by filing a statement of disassociation with the secretary of state.

- **Restrictions on Contracting Authority** – The LLC's articles of organization or the operating agreement may contain provisions to restrict the members' and managers' authority to bind the LLC to contracts.

- **Division of LLC's Profits and Losses** – Generally speaking, a member has the right to an equal share in the LLC's profits. The members of the LLC may agree otherwise though.

- **Compensation and Reimbursement** – An LLC is required to reimburse members and manager for payments made on behalf of the LLC and to indemnify managers and members for liabilities incurred.

- **Members' Distributional Interest** – The ownership share of a member is called the distributional interest. A member's interest may be transferred.

- **Fiduciary Duties of Loyalty and Care Owed to LLC** – Regardless if a person is a member or a manager of a LLC, the duties of loyalty and care are fiduciary duties owed to the LLC. The duty of loyalty means that the parties must act honestly which means no usurping of LLC opportunities, no self-dealing, no competition with the LLC, and no making of secret profits. There is a limited duty of care owed to the LLC which means that a manger or member must not engage in a known violation of the law, grossly negligent conduct, reckless conduct, a known violation of the law, etc. Liability for ordinary negligence will be assessed against a member or manager of a LLC.

- **Duty of Good Faith and Fair Dealing** – A member of a LLC who is not a manger does **not** owe a duty of loyalty or care or duty of good faith and fair dealing.

- **Continuation of an LLC** –An LLC may be continued in two instances. The first situation is where the **members unanimously vote** prior to the expiration of the current LLC. The second situation is where there is **a simple majority vote** of the at-will LLC members.

- **Winding Up and LLC's Business** – Winding up is "the process of preserving and selling the assets of the LLC and distributing the money and property to creditors and members." Assets of the LLC must be used to pay the **creditors first**, followed by any surplus left over to be distributed to the members in equal shares unless the operating agreement provides otherwise. After dissolution and winding up, articles of termination may be filed with the secretary of state.

Refresh Your Memory

The following exercise will enable you to refresh your memory on the rules and principles presented to you in this chapter. Read each question twice and place your answer in the blanks provided. Review the chapter material for any question you miss or are unable to remember.

1. Limited liability companies are created by ________________ law.

2. A limited liability company is a separate legal ___________________________.

3. Owners of the LLC are usually called ____________________________.

4. The main objective of the Uniform Limited Liability Act is to ____________________
____

5. When selecting a name for a new LLC, what words must be contained in the name? _____
____

6. What is the main benefit of opting for an LLC instead of a general partnership for conducting business? ______________________________

7. What is the primary advantage of an LLC as opposed to a limited partnership? ________
____

8. What is an at-will Limited Liability Company? ______________________________
____

9. What form may a member's capital contribution be to an LLC? ______________________________
____

10. What document provides a member's ownership interest in an LLC? ______________________________
____

Critical Thought Exercise

Hal, Mike, Sue, and Gail are college friends and have talents in the areas of e-commerce, marketing, product development, and business management. The four meet with a fifth friend, Karl, who is a second–year law student. They explain to Karl their idea for an Internet business that sends local cuisine from participating restaurants and caterers to students and military personnel who are away from home and miss their favorite food. Karl draws up the articles of organization as his contribution to being brought in as a member of the new limited liability company, "GoodGrub.com, LLC." Karl then decides that he does not have the time or energy to devote to the business. Karl declines the offer to join the LLC. Sue files the articles of organization with the secretary of state, but there is no mention of whether GoodGrub.com will be a manager-managed or member managed LLC. It was originally anticipated that Hal would be the manager of the LLC but all four members begin to manage Good Grub.com and it is very successful. To keep up with demand and to expand their business into new markets, Hal and Gail secure a $200,000 loan from Jefferson Bank. When Hal is dividing up yearly profits, he gives each member 15% of the profits and invests the other 40% in the expansion efforts.

The resulting dispute over profits and quick expansion of the business leads to turmoil. GoodGrub.com is unable to meet its financial obligations. Mike, Sue, and Gail sue Hal for a full distribution of profits. Jefferson bank sues GoodGrub.com, Hal, Mike, Sue, and Gail to recover the $200,000 loan.

Did Hal have the authority to withhold distribution of profits? Who is liable to Jefferson Bank?

Answer. ______________________________
____
____
____
____
____
____
____

____

____

____

____

____

____

____

____

____

____

Practice Quiz

True/False:

1. ___ Owners of an LLC are called legal entities. [p 639]

2. ___ If a member agrees in the LLC's articles of organization to be personally liable for the debts of the LLC, this is still insufficient. [p 640]

3. ___ LLC's are often utilized for businesses other than professional associations. [p 642]

4. ___ The mere filing of the articles of organization by the secretary of state is conclusive proof that the organizers have fulfilled all conditions required to create an LLC. [p 643]

5. ___ An LLC without a specified term of duration is called an at-will LLC. [p 643]

6. ___ A term LLC is another name for an at-will LLC. [p 643]

7. ___ A general partner who becomes a member of an LLC as a result of a conversion remains personally liable for the debts and obligations incurred by the partnership before the conversion is applicable. [p 646]

8. ___ An LLC may own and transfer personal property. [p 643]

9. ___ The operating agreement of an LLC may only be oral. [p 645]

10. ___ An LLC is a member-managed LLC unless it is designated as a manager-managed LLC in the articles of organization. [p 647]

11. ___ If Henrietta as a member of an LLC disassociates herself from a term LLC before the expiration of a specified term, her action will not be considered wrongful. [p 650]

12. ___ One way for the Tiny Toy Company to give notice of a member's disassociation is by filing a statement of disassociation with the secretary of state. [p 651]

13. ___ A member does have the right to an equal share in the LLC's profits. [p 646]

14. ___ All members, including those who have wrongfully disassociated from the LLC may participate in the winding-up of the LLC's business. [p 654]

15. ____ Certain formalities including statutory requirements must be met when forming an LLC. [p 643]

Multiple Choice:

16. Which of the following does not need to be placed in the articles of organization of an LLC? [p 643]
    a. The name and address of the initial agent for service of process
    b. The name and address of each organizer
    c. The name and address where the limited partnership will be primarily operating
    d. Whether the LLC is a term LLC and if so, the term specified

17. If an LLC is debating on which state to organize itself in, and cannot decide which one to choose between Maine and Vermont, what should it consider? [p 643]
    a. It should try to be an LLC as to both states.
    b. It should consider organizing in a state that it feels most comfortable with.
    c. It should consider the codes of the state as well as the state in which it will be doing most of its business.
    d. It should consider the government of the state in which it wants to operate.

18. Before Edward decides upon the way he wants to operate a business, he comes to you and asks about the powers that an LLC has. Which of the following best describes these powers? [p 642]
    a. An LLC has the power to waive the distribution of assets upon winding-up the LLC.
    b. An LLC has the power to own and transfer personal property.
    c. An LLC has the power to refuse reimbursement to members and managers for payments made on behalf of the LLC for business expenses.
    d. All of the above.

19. What does the duty of good faith and fair dealing impose upon a member of the member-managed LLC in discharging his or her duties to the LLC and its other members? [p 649]
    a. The members of a member-managed LLC are held to the express terms of the articles of organization and operating agreement and are required to act in "good faith" and deal fairly in all regards in achieving the objectives of the LLC.
    b. The members of a member-managed LLC are held to the express terms of the articles of organization, however, a member is not held to achieving the objectives of the LLC when discharging his or her duties to the LLC and its other members.
    c. The members must not usurp an LLC business opportunity.
    d. None of the above.

20. If Brenda wants to operate an LLC under the name of Brenda's Beautiful Babes, which of the following must she be aware of? [p 643]
    a. She must be aware that LLC's have no restrictions on shareholders.
    b. She must be aware that the name she has chosen must contain the words limited liability company or an acceptable abbreviation as per the ULLCA code.

c. She must be aware that the name she has chosen may not make a profit for her.
d. She must be aware that trademark issues are not applicable to her.

21. If a member of an LLC cannot make the required contribution of property or services, he or she is obligated to [p 644]
    a. pay creditors who relied on his or he statements.
    b. contribute money equal to the value of the promised contribution.
    c. contribute money less than the value of the promised contribution.
    d. do nothing and is excused at least once from his or her obligation.

22. If an LLC is formed between two people but they do not have an agreement as to how profits are to be shared, the most probably outcome under the ULLCA would be [p 646]
    a. that each member has the right to an equal share in the LLC's profits.
    b. that each member has no right to any share in the LLC's profits.
    c. that the two members must dissolve their LLC and reform it with an agreement as to profit distribution.
    d. all of the above

23. What do an LLC's income or losses flow through? [p 642]
    a. a trust account
    b. the entity level
    c. the members' individual income tax returns
    d. at an entrepreneurial level

24. If a member or a manager of an LLC negligently causes injury or death to another person, he or she is [p 642]
    a. not personally liable as the corporate veil of the LLC shields the member or manager from liability.
    b. personally liable if it is a member only who is negligent.
    c. personally liable if it is a manager only who is negligent.
    d. personally liable to the injured person or the heirs of a deceased person.

25. An LLC is often used instead of an S corporation because [p 642]
    a. an S corporation cannot have any more than 75 shareholders and one class of stock
    b. the members of an LLC have limited liability
    c. an LLC's provides limited liability to all members regardless of their participation in management of the business.
    d. all of the above

Short Answer:

26. How many persons may organize an LLC? [p 643] ________________________________

27. The ______________________ is similar to a stock certificate issued by a corporation as it identifies a member's ownership interest in an LLC. [p 644]

28. In a member-managed LLC, who has the authority to bind the LLC to contracts? [p 648]

____

29. In a manager-managed LLC, who has the authority to bind the LLC to contracts? [p 643]

____

30. When is an LLC bound to contracts? [p 649] ______________________________

____

31. What effect does a member's disassociation from an LLC have on the member with respect to the LLC? [p 650] ____

____

32. How may an LLC terminate its existence after it has dissolved or wound-up its operations? [p 652]

____

33. When does the existence of an LLC begin? [p 643] ______________________________

34. How may the articles of organization be amended in an LLC? [p 643] ______________

____

35. As it pertains to member-managed LLC's and manager-managed LLC's, what does the duty of loyalty include? [p 649] ______________________________________

____

Chapter 30

FRANCHISES, LICENSING, AND STRATEGIC ALLIANCES

Chapter Overview

Franchising has become an extremely important method of distributing goods and services to the public. Franchises account for 25% of all retail sales. This method of doing business can have risks for the franchisee, especially when the franchise contract is drafted solely by the franchisor. There bulk of law controlling the area of franchises and franchise agreements comes from contract law (chapters 9-16), sales (chapters 19-22), and intellectual property law (chapter 17). This chapter discusses the creation of a franchise, the rights and duties that arise in a franchise relationship, and the termination of a franchise.

Objectives

Upon completion of the exercises in this chapter, you should be able to:
1. Describe a franchise.
2. List the various forms of franchises.
3. Describe the rights and duties of the parties to a franchise agreement.
4. Explain the various forms of franchise fees.
5. Explain how intellectual property rights apply to franchises.
6. Describe the contract liability of franchisors and franchisees.
7. Understand the tort liability of franchisors and franchisees.
8. Describe international franchise formation.

Practical Application

You should be able to understand and analyze the problem areas in franchise formation. This will entail applying contract law principles to the special issues created in a franchise arrangement. Further, you will be able to comprehend the rights and liabilities associated with use of trademarks, service marks, patents, copyrights, trade name, and trade dress as they apply to franchises.

Helpful Hints

The biggest problem areas concerning franchises are in the areas of genuineness of assent, discharge, remedies, and intellectual property. It will be very helpful to review the pertinent chapters presented earlier in this test as part of the overall understanding of franchises.

Study Tips

The study of franchise law requires a basic understanding of the following concepts and principles:

franchise – a business arrangement that is established when one party licenses another party to use the franchisor's trade name, trademarks, patents, copyrights, and other property in the distribution and selling of goods and services.

distributorship franchise – the franchisor manufactures a product and licenses a retail franchisee to distribute the product to the public.

processing plant franchise – the franchisor provides a secret formula or process to the franchisee, and the franchisee manufactures the product and distributes it to retail dealers.

chain-style franchises – the franchisor licenses the franchisee to make and sell its products or distribute services to the public from a retail outlet serving an exclusive territory.

area franchise – the franchisor grants the franchisee a franchise for an agreed-upon geographical area within which the franchisee may determine the location of outlets.

Uniform Franchise Offering Circular (UFOC) – a uniform disclosure document that requires the franchisor to make specific presale disclosures to prospective franchisees.

FTC franchise rule – a rule set out by the FTC that requires franchisors to make full presale disclosures to prospective franchisees.

quality control standards – standards or performance and product quality set forth in the franchise agreement to preserve the franchisor's market name and reputation.

training requirements – employee standards that meet the franchisor's specifications

covenant not to compete – an agreement by the franchisee to not compete with the franchisor for a period of time in a specified area after the termination of the franchise.

franchise fees – fees payable by the franchisee as set forth in the franchise agreement.

initial license fee – a lump-sum payment to obtain a franchise.

royalty fee – fee for use of franchisor's trade name, property, and assistance that is computed as a percentage of the franchisee's gross sales.

assessment fee – fee for advertising and administrative costs.

lease fee – payment for land or equipment leased from the franchisor.

cost of supplies – payment for supplies purchased from the franchisor.

breach of franchise agreement – aggrieved party can sue the breaching party for rescission of the agreement, restitution, and damages.

trademarks – a distinctive mark, symbol, name, word, motto, or device that identifies the goods or products of the trademark owner.

service mark – mark, symbol, name, word, motto, or device that identifies the service provided by the service mark owner.

trade secrets – ideas that make a franchise successful but that do not qualify for trademark, patent, or copyright protection.

tort liability – franchisors and franchisees are liable for their own torts.

independent contractor status – the franchisee is an independent contractor, preventing the franchisor from being liable for the franchisee's torts and contracts.

apparent agency – agency that arises when a franchisor creates the appearance that a franchisee is its agent when in fact an actual agency does not exist.

termination of franchise – the franchise agreement usually states reasons or conditions that allow the franchisor or franchisee to terminate the franchise agreement.

termination "for cause" – termination of franchise agreement for failure to fulfill the duties imposed by the agreement.

wrongful termination – termination of the franchise agreement when cause for such action does not exist.

Refresh Your Memory

The following exercises will enable you to refresh your memory of the principles presented in this chapter. Read each question carefully and place your answer in the blanks provided. Review the chapter material for any question you miss or are unable to remember.

1. When one party ___________ another party to use the franchisor's name, trademarks, patents, copyrights, and other property, a franchise is formed.

2. In a distributorship franchise, the franchisor ______________ a product and licenses a retail franchisee for _______________.

3. In a ___________ _______ franchise, the franchisor provides a secret formula or process to the franchisee, and the franchisee manufactures the product and distributes it to retailers.

4. In a ______-______ franchise, the franchisor licenses the franchisee to make and sell its products or distribute services to the public from a retail outlet serving an __________________ territory.

5. The Uniform Franchise Offering Circular is a uniform __________________ document.

6. The FTC franchise rule requires franchisors to make full ____________ disclosures to prospective franchisees.

7. The _________ license fee is a lump-sum payment to obtain a franchise.

8. A __________ fee is assessed for use of the franchisor's name, property and ___________.

9. An assessment fee is for ______________ and administrative costs.

10. A ___________ is a distinctive mark, symbol, name, ______, _______, or device that identifies the goods or products of the owner.

Critical Thought Exercise

Federal Foods, Inc., runs company stores and sells franchises for its restaurants, known as Yum-Me's. Under the franchise agreement with Federal, each franchisee agrees to hire and train all employees and staff in strict compliance with Yum-Me's standards and policies. Federal employs area supervisors who are responsible for reviewing and approving all personnel actions at any restaurant within the four restaurant chains owned by Federal. This includes comprehensive policies relating to employee hiring, training, discipline, and work performance. As part of the franchise agreement, Federal retains the right to terminate any franchise that violates the rules or policies of the franchisor. In practice, the area managers approve the hiring of whatever employees the franchisee desire and the policies that the franchisee desires to create and implement. The area managers inspect each franchise, dictate the food production method, and enforce customer relations policies that were created by Federal.

Ned, a crew leader at a Yum-Me's restaurant, has repeatedly harassed female employees and customers by making rude and explicit sexual remarks. The franchisee and the on-site manager have done nothing to correct Ned's behavior. Two female employees and three customers have filed suit in federal court against Federal based upon Ned's acts. Federal argues that a franchisor cannot be held liable for harassment by franchise employees. Who should prevail?

Answer. ____

Sample Quiz

True/False:

1. ___ A franchisor and franchisee are established as separate corporations. [p 658]

2. ___ A franchise is any arrangement other than one in which the owner of a trademark, a trade name, or a copyright has licensed a franchisee to use it in selling goods or services. [p 658]

3. ___ An automobile dealership is not an example of a distributorship type of franchise. [p 658]

4. ___ The party who is granted a franchise is a franchisor. [p 658]

5. ___ A Coca-Cola bottling franchise is an example of a processing plant franchise. [p 659]

6. ___ Burger King is an area style franchise. [p 659]

7. ___ Area franchises are a useful business arrangement for expanding into foreign markets. [p 659]

8. ___ A Uniform Franchise Offering Circular requires the franchisor to make specific disclosures to prospective franchisees. [p 659]

9. ___ There was an abundance of governmental regulations pertaining to franchising [p 659]

10. ___ The FTC franchise rule requires the same disclosures to be made by franchisors in all states. [p 660]

11. ___ The least important assets of a franchisor are its name and reputation. [p 662]

12. ___ The franchisee's use of the franchisor's name and reputation are still subject to control by the franchisor with respect to the quality of the franchisee's goods or services. [p 662]

13. ___ Franchisees and their personnel are not required to attend training programs. [p 662]

14. ___ A franchisor cannot protect itself from a franchisee that opens a competing business in the same area after termination of the franchise. [p 662]

15. ___ Franchisees ordinarily make payments for a franchise license and separate fees for other products and services obtained from the franchisor. [p 662]

Multiple Choice:

16. An automobile dealership is [p 768]
    a. a chain-style franchise.
    b. a distributorship franchise.
    c. a processing plant franchise.
    d. an area franchise.
17. The party to whom a franchise is granted is the [p 768]
    a. franchisor.
    b. franchisee.
    c. principal.
    d. agent.

18. Bogart enters into an agreement whereby he receives an exclusive territory covering four states in which he is authorized to establish a plant to manufacture Fizzy Beer. After receiving Fizzy's secret formula, Bogart begins making beer. This is a [p 768]

a. processing plant franchise.
b. chain-style franchise.
c. distributorship.
d. none of the above.

19. For which type of franchise does the franchisee have the right to grant franchises to others within a geographical area? [p 769]
a. Processing plant franchise
b. Chain-style franchise
c. Area franchise
d. Distributorship franchise

20. The FTC franchise rule requires franchisors to [p 770]
a. share profits with franchisees.
b. supply advertising and administrative services to the franchisee.
c. supply trademarks and secret formulas to the franchisee.
d. make presale disclosures to prospective franchisees.

21. A payment for any land equipment obtained from the franchisor, that is billed either as a flat monthly or annual fee or as a percentage of gross sales or another agreed-upon amount is known as [p 662]
a. cost of supplies fee
b. lease fees
c. royalty fees
d. none of the above

22. A fee that is for the continued use of the franchisor's trade name, property, and assistance that is often computed as a percentage of the franchisee's gross sales is a [p 662]
a. covenant not to compete fee
b. arbitration fee
c. royalty fee
d. supply fee

23. A clause that provides that any claim or controversy arising from the franchise agreement or an alleged breach thereof would most likely be a(n) [p 662]
a. arbitration clause
b. training requirement
c. capital requirement
d. quality control clause

24. Since the franchisor and franchisee are separate legal entities, the franchisor deals with the franchisee as [p 664]
a. a banker
b. an employee
c. an agent
d. an independent contractor

25. If a franchise is terminated without just cause, the franchisee can sue the franchisor for [p 664]
a. assault
b. breach of covenant not to compete
c. general liability
d. wrongful termination

Short Answer:

26. What is a processing plant franchise? [p 659] ______________________________

27. Why is Mc Donald's not a processing plant franchise? [p 659]

28. Why are quality control standards important to the franchisor? [p 662] ______________________________

29. Give five examples of a type of franchise fee. [p 662] ______________________________

30. What is the purpose of an assessment fee and what does it cover? [p 662] ______________________________

31. What may an aggrieved party recover in a suit for breach of a franchise agreement? [p 662]

32. What is a strategic alliance? [p 669] ______________________________

33. What is a joint venture? [p 668]______________________________

34. What is an apparent agency? [p 667] ______________________________

35. What is wrongful termination of a franchise agreement? [p 664] ______________________________

Chapter 31
INVESTOR PROTECTION

Chapter Overview

The stock market crash of 1929 motivated Congress to make investor security a priority. Up to this time, fraud and dealing on inside information was rampant. Congress passed two key pieces of legislation in an attempt to remedy the problem. The Securities Act of 1933 requires public disclosure of material information by companies and others who issue securities to the public. The Securities Exchange Act of 1934 was enacted to prevent fraud in the trading of securities, especially insider trading. Additional statutes have been passed by the states. These federal and state statutes are still the cornerstone that forms the protection for investors in securities. This chapter examines these protections.

Chapter Objectives

Upon Completion of the exercises in this chapter, you should be able to:
1. Describe public offerings of securities and registration of those securities with the SEC.
2. Describe the exemptions from registration.
3. Define insider trading violations of Section 10(b) of the Securities Exchange Act of 1934.
4. Explain how tippers and tippees become liable for insider trading.
5. Understand how the SEC is addressing Internet stock fraud.
6. Explain the meaning of short-swing profits that violate Section 16(b) of the SEC Act of 1934.

Practical Application

This chapter has application from several viewpoints. The investor, which includes individuals, employee groups, and businesses, needs to know the protections that are available under federal state law that prevent fraudulent loss of their investment. Those persons and businesses that issue securities, and the people who work for them, need to know the standards to which the federal government will hold them. Lastly, the unsuspecting investor needs to know what acts may make them part of a fraudulent or criminal transaction so that liability can be avoided. Unless each person familiarizes himself with federal securities law, there is an increased risk of financial loss, damage to their business, and exposure to criminal prosecution.

Helpful Hints

The securities laws are geared to regulating transactions involving the issuance and trading of securities. Focus on the individual transaction or related transactions and the information that was exchanged or withheld as to the particular transaction. It is the improper release or suppression of material information and trading upon that information that triggers the application of the securities laws.

Study Tips

The following terms and sections of the securities laws are key to understanding the material in this chapter. You should develop a working knowledge of these key terms and pay attention to how they are applied by the courts.

security – (1) An interest or instrument that is common stock, preferred stock, a bond, a debenture, or a warrant, (2) an interest or instrument that is expressly mentioned in securities acts, and (3) an investment contract.

Securities Exchange Act of 1934 – A federal statute that primarily regulates the trading in securities.

Securities Act of 1933 – A federal statute that primarily regulates the issuance of securities by a corporation, a general or limited partnership, an unincorporated association, or an individual.

Securities and Exchange Commission (SEC) – A federal administrative agency that is empowered to administer federal securities laws. The SEC can adopt rules and regulations to interpret and implement federal securities laws. Violations of these rules carry civil and criminal penalties.

registration statement – Document that an issuer of securities files with the SEC that contains required information about the issuer, the securities to be issued, and other relevant information.

prospectus – A written disclosure document that must be submitted to the SEC along with the registration statement and given to prospective purchasers of the securities.

prefiling period – A period of time that begins when the issuer first contemplates issuing securities and ends when the registration statement is filed. The issuer may not condition the market by engaging in a public relation campaign during this period.

waiting period – A period of time that begins when the registration statement is filed with the SEC and continues until the registration statement is declared effective. The issuer is encouraged to condition the market during this time.

posteffective period – The period that begins when the registration statement becomes effective and runs until the issuer either sells all of the offered securities or withdraws them from sale.

final prospectus – A final version of the prospectus that must be delivered by the issuer to the investor prior to or at the time of confirming a sale or sending a security to a purchaser.

exempt securities transactions – Transactions that are exempt from registration but must still comply with antifraud provisions of the federal securities laws.

nonissuer exemption – An exemption from registration that permits average investors from registering the resale of their securities because they are not the issuer, an underwriter, or a dealer in securities.

intrastate offerings exemption – An exemption from registration that permits local businesses to raise capital from local investors to be used in the local economy without the need to register with the SEC. The three requirements for this exemption are:

1. The issuer must be a resident of the state for which the exemption is claimed
2. The issuer must be doing business in that state.
3. The purchasers of all securities must be residents of that state.

private placement exemption – An exemption from registration that permits issuers to raise capital from an unlimited number of accredited investors and no more than 35 nonaccredited investors without having to register the offering with the SEC. An accredited investor may be:

1. Any person with a net worth of at least $1 million.
2. Any person who has had an annual income of $200,000 for the previous two years and expects to make $200,000 in the current year.
3. Any corporation, partnership, or business trust with assets of $5 million.
4. Insiders of the issuers, such as officers and directors of corporate issuers and general partners of partnership issuers.
5. Institutional investors such as registered investment companies, pension plans, and colleges and universities.

small offerings exemption – An exemption from registration for the sale of securities not exceeding $1 million during a 12-month period.

restricted securities – Securities that were issued for investment purposes pursuant to the intrastate private placement, or small offering exemption. They cannot be resold for a limited period of time after their initial issue.

Rule 144 – Provides that securities sold pursuant to the private placement or small offering exemptions must be held for one year from the date when the securities are last sold by the issuer.

Rule 147 – Securities sold pursuant to an intrastate offering exemption cannot be sold to nonresidents for a period of nine months.

Rule 144A – The SEC rule permits qualified institutional investors to buy unregistered securities without being subject to the holding periods of Rule 144.

Section 24 of the Securities Act of 1933 – Imposes criminal liability of up to five years prison for violating the act or the rules and regulations adopted thereunder.

SEC actions for violating 1933 act – the SEC may:

1. issue a consent order
2. bring an action seeking an injunction
3. request disgorgement of profits by the court

Section 12 of the 1933 act – Imposes civil liability who violates Section 5 of the act. Under Section 12, a purchaser may rescind the purchase or sue for damages.

Section 11 – A provision of the Securities Act of 1933 that imposes civil liability on persons who intentionally defraud investors who intentionally defraud investors by making misrepresentations or omissions of material facts in the registration statement or who are negligent for not discovering the fraud.

Section 10(b) – A provision of the Securities Exchange Act of 1934 that prohibits the use of manipulative and deceptive devices in the purchase or sale of securities in contravention of the rules and regulations prescribed by the SEC.

Rule 10b-5 – A rule adopted by the SEC to clarify the reach of Section 10(b) against deceptive and fraudulent activities in the purchase and sale of securities.

scienter – means intentional conduct

Regulation Fair Disclosure – Prohibits companies from leaking important information to securities professionals before the information is disclosed to the public.

insider trading – When an insider makes a profit by personally purchasing shares of the corporation prior to public release of favorable information or by selling shares of the corporation prior to the public disclosure of unfavorable information. **Insiders** are:

1. officers, directors and employees at all levels of the company
2. lawyers, accountants, consultants, and other agents hired by the company to provide services or work to the company
3. others who owe a fiduciary duty to the company

tipper – A person who discloses material nonpublic information to another person.

tippee – The person who receives material nonpublic information from a tipper.

Liability Provisions of the Securities Exchange Act of 1934

Section 32 – Makes it a criminal offense to willfully violate the 1934 act or the rules or regulations adopted thereunder.

SEC actions – The SEC may enter into consent orders, seek injunctions, or seek disgorgement of profits by court order.

Insider Trading Sanctions Act – Permits SEC to obtain civil penalty of up to three times the illegal profits gained or losses avoided by insider trading.

Section 16(a) – A section of the Securities Exchange Act of 1934 that defines any person who is an executive officer, a director, or a 10% shareholder or an equity security of a reporting company as a statutory insider for Section 16 purposes.

Section 16(b) – A section of the Securities Exchange Act of 1934 that requires that any profits made by a statutory insider on transactions involving short-swing profits belong to the corporation.

Short-swing profits – Trades involving equity securities occurring within six months of each other.

Commodity Exchange Act (CEA) – Enacted in 1936 to regulate the trading of commodity futures contracts.

Commodity Futures Trading Commission Act amended the 1936 act significantly.

Section 4b of the CEA - Prohibits fraudulent conduct in connection with any order or contract of sale or any commodity for future delivery.

Commodity Futures Trading Commission – Five member federal agency appointed by the President to regulate trading in commodities futures contracts.

Refresh Your Memory

The following exercises will enable you to refresh your memory as to the key principles and concepts given to you in this chapter. Read each question carefully and put your answer in the blanks provided. Review the chapter material for any question you miss or are unable to remember.

1. What is the federal agency that is empowered to administer federal securities laws called?

   ______________ _____ _____________ ________________

2. A document that an issuer of securities files with the SEC that contains required information about the issuer, the securities to be issued, and other relevant information is a ____________________ ___________________.

3. A written disclosure document that must be submitted to the SEC along with the registration statement and given to prospective purchasers of the securities is a _________________.

4. The ___________ __________ is a period of time that begins when the registration statement is filed with the SEC and continues until the registration statement is declared effective.

5. An exemption from registration that permits average investors from registering the resale of their securities is a ______________________ exemption.

6. The _____________ ____________ exemption from registration permits local business to raise capital from local investors to be used in the local economy without the need to register with the SEC.

7. _______________ securities are securities that were issued for investment purposes pursuant to an exemption. They cannot be resold for a limited period of time after their initial issue.

8. Rule ____ provides that securities sold pursuant to the private placement or small offering exemptions must be held for _____ year(s) from the date when the securities are last sold by the issuer.

9. Section 24 of the Securities Act of 1933 imposes criminal liability of up to ______ years per violation of the act.

10. ______________________ means intentional conduct.

Critical Thought Exercise

Jerry Dallas is a corporate officer for CompuGames (CG), the leading manufacturer of hand-held computer games. The profit margin of CG is greatly impacted by the cost of the microprocessor it purchases for its games from Mini-Micro. Dallas tells his girlfriend, Julie Profit, that she should watch for any announcement of a price increase of 20% or more by Mini-Micro and sell her stock in CG if there is such a large price increase. Profit has a friend, Louis Nooze, who works in the public relations department at Mini-Micro. She asks Nooze to tell her if he hears of an announcement of price increases by Mini-Micro. Two days before a 33% price increase is to be announced by Mini-Micro, Nooze gives the news to Profit. Profit calls her stockbroker and sells all her stock in CG. When the price increase is announced, CG stock falls from $38 per share to $22 per share. By selling her stock before the announcement by Mini-Micro, Profit realizes a profit of $800,000.

If a stockholder initiates a suit against Dallas, Profit, and Nooze, will any of these people be liable for realizing illegal profits based upon insider trading or misappropriation?

Answer. ____

Sample Quiz

True/False:

1. ___ A security may not consist of an investment contract. [p 676]

2. ___ The Securities Act of 1934 is a federal statute that primarily regulates the trading in securities. [p 676]

3. ___ The Securities and Exchange Commission cannot adopt rules and regulations to interpret and implement federal securities laws. [p 676]

4. ___ A registration statement must be filed, but specific contents are mandatory. [p 678]

5. ___ A prospectus is a written disclosure document that is filed with the SEC and provided to prospective investors. [p 678]

6. ___ The registration period for securities offerings is divided into three time periods. [p 680]

7. ___ The prefiling period ends before the registration statement is filed. [p 680]

8. ___ The issuer is discouraged from conditioning the market during the waiting period. [p 680]

9. ___ The posteffective period begins when the registration statement becomes effective. [p 680]

10. ___ The issuer must deliver a final prospectus prior to or at the time of confirming a sale. [p 680]

11. ___ Securities issued by the government and common carriers are exempt from registration requirements. [p 681]

12. ___ The Securities Act of 1933 exempts securities transactions not made by an issuer, an underwriter, or a dealer from registration. [p 682]

13. ___ The intrastate offerings exemption requires that the issuer be a resident of the state for which the exemption is claimed, and the purchasers of the securities must be residents of that state. [p 682]

14. ___ An accredited investor may under the private placement exemption include any person with a net worth of at least $1 million. [p 682]

15. ___ Restricted securities can be resold for a limited period of time after their initial issue. [p 683]

Multiple Choice:

16. The securities Act of 1933 primarily regulates [p 677]
    a. short-swing profits.
    b. issuance of securities.
    c. insider trading.
    d. none of the above.

17. Which of the following descriptions does not need to be contained in a registration statement? [p 678]
    a. The securities being offered for sale
    b. The registrant's business
    c. The degree of competition in the industry
    d. The SEC's opinion as to the merits of the securities offered

18. The written disclosure document that must be submitted to the SEC and is given to all prospective investors to enable them to evaluate the financial risk of the investments is called a(n) [p 678]
    a. registration statement.
    b. prospectus.
    c. tombstone advertisement.
    d. offering statement.

19. The time period of the registration process during which the issuer cannot tout the prospectus to potential purchasers is the [p 680]
    a. prefiling period.
    b. waiting period.
    c. posteffective period.
    d. all of the above.

20. Lansing & Bismarck is a consulting firm that specializes in corporate reorganizations. Toji Bismarck learns that Superior Corp., a pharmaceutical company for whom he is doing temporary work, is about to announce that its scientists have developed a totally effective drug that will both prevent and cure lung cancer. Bismarck tells his wife, Sue, to buy the stock. Sue purchases $10 worth of Superior stock. Sue calls her brother, Ned, the next day. Ned purchases $50,000 worth of Superior stock that immediately climbs to $2.5 million when the drug discovery is announced. Sue's stock climbs to $500. Toji is liable for [p 687]
    a. only the $490 profit made by Sue.
    b. all the profit made by both Sue and Ned, if Ned knew the tip was material inside information.
    c. all the profit made on both Sue's and Ned's trades, regardless of the tippees knowledge.
    d. none of the profits made on the trades because Toji lacked scienter.

21. Section 24 of the Securities Act of 1933 imposes which of the following on individuals who willfully violates either the act or the rules and regulations imposed within it? [p 685]
    a. fined up to $10,000
    b. imprisoned up to five years
    c. both a and c
    d. none of the above

22. Which of the following prohibits the use of manipulative and deceptive devices in contravention of the rules and regulations prescribed by the SEC? [p 686]
    a. Rule 504
    b. Section 10 (b)
    c. Section 16 (b)
    d. All of the above

Short Answer:

23. Explain what a security is? [p 676] ____

____

____

____

24. If your lawyer was preparing a registration statement, what must be contained within it? [p 678]

____

____

____

____

25. What is the "plain English" rule adopted by the SEC for securities offerings? [p 681] __________

____

26. What are the three time periods during the registrations process? [p 680]
(1) ____________________ (2) ____________________ (3) ____________________

27. What is a Regulation A offering? [p 680] ____
____

28. What is a nonissuer exemption from registration? [p 682] ______________________________
____
____

29. What are restricted securities? [p 683] ____
____

30. What is prohibited by Section 10(b) of the Securities Exchange Act of 1934? [p 686] __________
____
____

31. What does Regulation Fair Disclosure (Reg FD) prohibit? [p 689] ________________________
____

32. What is required by Section 16(b) of the Securities Exchange Act of 1934? [p 690] ___________
____

33. What defense may be asserted against the imposition of a Section 11 liability action? [p 685]
____
____
____

Chapter 32

ANTITRUST LAW

Chapter Overview

After the Civil War, America changed from an agricultural to an industrialized nation. Freedom of competition took a huge blow with the formation of powerful business trusts that monopolized large segments of the country's economy. The anticompetitive practices of these large corporate enterprises resulted in monopolies in the oil, gas, sugar, cotton, and whiskey industries. Congress then stepped in and passed antitrust laws to limit the anticompetitive behavior of powerful trusts. The laws were written in general language, much like the Constitution, so that they could be applied to a broad range of activity and have the ability to respond to economic, business, and technological changes. This chapter examines the antitrust laws that strive to preserve freedom in the marketplace.

Objectives

Upon completion of the exercises in this chapter you should be able to

1. Explain the purpose of antitrust laws and describe the federal antitrust statutes.
2. Describe horizontal and vertical restraints of trade that violate Section 1 of the Sherman Antitrust Act.
3. Explain acts of monopolization that violate Section 2 of the Sherman Antitrust Act.
4. Describe the scope of Section 7 of the Clayton Act as it relates to mergers.
5. Apply Section 5 of the Federal Trade Commission Act to antitrust cases.
6. Explain the exemptions from antitrust laws.

Practical Application

As seen in the application of antitrust laws in the case of *United States v Microsoft Corp.*, antitrust laws remain a vital part of the federal government's enforcement of freedom of competition. Whether it is the small investor, consumer, or business partners of large corporations, anticompetitive behavior can still damage many economic interests. When corporations are allowed to dominate large segments of the economy, their failure is more devastating because there is a void that is unfilled by an able competitor. The government will continue to examine each merger, acquisition, and anti-competitive contract through the scope of the federal antitrust laws. Our economy depends upon their existence and enforcement.

Helpful Hints

There can be no meaningful discussion of antitrust law until you understand the mandates of the major federal antitrust laws and the activities that trigger their application to the conduct of an individual, small business, or corporation. Examine each act individually and pay close attention to the type of conduct that it prohibits. Then focus on the types of activity that have triggered federal intervention in the past. This will make you better able to predict what type of behavior will be called into question in the future.

Study Tips

An organized examination of the individual antitrust laws and acts forbidden by the important sections is key to your understanding of antitrust law. You need to understand the general proposition or prohibition of each section and the specific practice or activity that violates the section.

Enforcement of Antitrust Laws

Government actions – Enforcement of antitrust laws is divided between the Antitrust Division of the Justice Department and the Bureau of Competition of the Federal Trade Commission (FTC). The Sherman Act is the only major act with criminal sanctions. The government may seek civil damages, including treble damages for antitrust violations. The courts can also order divestiture of assets, cancellation of contracts, liquidation of businesses, any other reasonable remedy that will effectuate freedom of competition.

Private actions – Any private person who suffers antitrust injury to his or her business or property can bring a private civil action against the offenders. They may recover treble damages, costs of suit, and attorneys' fees.

Section 1 of the Sherman Antitrust Act

Section 1 outlaws restraints of trade. To determine the lawfulness of a restraint, the court applies the *rule of reason* and the *per se rule.*

Rule of Reason – The Supreme Court held that only unreasonable restraints of trade violate Section 1. The courts examine the following factor when trying to apply the rule of reason:

- The pro- and anticompetitive effects of the challenged restraint
- The competitive structure of the industry
- The firm's market share and power
- The history and duration of the restraint
- Other relevant factors

Per Se Rule – Some restraints are automatically a violation of Section 1 and no balancing of pro- and anticompetitive effects is necessary. Once a restraint is characterized as a per se violation, there is not defense or justifications for the restraint. If a restraint is a not per se violation, it is examined under the rule of reason.

Horizontal Restraints of Trade

A horizontal restraint of trade occurs when two or more competitors at the same level of distribution enter into a contract, combination, or conspiracy to restrain trade. These horizontal restraints include:

- *Price-Fixing* – Occurs where competitors in the same line of business agree to set the price of the goods or services they sell: raising, depressing, fixing, pegging, or stabilizing the price of a commodity or service. Price-fixing is a per se violation.
- *Division of Markets* – Occurs when competitors agree that each will serve only a designated portion of the market. It is a per se violation to enter into a market-sharing arrangement that divides customers, geographical area, or products.
- *Group Boycotts* – Occurs when two or more competitors at one level of distribution agree not to deal with others at another level of distribution.
- *Lawful Horizontal Agreements* – Some agreements at the same level are lawful, such as trade association rules, exchanging non-price information, and participating in joint ventures. These horizontal restraints are examined using the rule of reason.

Vertical Restraints of Trade

A vertical restraint of trade occurs when two or more parties on different levels of distribution enter into a contract, combination, or conspiracy to restrain trade. The Supreme Court has applied both the per se rule and the rule of reason in determining the legality of vertical restraints of trade under Section 1. These vertical restraints include:

- *Resale Price Maintenance* – Occurs when a party at one level of distribution enters into an agreement with a party at another level to adhere to a price schedule that either sets or stabilizes prices.
- *Nonprice Vertical Restraints* – These restraints are examined using the rule of reason. They are unlawful if their anticompetitive effects outweigh their procompetitive effects. Nonprice vertical restraints occur when a manufacturer assigns exclusive territories to retail dealers or limits the number of dealers in a geographical area.

Defenses to Section 1 of the Sherman Trust Act

- *Unilateral Refusal to Deal* – A unilateral choice by one party to refuse to deal with another party does not violate Section 1 as long as there was no action by two or more parties in concert. This rule is known as the ***Colgate doctrine***.
- Conscious Parallelism – This defense applies if two or more firms act the same but no concerted action is shown.
- Noerr Doctrine – Under this doctrine two or more persons may petition the executive, legislative, or judicial branch of the government or administrative agencies to enact laws or take other action without violating antitrust laws.

Section 2 of the Sherman Act

Section 2 prohibits the act of monopolization and attempts or conspiracies to monopolize trade. To prove a violation of Section 2, requires showing that the defendant possesses monopoly power in the relevant market and is engaged in a willful act of monopolization to acquire or maintain the power. The court will examine the following elements and defenses in determining the existence of a Section 2 violation:

- *Defining the Relevant Market* – This requires defining the relevant product or service market and geographical market. The relevant market generally includes substitute products or services that are reasonably interchangeable with the defendant's products or services. The relevant geographical market is defined as the area in which the defendant and its competitors sell the product or service.
- *Monopoly Power* – This is the power to control prices or exclude competition measured by the market share the defendant possesses in the relevant market.
- *Willful Act of Monopolizing* – A requires act for there to be a violation of Section 2. Possession of monopoly power without such act does not violate Section 2.
- *Defenses to Monopolization* – Only two defenses to a charge of monopolization have been recognized:
    1. innocent acquisition (acquisition because of superior business acumen, skill, foresight, or industry)
    2. natural monopoly (a small market that can only support one competitor)
- Attempts and Conspiracies to Monopolize – A single firm may attempt to monopolize. Two or more firms are required for a conspiracy to monopolize.

Clayton Act Section 7

Section 7 provides that it is unlawful for a person or business to acquire stock or assets of another where in any line of commerce or in any activity affecting commerce in any section of the country, the effect of such acquisition may be substantially to lessen competition or to tend to create a monopoly. In order to determine whether a merger is lawful under Section 7, the court must examine the following elements:

- *Line of Commerce* – Determining the line of commerce that will be affected by the merger involves defining the relevant product or service market. It includes products or services that consumers use as substitutes. If an increase in the price of one product or service leads consumers to purchase another product or service, the two products are substitutes for each other. The two products are part of the same line of commerce because they are interchangeable.
- *Section of the Country* – Defining the relevant section of the country consists of defining the relevant geographical market that will feel the direct and immediate effects of the merger.
- *Probability of a Substantial Lessening of Competition* – If there is a probability that a merger will substantially lessen competition or create a monopoly, the court may prevent the merger under Section 7.

In applying Section 7, mergers are generally classified as one of the following:

- *Horizontal Merger* – A merger between two or more companies that compete in the same business and geographical market. The court uses the presumptive illegality test for determining the lawfulness of horizontal mergers. Under this test the merger is illegal under Section 7 if:
    1. the merged firm would have a 30 percent or more market share in the relevant market and
    2. the merger would cause an increase in concentration of 33 percent or more in the relevant market.

  Other factors are also considered such as the past history of the firms involved, the aggressiveness of the merged firms, the economic efficiency of the proposed merger, and consumer welfare.
- *Vertical Mergers* – A vertical merger is a merger that integrates the operations of a supplier and a customer. In a backward vertical merger, the customer acquires the supplier. In a forward vertical merger, the supplier acquires the customer. Vertical mergers do not increase market share but may cause anticompetitive effects.
- *Market Extension Mergers* – A merger between two companies in similar fields whose sales do not overlap. They are treated like conglomerate mergers under Section 7.
- *Conglomerate Mergers* – Are mergers between firms in totally unrelated businesses. Section 7 examines the lawfulness of such mergers under the following theories:

  The ***Unfair Advantage Theory*** holds that a merger may not give the acquiring firm an unfair advantage over its competitors in finance, marketing, or expertise.

  The ***Potential Competition Theory*** reasons that the real or implied threat of increased competition keeps businesses more competitive. A merger that would eliminate this perception can be enjoined under Section 7.

  The ***Potential Reciprocity Theory*** says if Company A, which supplies materials to Company B, merges with Company C (which in turn gets its supplies from Company B), the newly merged company can coerce Company b into dealing exclusively with it.
- *Defenses to Section 7 Actions*

  The ***Failing Company Doctrine*** – Under this defense, a competitor may merge with a failing company if:
    1. there is no other reasonable alternative for the failing company
    2. no other purchaser is available
    3. the assets of the failing company would disappear from the market if the merger did not proceed

  The ***Small Company Doctrine*** – Two small companies are permitted to merge if it would make them more competitive with a large company.

- *Hart-Scott-Rodino Antitrust Improvement Act* – Requires certain firms to notify the FTC and the Justice Department in advance of a proposed merger. Unless the government challenges the proposed merger within 30 days, the merger may proceed.

Section 3 of the Clayton Act – Prohibiting Tying Arrangements

Section 3 prohibits tying arrangements involving sales and leases of goods. Tying arrangements are vertical restraints where a seller refuses to sell one product to a customer unless the customer agrees to purchase a second product from the seller. The defendant must be shown to have sufficient economic power in the tying product market to restrain competition.

Section 2 of the Clayton Act – Price Discrimination

Section 2(a) prohibits direct and indirect price discrimination by sellers or a commodity of a like grade and quality where the effect of such discrimination may be to substantially lessen competition or to tend to create a monopoly in any line of commerce.

- *Elements of a Section (2)a violation* - To prove a violation of Section 2(a), the plaintiff must show sales to two or more purchasers involving goods of like grade and quality that results in actual injury.
- *Indirect Price Discrimination* – This is a form of price discrimination (favorable credit terms, reduced shipping charges) that is less readily apparent than direct forms of price discrimination.
- *Defenses to Section 2(a) Actions* – There are three statutory defenses:

  Cost Justification A seller's price discrimination is not unlawful if the price differential is due to "differences in the cost of manufacture, sale, or delivery" of the product. Quantity or volume discounts are lawful to the extent they are supported by cost savings.

  Changing Conditions Price discrimination is not unlawful if it is in response to "changing conditions in the market for or the marketability of the goods." Reduction in price of winter coats would be lawful when the spring line of clothing comes out.

  Meeting the Competition A seller may engage in price discrimination to meet a competitor's price.

Section 5 of the Federal Trade Commission Act

Section 5 prohibits unfair methods of competition and unfair or deceptive acts or practices in or affecting commerce. Section 5 covers conduct that (1) violates any provision of the Sherman Act of the Clayton Act, (2) violates the spirit of those acts, (3) fills the gaps of those acts, and (4) offends public policy, or is immoral, oppressive, unscrupulous, or unethical, or causes substantial injury to competition or consumers.

Section 5 of the FTC Act and the Internet

Section 5 prohibits unfair and deceptive acts affecting commerce. When Internet site operators use deceptive methods to capture Internet traffic, such as disguising the true nature of their site, this practice violates Section 5. The FTC used Section 5 to shut down the "page-jacking" and "mouse-trapping" used by Internet porn sites.

Exemptions From Antitrust Laws

Statutory exemptions include labor unions, agricultural cooperatives, export activities of American companies, and insurance business that is regulated by a state. Other statutes exempt railroad, shipping, utility, and securities industries from most of the reach of antitrust law.

Implied exceptions are given by federal court decision. Two such exemptions include professional baseball and the airline industry.

State action exemptions are economic regulations, such as utility rates, mandated by state law. Though it is a form or price-fixing, the states and utilities are not liable under for anti-trust violations.

Refresh Your Memory

The following exercise will enable you to refresh your memory on the rules of law and principles presented to you in this chapter. Read each question twice and place your answer in the blanks provided. Review the chapter material for any question you miss or are unable to remember.

1. The Sherman Act is the only major antitrust act with ____________________ sanctions.

2. Section 1 of the Sherman Act prohibits contracts, combinations, and conspiracies in ____________ of trade.

3. The rule of ______________ holds that only ______________________ restraints of trade violate Section 1 of the Sherman Act.

4. Horizontal __________ ___________ occurs when the competitors in the same line of business agree to set the price of goods or services they sell.

5. Section 2 of the Sherman Act prohibits the act of ______________________ and attempts or ____________________ to monopolize trade.

6. A merger is illegal if it will lessen the competition in any _______________ of commerce.

7. A ___________ _______________ merger is a merger between two companies in similar fields whose sales do not overlap.

8. The _____ _________ _________ is a defense to a Section 7 violation under the Clayton Act that allows two or more _________ companies to merge without liability if the merger allows them to compete more effectively with a large company.

9. The Robinson-Patman Act prohibits price ______________________ in the sale of goods.

10. Quantity or volume discounts are lawful under Section 2 of the Clayton Act because of the ___________-____________________ defense.

Critical Thought Exercise

When the partners of The Four Brothers Pizza Shoppe terminated the partnership, they divided the greater Chicago area into four parts and agreed to restrict the geographical area within which each would advertise and deliver pizzas. Two years later one partner filed suit against the other three alleging in part that the restriction on advertising and delivery area was a per se violation of the Sherman Act. Was the agreement made as part of a breakup of a partnership that divided a city into geographical areas for advertising and delivery a violation of antitrust law?

Answer. ____

____

____

____

____

____

Sample Quiz

True/False:

1. ___ The rule or reason holds that any unreasonable restraints of trade violate the Sherman Act. [p 702]

2. ___ A horizontal restraint of trade occurs when two companies at the same levels of distribution enter into an agreement to restrain trade. [p 703]

3. ___ Price-fixing agreements occur between sellers. Agreements between buyers are not price-fixing restraints of trade under the Sherman Act. [p 703]

4. ___ Division of markets is a per se violation of Section 1. [p 703]

5. ___ A group boycott would occur if a group of television manufacturers agreed not to sell their products to certain discount retailers. [p 704]

6. ___ A vertical restraint of trade occurs when two or more parties on different levels of distribution enter into an agreement to restrain trade. [p 705]

7. ___ Trade associations can help avoid antitrust liability by discussing or exchanging price information about current or future sales to customers. [p 707]

8. ___ Conscious parallelism is when two or more firms act the same but no concerted action is shown. [p 707]

9. ___ As part of its burden of proof regarding violation of Section 2 of the Sherman Act, the government needs to prove that a defendant possesses monopoly power in the relevant market. [p 708]

10. ___ The relevant geographical market, for Section 2 analysis, is defined as the area in which the defendant and its competitors sell the product or service. [p 708]

11. ___ For an antitrust action to be sustained, the defendant must not possess monopoly power in the relevant market. [p 708]

12. ___ There are only two defenses to a charge of monopolizing: innocent acquisition and natural monopoly. [p 079]

13. ___ Section 7 of the Clayton Act only applies to all methods of external expansion. [p 710]

14. ___ If ABC Beer, a beer that is sold nationally, desires to merge with Little Beer, which is sold in Ohio, Indiana, and Michigan, the relevant geographical market for this merger will be the direct and immediate effects of the merger which would be in the area of the three states. [p 708]

15. ___ The test for determining the lawfulness of horizontal mergers is the presumptive illegality test. [p 711]

Multiple Choice:

16. Section 1 of the Sherman Act outlaws certain [p 702]
    a. restraints of trade.
    b. monopolization.
    c. mergers.
    d. tying arrangements.

17. Which of the following is a defense to a Section 1 violation? [p 706]
    a. Innocent acquisition
    b. Unilateral refusal to deal
    c. The failing company doctrine
    d. Meeting the competition

18. Section 2 of the Sherman Act prohibits [p 707]
    a. restraint of trade.
    b. mergers.
    c. monopolization.
    d. tying arrangements.

19. The power to control prices or exclude competition measured by the market share the defendant possesses in the relevant market is [p 708]
    a. price-fixing.
    b. a tying arrangement.
    c. the unfair advantage theory.
    d. monopoly power.

20. The protection of quality control coupled with a trade secret may save a [p 713]
    a. tie-in arrangement.
    b. price-fixing arrangement.
    c. division of markets arrangement.
    d. resale price maintenance arrangement.

21. When a party at one level of distribution enters into an agreement with a party at another level to adhere to a price schedule that either sets or stabilizes prices, this is known as [p 705]
    a. resale pricing maintenance.
    b. the Colgate doctrine.
    c. a unilateral refusal to deal.
    d. none of the above

22. Which of the following holds that two or more persons may petition the executive, legislative, or judicial branch of the government or administrative agencies to enact or to take other action without violating the antitrust laws? [p 707]
    a. Section 2 of the Sherman Act

b. conscious parallelism
c. The Noerr doctrine
d. The Online Commerce and Internet Law Doctrine

23. Mergers between firms in unrelated businesses are often termed [p 711]
a. market extension mergers
b. horizontal mergers
c. vertical mergers
d. conglomerate mergers

24. The failing company doctrine is [p 712]
a. a defense whereby a competitor may merge with a failing company.
b. used if there is no other reasonable alternative for a failing company.
c. available if the assets of the failing company would completely disappear from the market if the anticompetitive merger were not allowed to go through.
d. all of the above

25. Which of the following best describes when price discrimination is not unlawful? [p 714]
a. When the price of goods is raised to reflect deterioration of goods.
b. When the price of goods is raised to make a profit.
c. If it is in response to changing conditions in the market for or the marketability of goods.
d. None of the above

Short Answer:

26. What is meant by the term price-fixing ? [p 703]

____

____

____

27. Describe an example of the doctrine of conscious parallelism. [p 707] ______________________________

____

____

28. Name two defenses to a monopolization charge and give an example of each. [p 709]
(1) ______________________________
(2) ______________________________

29. What test does the court apply to determine the relevant product or service market in Section 7 analysis under the Clayton Act? [p 710] ______________________________

____

____

30. Explain the difference between a forward vertical merger and a backward vertical merger. [p 711] ______________________________

____

31. What is a conglomerate merger? [p 711] ______________________________

____

32. If two companies are proposing a merger, what must they do to comply with the Hart-Scott-Rodino Antitrust Improvement Act? [p 712] ____

____

33. If a doctor charges one patient $200 for the same procedure as she charged another patient only $55, is this price discrimination a violation of the Robinson-Patman Act? [p 713] ____________

____

Chapter 33

CONSUMER AND ENVIRONMENTAL PROTECTION

Chapter Overview

Starting in the 1960s and continuing into the early 1980s, federal and state governments enacted numerous statutes in order to regulate the behavior of businesses that deal with consumers. The goal of the legislation was to promote product safety and prohibit abusive, unfair, and deceptive selling practices. This was a drastic change from earlier days when sales to consumers were governed by the principle of *caveat emptor*, which means "let the buyer beware."

With great increase in population growth, urbanization, and all forms of industry, our desire for higher profits, more products, and technological advancement lead to damage to the environment on a worldwide basis. In an effort to curtail the damaging effects of pollution, the federal government and states have created environmental protection laws that apply to all businesses and individuals. In part, this chapter examines the efforts of the government to contain the levels of pollution that is still being made, while cleaning up huge amounts of pollution and hazardous waste that have been dumped into the environment.

Additionally, this chapter presents the statutes, rules, and cases that allow consumers greater protection and have increased the ability of consumers to sue businesses for damages caused by their dangerous, fraudulent, and deceptive methods. Legal theories have developed in the areas of breach of warranty, negligence, and strict liability. Government mandates and regulation by administrative agencies has mushroomed in the area of consumer protection. These laws and regulations form the consumer protection laws that are examined in this chapter.

Objectives

Upon completion of the exercises in this chapter, you should be able to:

1. Describe the authority and responsibilities of the Food and Drug Administration.
2. Describe the regulation of drugs, cosmetics, and medical devices.
3. Describe the scope of the Consumer Product Safety Act and its effect on product safety.
4. Describe the regulation of packaging, labeling, and poison prevent labeling.
5. Understand the key elements of consumer credit protection statutes.
6. Describe the mandates of the Clean Air Act.
7. Explain the effluent water standards of the Clean Water Act.
8. Explain how environmental laws regulate the use of toxic substances.

Practical Application

Upon learning the main legislative protections for consumers in this chapter, you will understand the duties, obligations, and requirements placed upon businesses when they deal in the manufacture, sale, or distribution of consumer goods or services. This information will allow you to determine your specific rights and obligations whether you are a business that must comply with the law or a consumer who is seeking to enforce a protected right.

Helpful Hints

As with all law, your analysis of a situation must begin with the basis definitions and requirements as contained in the statutes. Once you have that foundation, your focus should turn to the act or nature of the product. By determining where the act or product fits in the legislative scheme of consumer protection, you can alleviate the illegality or enforce the mandates contained in a consumer law. Also, many of the statutes require a mental element in combination with the conduct. Examine the intent of the business employee to determine if the statute has been violated.

With all of the different regulations that have been enacted to curtail pollution and its effects upon the environment, it is helpful if you organize your analysis of any situation based upon the type of damage done or the segment of the environment that is at risk. This will lead you to the correct statute or regulation for guidance as to how the situation will be handled by the appropriate agency or the courts.

Study Tips

It is important that you become familiar with the following consumer protections if you are going to be able to analyze actual business situations where the statutes are implicated.

You should organize your study of environmental protection by looking at the areas of the environment that are protected. Examine the laws and cases within the areas of air, water, toxic and hazardous substances, nuclear waste, endangered species, and noise.

Under the common law, both an individual and the government could bring a suit for negligence. The individual could bring an action for private nuisance and the government could maintain an action against a polluter for public nuisance. This was a very ineffective way of controlling pollution. With the creation of the Environmental Protection Agency (EPA) by Congress in 1970, the federal government had a vehicle for implementing and enforcing federal environmental protection laws. The EPA can make rules, adopt regulations, hold hearings, make decisions, and order remedies for violation of federal environmental laws. The EPA can also initiate judicial proceedings against violators.

The National Environmental Policy Act was created in 1969. Under this act, an environmental impact statement must be prepared to assess the adverse impact that any legislation or federal action will have upon the environment. This study is required before the project or legislation can be approved. Each state has a similar statute.

Food, Drug, and Cosmetic Act (FDCA)

This act regulates much of the testing, manufacture, distribution, and sale of foods, drugs, cosmetics, and medical products and devices in the United States. The **Food and Drug Administration (FDA)** administers the act. The FDA implements the FDCA as follows:

- *Regulation of Food* – The FDCA prohibits the shipment, distribution, or sale of aldulterated food, which is any food that consists in whole or in part of any "filthy, putrid, or decomposed substance" that is unfit for consumption. The FDA allows certain amounts of contaminants up to the amount set by their "action levels." For example, tomato juice is allowed to have 10 fly eggs per 3 ½ ounces. Anything below the action level is considered safe to eat.
- **Nutritional Labeling and Education Act** – requires food manufacturers and processors to provide more nutritional information on virtually all foods and forbids them from making scientifically unsubstantiated heath claims. The law requires labels on food items with information on calories, fat, fiber, cholesterol and other substances. The FDA regulations adopted to implement the act, required information on serving size and nutrients. Definitions were developed for *light, low fat*, and *natural.*
- *Regulation of Drugs* – The FDA regulates the testing, licensing, manufacturing, distribution, and sale of drugs. The licensing process is long and thorough. Users of drugs must be

provided with a copy of detailed directions that include any warnings and list possible side effects.

- *Regulation of Cosmetics* – The FDA regulations require cosmetics to be labeled, to disclose ingredients, and to contain warnings as to any carcinogenic ingredients. The FDA may remove from the market any product that makes a false claim of preserving youth, increasing virility, or growing hair.
- *Regulation of Medicinal Devices* – The FDA has authority under the Medicinal Device Amendment to the FDCA to regulate medicinal devices, such as heart pacemakers, surgical equipment, and other diagnostic, therapeutic, and health devices. The FDA is empowered to remove quack devices from the market.
- *Other acts and amendments* – The FDA has been empowered by numerous other acts and amendments to the FDCA to regulate pesticides, food additives, color additives, animal drugs and food, biological material (blood, vaccines), food service sanitation, and radiation products (X-ray machines, mircowave ovens, etc.).

United Nations Biosafety Protocol for Genetically Altered Foods

The Biosafety Protocol was passed to resolve a dispute between exporters of genetically modified agricultural products and countries that desired to keep the products out of their country. As a compromise, the 138 countries that signed the protocol agreed to allow the importation of genetically engineered foods as long as they were clearly labeled with the phrase "May contain living modified organisms." This allows consumers to decide themselves whether to purchase altered food products.

Product Safety

The federal government has enacted several statutes that regulate the manufacture and distribution of consumer products. Some of these are:

- The *Consumer Product Safety Act* regulates potentially dangerous consumer products and created the **Consumer Product Safety Commission (CPSC)**. The CPSC is an independent federal agency that is not attached to any department. It interprets the CPSA, conducts research on the safety of products, and collects data and regarding injuries caused by products. The CPSC sets safety standards for consumer products and has the power to compel a manufacturer to recall, repair, or replace a hazardous product. Alternatively, the CPSC can seek injunctions and seize hazardous products. It can also seek civil and criminal penalties.
- *Fair Packaging and Labeling Act* requires the labels on consumer goods to identify the product, the manufacturer, processor, or packager of the product and its address; the net quantity of the contents of the package; and the quantity of each serving. The label must use simple and clear language that a consumer can understand. The act is administered by the Federal Trade Commission and the Department of Health and Human Services.
- *The Poison Protection Packaging Act* requires manufacturers to provide "childproof" containers and packages for all household products.

Unfair and Deceptive Practices

When sellers engage in unfair, deceptive, or abusive techniques, the **Federal Trade Commission (FTC)**, under the authority of the **Federal Trade Commission Act (FTC Act)**, is authorized to bring an administrative proceeding to attack the unfair or deceptive practice. IF the FTC finds a violation under **Section 5 of the FTC Act**, it may order a cease-and-desist order, an affirmative disclosure to consumers, or corrective advertising. The FTC may sue for damages on behalf of consumers in either state or federal court. Improper acts by sellers that are addressed by the FTC include:

- *False and Deceptive Advertising* is prohibited under Section 5 when advertising
  1. contains misinformation or omits important information that is likely to mislead a "reasonable consumer" or
  2. makes an unsubstantiated claim (e.g., "This pain reliever works 50% faster on your headache than our competitors.").
- *Bait and Switch* is another type of deceptive advertising that occurs whena seller advertises the availability of a low-cost discounted item but thenpressures the buyer into purchasing more expensive merchandise. Bait and switch occurs when if
  1. the seller refuses to show consumers the advertised merchandise
  2. discourages employees from selling the advertised merchandise or
  3. fails to have adequate quantities of the merchandise available.
- *Door-to Door Sales* may entail overaggressive or abusive practices. These tactics are handles on a state level where laws give consumers a certain number of days to rescind door-to-door sales, usually three.
- *Unsolicited Merchandise* is handled under the **Postal Reorganization Act**. The act permits persons who have received unsolicited merchandise through the mail to retain, use, disregard, or dispose of the merchandise without having to pay for it or return it.
- *Anti-Spam Statutes* have been enacted by many states to prevent the sending of unsolicited commercial e-mail messages with misleading information in the subject line or transmission path. Courts have held that the benefits of the act outweigh any burden upon commerce.

Federal Consumer-Debtor Protection Laws

The federal government protects consumer-debtors (borrowers) from abusive, deceptive, and unfair practices by creditors (lenders) through a comprehensive scheme of laws concerning the extension and collection of credit. These laws include

- The *Truth-In-Lending Act* requires creditors to make certain disclosures when the creditor regularly
  1. extends credit for goods or services to consumers or
  2. arranges such credit in the ordinary course of their business.

  The TILA is administered by the Federal Reserve Board who adopted a laundry list of disclosures under **Regulation Z**. These disclosures include the finance charge, interest, points, annual percentage rate, due dates of payments, and late payment penalties.
- The *Consumer Leasing Act (CLA)* extended the TILA's coverage to lease terms in consumer leases.
- The *Fair Credit and Charge Card Disclosure Act of 1988* amended TILA to require disclosure of credit terms on credit-and charge-card solicitations and applications. The act requires, in tabular form, disclosure of
  1. the APR
  2. any annual membership fee
  3. any minimum or fixed finance charge
  4. any transaction charge for use of the card for purchases, and
  5. a statement that charges are due when the periodic statement is received by the debtor.
- The *Equal Credit Opportunity Act (ECOA)* prohibits discrimination in the extension of credit based on sex, marital status, race, color, national origin, religion, age, or receipt of income from public assistance programs.
- The *Fair Credit Reporting Act (FCRA)* is located under **Title VI** of TILA. It protects consumers who are subjects of a credit report by setting out guidelines for credit bureaus. The act gives consumers the right to request information on the nature and substance of their credit report, the sources of this information, and the names of recipients of the report.
- The Fair Debt Collection Practices Act protects consumer-debtors from abusive, deceptive, and unfair practices used by debt collectors. The practices prohibited by the FDCPA include:
  1. harassing, abusive, or intimidating tactics (threatening or abusive language)
  2. false or misleading representations (posing as police officer or attorney)

3. unfair or un conscionable practices (threatening to take illegal action)

The debt collector may not contact the debtor:
1. At an inconvenient time
2. At inconvenient places
3. At the debtor's place of employment if the employer objects
4. If the debtor is represented by an attorney
5. If the debtor gives written notice that the debtor refuses to pay the debt or does not want to have any further contact with the debt collector.

Air Pollution

- The *Clean Air Act* provides comprehensive regulation of air quality in the United States. It directs the EPA to establish national ambient air quality standards (NAAQS) for certain pollutants. There are primary levels to protect humans and secondary levels to protect vegetation, climate, visibility, and economic values. The states are responsible for enforcing these levels. The Clean Air Act regulates both stationary (manufacturing plants) and mobile (automobiles) sources.
- *Nonattainment areas* are regions that do not meet air quality standards. Deadlines are established for areas to meet attainment levels. States must submit compliance plans that
  1. identify major sources of air pollution and require them to install pollution control equipment
  2. institute permit systems for new stationary courses
  3. implement inspection programs to monitor mobile sources

  States that fail to develop and implement a plan are subject to the following sanctions:
  1. loss of federal highway finds
  2. limitations on new sources of emissions (prohibits new construction of industrial plants in the nonattainment area)
- The *Clean Air Act Amendment of 1990* allows companies to trade sulfur dioxide emissions (the pollutant that causes acid rain). Companies still face strict quotas, but they are free to satisfy their limits by buying pollution credits from other companies. These credits are actually traded on the Chicago futures market.
- *Toxic air pollutants* cause serious illness or death to humans. The EPA must identify toxic pollutants, set standards for these chemicals, and require stationary sources to install equipment to control emissions of toxic substances. These standards are set without regard to technological or economic feasibility.
- *Indoor air pollution* is a serious problem that is not regulated. Some buildings have air that is 100 times more polluted than the outdoor air. This is caused mainly by tightly sealed buildings and exposure to indoor chemicals and construction materials.

Water Pollution

Any person who wants to discharge pollution into water must obtain a permit from the EPA. This permit system is called the National Pollutant Discharge Elimination System (NPDES). The EPA can deny a permit or set restrictions as to amount and frequency of discharge.

- The *Clean Water Act* has been updated and amended several times from 1948 to 1987. Pursuant to the act, the EPA has established water quality standards that define which bodies of water can be use drinking water, recreation, wildlife, and agricultural and industrial uses.
- The Clean Water Act authorizes the EPA to establish water pollution standards for **point sources** of water pollution, which are stationary sources of pollution such as paper mills, manufacturing plants, electric utility plants, and sewage plants. The EPA sets standards for technology that must be used and requires dischargers of pollution to keep records, maintain monitoring equipment, and keep samples of discharges.
- The Clean Water Act prohibits **thermal pollution** because it damages the ecological balance and decreases oxygen in a waterway.
- The Clean Water Act forbids the filling or dredging of **wetlands** unless a permit has been obtained from the Army Corps of Engineers. Wetlands include swamps. Bogs, marshes, and similar areas that support birds, animals, and vegetative life.

- The *Safe Drinking Water Act* authorizes the EPA to establish national primary drinking water standards. The act prohibits dumping of waste into wells.
- The *Marine Protection, Research, and Sanctuaries Act* requires a permit for dumping waste and foreign material into ocean waters and establishes marine sanctuaries as far seaward as the Continental Shelf and in the Great Lakes and their connecting waters.
- The Clean Water Act authorizes the U.S. government to clean up **oil spills** within 12 miles of shore and on the Continental Shelf and to recover the cleanup costs from responsible parties.
- The *Oil Pollution Act of 1990*, which is administered by the Coast Guard, requires the oil industry to adopt procedures that can more readily respond to oil spills.
- The United Nations Conference on the Law of the Sea (LOS Convention) established a 200-mile exclusive economic zone (EEZ) for coastal nations. This convention grants sovereign rights to coastal nations to explore, exploit, conserve, and manage living resources in their EEZs. The coastal nations have the right to board and inspect ships, arrest a ship and its crew, and instigate legal proceedings against violators of its EEZ rights.

Toxic Substances

Many of the chemicals used for agriculture, mining, and industry contain toxic substances that cause birth defects, cancer, and other health-related problems. Because of the grave danger posed by these chemicals, the federal government has enacted legislation to regulate their use.

- The *Insecticide, Fungicide, and Rodenticide Act* requires pesticides, herbicides, fungicides, and rodenticides to be registered with the EPA. The EPA may deny, suspend, or cancel the registration if it finds that the chemical poses an imminent danger. The EPA sets standards for the amount of residue that is permitted on crops sold for human and animal consumption.
- The Toxic Substances Control Act requires manufacturers and processors to test new chemicals to determine their effect on human health and the environment before the EPA will allow them to be marketed. The EPA requires special labeling for toxic substances and may limit or prohibit their manufacture and sale. A toxic substance that poses an imminent hazard may be removed from commerce.

Hazardous Waste

Solid waste may cause of significantly contribute to an increase in mortality or serious illness or pose a hazard to human health or the environment if they are not handled properly. These wastes consist of garbage, sewage, industrial discharge, and old equipment. If these wastes are mishandled they can cause air, water, and land pollution. They are regulated as follows:

- Congress enacted the *Resource Conservation and Recovery Act* to regulate the disposal of new hazardous waste. The act authorizes the EPA to regulate facilities that generate, treat, store, transport, and dispose of hazardous wastes. Any substance that is toxic, radioactive, or corrosive or can ignite is a hazardous material. Hazardous wastes are tracked and regulated from the moment they are created to the time of their final disposal or storage.
- The *Comprehensive Environmental Response, Compensation, and Liability Act*, which is known as the "**Superfund**" gave the federal government a mandate to deal with years of abuse and neglect in the disposal of hazardous waste. The EPA is required by the Superfund to:
    1. identify sites in the United States where hazardous wastes have been disposed, stored, abandoned, or spilled, and
    2. rank these sites regarding the severity of the risk they pose.

    The sites with the highest ranking are put on a National Priority List. The sites on this list receive first priority for cleanup. Studies are conducted to determine the best method for cleaning up the waste site. The Superfund provides for the creation of a fund to finance the cleanup of sites. The EPA can order a responsible party to clean up a hazardous waste site. If the party fails to do so, the EPA can clean up the site and recover the cost from any responsible party under a theory of strict liability. The cost of cleanup can be recovered from:

1. the generator who deposited the wastes
2. the transporter of the wastes to the site
3. The owner of the site at the time of disposal
4. the current owner and operator of the site

The Superfund contains a right to know provision that requires businesses to:

1. disclose the presence of certain listed chemicals to the community
2. annually disclosure emissions of chemical substances released into the environment, and
3. immediately notify the government of spills, accidents, and other emergencies involving hazardous substances.

Nuclear Waste

Nuclear power plants create radioactive waste that maintains a high level of radioactivity for a very long period of time. Two federal agencies monitor and regulate nuclear energy in the United States.

- The Nuclear Regulatory Commission (NRC)regulates the construction and opening of commercial nuclear power plants. The NRC monitors the plants and may close an unsafe plant.
- The EPA sets standards for allowable levels of radioactivity in the environment and regulates the disposal of radioactive waste. The EPA also regulates thermal pollution caused by the nuclear power plants and emissions and uranium production.

Endangered Species

The Endangered Species Act protects endangered species and threatened species of animals. The EPA and the Department of Commerce designate critical habitats for each endangered and threatened species. Real estate or other development in these habitats is prohibited or severely limited. In addition to the Endangered Species Act, there are numerous other acts that protect migratory birds, eagles, horses, burros, marine mammals, and fish.

Noise Pollution

Noise pollution is created by planes, automobiles, manufacturing plants, construction equipment, audio equipment, and the like. Because noise pollution has a direct impact on humab health, the federal government has addressed the need to decrease noise pollution.

- The Noise Control Act authorizes the EPA to establish noise standards for products sold in the United States. The EPA and Federal Aviation Administration jointly establish noise limitations for airplanes. The Department of Transportation and EPA regulate noise from trucks, railroads, and interstate carriers. The Occupational Safety and Health Administration (OSHA) regulates noise levels in the workplace.
- The Quiet Communities Act authorizes the federal government to provide financial and technnical assistance to state and local governments to help control noise pollution.

Transborder Pollution

When another country is the source of pollution in an affected country, the countries must deal with transborder pollution. The regulation of this type of pollution depends upon the existence of a treaty between the offending and affected countries. The United States had several treaties with Canada and Mexico to address many transborder pollution issues. The whole issue of transborder pollution and regulation of global pollution is in its infancy.

Refresh Your Memory

The following exercises are intended to aid you in refreshing your memory in regards to the important concepts and rules contained in the consumer protection laws that have been presented in this chapter. Answer all the questions in the blanks provided before referring to the chapter material. Review the material for any question that you got wrong or were unable to remember.

1. The FDCA regulates the testing, ____________________, distribution, and ________________ of food, drugs, ____________________, and medicinal products and devices in the United States.

2. The FDCA prohibits the shipment, distribution, or sale of ________________________ food.

3. The FDA is empowered to remove "_____________________" medicinal devices from the market.

4. As part of its powers under the Consumer Product Safety Act, the CPSA is authorized to collect data regarding ____________________ caused by consumer products.

5. If a consumer product is found to be imminently hazardous, the manufacturer can be required to ________________, repair, or __________________ the product.

6. The ________________ ________________ ____________ coordinates the implementation and enforcement of the federal environmental protection laws.

7. The National Environmental Policy Act requires that an _____________________ ____________ ______________ be prepared for all proposed legislation and major federal action that significantly affects the quality of the human environment.

8. The _________ _______ _______ was enacted in 1963 to assist states in dealing with air pollution.

9. The Clean Air Act directs the EPA to establish ___________ ___________ _____ ___________ _______________ for certain pollutants at two different levels: primary and secondary.

10. Industrial plants, oil refineries, and public utilities are examples of ______________ sources of air pollution.

Practice Quiz

True/False:

1. ___ The FDCA prohibits the sale of adulterated food, and regulates the misleading labeling of food. [p 728-729]

2. ___ Testing of cosmetics is not done by the Food and Drug Administration. [p 728]

3. ___ The FDA can obtain orders for the seizure, recall, and condemnation of adulterated food. [p 728]

4. ___ The FDA does not allow defects or contaminants to be in food without the food being deemed adulterated. [p 729]

5. ___ Terms such as *low fat, light,* and *natural* have standards that can be enforced by the FDA. [p 730]

6. ___ Before a new miracle drug can be sold to needy patients, the drug manufacturer must go through a brief licensing process by the FDA. [p 730]

7. ___ Manufacturers are prohibited from touting the medical benefits of charms and bracelets. [p 731]

8. ___ Motor Vehicles, boats, aircraft and firearms are regulated by the Consumer Product Safety Commission. [p 884]

9. ___ The FTC may not force a company to purchase corrective advertising to remedy an unfair or deceptive practice. [p 732]

10. ___ The FTC may sue for damages on behalf of an individual consumer for false advertising. [p 732]

11. ___ If a business makes an unsubstantiated claim, such as "Our juice is 20% more nutritional than XYZ Juice," the FTC may pursue a violation of Section 5 of the FCT Act. [p 732]

12. ___ The purpose of an environmental impact statement is to provide enough information about the environment to enable the federal government to determine the feasibility of a project. [p 734]

13. ___ Although the EPA establishes air quality standards, the states are not responsible for their enforcement. [p 735]

14. ___ Automobile and other vehicle emissions are not considered mobile sources of air pollution under the Clean Air Act. [p 735]

15. ___ The Clean Water Act forbids the filling or dredging of wetlands unless a permit is obtained from the Army Corps of Engineers. [p 738]

Multiple Choice:

16. False and misleading labeling of food products is prohibited by the [p 728]
    a. Consumer Product Safety Act.
    b. Fair Packaging and Labeling Act.
    c. Poison Prevention Packaging Act.
    d. Food, Drug, and Cosmetic Act.

17. Food is deemed adulterated if it consists in whole or in part of any [p 728]
    a. filthy, putrid, or decomposed substance.
    b. food that is improperly labeled.
    c. food that does not contain the correct amount in the container.
    d. incorrectly colored or misshaped food.

18. Tolerances for pesticides used on agricultural products are regulated by the [p 731]
    a. Federal Trade Commission.
    b. Food and Drug Administration.
    c. Consumer Product Safety Commission.
    d. Department of Justice.

19. Because the CPSC regulates potentially dangerous consumer products, it [p 731]
    a. seeks injunctions to stop anyone from making products.
    b. seeks criminal penalties for the manufacture of potentially dangerous products.
    c. issues product safety standards for consumer products that pose an unreasonable risk of injury.
    d. makes private parties file all suits and requests for injunctions.

20. Under the Clean Air Act, the EPA establishes primary and secondary levels of allowable pollution. These standards are called [p 735]
    a. adverse impact.
    b. national ambient air quality standards.
    c. pollution credits.
    d. the National Pollutant Discharge Elimination System.

21. The trading of pollution credits is allowed under the [p 735]
    a. Clean Air Act Amendments of 1990.
    b. Clean Water Act.
    c. River and Harbor Act.
    d. Safe Drinking Water Act.

22. Under the Clean Water Act, dischargers of pollution are required to [p 735]
    a. pay a "use fee" each time they discharge pollutants.
    b. keep records.
    c. maintain monitoring equipment.
    d. keep samples of discharges

23. The Clean Water Act does not regulate [p 735]
    a. thermal pollution.
    b. national primary drinking water standards.
    c. wetlands.
    d. oil spills.

24. The operator of a hazardous waste disposal site will have to clean up contamination caused by improper dumping of hazardous waste over 30 years ago by a previous owner of the waste site pursuant to the [p 741]
    a. Toxic Substances Control Act.
    b. Insecticide, Fungicide, and Rodenticide Act.
    c. Resource Conservation and Recovery Act.
    d. Comprehensive Environmental Response, Compensation, and Liability Act.

35. Under the Endangered Species Act, a wildlife form may be declared threatened or endangered by [p 741]
    a. the EPA.
    b. the Department of Commerce.
    c. the secretary of the interior.
    d. the Endangered Species Commission.

Short Answer:

26. Explain the meaning of adulterated food. [p 728] ____
____
____
____

27. The ___________ is empowered to regulate food, food additives, drugs, cosmetics, and medicinal devices. [p 728]

28. What is required of food manufacturers and processors under the Nutrition Labeling and Education Act? [p 729]
____
____
____
____

29. List three examples of "action levels." [p 729] (1) ____
(2) _____________________________________ (3) ____

30. Name three of the FDA requirements for cosmetics. [p 731] (1) ________________________________
_____________________________ (2) ____
(3) ____
___

31. List four types of medicinal devices controlled by the FDCA. [p 731]
(1) ____________________________ (2) ____________________________
(3) ____________________________ (4) ____________________________

32. Explain why the United States felt that trade barriers were being used against genetically modified foods and what the United States had to concede to get its exports into foreign countries. [p 731]
____
____
____
____
____

33. What are three things that the Consumer Product Safety Commission is empowered to do? [p 731]
____
____
____
____

34. What is false and deceptive advertising under Section 5 of the FTC Act? [p 732]

____
____
____

35. What can a person do if they receive unsolicited merchandise in the mail? [p 733]

____
____
____
____

Chapter 34

LABOR AND EMPLOYMENT LAW

Chapter Overview

When the United States became industrialized in the late 1800's, large corporate employers assumed much greater power than their employees. It was not until the 1930's, during the Great Depression, that state and federal governments began to regulate employment relationships. Legislation granted employees the right to form labor unions and bargain with management for improved working conditions, better pay, and benefits. Further legislation guaranteed the right to strike and picket. This chapter discusses the creation of labor unions and regulation of labor relations.

This chapter also examines employment contracts and the exceptions to the at-will doctrine that applies to a majority of employment contracts. It also examines the statutes that have been enacted to protect workers. These laws include workers' compensation, minimum wage and overtime pay, occupational safety, pension, immigration, unemployment, Social Security, and other laws that protect employees from unfair treatment.

Objectives

Upon completion of the exercises in this chapter, you should be able to:

1. Describe how state workers' compensation laws function and the benefits that are available.
2. Explain employer's obligation under OSHA to provide and maintain safe work conditions..
3. Understand unemployment compensation benefits and Social Security laws.
4. Describe the rights granted by the Family and Medical Leave Act.
5. Explain how a union is formed.
6. Describe union elections and the consequences of interfering with union elections.
7. Understand the process of collective bargaining and compulsory subjects of collective bargaining.
8. Describe the right to picket and its limitations.

Practical Applications

Upon mastering the concepts in this chapter, you should be able to recognize when the conduct involved in a particular labor relationship is legal or illegal. Further, should be able to recognize the general legal principle that applies to a dispute and understand the likely outcome.

Additionally, you should be able to recognize the situations where employee rights and protections are applicable and the specific laws that cover a dispute or loss of income. You will understand the limits of the protections and the employee's requirements that must be met to gain protection under the various statutes.

Helpful Hints

When there is a labor dispute, emotions are often frayed and the parties are likely to react impulsively. It is helpful to realize that both state and federal governments and the courts have created a large amount of statutory and case law that will dictate the proper conduct of the parties and the consequences of illegal activity. Examine each statute and case closely for the precise conduct that was either condoned or forbidden. By understanding what conduct triggers which rule of law, you will be more effective in your labor relationships.

Further, both the employee and employer benefit by a clear understanding of how the various employment protection statutes function. The requirements of some laws apply only to specific employers based upon the qualifying language of the statute. Employees often have requirements of notice and cooperation built into the statute with which they must comply to gain enforcement of their rights. Employers must understand and adhere to the requirements imposed by government regulation in the workplace or they subject themselves to the high costs of law suits and lost production in the workplace.

Study Tips

It is crucial for you to understand the following rules of law and mandates that must be followed when you are involved in a labor action or negotiations.

Norris-*LaGuardia Act.* Made it legal for employees to organize.

Nat*ional Labor Relations Act.* Established the right of employees to form, join, and participate in unions. Placed a duty on employers to bargain and deal in good faith with unions.

Labor-*Management Relations Act.* Expanded the activities that union were allowed to engage in. Gave employers the right to speak out against the unions. Gave the President the right to enjoin a strike for up to 80 days if the strike would create a national emergency.

Labor-*Management Reporting and Disclosure Act.* This act regulates internal union affairs related to union elections, who can hold office, and makes union officials accountable for union funds.

Railway Labor Act. This act allows railroad and airline employees to organize and created a mechanism for the adjudication of grievances.

National Labor Relations Board (NLRB). Appointed by the President, the five members of the NLRB oversee union elections, prevent unfair labor practices, and enforces federal labor laws.

NLRB v. ILA, AFL-*CIO (1985).* This Supreme Court case upheld negotiated contracts that preserved work for the longshoremen. The court felt that allowing the longshoremen to negotiate a contract by which they were required to unload containers that didn't need unloading was beneficial to the national economy and "work preservation" for the longshoremen was a legitimate goal of federal labor policy.

Lechmere v. NLRB (1992). Labor organizers have no right to trespass onto the employer's property to organize the employees when they can have access to the employees via nontrespassory means. Even if it is difficult to contact employees away from work, this does not give the organizers the right to trespass onto the employer's property to pass out leaflets.

NLRB v. Exchange Parts Co. (1964). The Supreme Court ruled that giving increased benefits to the employees on the eve of a union election for the purpose of forming a union was designed to affect the outcome of the election and was therefore, an unfair labor practice.

Plant Closing Act. Requires employers to give their employees 60 days' notice before engaging in certain plant closings or layoffs.

First Nat'l Maintenance Corp v. NLRB (1981). An employer's decision to close a business unit is not part of the terms and conditions that the union can force the employer to negotiate.

Union Security Agreements. If the union obtains a union shop agreement with the employer, all employees must join the union within a certain number of days or they will be terminated. In an agency shop, the employee do not have to join the union, but they have to pay an agency fee equal to union dues.

State Right-To-Work Laws. States are free to enact laws that outlaw union and agency shops. Today, there are 21 states that have enacted right-to-work laws.

It is just as important to understand when the employment laws may apply as it is to understand the technical requirements built into the individual statutes. You should develop your understanding of employment laws by organizing the material into general areas.

Protective Statutes

The following statutes and legislative schemes protect both substantive and procedural rights of employees in their dealings with employers.

Workers' Compensation Acts

These acts were enacted to compensate employees for injuries that occurred on the job regardless of fault. The amount of compensation payable to the employee is set by statute. Payment under the workers' compensation statute is the employee's exclusive remedy, meaning that an employee cannot sue their employee when they are injured on the job.

Occupational Safety and Health Act

The Act was enacted to promote safety in the workplace. It imposes recordkeeping and reporting requirements upon the employer. The enforcement arm created by the act is the Occupational Safety and Health Administration (OSHA). OSHA has adopted regulations to enforce the safety standards created by the act. OSHA may inspect places of employment and cite the employer for violations. OSHA violations carry both civil and criminal penalties.

Fair Labor Standards Act (FSLA)

The FSLA prohibits child labor and establishes minimum wage and overtime pay requirements.

Employee Retirement Income Security Act (ERISA)

ERISA is designed to prevent fraud and abuses associated with private pension funds. Requires that the pension plan be in writing and name a pension fund manager. ERISA dictates how the pension funds can be invested and sets time limits for when pension rights must vest.

Consolidated Omnibus Budget Reconciliation Act (COBRA)

Provides that employee or his beneficiaries must have the opportunity to maintain group health coverage upon dismissal or death due to certain events. Government employees are covered by the Public Health Service Act.

Family and Medical Leave Act

The act guarantees workers unpaid time off for medical emergencies. Applies to employers with 50 or more employees. Employee must have worked for at least one year and performed at least 1,250 hours of work. Covers time off for birth or care of child, serious health condition, and care for spouse, parent, or child with a serious health problem. Employee must be restored to their same or a similar position upon their return.

Immigration Reform and Control Act

Forbids employer from hiring illegal immigrants. Employer must examine documents to determine employees right to work in the country.

Federal Unemployment Tax Act

Employers must pay unemployment taxes to compensate employees during periods of unemployment. Employee does not receive benefits if they are discharged for misconduct or quit without cause.

Social Security

Under the Federal Insurance Contributions Act (FICA) employees and employers make contributions to the Social Security Fund. The funds are used to pay current recipients of Social Security.

Refresh Your Memory

The following exercise will enable you to refresh your memory of the main points given in this chapter. Read the question twice and place your answer in the blanks provided. If you do not remember the principle, go to the next question and come back to the ones you did not answer.

1. The relationship between employers and employees changed dramatically when the United States became ____________________________ in the late 1880s.

2. As a reaction to employment abuses, workers organized unions to gain _________________ strength.

3. Approximately _______ percent of private-sector workers belong to labor unions.

4. In 1932, the _______________________________ Act created the right of workers to organize.

5. The NLRA, also known as the _____________________ Act, placed an affirmative duty on employers to bargain and deal in good faith.

6. To recover under workers' compensation, the workers' injuries must have been ___________-______________________.

7. In the interest of promoting ___________ in the workplace, Congress, in 1970, enacted the Occupational Safety and Health Act.

8. The Fair Labor Standards Act forbids the use of ____________ ______ ______ and makes it unlawful to ship goods produced by businesses that use ______________ _____ ___________.

9. The FSLA establishes _________ wage and __________ pay requirement for workers.

10. COBRA provides that an employee of a private employer or the employee's __________ must be offered the opportunity to continue his or her group _______ insurance after the dismissal or death of the employee or the loss of coverage due to certain qualifying events.

Critical Thought Exercise

Sid Frost worked as a merchandising supervisor for Global-Mart, Inc., a large discount store employing over 26,000 people. When Frost suffered his third stroke in April 1999, he took leave from work, which was covered by the Family and Medical Leave Act (FMLA) of 1993. The Vice-President of Personnel for Global-Mart approved the leave. Mike Allen, who had been hired only two months after Frost in 1984, temporarily filled Frost's position. When Frost returned to work, he discovered that Allen had been promoted to senior supervisor and given a $7,000 raise. The senior supervisor position is filled from the supervisor classification based upon seniority. Global-Mart refused to allow Frost to return to his position as a supervisor and demoted him to a senior salesman position that required travel away from home on a weekly basis. Six weeks later Global-Mart fired Frost because he was unable to keep up the schedule required by his position and because his expense account was not timely filed by the end of the month.

Frost sues Global-Mart for violation of the FMLA based upon Global-Mart's failure to promote him to senior supervisor or return him to his prior position. Did Global-Mart violate the FMLA?

Answer.

Practice Quiz

True/False:

1. ___ Accidents that occur at a company cafeteria or while on a business lunch for an employer are not covered by workers' compensation. [p 760]

2. ___ If an employer intentionally injures a worker during work hours, the employee's remedy is not limited to workers' compensation benefits. [p 760]

3. ___ Federal, State and local governments do not have to comply with the Occupational Safety and Health Act. [p 761]

4. ___ OSHA is empowered to enter a business of the employer to inspect for health hazards and safety violations. [p 761]

5. ___ Under the Fair Labor Standards Act, children ages 14 and 15 may work unlimited hours but only in hazardous jobs. [p 762]

6. ___ If an employee works 50 hours one week he or she is entitled to any overtime pay because they worked over 40 hours per week. [p 762]

7. ___ The Family Medical Leave Act applies to private employers with 50 or more employees, as well as to federal, state, and local governments. [p 763]

8. ___ Employers covered by the Family and Medical Leave Act are entitled receive up to 16 weeks of unpaid leave during any 12-month period. [p 763]

9. ___ Only semiskilled and unskilled worker were permitted to join the American Federation of Labor (AFL). [p 752]

10. ___ During the Great Depression of the 1930s, several federal statutes were enacted giving workers certain rights and protections. [p 752]

11. ___ The right to bargain collectively with employers was granted by the Norris-LaGuardia Act. [p 752]

12. ___ The NLRB oversees union elections [p 753]

13. ___ If at least 30% of the employees in the bargaining unit are interested in forming a union, the NLRB can be petitioned to investigate and set an election date. [p 754]

14. ___ Illegal strikers may not be discharged by the employer with no rights to reinstatement. [p 758]

15. ___ Unions may not adopt internal rules to regulate the union.

Multiple Choice:

16. OSHA standards establish rules pertaining to [p 761]
    a. minimum wage.
    b. amounts of compensation after a work-related injury.
    c. maximum levels for exposure to hazardous chemicals.
    d. age requirements for use of child labor.

17. Employers who establish pension plans for their employees are subject to the recordkeeping, disclosure, and other requirements of [p 764]
    a. COBRA.
    b. ERISA.
    c. FUTA.
    d. FICA.

18. An eligible employee under the Family and Medical Leave Act who takes leave must, upon returning to work [p 763]
    a. accept whatever position is open at the tine.
    b. accept a reduction in pay if someone else has been promoted.
    c. forfeit benefits equal to the value of the leave.
    d. be restored to either the same or an equivalent position with equivalent employment benefits and pay.

19. Social Security benefits include [p 765]
    a. survivors' benefits to family members of deceased workers.
    b. the right to continue group health insurance provided by the employer.
    c. the right to take time off for the birth of a child.
    d. payments for a period of time when the employee is temporarily unemployed.

20. The act that placed an affirmative duty on employers to bargain and deal in good faith with union was the [p 752]
    a. Norris-LaGuardia Act.
    b. National Labor Relations Act.
    c. The Railway Labor Act.
    d. none of the Above.

21. The Landrum-Griffin Act includes a rule that [p 758]
    a. gives employees the right to form unions.
    b. allows an injunction to be issued to stop unfair labor practices.
    c. makes union officials accountable for union funds and property.
    d. requires a 60-day notice for certain plant closures.

22. The administrative agency created to enforce the Wagner Act (NLRA) is the [p 752]
    a. NLRB.
    b. AFL.
    c. CIO.
    d. Labor Board of Conciliation and Arbitration.

23. The act of negotiating by a union with an employer is called [p 756]
    a. collective bargaining.
    b. picketing.
    c. a wildcat action.
    d. a secondary boycott.

24. A wildcat strike takes place when [p 758]
    a. striking employees continue to occupy the premises of the employer.
    b. individual union members to out on strike without proper authorization from the union.
    c. employees strike part of the day and work part of the day.
    d. striking employees cause substantial damage to the property of the employer.

25. Picketing is unlawful unless it [p 757]
    a. is accompanied by violence.
    b. obstructs customers from entering the employer's place of business or prevents nonstriking employees from entering the premises.
    c. prevents pickups and deliveries at the employer's of business.
    d. all of the above.

Short Answer:

26. Why were workers' compensation laws created? [p 759]

27. Describe four examples of specific duty standards created by OSHA. [p 791]

28. What can OSHA do upon finding a safety violation following an inspection of a place of employment? [p 761]

29. According to the Fair Labor Standards Act, what type or work can a child under 14 accept? [p 762]

30. If children cannot work in hazardous jobs, who determines what job is hazardous? [p 762]

31. To whom may an employer pay less than minimum wage? [p 762]

32. What is the prerequisite for an employee to be covered by the Family and Medical Leave Act? [p 763]

33. Under the Immigration Reform and Control Act of 1986, an employer must attest to what facts before an employee may be hired? [p 764]

34. How much must a self-employed person contribute to Social Security? [p 765]
    ____
    ____

35. Which Act helped to implement a program whereby employers are now required to pay unemployment taxes? [p 764]
    ____

Chapter 35

EQUAL OPPORTUNITY IN EMPLOYMENT

Chapter Overview

Prior to the 1960's, there was little that an employee could do to address discrimination by the employer in regards to hiring, discharge, promotion, pay, and work assignments. Congress addressed discrimination by passing a comprehensive set of law that made it actionable to discriminate against a person because of race, sex, religion, national origin, age, or disability. The interpretation of these federal statutes has created a large body of law that has created a much more level playing field in the workplace. The chapter examines the major legislation and the application of these laws by the courts.

Objectives

Upon completion of the exercises in this chapter, you should be able to:

1. Describe the protection provided by Title VII of the Civil Rights Act of 1964.
2. Identify examples of discrimination based upon race, color, and national origin.
3. Describe conduct that creates sex discrimination, including sexual harassment.
4 Discuss the important protections contained in the Equal Pay Act of 1963.
5. Explain the protections provided by the Age Discrimination in employment Act.
6. Describe the scope of the Americans with Disabilities Act and the protections it affords person with a disability.
7. Define the doctrine of affirmative action and describe how it is used.

Practical Application

Antidiscrimination laws set forth mandates for employers and protection for employees that alter the course of conduct of people in the business environment. You should be able to recognize the situations where discrimination is unlawful and instances where a defense to discrimination may apply. This will allow you to make decisions that stay within the requirements set forth by the federal laws.

Helpful Hints

Since most of this chapter concentrates on specific laws and cases that interpret the laws, it is beneficial to know the basic definition or content of each law and understand the examples of how they are applied in the real world. You should focus on the type of conduct that is involved in a situation to determine which area of law is applicable and what actions must be taken to correct the action, if at all possible.

Study Tips

Enforcement of federal antidiscrimination laws

The Equal Employment Opportunity Commission (EEOC) is appointed by the President and is responsible for enforcing the provisions of all the federal laws that address areas of discrimination in the workplace. The EEOC is empowered to not only investigate, but also to issue opinions and directives to offending employers, bring suit against the violator, and even seek injunctive relief to stop the actual conduct that violated a particular law. Though an employee can file suit directly against the employer if the EEOC gives permission, action by the EEOC is the best actions available to force a stop to the illegal conduct.

Title VII of the Civil Rights Act of 1964

Overall, Title VII is the most important piece of legislation ever passed to address discrimination. As such, it provides the authority for the largest number of cases brought to rectify discrimination. The conduct that will trigger a Title VII action will be within the areas of:

- Hiring
- Discharge
- Compensation (rate of pay and classification that affects pay)
- Terms of employment (work schedule, fringe benefits)
- Conditions of the employment (rules, policies and procedures)
- Privileges granted as part of employment (honorary positions, use of company assets)
- Promotion (not promoted when qualified)
- Work assignment (given less desirable assignments that prevent growth)

If any action on the above list is made by an employer based upon a person's race, color, religion, sex, or national origin; or the employee is limited in any way that deprives them of an opportunity based upon race, color, religion, sex, or national origin, a violation of Title VII has been committed.

Title VII applies to:

- employers with 15 or more employees
- employment agencies
- labor union with 15 or more employees
- state and local governments
- most federal employees
- undocumented aliens

Title VII does not apply to:

- Indian tribes
- tax-exempt private clubs

There are two types of discrimination that Title VII addresses:

- Disparate treatment: employer discriminates against individual
- Disparate impact: employer discriminates against entire protected class

Procedure for bringing Title VII action consists of these steps:

- Private complainant must file complaint with EEOC
- EEOC given opportunity to sue on behalf of complainant
- If EEOC chooses not to sue, issues right to sue letter
- Complainant now has right to sue employer

Remedies for violation of Title VII include:

- Recovery by employee of up to two years' back pay
- If malice or reckless indifference to rights is shown, aggrieved party may recover compensatory and punitive damages
- Statutory damages from $50,000 to $300,000 may be awarded depending upon the size of the employer
- Court may order reinstatement, including seniority rights
- Court may issue injunctions to compel compliance

The **Pregnancy Discrimination Act** was added to Title VII in 1978 to forbid discrimination because of pregnancy, birth, or related medical conditions. The effect that pregnancy or giving birth to a new baby may have upon a woman cannot be raised in a job interview or used as the basis for not offering a position. It also forbids the use of pregnancy, giving birth, or a related medical condition, as a basis for making a decision in any of the other employment areas listed above.

Sexual Harassment

Lewd remarks, touching, intimidation, posting pinups, and other verbal of physical conduct of a sexual nature that occur on the job are sexual harassment and violate Title VII. Requesting that an employee has sex with the employer to get hired, receive a promotion, or prevent discharge, are all forms of sexual harassment prohibited by Title VII. When the workplace is permeated with discriminatory intimidation, ridicule, and insult, that is sufficiently severe or pervasive to alter the conditions of the victim's employment and create an abusive working environment, Title VII is violated. In evaluating the severity ands pervasiveness of sexual harassment, a court will focus on the perspective of the victim and ask whether a "reasonable woman" would consider the conduct to be offensive. Evidence of the offending conduct may come from words, physical acts, e-mails distributed within or outside the office, pictures (including material on computers), jokes, threats, and both employer and employee communications. The court will consider the overall effect that several acts have upon the victim.

Defense To Sexual Harassment

An employer may raise an affirmative defense against liability or damages for sexual harassment by proving that:

1. The employer exercised reasonable care to prevent and correct promptly any sexually-harassing behavior, and
2. The plaintiff employee unreasonably failed to take advantage of any preventive of coercive opportunities by the employer or to otherwise avoid harm

Religious Discrimination

Under Title VII, the employer is under a duty to reasonably accommodate the religious observances, practices, or beliefs of its employees if it does not cause undue hardship on the employer.

Defenses To A Title VII Action

Merit. Employers can select or promote employees based on merit. Thus, a promotion can lawfully be based upon experience, skill, education, and ability tests. A test or condition that has no relevance to the position may not be used to prevent a protected class or individual from qualifying for employment.

Seniority. An employer may maintain a seniority system that rewards long-term employees. The system is lawful unless persons in a position of seniority achieved their position through intentional discrimination in the past.

Bona Fide Occupational Qualification. Employment discrimination based on a protect class (such as sex, but other than race or color), is lawful if it is job related and a business necessity. Hiring only women to work in a women's health spa would be legal but hiring only women for a women's clothing store in the mall would be a violation of Title VII.

Equal Pay Act of 1963

Protects both sexes from pay discrimination based on sex. The act prohibits disparity in pay for jogs that require equal skill, equal effort, equal responsibility, or similar working conditions. If two jobs are determined to be equal and similar, an employer cannot pay disparate wages to members of different sexes.

Ex: Sue is paid $8.50 an hour to climb a 30-foot ladder and clean the light fixtures in the ceilings of the employer's warehouses. Mike is paid $14.00 per hour to climb the same ladder and change burned out light bulbs in the same fixtures that Sue is paid to clean. Sue and Mike are doing jobs that require low skill levels and require the same physical risk. The only basis for the disparate pay is the sex of the employees, making this a violation of the Equal Pay Act.

Disparate pay is allowed when it is based upon:

- Seniority
- Merit
- Quantity of quality of product (commissions)
- A differential based on any factor other than sex (shift differential)

Age Discrimination in Employment Act of 1967

The ADEA prohibits are discrimination in all employment decisions, including hiring, promotions, compensation, and other terms and conditions of employment. The Older Worker Benefit Protection Act amended the ADEA to prohibit age discrimination with regard to employee benefits. The ADEA applies to all employees over age 40.

The Americans With Disabilities Act of 1990

The ADA imposes obligations on employers and providers of public transportation, telecommunications, and public accommodations to accommodate individuals with disabilities. Title I of the ADA prohibits employment discrimination against qualified individuals with disabilities in regard to job application procedures, hiring, compensation, training, promotion, and termination. Title I requires an employer to make reasonable accommodations to individuals with disabilities that do not cause hardship to the employer. Employers may not inquire into the existence, nature, or severity of a disability during the application process.

Civil Rights Act of 1866

Section 1981 of this act gives all persons equal contract rights. Section 1981 also prohibits racial discrimination and discrimination based upon national origin. Though most discrimination cased are brought under Title VII, there are two good reasons to bring an action under Section 1981: (1) A private plaintiff can bring an action without going through the procedural requirements of Title VII, and (2) there is no limitation period on the recovery of back pay (claimant can only go back two years under Title VII) and no cap on the recovery of compensatory or punitive damages.

Affirmative Action

This is a policy that provides that certain job preferences will be given to minority or other protected class applicants when an employer makes an employment decision. Affirmative action plans will not be upheld when they discriminate against a majority after past discriminatory practices have already been rectified. Additionally, the courts will not allow employers to give a preference to a minority when another employee is far better qualified for a position.

Ex: Bob is white and has both a master's degree and doctorate in psychology. Bob has 25 years of experience in a supervisory position at Major University Psychological Services Center. Keith is black and only has a bachelor's degree. Keith has worked at Major University for only 2 years and has never held any supervisory position. If

Keith is hired as the new director of the entire Psychological Services Center because he is black, Bob will have a cause of action under Title VII for racial discrimination.

Refresh Your Memory

The following exercise will enable you to refresh your memory of the important rules and concepts set forth in this chapter. Read each question twice and put your answer in the blanks provided. Answer the entire exercise, then review questions and the text in areas you did not remember.

1. The federal agency responsible for enforcing most federal antidiscrimination laws is the ______ ____________ _____________ _____________.

2. Title ____ of the ______ _______ ____ of 1964 was intended to eliminate job discrimination based on five protected classes. Those classes are: ______, _______, _____________________, _____ and ____________.

3. Title VII applies to employers with ______ or more employees.

4. _______________ _______________ discrimination occurs when an employer treats a specific individual less favorably because of their membership in a protected class.

5. A ________ to ______ letter is issued if the EEOC refuses to file suit on behalf of a claimant.

6. ____________ __________ refers to the country of a person's ancestors or cultural characteristics.

7. The Pregnancy Discrimination Act forbids employment discrimination because of pregnancy, _________________, or related ______________ conditions.

8. Refusing to hire someone unless they have sex with the manager is a form of _______________ _______________________.

9. The frequency and severity of sexual harassment are two factors considered in determining whether the employee is being subjected to a __________ _______ _______________.

10. Under Title VII, an employer is under a duty to _______________ _______________ the religious observances, practices, or beliefs of its employees.

Critical Thought Exercise

Carol Jones was employed with Richmond Components, Inc. (RCI), an electrical engineering and manufacturing company that supplied parts and guidance system development for the United States Air Force. Jones was a public relations and communications manager for RCI at their facility located on Davis Air Force Base for over nine years. Of the 135 employees at the RCI facility at Davis AFB, only 9 women were in professional positions. Employees in the office where Jones worked used e-mail as the major form of communication between employees. Jones was sent sexually explicit material via e-mail, including pictures that had been downloaded from the Internet. Two male engineers in her work area used semi-nude swimsuit pictures as the screensaver on their computer. Pictures of nude women from magazines were cut out and put in her mailbox with notes, such as,

"Will you pose like this for us?" When Jones requested that information for press releases be given to her by a stated deadline, she was told to, "Go have sex and chill out," along with other sexually demeaning comments about her anatomy. When Jones complained to the vice-president in charge of personnel, she was told that she worked in a high-stress 'boys' club" and she had better learn to accept the "give-and-take" environment at RCI. Jones quit her job and filed an action under Title VII. Will she prevail?

Answer.

Practice Quiz

True/False:

1. ___ The EEOC is not empowered to bring suit to enforce Title VII of the Civil Rights Act of 1964.
[p 774]

2. ___ Discrimination based upon race, color, sex, national origin and religion are covered by Title VII. [p 774]

3. ___ The requirements of Title VII also apply to state and local governments and their agencies. [p 774]

4. ___ In an action for disparate treatment discrimination, the complainant need not prove that he or she applied for and was qualified for the employment position. [p 775]

5. ___ When bringing an action under Title VII, it is not necessary for a private person to first file a complaint with the EEOC. [p 775]

6. ___ Under title VII, race is not referred to in broad categories such as Black, Caucasian, Asian, and Native American. [p 776]

7. ___ Conduct need not seriously affect the victim's psychological well-being to be actionable as abusive work environment harassment. [p 778]

8. ___ When asserting an affirmative defense to sexual harassment, the employer need not prove that employees were informed of the employer's anti-harassment policy and the complaint procedure put in place by the employer. [p 779]

9. ___ Many religious discrimination cases involve a conflict between an employer's work rule and an employee's religious beliefs. [p 780]

10. ___ An employer has to accommodate an employee's request to have Saturday off from work for religious services even if the employer has no other employee that can work on that day.
[p 780]

11. ___ To be legal, a bona fide occupational requirement must be job related, and a business necessity. [p 781]

12. ___ If an employer violated the Equal Pay Act, he must decrease the wages of the discriminated-against employee to eliminate the unlawful disparity of wages. [p 783]

13. ___ Under the Equal Pay Act, an employer may not pay disparate wages to members of different sexes if the difference is based on a seniority system. [p 783]

14. ___ Under the Equal Pay Act, an employer may not pay disparate wages to members of different sexes if one employee works the night shift for which higher wages are paid. [p 783]

15. ___ Under the ADA, an employer may not inquire about the applicant's ability to perform job-related functions. [p 786]

Multiple Choice:

16. The enforcement of federal antidiscrimination laws is the responsibility of the [p 774]
   a. OWBPA.
   b. EEOC.
   c. ADEA.
   d. ADA.

27. The definition of what constitutes an "unlawful employment practice" was amended to Title VII by
[p 774]
   a. the Equal Employment Practices Act of 1972.
   b. a decision of the United States Supreme Court.
   c. the Americans with Disabilities Act.
   d. the Pregnancy Discrimination Act in 1978.

18. Title VII applies to employers with [p 774]
   a. 8 or more employees.
   b. 12 or more employees.
   c. 15 or more employees.

d. 33 or more employees.

19. Title VII prohibits discrimination in [p 774]
    a. hiring.
    b. promotion or demotion.
    c. payment of compensation.
    d. all of the above.

20. To bring an action under Title VII, a private complainant must first file a complaint [p 775]
    a. in federal district court.
    b. in the trial court in the state where they reside.
    c. with the EEOC.
    d. with the Commerce Department.

21. What do employers adopt that provide that certain job preferences will be given to members of minority racial and ethnic groups, females,. and other protected-class applicants when an employer makes an employment decision? [p 787]
    a. an international antidiscrimination law.
    b. employment quotas based on a specified number or percentage of minority applicants or employees
    c. affirmative action plans
    d. none of the above.

22. Which of the following are forbidden under Title I of the ADA? [p 786]
    a. preemployment medical exams
    b. inquiring about the existence, nature and severity of a disability
    c. conditioning the job offer on passage of a medical exam only as to one entering employee
    d. all of the above

23. Which of the following is not a protected age category under the ADEA? [p 784]
    a. persons under age 40
    b. persons over age 40
    c. persons over age 50
    d. persons over age 60

24. Which of the following remedies may a court award against an employer based on violations of Title
    VII? [p 775]
    a. punitive damages
    b. compensatory damages
    c. fictional seniority
    d. All of the above

25. Disparate-impact discrimination happens when [p 775]
    a. an employer treats a specific individual less favorably than others based on that person's race, national origin, sex, religion or color.
    b. the EEOC issues a right to sue letter.
    c. an employer adopts a work rule that is neutral on its face but is shown to cause an adverse impact on a protected class.
    d. when an employer adopts a work rule that is related to performance.

Short Answer:

26. List the five protected classes under Title VII. [p 774] (1) ______________
(2) ______________ (3) ______________ (4) ______________
(5) ______________

27. Disparate impact discrimination is often proven through ________________________ data about the employer's employment practices. [p 775]

28. What two things must happen before a claimant can sue their employer for a Title VII violation?
[p 775] (1)
____
(2)
____
____

29. If a male applicant is not hired by an airline as a flight attendant because "women are more compassionate towards passengers," he is a victim of _____ _________________. [p 777]

30. Hanging a provocative male Chippendale's calendar in your office may be ____________ ________________. [p 778]

31. Failing to accommodate an employee and forcing him or her to work on their Sabbath when it is not necessary is a form of ______________ __________________. [p 780]

32. Promoting your top salesman, Frank, to the position of senior salesperson even though Hanah has worked for you for one year longer is legal because the promotion was based on ________________. [p 781]

33. Seniority systems are lawful as long as they are not the result of ______________ ______________. [p 781]

34. If two jobs are determined to be equal and ___________, an employer cannot pay _______________ wages to members of different sexes. [p 783]

35. The Older Workers Benefit Protection Act amended the ADEA to prohibit ______ discrimination with regard to employee _________. [p 784]

Chapter 36

PERSONAL PROPERTY AND BAILMENTS

Chapter Overview

Property would have little if any value if the law did not protect the rights of owners to use, sell, dispose of, control, and prevent others from trespassing upon their property. Property may be either real property (buildings and land) or personal property. In this chapter we examine the types of personal property, the methods of acquiring ownership in personal property, and property rights in mislaid, lost, and abandoned property. The chapter then discusses bailment of property, situations where possession of (but not title to) property is delivered to another party for transfer, safekeeping, or use. The typical rental of equipment is a bailment.

Objectives

Upon completion of the exercises in this chapter, you should be able to

1. Define personal property.
2. Describe the methods for acquiring ownership in personal property.
3. Understand how title to personal property is acquired by purchase, production, accession, and confusion.
4. Apply the rules relating to lost, mislaid, and abandoned property.
5. Define ordinary bailments and list the elements of a bailment.
6. Explain bailee liability for lost, damaged, or destroyed property.

Practical Application

Businesses are constantly transferring ownership of personal property or creating personal property for sale. Additionally, temporary use of property, whether by borrowing or renting, is a common commercial practice. The material in this chapter has valuable application to everyday business practices. Knowledge of the rights and duties relating to ownership and bailment of personal property helps anyone to make informed and reasoned choices when deciding how to deal with a personal property issue.

Helpful Hints

Once it is determined that something is personal property, it is wise to focus on the treatment of the property to determine who has rights in it and what duties may have arisen in regards to the property. The circumstances under which possession of property is accomplished from person to person or business to business will determine who may ultimately be responsible for damage to or loss of the property. The law differentiates the rights of people depending upon how they came into possession of the property and the circumstances surrounding the acquisition of possession.

As you study this material, look at the status of the property as it changes possession. This will guide you in applying the correct law to solve a personal property issue.

Study Tips

In order to answer questions or resolve disputes relating to personal property, it is wise to examine personal property from the perspective of creation and acquisition, transfer by gift, temporary or permanent loss, and rights and duties associated with bailments. The following terms and rules of law are essential to that understanding.

Acquiring Ownership in Personal Property

The methods for acquiring personal property are:

- *By Possession* – Property can be acquired by capturing it.
- *By Purchase or Production* – The most common way to obtain property is to purchase it. Production is another common method. A manufacturer who turns raw materials into a product acquires ownership of the product.
- *By Gift* – A gift is a voluntary transfer of property without consideration. The person making the gift is the donor and the person receiving the gift is the donee. The three elements of a valid gift are:
  1. **Donative intent** For a gift to be effective, the donor must have intended to make a gift.
  2. **Delivery** Delivery must occur for there to be a valid gift. Delivery can either be physical or constructive (giving title documents to a car).
  3. **Acceptance** This is usually not a problem unless the gift is refused.

  Gifts ***inter vivos*** are made during a person's lifetime while a gift ***causa mortis*** is made in contemplation of death. Gifts causa mortis can be revoked up until the time of death. ***Uniform Gifts to Minor Acts*** allow adults to make irrevocable gifts to minors. The custodian of the gift has broad discretionary powers to invest the money or securities for the benefit of the minor.
- *By Will or Inheritance* – If a person who dies has a valid will, the property is distributed to the beneficiaries, pursuant to the provisions of the will.
- *By Accession* – Accession occurs when the value of personal property increases because it is added to or improved by natural or manufactured means.
- *By Confusion* – Confusion occurs if two or more persons commingle fungible goods. The owners share ownership in the commingled goods to the amount of the goods contributed.
- *By Divorce* – Parties obtain property rights in the property of the marital estate.

Mislaid, Lost, and Abandoned Property

People find property belonging to others and ownership rights to the property differs depending on whether the property was mislaid, lost, or abandoned. These are the rules that apply to property in those categories.

- *Mislaid Property* – Property is mislaid when the owner places it somewhere and forgets it. The owner will probably return when it is discovered that the property was mislaid. The owner of the property where it was found has the right to take possession. The owner of the premises becomes an involuntary bailee and must take reasonable care of the property until it is reclaimed. The typical situation for this is when a patron leaves their glasses or jacket at a business.
- *Lost Property* – Property is lost when the owner negligently, carelessly, or inadvertently leaves it somewhere. The finder of the property takes title against the world except the true owner. The finder must make efforts to return the property.

- *Abandoned Property* – Property is classified as abandoned if the owner discards the property with the intent to relinquish his rights in it or he gives up all attempts to locate lost or misplaced property.
- **Estray Statutes** – most states have an estray statute, which dictates what the finder of lost or misplaced property must do to acquire title to the property. This usually includes turning the property over to the police, giving notice that the property was found, and waiting for a time period to pass. The finder can then claim ownership.

Bailments

A bailment is a transaction where the owner transfers his or her personal property to another to be held, stored, delivered, or for some other purpose. Title to the property remains in the owner. The owner of the property is the bailor and the party who received the property is the bailee.

- There are three essential elements that must be present to create a bailment:
  1. Only person property can be bailed.
  2. There must be delivery of possession which also involves two elements:
     - (i) The bailee has exclusive control over the personal property
     - (ii) The bailee must knowingly accept the personal property.
  3. There must be a bailment agreement, which may be either express or implied.

Ordinary Bailments

There are three classifications of ordinary bailments. The importance of these categories is that they determine the degree of care owed by the bailee in protecting the bailed property. The three categories are:

- Bailments for the sole benefit of the bailor are gratuitous bailments that benefit only the bailor. The typical gratuitous bailment involves the bailee watching the bailor's property as a favor without compensation. The bailee only owed a duty of slight care. As long as the bailee is not grossly negligent, no liability will be incurred for loss or damage.
- Bailments for the sole benefit of the bailee are gratuitous bailments for the sole benefit of the bailee. This is the typical "borrowing the lawnmower" situation. The bailee owes a duty of great care. The bailee is responsible for even the slightest negligence.
- Mutual benefit bailments are made for the benefit of both the bailor and bailee. The bailee has a duty of reasonable care, making the bailee liable for any goods that are lost, damages, or destroyed because of his or her negligence. This is the typical paid storage or valet parking situation.

Special Bailments

Special bailees include common carriers, innkeepers, and warehouse companies. In addition to the rules applicable to ordinary bailees, they are subject to the special liability rules contained in Article 7 of the Uniform Commercial Code (UCC).

- Common Carriers – These bailees offer transportation to the public. They include airlines, railroads, bus companies, trucking companies, and public pipeline carriers. The delivery of goods to a common carrier creates a mutual benefit bailment. Unlike an ordinary bailment, common carriers are held to a duty of strict liability. If goods are lost, damaged, or stolen, the common carrier is liable even if it was not at fault. The liability of airlines for lost luggage is limited to $1,250 per piece of luggage for a domestic flight.
- Warehouse Companies - These bailees contract for the storage of goods for compensation. They are held to a duty of reasonable case. They are not liable for the negligence of others that causes loss or damage.
- Innkeepers – An innkeeper owns a facility that provides lodging for compensation. Under common law, innkeepers are held to strict liability for the loss or damage to the property of

guests. Most all states have innkeepers' statutes that limit the liability of innkeepers. To limit their liability, the innkeeper must provide a safe and make guests aware of its availability for their use.

Documents of Title

A document of title generally serves as a receipt for the goods, establishes the terms of the bailment contract, and evidences title to the goods. It is evidence that the holder of the receipt is entitled to receive, hold, and dispose of the document and the goods that it covers.

- Warehouse Receipts – This is a written document issued by a warehouseman. It contains the terms of the bailment. The warehouse has a lien on the goods until all expenses incurred have been satisfied.
- Bill of Lading – This document of title is issued by a carrier when goods are received for shipment. Bills of lading are issued by common carriers, contract carriers and others engaged in the business of transporting goods. A through bill of lading provides that connecting carriers may be used to transport the goods. The original carrier is liable to the bailor for loss or damage caused by the connecting carrier.

Refresh Your Memory

The following exercise will enable you to refresh your memory of the principles presented to you in this chapter. Read each question twice and place your answer in the blanks provided. Complete the entire exercise, and then review the chapter material for any question you miss or are unable to remember.

1. A person can acquire ownership of a wild animal by ____________ ________________ of it or ________________ it.

2. ____________________ the property from its owner is the most common method of acquiring title to personal property.

3. A voluntary transfer of property without consideration is known as a ____________.

4. A gift made during a person's lifetime is an _______ _______ gift that is an ___________________ present transfer of ownership.

5. If a person dies with a valid will, the property is distributed to the ________________. If there is not will, the property is distributed to the _____________ as provided for in an inheritance statute.

6. When the value of personal property increases because it is added to or improved by natural or ____________________ means, this is known as _______________.

7. When an owner voluntarily places his or her property somewhere and then inadvertently forgets it, the property is considered to be ________________.

8. The finder of _____________ property obtains title to the found property against everyone except the ______________ owner.

9. The finder of lost or misplaced property to obtain title to the property if they follow the procedure set forth in ____________ statutes.

10. If the owner discards the property with the intent to relinquish his or her rights in it, the property is considered to be ________________________.

Critical Thought Exercise

Tom Cruel, chairman of the Central Republican Committee for Rashaw County, was transporting a valuable painting in his trunk to a friend's home where it was to be displayed during a fundraiser. Cruel stopped at the country club for lunch and left his Mercedes in the care of a parking attendant who worked for Jiffy Parking Service, Inc. The attendant left the key box unattended while taking a break. The car and its contents were stolen. The car was recovered by police using a global positioning system, but the trunk was empty upon its return. Cruel was missing the painting worth $30,000, a golf bag and clubs valued at $1,400, and a CD case containing 120 music compact discs worth an estimated $1,500. Cruel has filed suit against Jiffy for the value of all the items taken from the trunk, including the painting. Is Jiffy liable to Cruel? If so, for which stolen items must it pay damages to Cruel?

Answer. ____

Sample Quiz

True/False:

1. ___ Intangible property includes stock certificates, bonds, and copyrights. [p 795]

2. ___ Taking possession or capturing property is not the most common method of acquiring property. [p 796]

3. ___ A constructive delivery will not be found for a gift despite such actions as giving the key to a safe-deposit box where the gift is located is handed over to the donee. [p 797]

4. ___ A gift cause mortis is made in contemplation of death. [p 797]

5. ___ The Uniform Gift To Minors Act is used by adults whenever they want to give a gift of money or securities to a minor. [p 798]

6. ___ If a person dies with a will, their property will be distributed to the beneficiaries. [p 798]

7. ___ A business owner who has an addition built on his building acquires ownership by accession. [p 798]

8. ___ If an improvement is made to the owner's property by mistake and the improvement cannot be removed, the owner obtains title to the improvement does not have to pay for it. [p 799]

9. ___ Confusion does not occur if two or more persons commingle fungible goods. [p 799]

10. ___ The owner of premises where personal property is mislaid is not entitled to take possession of the property against all except the rightful owner. [p 800]

11. ___ The finder of lost property does not obtain title to such property against the whole world. [p 800]

12. ___ Most estray statutes require that the property be turned over to a government agency. [p 800]

13. ___ If an owner of mislaid or lost property does not give up any further attempts to locate the property, the property is abandoned. [p 801]

14. ___ In a bailment, the owner of the property is the bailor. [p 802]

15. ___ A bailment is different than a sale or a gift because title to the goods does not transfer to the bailee. [p 802]

Multiple Choice:

16. Animals and minerals are [p 795]
    a. real property.
    b. a fixture.
    c. tangible property.
    d. intangible property.

17. Which of the following is method of acquiring ownership in personal property? [p 796-797]
    a. By possession
    b. By purchase or production
    c. By gift
    d. All of the above

18. A gift made in contemplation of death is a gift [p 797]
    a. inter vivos.
    b. causa mortis.
    c. by will or inheritance.
    d. by accession.

19. When a person cuts a car in half, adds a middle section, and creates a limousine, he has acquired ownership to the limousine by [p 798]
    a. purchase or production.

b. gift.
c. confusion.
d. accession.

20. If Janice hangs her jacket in a coatroom at a restaurant and forgets to take it home, her jacket will be considered [p 800]
    a. mislaid property.
    b. lost property.
    c. abandoned property.
    d. intangible property.

21. If Sue put her purse on the top of her car and it is blown off the roof as she drives to work, the purse is [p 800]
    a. mislaid property.
    b. lost property.
    c. abandoned property.
    d. intangible property.

22. Which of the following can be bailed? [p 802]
    a. promissory notes
    b. jewelry
    c. animals
    d. all of the above

23. Which of the following is true with respect to bailments? [p 803]
    a. The creation of a bailment requires certain formalities.
    b. A bailment may not be implied.
    c. A bailment must b in writing if it is for more than one year.
    d. A bailment may not be expressed.

24. What type of care does a bailee owe when the bailment is for the sole benefit of the bailee? [p 804]
    a. slight care
    b. utmost care
    c. reasonable care
    d. ordinary care

25. What type of care does the bailee owe in a mutual benefit bailment situation? [p 804]
    a. duty of reasonable or ordinary care
    b. duty of utmost care
    c. duty of slight care
    d. none of the above.

Short Answer:

26. Define the meaning of tangible property? [p 795]

____

____

27. List seven ways to acquire personal property? [p 796] ______________________________

____

28. What makes property "abandoned." [p 801] ____
____
____

29. Define bailment? [p 802] ____
____
____

30. What must a bailee do at the termination of a bailment? [p 805] ____________________
____

31. Provide an example of a bailment for the sole benefit of the bailee. [p 804]
____
____

32. What sort of duty of care is owed by someone who borrows a power tool from a neighbor? [p 804]
____

33. What is a mutual benefit bailment? [p 804] ______________________________________
____

34. When are warehouses liable for loss or damage to the bailed property? [p 805] __________
____

35. What is an innkeeper? [p 805] ____

Chapter 37

REAL PROPERTY AND LANDLORD-TENANT RELATIONSHIP

Chapter Overview

In the Western world, we have come to value real property more than most any other possession. To the ownership of land attaches wealth and influence in western society. More importantly, the privacy rights associated with property ownership are assigned great personal worth and psychological value. Even in the face of government power, we proclaim, "A man's home is his castle." In this chapter we focus on the legal rights associated with ownership, occupation, use, and transfer of real property.

Further, the average business does not have the resources to buy land and build its store, offices, manufacturing facilities, or other commercial facilities. Renting or leasing real property is a necessary part of doing business. This chapter covers law in the areas of contracts and real property that relate to the landlord-tenant relationship. It also discusses the regulation of land use by the government.

Chapter Objectives

Upon completion of the exercises contained in this chapter, you should be able to

1. Describe the different types of ownership interests in real property.
2. Explain ownership interests in surface, subsurface, and air rights.
3. Describe the various kinds of freehold estates, concurrent ownership and future interests in land.
6. Describe the different types of tenancy
7. Understand landlord as well as tenant duties
8. Understand how zoning laws regulate the use of land.
9. Describe the acquisition of property by the government by the use of eminent domain.

Practical Application

Upon mastering the concepts in this chapter, you should be able to recognize how a piece of real property is held by the owner and what affect that has upon its use, transfer, and value. As an example, real estate that has an easement attached to it is worth less because another party has the right to use the property for their own purposes as specified in the easement. When the property is transferred to another owner, that owner may have to accept the easement, depending on whether legal requirements have been met.

In addition to learning the objectives in this chapter, you should understand the duties and rights of landlords and tenants in the common leasing of real property. Failure to meet the duties imposed at common law and by statute may cause a tenant to lose their tenancy. A landlord who violates their duties is subjected to damages and sanctions. A businessperson who is leasing a storefront or commercial building must understand the restrictions on the use of the building and what affirmative tasks must be undertaken to keep them out of breach of contract.

Helpful Hints

There are many rules created by common law, statute, and current case law. A logical order can be created to this large volume of law if you focus on the creation of the right in the land, its transfer, and perfecting the right by giving notice to the rest of the world. When you are faced with a real property problem, you need to know how the person or company obtained its interest in the real property, what rights go with that interest, if any other party claims a joint interest in the same property, and how that interest is protected or sold to another. Unlike personal property that is usually not granted to a beneficiary until a will becomes effective, the transfer of an interest in real property may be dictated by the language and conditions contained in the deed. It is often necessary to look backwards in the line of owners to determine who will own the interest in the future.

It is also important that you learn the terminology associated with the rights and duties that arise from the landlord-tenant relationship. In each lease of real property, whether you are the landlord or the tenant, you must understand your obligations and know how those obligations are created in a written lease. You must also understand the obligations that are created by statute and remain in effect even if they are not included in the lease. As you examine each right and duty, determine the type of land use that is proper and improper in each situation.

Study Tips

The following outline will help you create a mental checklist of the main issues and rights involved in ownership and transfer of rights in real property. This "checklist" is constantly trying to answer the following questions:

- Is this real or personal property?
- In what form is the reap property currently owned?
- Does anyone hold a future interest in this land?
- Does anyone a co-owner of this real property?
- Was there a legal transfer of an ownership interest?
- Was the transfer of the ownership interest property recorded by deed?
- Does anyone own a nonpossessory interest in this real property?
- Is any legal action being taken against the real property?

Nature of Real Property

Real property is the land itself and any buildings, trees, soil, minerals, timber, plants and other things that are permanently affixed to the land. Any building or permanent structure that is built upon the land becomes part of the real property. The owner of the property also owns the subsurface rights to any minerals, oil, gas, or other commodity that may be under the surface. These subsurface rights may be sold separate from the rest of the real property. Both natural and cultivated plants are part of the real property. They become personal property if the owner severs them from the land. Items that are permanently affixed to the land or a building become part of the real property if they cannot be removed without causing substantial damage to the realty. A regular refrigerator would remain personal property and may be removed when the realty is sold. A built-in commercial refrigerator becomes a ***fixture*** and is sold with the realty. One other type of property is the air space above the surface of realty. This space may be sold or leased separate from the realty like a subsurface right.

Ownership Rights

The ownership rights one possesses in real property is called an estate in land. An estate is defined as the bundle of legal rights that the owner has to possess, use, and enjoy the property. The type of estate an owner possesses is determined by the deed, will, lease or other document that created or transferred ownership rights.

- A *freehold estate* is an estate where the owner has a present possessory interest in the real property. Two types of freehold estates are estates in fee and life estates.
  - A *fee simple absolute* is a type of ownership of real property that grants the owner the fullest bundle of legal rights that a person can hold in real property.
  - A *fee simple defeasible* grants the owner all the incidents of a fee simple absolute except that it may be taken away if a specified condition occurs or does not occur.
  - A *life estate* is an interest in land for a person's lifetime. Upon that person's death, the interest will be transferred to another party.

Future Interests

A person may be given the right to possess property in the future rather than in the present. The two forms of future interests are:

- *Reversion* – A right of possession that returns to the grantor after the expiration of a limited or contingent estate.
- *Remainder* – If the right of possession returns to a third party upon the expiration of a limited or contingent estate.

Concurrent Ownership

The forms of co-ownership or concurrent ownership are

- *Joint Tenancy* – Upon the death of one owner, the property passes to the other joint tenants automatically. This is called the right of survivorship.
- *Tenancy in Common* – The interest of a surviving tenant in common passes to the deceased tenant's estate and not to the co-tenants.
- *Tenancy by the Entirety* – This form can only be used by married couples. This also has a right of survivorship, but unlike a joint tenancy, one tenant cannot sell their interest in the realty.
- *Community Property* – None states recognize community property rights. Upon the death of one spouse, one-half of the community assets automatically pass to the surviving spouse. The other half passes by will or by the state's intestate statute.
- *Condominium* – A form of ownership in a multiple-dwelling building where the purchaser has title to an individual unit and owns the common areas as a tenant in common.
- *Cooperative* – A form of ownership of a multiple-dwelling building where a corporation owns the building and the residents own shares in the corporation.

Transfer of Ownership of Real Property

An owner may transfer their interest in realty by one of the following methods:

- *Sale* – This is the passing of title from a seller to a buyer for a price. It is also called a conveyance.
- *Tax Sale* – The government may obtain a tax lien against property for unpaid property taxes. If the lien remains unpaid, a tax sale is held to satisfy the lien.
- *Gift, Will, Inheritance* – These forms of transfer involve granting title to another without the payment of any consideration.
- *Adverse Possession* – When a person openly possesses the property of another, they may acquire title if certain statutory requirements are met. The owner must have notice that his or her land is being wrongfully possesses and take no steps to eject the adverse possessor.

Deeds and Recording Statutes

Deeds are used to convey property by sale or gift. The seller or donor is called the *grantor*. The buyer or recipient is the *grantee*. A *warranty deed* has the greatest number of warranties or guarantees.

The *quitclaim deed* provides no protection for the buyer, granting only whatever interest the grantor possesses.

A *recording statute* provides that copies of the deed and other documents, such as mortgages and deeds of trust, may be filed with the *county recorder's office* to give constructive notice of the ownership to the world. Recording statutes are intended to prevent fraud and to establish certainty in the ownership and transfer of property.

A seller has the obligation to transfer *marketable title* to the grantee. Marketable title means that the title is free from encumbrances, defects in title, or other defects that would affect the value of the property.

Nonpossessory Interests

Nonpossessory interests exist when a person holds an interest in another person's property without actually owning any part of the property. The three nonpossesory interests are

- **Easements** – An easement is a given or required right to make limited use of someone else's land without owning or leasing it.
  Easements may be **expressly** created by
  1. *grant* – where the owner gives another party an easement across his or her property
  2. *reservation* – where an owner sells his or her land but keeps an easement on the land

  Easements may be **implied** by
  1. *implication* – where an owner subdivides a piece of property with a well, path, road or other beneficial appurtenant that serves the entire parcel, or by
  2. *necessity* – where a landlocked parcel must have egress and ingress
- There are two types of easements
  1. Easements Appurtenant – A situation created when the owner of a piece of land is given an easement over an adjacent piece of land.
  2. Easements in Gross – An easement that authorizes a person who does not own adjacent land the right to use another's land. Examples include easements granted for power lines, telephone lines, gas lines, and cable lines.

  The easement holder owes a duty to maintain and repair the easement.
- **Licenses** – A license grants a person the right to enter upon another's property for a specified and usually short period of time. A ticket to a football game gives you a license to use a seat in the stadium for a period of time.
- **Profit** – Grants a person the right to remove something from another's real property.

A landlord or tenant can have obligations created by the lease, by statute, or by common law doctrines such as negligence. Examine each of these areas individually to discover the specific rights and duties that are created for the landlord and tenant.

Landlord-Tenant Relationship

This relationship is created when the owner of a freehold estate transfers a right to exclusively and temporarily possess the owner's property. The tenant receives a leasehold estate.

The types of tenancy are:

- *tenancy for years* – a tenancy created when the landlord and the tenant agree on a specific duration for the lease.
- *periodic tenancy* – a tenancy created when a lease specifies intervals at which payments are due but does not specify how long the lease is for.
- *tenancy at will* – a lease that may be terminated at any time by either party.
- *tenancy at sufferance* – a tenancy created when a tenant retains possession of property after the expiration of another tenancy or a life estate without the owner's consent.

Duties Owed by the Landlord

The landlord has the following duties:

- *duty to deliver possession*
- *duty not to interfere with the tenant's right of quiet enjoyment* – the law implies a covenant of quiet enjoyment in all leases. The landlord may not interfere with the tenant's quiet and peaceful possession, use, and enjoyment of the leased premises.
- *duty to maintain the leased premises* – the landlord must comply with the requirements imposed by building and housing codes. Under an implied warranty of habitability, the leased premised must be fit, safe, and suitable for ordinary residential use.

Duties Owed by the Tenant

A tenant owes the landlord the duties agreed to in the lease and any duties imposed by law. These include:

- *duty not to use leased premises for illegal or nonstipulated purposes*
- *duty not to commit waste* – waste occurs when a tenant causes substantial and permanent damages to the leased premises that decreases the value of the property and the landlord's reversionary interest in it.
- *duty not to disturb other tenants* – a landlord may evict the tenant who interferes with the quiet enjoyment of other tenants.

Tort Liability of Landlords and Tenants

Landlords and tenants owe a duty of reasonable care to third parties not to negligently cause injury to them. The landlord also owes this duty to the tenant.

Transferring Rights to Leased Property

Landlords may sell, gift, devise, or otherwise transfer their interests in leased property. The new landlord cannot alter the terms of an existing lease.

The tenant may transfer his or her rights under a lease to another by way of an assignment. The new tenant is the assignee and is obligated to perform the duties that the assignor had under the lease. The assignor remains responsible for his or her obligations under the lease unless released by the landlord.

If a tenant transfers only some of his or her rights under the lease, it is a sublease. The sublessor is still responsible under the lease and the sublessee does not obtain any rights under the original lease.

Land Use Control

Land use control is the collective term for the laws that regulate the possession, ownership, and use of real property. Forms of land use control include:

- *private nuisance* – a landowner or tenant who is affected in the use and enjoyment of real property by the use of adjoining or nearby property may bring a private nuisance action for damages.
- *restrictive covenants* – this is a private agreement between landowners that restricts the use of their land. They are often used by residential developers and condominium buildings to establish uniform rules for all occupants.
- *public nuisance* – this is a nuisance that effects or disturbs the public in general.
- *zoning* – zoning ordinances are local laws that are adopted by municipalities and local governments to regulate land use within their boundaries. Zoning ordinances are adopted and enforced to protect the health, safety, morals, and general welfare of the community. A

landowner may obtain a variance that permits a type of building or use that would not otherwise be allowed by a zoning ordinance.

Refresh Your Memory

The following exercise will enable you to refresh your memory on the rules of law and principles presented to you in this chapter. Read each question twice and put your answer in the blanks provided. Review the chapter material for any question that you miss or are unable to remember.

1. Houses, farms, and buildings are all forms of ______________________________ property.

2. Items of personal property, that are affixed to real property are called ____________________

3. Rights to minerals and other things under the surface of land are called _________________ rights.

4. A person's ownership rights in real property are called an _____________ ______ ____________.

5. The highest form of ownership of real property is a _____________ _______________ _______________.

6. An estate that may be taken away if a specified condition occurs or does not occur is a __________ ____________ _________________.

7. A landlord holds a _________________ estate that he or she can transfer to a tenant for their use.

8. The tenant's interest in property is called a __________________ _________________.

9. The rental agreement between the landlord and tenant is called the __________________.

10. When the landlord and tenant agree on a specific duration for the lease, it is a tenancy ____________________ _____________________________________.

11. Which federal statute makes it unlawful for a party to refuse to rent or sell a dwelling to any person because of his or her race, color, national origin, sex, or religion? ________________ _________________________

12. Which power may the government use to acquire private property for public purposes? ____

13. Which federal statute prohibits racial discrimination in the transfer of real property, including housing, commercial and industrial property? _____________________________________

14. Which type of easement authorizes a person who does not own adjacent land the right to use another's land? _______________________________________

15. An easement __________________________ is created when the owner of one piece of land is given an easement over an adjacent piece of land.

Critical Thought Exercise

Jim Lewis and Dale Tingle decided to form a partnership for the purpose of entering the restaurant business. Prior to forming the partnership, Lewis and Tingle purchased a large Victorian house in Sacramento with the idea that they would convert the first floor into a restaurant and the upper floors into office space. Lewis contributed $90,000 to the purchase and Tingle contributed $10,000. Lewis and Tingle took title as joint tenants with the right of survivorship. The partnership was formed five months later and the Sacramento property was converted into a restaurant and offices as planned. When Lewis and Tingle purchased another house in Davis, California, they took title as tenants in common. Tingle contributed $100,000 as the down payment for the Davis property. When the partnership was dissolved, the court ordered that both properties be sold. Lewis was given a reimbursement for the Sacramento property in the amount of $80,000. The Davis property was sold for $320,000 and the proceeds of the sale were divided equally between Lewis and Tingle. Did the court divide the proceeds from the sale of the two properties properly?

Answer. ____

Practice Quiz

True/False:

1. ___ Buildings constructed on land are not personal property. [p 813]

2. ___ Subsurface rights may not be sold separately from surface rights. [p 813]

3. ___ Natural plants such as trees are real property, as are cultivated plants such as a corn crop. [p 813]

4. ___ Door knobs are not fixtures and are part of the realty. [p 813]

5. ___ An easement is the bundle of legal rights that the owner has to possess, use, and enjoy the property. [p 822]

6. ___ A life estate is an interest in real property that lasts forever. [p 815]

7. ___ When a life estate or contingent estate terminates, the right of possession does not revert to the grantor. [p 818]

8. ___ A remainder is not a right of possession that returns to the grantor after the expiration of limited or contingent estate. [p 818]

9. ___ If the right of possession returns to a third party upon the expiration of a limited or contingent estate, it is called a remainder. [p 816]

10. ___ Tenancy in common is not a form of co-ownership that includes the right of survivorship. [p 816]

11. ___ In a tenancy in common, the interests of a surviving tenant in common pass to the deceased tenant's estate. [p 816]

12. ___ Tenancy by the entirety is form of co-ownership of real property that can be used only by anyone. [p 816]

Multiple Choice:

13. Which of the following is real property? [p 813]
    a. The tables and chairs in a restaurant
    b. A portable hot tub
    c. A camper in which a family is living
    d. An in-ground swimming pool

14. The rights to natural gas under Sue's home are her [p 813]
    a. easement rights.
    b. profit.
    c. personal property.
    d. subsurface rights.

15. Larry conveys Blackacre to "Jim Smith and Greg Brown, as tenants in common." Jim Smith has a will that leaves his entire estate to Ned Green. If Smith dies, his interest in Blackacre will pass to [p 816]
    a. Smith's heirs under the state's intestate statute.
    b. Green.
    c. Brown.
    d. none of the above.

16. The owner of a condominium [p 818]
    a. has title to their individual unit.
    b. owns the common areas as tenants in common with the other owners.
    c. may sell or mortgage their unit without the permission of the other owners.
    d. all of the above.

17. Gus has a home on a 10-acre parcel that he subdivides into two 5-acre parcels. Gus builds a new house on the subdivided parcel. The only way for the new homeowner to get to the main road is to drive across Gus's parcel. The new homeowner has acquired an [p 822]
   a. easement by express grant.
   b. easement by implication.
   c. license.
   d. profit a'pendre.

18. The government must compensate a property owner when the government takes his or her property by eminent domain under the mandate of the [p 830]
   a. Just Compensation Clause.
   b. action to quiet title.
   c. Statute for the Regulation of Open Property.
   d. profit a'pendre.

19. Kyle, a landlord, has always rented his apartments to female schoolteachers. Kyle believes that schoolteachers, especially women, are neat and quiet and make the best tenants. Does Kyle have the right to discriminate against others in favor or female schoolteachers in this manner? [p 829]
   a. Yes, because Kyle owns the premises and is free to contract with whomever he pleases.
   b. Yes, because Kyle is free to rent his freehold estate to anyone he desires.
   c. No, because there is no proof that schoolteachers are neat.
   d. No, because Kyle is prohibited by the Civil Rights Act from discriminating against tenants on the basis of their sex.

20. The Country Inn rents efficiency suites by the day, week, and month. The Inn has staircases and steps leading into all suites as part of its Victorian architecture. The Inn tells all disabled persons that it is unable to accommodate physical handicaps. The policy of the Country Inn [p 829]
   a. is lawful because private businesses do not have to accommodate handicapped persons.
   b. is lawful because an owner may design their hotel to fit their own style and budget.
   c. is unlawful because the Americans with Disabilities Act prohibits discrimination on the basis of disability in places of public accommodation operated by private entities.
   d. is unlawful because it violates the Fair Housing Act.

Short Answer:

21. Things such as radio towers, bridges, and grain silos are considered __________ property. [p 813]

22. Give four examples of things that may be removed from the earth or sold as part of an owners subsurface rights. [p 813] ____

____

23. Give four examples of things in a home that are fixtures and cannot be removed upon a sale of the real property. [p 813]____

____

24. Three types of estates are [pp 814-815] ______________, ______________,

____

25. A life estate that is measured in the life of third party is an [p 815] ______________.

26. The interest that the grantor retains for him- or herself or a third party is a [p 818] ________________ ________________.

27. Name and define two future interests. [p 818]
1) ________________
2) ________________

28. What is a joint tenancy and how should it be created in a deed? [p 815] ________________
____
____

29. What is a cooperative? [p 818]
____
____

30. What is adverse possession? [p 821] ________________
____

31. What is a marketable title? [p 819] ________________
____
____

Chapter 38

INSURANCE, WILLS, AND ESTATES

Chapter Overview

The potential risk of loss that a business or individual faces due to death, fire, or injury may be staggering. Insurance is a crucial part of business planning. This chapter examines the insurance contract, types and uses of insurance, defenses used by insurance companies to avoid liability, and secondary liability for losses. The businessperson should understand the types of insurance coverage that are necessary for the proper protection of personal and business assets.

Wills and trusts are the two main ways that a person disposes of their assets prior to or upon their death. These assets may include business ownership, intellectual property, stocks and bonds, real estate, and personal property. A person who dies intestate, or without a will, will have his or her estate distributed according to a state statute. A trust may be created before death so that property may be held and managed for the benefit of another.

Objectives

Upon completion of the exercises in this chapter, you should be able to:

1. Describe the essential parts of an insurance contract.
2. Describe various types of life, health, and disability insurance.
3. Explain uninsured motorist and no-fault insurance.
4. Understand the various forms of business insurance.
5. Describe the requirements for making a valid will.
6. Explain the types of gifts that can be contained in a will.
7. Explain *per stirpes* and *per capita* distribution of an estate.
8. Describe the application of an intestacy statute.
9. Describe the formation and functioning of a trust.
10. Differentiate between a trust and a living trust and the purposes of each.

Practical Application

Even the most successful business has limited resources. This chapter will help you develop a greater understanding of the role that insurance plays in the overall business plan and estate planning of the individual. By understanding the coverage provided by different insurance products, you can make an informed decision as to the type and amount of insurance that is needed to achieve business and personal goals that have been set. Just as import is an understanding of your rights as an insured and the potential defenses that an insurance company will use to avoid paying a claim.

When a businessperson acquires assets, it is wise to know how those will be distributed upon their death. The fruits of years of hard work may be wasted if a person does not take adequate steps to preserve their estate and ensure that the estate will be distributed as they wish. As discussed in Chapter 51, insurance, especially key-person insurance, is an integral part of the estate planning process. A business may have to be dissolved if the owners do not take estate planning into account.

Helpful Hints

You should examine insurance products and incorporate them into any business plan and personal estate plan. When a businessperson is making a decision as the type and amount of coverage needed, he or she must first determine the asset or risk for which protection is needed. The coverage must then be matched to that risk. The needs of a business will vary depending upon the type of business activity, product produced or sold, importance of key personnel, and exposure to liability based upon the risk created by the business to its employees and members of the general public.

The main purpose of entering into business is to acquire wealth and provide the necessities of life for yourself, family, and others that depend upon you. Regardless of the amount of current assets held by a person, everyone should have an estate plan. It may be as simple as a will or may involve complex estate planning with the use of trusts, tax consultation, and use of joint tenancy. If an estate plan is in place, it will provide the distribution of assets as desired by the businessperson even if the assets grow or change. Periodic updates of the estate plan are advisable

Study Tips

In order to accomplish their business goals, each businessperson should understand the important points contained in the following outline. This laundry list of insurance terms and principles is indispensable.

Regulation of the Insurance Industry

Each state has enacted statutes that regulate the insurance industry that operates within the state. State regulation covers all aspects of insurance company incorporation, licensing, oversight, termination of business, and the licensing of agents and brokers.

Insurance Contracts

- The ***insurance contract*** is a form of third party beneficiary contract, as was discussed in Chapter 15. The insurance contract, or ***policy***, is purchased by the ***insured*** who pays premiums to the insurance company or ***insurer***. The policy is usually sold by an ***agent*** who works for the insurance company or by an ***insurance broker*** who represents several insurance companies and is the agent of the insured.
- ***Mandatory provisions*** are required by statute and must be included in each policy. If mandatory provisions are omitted from the contract, they will still be implied. Examples of these provisions include coverage for certain losses and how limitations on coverage must be worded in the contract.
- The ***effective date of coverage*** is the first date when the insurer becomes obligated to pay for any loss suffered by the insured. This effective date may be when the application and first premium are paid, when a physical exam is passed, or when a broker obtains the insurance.
- Modification of an insurance contract by the parties is usually accomplished by adding an ***endorsement*** to the policy or by executing a document called a ***rider***.

- A person must have an insurable interest in anything he or she insures. For life insurance, a person must have a familiar relationship or an economic benefit from the continued life of another. For property insurance, anyone who would suffer a monetary loss from the destruction of the property has an insurable interest in that property.
- Coverage is limited by deductible clauses and exclusions from coverage.

Life Insurance

- *Life insurance* is a form of insurance where the insurer must pay a specific sum of money to a named **beneficiary** upon the death of another. There are numerous life insurance products, including whole life, limited-payment life, term life, universal life, and endorsement and annuity. The amount of **premiums** for a policy depends upon factors such as availability of a cash or surrender value, and the period over which premiums will be paid.
- *Key-person life insurance* is often purchased by business owners to finance **buy-sell agreements** upon the death of one of the owners of the business. If an insured owner dies, the insurance proceeds are paid to the deceased's beneficiaries. The deceased's interest in the business then reverts to the other owners of the business according to the terms of the buy-sell agreement. This allows a business to continue upon the death of an owner and prevents the beneficiaries from selling off the assets of the business.
- A *double indemnity clause* stipulates that the insurer will pay double the amount of the policy if death is caused by accident or criminal agency.
- *Exclusions from coverage* in many policies include death caused by military actions, executions by government, accidents in private aircraft, and suicide within one or two years.

Health and Disability Insurance

- *Health insurance* can be purchased to cover the costs of medical treatment. Plans vary from health maintenance organizations with low deductibles and co-payments to self-funded plans that have high deductibles, but have greater freedom in choosing doctors and much lower monthly premiums.
- *Disability insurance* provides a monthly income to an insured who is unable to work due to a non work-related disability.

Fire and Homeowners Insurance

- A standard *fire insurance policy* protects real and personal property against loss resulting from fire and certain related perils. Most policies provide for replacement cost insurance that pays the cost to replace the damaged or destroyed property at its current cost.
- A *homeowners policy* covers personal liability in addition to the risks covered by the fire insurance policy. The homeowners policy covers losses from a much wider range of causes, including negligence and theft.
- A *residence contents broadform* policy covers losses incurred by renters for damage or destruction to their possessions.

Automobile Insurance

Many states have mandatory automobile insurance statutes. Proof of insurance is required to be kept on file with the state department of motor vehicles. The basic types of automobile insurance are:

- *Collision insurance* insures the owner's car against the risk of loss or damage. The premium varies depending upon the amount of deductible paid towards any loss by the car owner.

- *Comprehensive insurance* insures an automobile from loss or damages from causes other than collision, such as fire, theft, hail, falling objects, earthquakes, floods, and vandalism.
- *Liability insurance* covers damages that the insured causes to third parties. This coverage usually has a limit for injury to each person in an accident, a limit for the total bodily injury for all persons injured, and a limit for property damage.
- *Medical payment coverage* covers medical expenses for the driver and his or her passengers who are injured in an accident.
- *Uninsured motorist coverage* provides coverage to the driver and passengers who are injured by an uninsured motorist or hit-and-run driver.
- *No-fault automobile insurance* has been enacted in some states. Under this system, a driver's insurance company pays for any injuries he or she suffered in an accident, no mater who caused the accident. Claimants may not sue to recover damages from the party who caused the accident unless the injured party suffered serious injury.

Business Insurance

The owner of real property and a business should purchase several types of insurance in addition to liability and fire insurance. These additional types of insurance include:

- *Business interruption insurance* that pays for lost revenues during the period a business is rebuilding after a fire or some other event.
- *Workers' compensation insurance* pays for injuries and lost wages of employees who are injured on the job. This insurance is mandatory in most states.
- *Fidelity insurance* covers the employer against losses caused by employee theft or fraud.
- *Directors' and officers' liability insurance* protects directors and officers from liability for their negligent actions that they take on behalf of the corporation.
- *Product liability insurance* protects against losses incurred by manufacturers and sellers for injuries caused by their defective products.

Other Types of Insurance

Some special types of insurance that a particular business or individual may desire include:

- *Professional malpractice insurance* which covers the injuries caused by professionals, such as doctors, lawyers, accountants, and architects, resulting from the negligent performance of their duties.
- *Title insurance* protects against defects in title and liens and encumbrances that are not disclosed on the title insurance policy. A lender often requires this insurance before it will fund a loan.
- *Credit insurance* may be purchased by either the creditor or debtor to protect against the debtor's inability to pay a debt. It usually consists of credit life insurance or credit disability insurance.
- *Marine insurance* protects owners and shippers against loss or damage to their ships and cargo.
- *Group insurance* is an insurance that is sold to all the members of a single group, often all the employees of one employer, union, or professional association.
- *Umbrella insurance* coverage pays only if the basic policy limits of a liability policy have been exceeded. This insurance is inexpensive and often extends coverage to $5 million.

Performance of Insurance Contracts

The parties to an insurance contract are obligated to perform the duties imposed by the contract. The duties of the insured are:

- *Duty to pay premiums* – the insured must pay the agreed-upon premiums. Many policies include a grace period during which an insured may pay an overdue premium.

- *Duty to notify insurer* – the insured must notify the insurer after the occurrence of an insured event.
- *Duty to cooperate* – the insured must cooperate with the insurer in investigating claims made against the insurer.

The duties of the insurer are:

- *Duty to defend* – the insurer has a duty to defend against any suit brought against the insured that involves a claim within the coverage of the policy.
- *Duty to pay insurance proceeds* – the insurer's primary duty is to pay legitimate claims up to the policy limit.

Defenses of the Insurer

The most common defenses that may be raised by the insurer to avoid liability are:

- *Misrepresentation and concealment* – the insurer may avoid liability if: 1) the applicant makes a material misrepresentation in the application that is relied upon by the insurer in deciding whether to issue the policy, or 2) the applicant concealed material information from the insurer. Many states have enacted incontestability clauses that prevent insurers from contesting the statements in an application after a number of years.
- *Breach of warranty* – the insured may be required to make affirmative or promissory warranties that certify that facts or conditions are true, such as there being no known structural defects in a building, or that facts will continue to be true while the policy is in effect. The breach of these promises by the insured will relieve the insurer of liability.

Subrogation

If an insurance company pays a claim to an insured for liability or property damage caused by a third party, the insurer succeeds to the right of the insured to recover from the third party.

In order to make informed judgments involving estate planning, the individual should understand the following principles law relating to wills and trusts.

Requirements for Making a Will

A will is a declaration of how a person wants his or her property distributed upon death. The person who makes this testamentary disposition of property is called the testator or testatrix. The persons designated to receive the property are the beneficiaries.

Every state has a Statute of Wills that sets forth the requirements for a valid will. They are

- Testamentary capacity – the testator must be of legal age and of sound mind
- Writing – the will must be in writing except for noncupative wills
- Testator's signature – the will must be signed at the end.

Attestation by Witnesses

Wills must be attested to by two or three objective and competent persons. The person need not live in the same state, but all the parties must be present when the will is attested to by all witnesses and signed by the testator.

Changing the Will

Wills may be changed by a codicil, a separate document that must be executed with the same formalities as a will. The codicil must incorporate by reference the will it is amending by referring to the testator by name and the date of the previous will. The codicil and will become one document that is read as a whole.

Revoking a Will

Any act that shows a desire to revoke a will shall be deemed a revocation. Making a new will, burning, tearing, or crossing out the pages are all forms of revocations. Wills may also be revoked by operation of law, such as when people get divorced or a spouse is convicted of the murder of the other spouse.

Special Types of Wills

- *Holographic will* are entirely handwritten by the testator, dated, and signed. They need not be witnessed.
- *Noncupative wills* are oral wills made before witnesses during a final illness. They are sometimes call deathbed wills.

Types of Testamentary Gifts

- A gift or real property is a *devise.*
- A gift of personal property is a *bequest* or *legacy.*
- *Specific gifts* are specifically named items of personal property, such as a ring.
- *General gifts* do not specify the source, such as a cash gift.
- *Residuary gifts* are established by a residuary clause that leaves the portion of the estate left over after all distributions and costs are satisfied.

Ademption and Abatement

- *Ademption* – the beneficiary receives nothing when the testator leaves a specific gift and that gift is not in the testator's estate when he or she dies.
- *Abatement* – if the testator's estate is not large enough to pay all of the devises and bequests, the doctrine of abatement applies. If the will has general and residuary gifts, the residuary gift is abated first. If the will only has general gifts, each gift is reduced proportionately.

Per Stirpes and Per Capita Distribution

When the will leaves the estate to the testator's lineal descendants, it will be distributed either per stipres or per capita.

- *Per stirpes* – the lineal descendants inherit by representation of their parents.
- *Per capita* – the lineal descendants equally share the property of the estate without regard to the degree of relationship to the testator. Children share equally with grandchildren.

Videotaped and Electronic Wills

Electronic wills and videotaped wills do not have any legal force by themselves. A written will is still required. The videotaped or electronically recorded will can be used to supplement the written will to show that the testator had testamentary capacity.

Reciprocal Wills

Reciprocal will arise where two or more testators execute separate wills that make testamentary dispositions of their property to each other on the condition that the survivor leave the remaining property on his or her death as agreed by the testators.

Undue Influence

A will may be invalidated if it was made as a result of undue influence upon the testator. Undue influence occurs when one person takes advantage of another person's mental, emotional, or physical weakness and unduly persuades that person to make a will. The persuasion by the wrongdoer must overcome the free will of the testator.

Murder Disqualification Doctrine

Most state statutes and court decisions provide that a person who murders another person cannot inherit the victim's property.

Intestate Succession

If a person dies without a will, or a will fails for some legal reason, the property is distributed to his or her relatives pursuant to the state's intestacy statute. Relatives who receive property under these statutes are called heirs. If there are no heirs, the property escheats (goes) to the state.

Probate

Probate is the process of a deceased's property being collected, debts and taxes being paid, and the remainder being distributed. A personal representative must be appointed to administer the estate. If the person is named in a will, they are called an executor. If the court appoints the representative, they are an administrator. A probate proceeding is administered and settled according to the state's probate code. Almost half of the states have adopted most or all of the Uniform Probate Code.

Living Wills

People who do not want their lives prolonged indefinitely by artificial means should sign a living will that stipulates their wishes before catastrophe strikes and they become unable to express it themselves.

Trusts

A trust is a legal arrangement established when one person, the settlor or trustor, transfers title to property to another person to be held and used for the benefit of a third person. The property held in trust is called the trust corpus or trust res. Trusts often give any trust income to an income beneficiary and the corpus is distributed to a remainderman upon termination of the trust. There are several kinds of trusts.

- **Express trust** – A trust created voluntarily by the settlor. Express trusts are either:
  - *inter vivos trust* – a trust that is created while the settlor is alive
  - *testamentary trust* – a trust created by will
- **Implied trust** – A trust that is implied by law or from the conduct of the parties. These trusts are either:
  - *constructive trust* – an equitable trust that is imposed by law to avoid fraud, unjust enrichment, and injustice
  - *resulting trust* – a trust created by the conduct of the parties
- **Charitable trust** – created for the benefit of a segment of society or society in general
- **Spendthrift trust** – designed to prevent a beneficiary's personal creditors from reaching his or her trust interest
- **Totten trust** – created when a person deposits money in a bank in their own name and holds it as trustee for the benefit of another

Refresh Your Memory

The following exercise will enable you to refresh your memory on the important principles presented to you in this chapter. Read each question twice and place your answer in the blanks provided. Review the chapter material for any question you miss or are unable to remember.

1. Under an insurance contract, the insurance company is the insurer who ____________________ the insurance coverage.

2. An insurance ________________________ usually works exclusively for one insurance company.

3. An ______________________________ is an addition to an insurance policy that modifies it.

4. Before a person can purchase insurance, they must have an _____________ _____________ in the insured item or person.

5. __________________________ clauses provide that insurance proceeds are payable only after the insured has paid a certain amount of the damage or loss.

6. ___________________ life insurance is issued for a limited period of time with premiums payable and coverage effective only during this term.

7. The ______________________ is the person who is to receive the insurance proceeds of a life insurance contract when the insured dies.

8. The standard fire insurance policy protects the homeowner from loss caused by ____________, lightning, _____________, and water damage.

9. Under _____- _______ _________________, a driver's insurance company pays for any injuries or death he or she suffered in an accident, no mater who caused the accident.

10. A policy called the _____________ ______________ covers the renters' possessions against the same perils as a homeowners policy and personal liability coverage.

Critical Thought Exercise

The five partners in the law firm of Higgins & Ford, LLP, purchased a $500,000 life insurance policy on the life of each partner from Celestial Insurance. The firm was listed as the beneficiary. On the application forms, the relationship pf the beneficiary to the insured was listed as "business/family association." The period of contestability was two years. Three years after the policy on the life of Victor Ford was purchased, Mr. Ford died in an automobile accident. Celestial refused to pay on the policy and filed suit in a federal district court against Higgins & Ford, seeking to have the policy declared void *ab initio* (from the beginning) on the ground that the law firm lacked an insurable interest.

Does the misleading statement regarding the relationship with the insured by the beneficiary or the lack of a personal relationship with Victor Ford prevent Higgins & ford from having an insurable interest?

Answer. ____

____

____

____

____

____

____

____

____

____

____

____

Sample Quiz

True/False:

1. ___ The party who pays a premium to a particular insurance company for insurance coverage is the insured. [p 838]

2. ___ An insurance agent is an independent contractor who usually represents one insurance company and is an agent of that company [p 838]

3. ___ In all situations, an insurable interest must be based upon a close family relationship, not a business relationship. [p 839]

4. ___ The owner of real or personal property is not the only person who may have an insurable interest in the property. [p 838]

5. ___ The owner of a life insurance policy is the person who contracts with the insurance company and pays the premium. [p 838]

6. ___ A double indemnity clause is a clause in many life insurance policies that allows for payment of double the amount of the policy if death is caused by accident. [p 840]

7. ___ Disability insurance payments made to an insured are usually based on the degree of disability. [p 840]

8. ___ A property owner who buys a homeowners policy does needs a separate fire insurance policy. [p 840]

9. ___ The persons designated to receive the property under a will are the beneficiaries. [p 844]

10. ___ A will must be signed at the end of the will if there is an attestation clause. [p 845]

11. ___ Written documents are the only way to show a desire to revoke a will. [p 847]

12. ___ A specific gift is an item of personal property, such as your great-grandmother's ring. [p 848]

13. ___ Abatement is applied if the property the testator leaves is not sufficient to satisfy all the beneficiaries named in a will. [p 848]

14. ___ When two people who would inherit property from each other die simultaneously, each deceased person's property is distributed as though he or she had not survived. [p 847]

15. ___ A will may be found to be valid if it was made as a result of undue influence on the testator. [p 847]

Multiple Choice:

16. Which of the following statements is accurate? [p 838]
    a. Insurance brokers work for an individual insurance company.
    b. Insurance brokers are independent contractors who represent a number of insurance companies.
    c. Insurance agents represent multiple insurance companies.
    d. Insurance agents and brokers are both independent contractors.

17. Mary is a partner in a very successful accounting firm, is married, and has two children. Who has an insurable interest that would allow them to purchase life insurance if Mary is the insured? [p 838]
    a. Mary's husband
    b. Mary's children
    c. Mary's partners in the accounting firm
    d. All of the above

18. The type of life insurance that has a cash value that grows at a variable interest rate is [p 840]
    a. universal life.
    b. whole life.
    c. term life.
    d. limited-payment life.

19. Small businesses, such as partnerships, limited liability companies, and close corporations, often purchase ________________ life insurance on the owners of the business. [p 840]
    a. whole
    b. key-person
    c. universal
    d. term

20. To protect against the risk of loss caused by property damage by the insured or members of the insured's immediate family, the insured should have [p 840]
    a. standard fire coverage.
    b. a personal articles floater.
    c. liability coverage.
    d. residence contents broad form coverage.

21. To protect against the risk of loss caused by theft of his or her vehicle, and insured should purchase [p 840]
    a. automobile collision insurance.
    b. automobile comprehensive insurance.
    c. automobile liability insurance.
    d. automobile medical payment coverage.

22. Which of the following is an insurance policy that provides coverage beyond the basic policy limits of the insured's other insurance policies? [p 840]
    a. Title insurance policy
    b. Credit insurance policy
    c. Group insurance policy

d. Umbrella insurance policy

23. Which of the following is not a duty of an insured under an insurance contract? [p 842]
    a. Duty to pay insurance proceeds
    b. Duty to pay premiums
    c. Duty to cooperate
    d. Duty to notify insurer

24. The person who makes a will is the [p 844]
    a. testator.
    b. executor.
    c. beneficiary.
    d. administrator.

25. When a testator leaves a specific devise of property to a beneficiary, but the property is no longer in the estate when the testator dies, the beneficiary receives nothing under the principle of [p 848]
    a. abatement.
    b. ademption.
    c. intestacy.
    d. per capita distribution.

Short Answer:

26. What is an insurable interest? [p 838] ______________________________

____

27. Differentiate between universal and term life insurance? [p 840] ______________

____

____

28. What is the difference between health insurance and disability insurance? [p 840] __________

____

____

____

29. What are three things covered by liability coverage under a homeowners policy? [p 840]
    (1) ______________________________
    (2) ______________________________
    (3) ______________________________

30. List four standard types of coverage that an automobile owner may purchase? [p 840]
    (1) ____________________ (2) ____________________
    (3) ____________________ (4) ____________________

31. Why may a business want to purchase marine insurance? [p 840] ____________________

____

32. Give an example of how an umbrella policy works [p 840] ____________________

____

____

33. Explain how the doctrine of subrogation is applied. [p 1016] ______________________

34. What are the three main requirements of a valid will? [p 844-845]

35. Explain per stirpes distribution. [p 849] ______________________

Chapter 39
INTERNATIONAL AND COMPARATIVE LAW

Chapter Overview

This chapter explores the federal government's power under the Foreign Commerce and Treaty Clauses of the U.S. Constitution as well as the sources of international law. It also details the functions and governance of the United Nations. Various economic organizations including the North American Free Trade Agreement are also examined. The other international facets that are discussed include international intellectual property rights provided by Internet treaties, sovereign immunity, the World Trade Organization's dispute resolution procedure, and the arbitration of international disputes.

Objectives

Upon completion of the exercises that follow, you should be able to:

1. Recognize the function of the federal government's power under the Foreign Commerce and Treaty Clauses of the U.S. Constitution.
2. List and differentiate between the different sources of international law.
3. Understand the functions and importance of the United Nations.
4. Be familiar with the North American Free Trade Agreement and other regional economic organizations.
5. Discuss how the World Trade Organization's dispute resolution procedure works.
6. Discuss the doctrine of sovereign immunity.
7. Discuss how international disputes are arbitrated.

Practical Application

You should be able to appreciate the importance of the Foreign Commerce and Treaty Clauses of the U.S. Constitution as well as the impact of sovereign immunity. Further, you should be familiar with the names and functions of the various regional organizations. Finally, you should be able to state how international disputes are arbitrated and how the World Trade Organization's dispute resolution procedure works.

Helpful Hints

One of the most helpful tools to understanding the importance of this chapter is to focus on the fact that the chapter involves the international spectrum of business. The study tips below are organized first by sources of international law, then by regional organization, followed by procedure for resolving international disputes. It is very beneficial to understand the functions of the various organizations in order to better understand the cases discussed in this chapter.

Study Tips

Background information – A legislative source of international law does not exist. A separate court for interpreting international law does not exist. Further, a world executive branch that could enforce the international laws is also non-existent. International law is very important with the increase in technology and transportation that is bringing businesses all over the world closer together.

The United States Constitution and International Affairs

Foreign Commerce Clause allows Congress to regulate commerce with foreign nations. Treaty Clause gives the president the power to make treaties as long as two-thirds of the senators present agree. States cannot unduly burden foreign commerce. State and local laws cannot conflict with treaties, as treaties are part of the Constitution.

Sources of International Law

- **Treaties and conventions** – These are like legislations that published by the United Nations and whose subject matter involves human rights, commerce, dispute settlements, foreign aid and navigation.
- **Treaty defined**- An agreement or contract between two or more nations, formally signed and ratified by the supreme power of each nation.
- **Conventions defined**- Treaties that are sponsored by international organizations and are signed by several signatories.
- **Customs**- A separate source of international law which defines a practice followed by two or more nations when interacting with one another. Requirements for a practice to become a custom include a repetitive action by two or more nations over a long period of time and acknowledgment that the custom is followed. Special note- Customs that have been followed for a considerable amount of time may become treaties.
- **General Principles of Law** – Many countries depend on general principles of law that are used in civilized nations in order to resolve international disputes. These principles may be derived from statutes, common law, regulations or other sources.
- **Judicial Decisions or Teaching** - This fourth source of law refers to the judicial teachings and decisions of scholars from the nations in dispute. Note: There is no precedent for international courts.

The United Nations and who governs it

- **The United Nations** - A very important international organization dedicated toward maintaining peace and security in the world, espousing economic and social cooperation and protecting human rights. A legislative body called the General Assembly, the Security Council and the Secretariat governs it. The General Assembly adopts resolutions and the council's duty is to maintain peace and security internationally. The United Nations is made up of several agencies including the United Nations Educational, Scientific, and Cultural Organization, the United Nations International Children's Emergency Fund and the International Monetary Fund, the World Bank International Fund for Agricultural Development.

Governance of the United Nations:

- **The General Assembly –** Comprised of all member nations. The assembly adopts resolutions regarding human rights, trade, finance and economics.
- **The Security Council** – A council made up of fifteen member nations, of which five are permanent. The five permanent members are China, Russia, France, the United States and the United Kingdom. The council's main responsibility is to maintain international peace and security and is authorized to use armed forces.

- **The Secretariat** – Administers the day-to-day operations of the UN. It is headed by the secretary-general and may use his office to help settle international disputes.

The International Court of Justice – A court located in The Hague, the Netherlands which is also called the **World Court**. Only nations may have this court decide cases. A nation may however seek redress on behalf of a business or individual who has a claim against another country.

UN Agencies – The United Nations is made up of many agencies to handle a variety of economic and social agencies. The International Monetary Fund (IMF) and the World Bank are among these agencies.

- **The International Monetary Fund (IMF)** – This agency was established to help promote the world economy, with its main focus on promoting sound monetary, fiscal and macroeconomic policies worldwide by giving aide to needy countries.
- **The World Bank** – The World Bank is made up of over 180 nations, and is financed by developed countries. It also provides money to developing countries to fund projects for humanitarian purposes and to help relieve poverty.

Regional International Organizations

The European Union - This international regional organization used to be referred to as the European Community or Common Market. It represents more than 300 million people and is made up of several countries of Western Europe. The European Commission acts solely in the best interests of the union. Customs duties have been abolished among member nations and customs tariffs have been enacted for European Union trade with the rest of the world.

The North American Free Trade Agreement - An agreement signed by Mexico, Canada and the United States that created a free-trade zone stretching from the Yukon to the Yucatan. This agreement dispensed with or reduced most of the quotas, tariffs and duties as well as other barriers to trade among these three countries. Benefits of the agreement include the provision that these countries may discriminate against other countries but provide for deals among themselves. Some economists feel that NAFTA is more of a managed trade agreement.

Asian Economic Communities - Several Asian countries have created the Association of South East Asian Nations (ASEAN). China and Japan are not members of this association, however, Japan has given financing for the countries that comprise this organization. China may one day become a member of ASEAN.

Latin, Central, and South American Economic Communities - There are several Latin American and Caribbean countries that have founded many regional organizations to further economic development and cooperation. They are the Central American Common Market, the Mercosur Common Market, the Caribbean Community and the Andean Common Market.

African Economic Communities - The economic communities that have been formed in Africa include the Economic and Customs Union of Central Africa, the Eat African Community, the Organization of African Unity, and the Economic Community of West African States.

Middle Eastern Economic Communities - The Organization of Petroleum Exporting Countries is the best-known Middle Eastern economic organization. The Gulf Cooperation Council was formed to develop an economic trade area.

World Trade Organization (WTO)

- **Basic Information** - The WTO was created as part of the Uruguay Round of trade negotiations concerning the General Agreement on Tariffs and Trade. It is located in Switzerland.
- **Function of the WTO** - The function of the WTO is to hear and decide trade disputes between nations that are members. A three-member panel hears the dispute, which then generates a report that is given to the dispute settlement body. The WTO has expunged the blocking ability of member nations. There is however an appellate body to appeal the dispute settlement body. Only issues of law, not fact may be appealed.
- **Findings of Trade Agreement Violations** - If a violation of a trade agreement is found, the offending nation may be ordered to stop participating in the violating practice, as well as to pay damages to the other party. If the violating nation does not comply with the order, retaliatory trade sanctions by other nations may be assessed against the offending nation.
- **WTO Jurisdiction** - The WTO is also known as the "Supreme Court of Trade." Its jurisdiction involves the enforcement of comprehensive and important world trade agreements. Note too that in 2002, China became a member of the WTO, opening its markets to foreign goods and services.

Jurisdiction of National Courts to Decide International Disputes

- **General Facts** - National courts of individual nations hear the bulk of disputes involving international law.
- **Judicial Procedure and the Problems Nations Face** - The main problems a party seeking judicial resolution of an international dispute faces are which court will hear the case and which law will be applied. Most cases are heard in the plaintiff's home country. However, many international contracts provide for a forum-selection clause as well as a choice of law clause. Dispute resolution becomes more difficult and often impossible without these two clauses.

Important Principles of International Law

- The **act of state doctrine** - This act proclaims that judges of one country cannot question the authority of an act committed by another country that occurs within that country's own borders.
- The **doctrine of sovereign immunity** - This doctrine states that countries are granted immunity from suits in courts in other countries.
- The **Foreign Sovereign Immunities Act** - This act provides a qualified or restricted immunity in two situations. The first instance in which a foreign country is not immune from lawsuits in the United States courts is if the foreign country has waived its immunity, either explicitly or by implication. The second instance is if the action is based upon a commercial activity carried on in the United States by the foreign country or carried on outside the United States but causing a direct effect in the United States.

- **Nationalization of Private Property owed by Foreigners** - This international law allows nations to nationalize private property owned by foreigners if it is for a public purpose. This can occur by expropriation whereby the owner is paid just compensation by the government that took the property or it can be accomplished by confiscation in which case the owner either receives an insufficient payment or no payment at all for the property seized.
- Political risk insurance as per the **Overseas Private Investment Corporation** - The Overseas Private Investment Corporation was created to help insure United States businesses and citizens against losses incurred from confiscation by foreign governments. The American businesses and citizens may purchase an insurance policy to protect their property.

Ways to Resolve International Disputes

International Arbitration is a nonjudicial method of resolving disputes whereby a neutral third party decides the case. The arbitrator will issue an award, not a judgment. The award wining party may attach property of the losing party regardless of which country the property is located in. Over fifty countries are signatories to the **United Nations Convention on the Recognition and Enforcement of Foreign Arbitral Awards.**

International Criminal Prosecutions

A nation may criminally prosecute a business or individual that commits crimes within its jurisdiction or that violate the nations laws. If the wrongdoer takes refuge in another country, the person may be sent back to the country that wants to prosecute him or her. Extradition is necessary in order to punish the perpetrator.

Jewish Law and the Torah

In addition to abiding by the criminal and civil laws of their host countries, the Jews also obey the legal principles of the Torah. The Torah is an exhaustive set of religious and political rules that are formulated from Jewish principles. The base of the Torah is to determine the truth.

Islamic Law and the Koran

Saudi Arabia has Islamic law as its only law. It is mainly used in matters involving divorce, marriage and inheritance with some criminal law. One main characteristic of Islamic law is that it prohibits the making of unjustified or unearned profit.

Hindu Law

The Hindu law is religious based, using scholarly decisions that have been handed down from century to century. It embodies the doctrine of proper behavior. Note, that outside of India, Anglo-Hindu law applies in many countries with Hindu populations.

Refresh Your Memory

The following exercise will enable you to refresh your memory on the rules and principles presented to you in this chapter. Read each question twice and place your answer in the blanks provided. Review the chapter material for any question you miss or are unable to remember.

1. There is no individual source of ____________ law.

2. Which clause of the United States Constitution gives Congress the power to regulate commerce with foreign nations? The ____________ ______________ __________.

3. What are the four sources of international law as listed by the Statute of the International Court of Justice?
____
____
____
____

4. What is the equivalent of legislation at the international level? ________________________ and ________________________.

5. What describes a practice followed by two or more nations when dealing with each other?
____
____

6. What do courts and tribunals that decide international disputes often rely upon to make their decisions? __________________ ______________________ of _________________.

7. What is known as the fourth source of law to which international tribunals can refer?
_____________ _____________ and _____________ of the most qualified scholars of the nations that are involved in the dispute.

8. What is the International Court of Justice also known as? The ____________ _________.

9. The purpose of the North American Free Trade Agreement was to create a
__________________-________________ zone.

10. What is one of the main functions of the World Trade Organization?
____
____
____

Critical Thought Exercise

Scientists at Cornell University engaged in genetic engineering and created a pear called the New York Sweetie that is resistant to bruising, browning, and insect infestation. The Sweetie grows approximately 30% larger than known pears and has both a higher water and sugar content, making the Sweetie highly desired by consumers worldwide. The only pear that can compete with the quality of the Sweetie is the Favlaka Beauty, grown exclusively in Favlaka. Favlaka is a large European nation with a population of over 300 million people. The country of Favlaka is a member of the European Union and the World Trade Organization. The residents of Favlaka consume over $1.2 billion worth of pears each year. All pears that are eaten on Favlaka are grown in Favlaka or a neighboring EU country. Favlaka will not allow the importation of fruit that has undergone any genetic engineering. The Favlaka Pear Cartel argues that the introduction of genetically engineered pears into their markets jeopardizes the Favlakan pear industry and the health of all Favlakans. They fear that future crops will become susceptible to insect infestation and attacks by mold and fungus. The United States Pear Growers argue that there is no scientific evidence that the NY Sweetie will cause damage to any other variety of pear or humans when it is grown or consumed. They further argue that the actions of the Favlakan government is banning the Sweetie are unfair trade practices under WTO agreements. It is argued that the Favlakan government is only motivated by the goal of preventing international competition for the Favlakan Beauty.

In what forum should this dispute be resolved? What procedure should be used to resolve this international dispute? What law should control the issues in this case? How should the WTO rule in this case?

Answer.

Practice Quiz

True/False:

1. ___ The Security Council for the United Nations is mainly responsible for maintaining national peace and security. [p 866]

2. ___ The Educational, Scientific, and Cultural Organization, the United Nations International Children's Emergency Fund and the International Monetary Fund are among the agencies that are included from the United Nations due to the Economic and social problems involved with these agencies. [p 867]

3. ___ Nations that have a claim against another country may have their cases decided by the International Court of Justice. [p 866]

4. ___ The European Union treaty opened borders for trade by providing for the free flow of capital, labor, goods and services among member nations. [p 869]

5. ___ In order to admit a new member to the European Union, there need not be a unanimous vote by existing European Union members. [p 869]

6. ___ The European Court of Justice does has jurisdiction to enforce European Union law. [p 866]

7. ___ The European Court of Justice is the final arbiter of European Union law. [p 869]

8. ___ The North American Free Trade Agreement provides for the addition of duties, tariffs, quotas and other various trade barriers between Canada, the United States and Mexico. [p 869]

9. ___ An important characteristic of the World Trade Organization is the elimination of the blocking power of member nations. [p 874]

10 ___ The World Trade Organization has competed with the "Supreme Court of Trade." [p 873]

11. ___ A general principle of international law is that a country has authority over what takes place within its own territory. [p 876]

12. ___ The Rabbi-judges sitting as Beis Din are more concerned with the truth than its adversarial process. [p 878]

13. ___ Islamic law provides the making of unearned or unjustified profit. [p 879]

14. ___ An arbitrator issues a judgment, not an award. [p 878]

15. ___ If there is no agreement providing where an international dispute will be brought, the case will not be brought at all. [p 875]

Multiple Choice:

16. What types of matters are treaties and conventions concerned with? [p 865]
    a. Statutes banning state governments from purchasing goods and services
    b. Human rights, foreign aid, navigation, commerce and dispute settlement
    c. Consistent and recurring action by two or more nations over a long period of time
    d. General principles of law that are recognized by civilized nations

17. Custom is often defined as [p 865]
    a an agreement between two nations.
    b. a principle of law that is common to the national law of the parties in dispute.
    c. a practice followed by two or more nations when dealing with each other.
    d. a goal to maintain peace and security in the world.

18. Which of the following is not a true statement? [p 876]
    a. Nations must obey international law enacted by other countries or international organizations.
    b. There is no world executive branch to enforce international laws.
    c. There is no individual world court that must interpret international laws.
    d. There is no individual legislative source of international law.

19. A choice of forum clause in an international contract is a clause that [p 876]
    a. states that commercial disputes between the United States and foreign governments or parties may be brought in federal district court.
    b. an agreement that designates which nation's laws will be applied in deciding the case.
    c. a trade pact giving nations much easier access to the United States' marketplace.
    d. designates which nation's court has jurisdiction to hear a case arising out of the contract.

20. The act of state doctrine states that [p 876]
    a. the restraint on the judiciary is not justified under the doctrine of separation of powers.
    b. a country has no authority over what transpires within its own territory.

c. judges of one country cannot question the strength of an act committed by another country within its own borders.
d. the courts may sit in judgment upon the acts of the government of another, done within its own borders.

21. Which of the following is true with respect to the goals of the United Nations? [p 866]
    a. One of its goals is to maintain peace and security in the world.
    b. It was created to promote economic and social copperation.
    c. It functions to protect human rights.
    d. all of the above

22. Which of the following is not an agency associated with the United Nations? [p 867]
    a. United Nations International Children's Emergency Fund
    b. the World Bank
    c. the International Monastery Fund
    d. the International Fund for Agricultural Development

23. Which of the following is the United Nations governed by? [p 866]
    a. the General Assembly
    b. the Secretariat
    c. the Security Council
    d. all of the above

24. Which doctrine states that an act of a government in a foreign country is not subject to suit in the
foreign country? [p. 877]
    a. the World Trade Organization Act
    b. the Sovereign Immunity Doctrine
    c. the Act of State Doctrine
    d. none of the above

25. Which of the following are agreements between nations that are formally ratified by the supreme
power of each signatory nation? [p 880]
    a. customs
    b. judicial decisions and teachings
    c. treaties and conventions
    d. general principles of law

Short Answer:

26. What are the two constitutional provisions that give power to the federal government to regulate international affairs? [p 863] The ____________________ ____________________ Clause and the ________________ Clause.

27. What is the name of the international organization that was created by a multinational treaty to promote social and economic cooperation among nations and to protect human rights? [p 866] ____________ ____________

28. What is the most well known Middle Eastern economic organization? [p 872] The _________ of _____________ _____________ _____________

29. Which organization has become the world's most important trade organization? [p 872]
____
____
____

30. Which court hears most of the international disputes? [p 875] The
____________________________ ______________ of the plaintiff's home country.

31. What is the most litigated aspect of the Foreign Sovereign Immunities Act? [p 877]
____
____

32. What are the benefits of having an arbitrator decide a dispute that arises between parties to a contract? [p 878]
____
____
____

33. If Rachel had an international dispute that she needed to have resolved, which two sources of international law would she encourage the court to rely on when making its decision? [p 865]
________________ and ________________

34. If Sue, an exporter of material from the United States has an excessive tariff placed upon her goods when they enter one of the World Trade Organization's member countries, what multilateral treaty might she rely upon to help limit the tariff? [p 872]
____
____
____

35. If a violation of a trade agreement is found, what can the general report and appellate decision order the offending nation to do? [p 874]
____
____
____
____